TOWARD
BETTER
TEACHING
IN
PHYSICAL
EDUCATION

TOWARD
TEACHING IN

1961

Englewood Cliffs, New Jersey

ELWOOD CRAIG DAVIS
Professor of Physical Education and Education
University of Southern California . . . . .
. . . . . **EARL L. WALLIS**
Associate Professor of Physical Education, San
Fernando Valley State College . . . . . .

BETTER PHYSICAL EDUCATION

PRENTICE-HALL, INC.

Preface

Physical education moves forward in sectors rather than in a frontal advance. These sectoral advances are the result of human needs and desires related to matters such as program, administration, and method. This last sector has received scant attention for several decades.

. . .

School administrators are now becoming dissatisfied with the quality of teaching in physical education. Pressures are at work in the teaching sector, forcing progress in certain directions.

. . .

We have known for some time that we do not teach physical education to a group but, rather, we teach an individual. Successful teaching demands more than this, however. We teach in a *given community,* for *certain purposes,* and according to *understood principles.*

. . .

Teaching is a skill that can always be improved. Changed conditions and new demands mean changed emphases, and tomorrow's teachers will be better prepared to meet these challenges. New activities and programs cannot substitute for teaching—successful teaching in physical education transcends the bounds of better methods of teaching or better physical education.

The above observations were made in the prefaces to the 1941 and 1948 editions of this book, but the improvement in teaching anticipated in the first edition has not been realized. The actual degree and pace of improvement have been inadequate to stem the spread of dissatisfaction with methods of physical education.

v

In spite of the better *prepared* teachers and better *methods* acknowledged in the second edition, better *teaching* is still not in evidence. We have not kept pace with the demands for change. Our attention has been more deeply focused on such matters as program and equipment, and we seem to be unaware of the need for improved teaching.

A great historian-philosopher warns that survival depends on identifying correctly the challenge that threatens, and then arising to meet it successfully. We have good intentions, but time, effort, and energy have been spent on matters unrelated to the *conditions* which control both survival and progress. Are we again to become aware of the *real* challenge only when it is too late to face up to it?

These comments indicate something of the concern of this third edition. The revision has been comprehensive, with new chapters on self-improvement, public relations, securing a position, adjustment and guidance, an analysis and synthesis of principles per se, and a challenge to the student about his future. Some chapters have been eliminated, others unified, and still others have undergone complete revision and reorganization.

Those emphases which formerly characterized this book, and which still point the way, have been retained. The need for the novice teacher to sense his obligation to the community, the forward-looking role that principles play in teaching, the key position of modern concepts of motor learning in physical education teaching, the honest facing of facts by the prospective teacher, the highlighting of purposes and their inescapable connection with teaching, and the challenging treatment of measurement and evaluation, with new suggestions for grading, are some topics which the reader familiar with this volume will find have been modified in terms of new ideas.

The authors are grateful to many professional colleagues around the country who have made helpful suggestions for this revision. It is their hope that this cooperative relationship may continue in any future editions.

The authors are grateful to Kathleen Skalley Davis, Betty Wallis, and Eleanor Wallis for their work in the preparation of this edition. Appreciation is also extended to Dr. Gene Logan for his graphic presentations of ideas that appear in the text. The authors also wish to acknowledge the expert typing of the entire revised manuscript by Mrs. June Brown.

Special acknowledgment and gratitude are due Dr. Minnie L. Lynn for her careful, detailed, and comprehensive criticism of the manuscript. Most of her suggestions have been incorporated.

Although all of this assistance leads to a deep appreciation and indebtedness to many people, the pages that follow, with their emphases, presentations, interpretations, and errors, are the responsibility of the authors alone.

ELWOOD CRAIG DAVIS
EARL L. WALLIS

Contents

Part Three | *YOUR PURPOSES AND VALUES: why teach physical education?*

TOWARD
BETTER
TEACHING
IN
PHYSICAL
EDUCATION

Part One

YOU AND TEACHING:
how ready are you?

The beginning teacher faces challenges

Without difficulties there are no challenges.
Without challenges there is no progress.

Adapted from Toynbee.

SOME MAJOR PROBLEMS. THE BEGINNING TEACHER HAS
usually heard about the many difficulties teachers experience in their first jobs. The beginning teacher is perplexed by
many new problems. Even though one may join a wonderful group
of people on a school faculty, maintaining one's energy and enthusiasm is a problem common to most new teachers. It takes bound-
less energy to maintain the constant alertness needed to handle large
groups of children, to guide them into profitable behavior, to observe necessary routines, and to radiate each hour, day after day,
enthusiasm for learning.

Fitting into the system of the school is a problem for some teachers.
Adjustment to administrative or supervising direction or lack of
direction may be a problem. One teacher recently said, "My big-
gest surprise in my first year of teaching was the lack of supervision
—I had to find my own way." Other beginning teachers find that
they must adjust to constant criticism and evaluation. It is difficult
to know what to expect.

3

Beginning teachers are sometimes surprised by the amount of clerical and outside work required of them. Extra duties, meetings, and club sponsorship demand time and energy. Evaluating progress of pupils, assigning marks or grades, making reports, and working effectively with parents are problems which perplex the beginner.

Organizing and preparing the daily program may be a problem. Adapting to the abilities of the very slow or the very fast pupils may be difficult. Handling problems of pupil behavior and maintaining good control is a problem for many teachers. Knowing how firm or lenient to be; knowing when to use a sense of humor without being too informal or familiar; being democratic and yet keeping classes under control; and, knowing how to motivate learning and stimulate pupils who lack interest are problems confronting many beginning teachers.

Occupational insecurity may disturb the teacher, particularly if he is coaching competitive sports. Moreover, there are a thousand and one detailed duties required of the teacher. He may find it extremely difficult to take care of these details, plan his work, simultaneously keep up his professional study and growth, and have some time and energy for recreation.

Some rewards. But teaching has its satisfactions. Teaching and working with young people are a most important responsibility of a democracy. One tends to preserve his youthful enthusiasms by working with young people and stimulating their development. The admiration and respect of youth is a reward in itself. Vacations offer opportunities for travel, recreation, self-improvement. The very nature of the teacher's work brings associations with interesting and stimulating people of the community.

One other satisfaction is worth noting. The teacher usually has relative freedom as to techniques of teaching. He can exercise his own ingenuity and creativeness in fostering the learning process. He can express and develop his own personality in interpreting mankind's accumulation of knowledge and skills to the fresh minds of youth.

The importance of teaching. A look at the history of American education may help the beginning teacher understand his responsibilities. In the simple life of American pioneer days, the parent was the teacher. The child imitated the adult and followed in his footsteps. The parent showed the child how to do things. The child learned by imitation and trial and error. He had to learn to survive.

Soon, greater security, improvement in economic status, and increase in population permitted social groups to try to provide a better life for their offspring. Education seemed the most promising means of attaining this better life.

Eventually the system of free public education developed to the degree that today high school graduation is thought to be the minimum education for American youth. The trend is toward more extended educational programs for all fields. Teachers need more and more education, both to provide basic understanding of the growing social accumulation and to provide techniques for short-cutting the student's vicarious experiencing of it.

The accumulating experience of generation after generation of man has been analyzed, epitomized, reduced to verbal or mathematical symbols, and turned over to the teachers to be made a part of the child's developing personality. The children are supposed to take on, in the few short years of formal schooling, the benefits of much of mankind's thousands of years of experience. The teacher's job is to foster the incorporation of his handed-down maturity in adjustment to life. This is a process of re-experiencing, symbolically and in epitomized form, eons of man's experience.

This vicarious and symbolic experiencing, called education, is of necessity highly artificial. The pain of man's original experience is removed. The blunders and failures of succeeding generations do not appear. Only the short-cuts to the successful experience remain.

To make these abstract summaries of the social heritage a part of the real life of the child is a very difficult task. Unless the teacher can make these experiences seem alive, real and applicable to life, the result is mummified erudition—a wide divergence from the ideal of a social Superman, wise from the experiences of all ages. Unless these school experiences reveal themselves in changed conduct and behavior outside the formal school atmosphere, the child has benefited very little.

Mental health, psychosomatic medicine, and common sense have combined to further the abandonment of the old religious concept of the "wickedness of the flesh." The dualistic mind and body theory is slowly changing even in practice to the "whole personality development" theory. A wholesome personality is usually developed in one whose needs have been met to a considerable degree and whose training will aid him in meeting his needs in the future. But these needs are many. They are physiological demands for food, air, water, shelter, and physical activity. They are needs for feelings of safety and security. They include needs for affection, for self-respect, and for approbation and respect from others. Moreover, the human personality needs that feeling of self-expression, of self-realization that accompanies individual achievement. In other words, basic body needs, security against pain or danger, affection, regard and esteem from others, self-respect, and a confidence in being able to meet life's problems are the necessities for normalcy and an approach to happiness. Parents want the teacher to help their children attain these needs. The basic principle of democratic government is that as many as possible of the present or future citizenry should be able to satisfy these personal needs.

Education by means of the physical. Physical education is one category of experiences through which the child's needs may be met. Functional efficiency is highly dependent on energy supplies, on growth and development, on fineness and nicety of body controls, and on habits of recreation. Moreover, physical development, socio-motor skills, posture, and group-cooperative experiences contribute to the child's social status. Social status is a very important aspect of the individual's self-evaluation. Social status refers to the degree of prestige one attains in the social groups with which one comes in contact. Physical experiences that (1) foster growth, (2) develop skilled movements, (3) increase and redirect energy supplies, (4) furnish opportunities for success in social experiences, and (5) resolve frustrations are examples of education by means of the physical.

Subjects an artificial division. Normal man is not split up into aspects. He is a physiological *unit,* a unit that makes all its contributions to the world through some phase of motor expression. Physical Education, as a school subject, has in real-life experiences no line of demarcation from other school subjects. However, the line is usually quite definite in the artificiality of school compartmentalization. The same statement could be made in reference to to any school subject. The very nature of the school organization at present makes it necessary that each teacher use a subject (teach it) as a means of helping the children satisfy other needs.

Learning social principles and disciplines. A person learns to get along with people. He learns social principles as guides for group-cooperative activity. He learns such characteristics of behavior as industry, exactness, promptness, objective evaluation, and the like, in a variety of experiences which require these disciplines for success. To claim for any subject the responsibility for teaching these aspects would be contrary to the nature of generalized experience. Social traits must appear in a variety of the child's experiences before they become a part of his personality. Only great teachers seem to be able to accelerate markedly this incorporation, this personality growth. Only such great teachers *teach the child.*

Subject material is a means. The subject field represents merely some of the material which the teacher finds useful in developing the child. Physical education furnishes experiences very helpful in meeting the child's developmental needs. The better teachers, however, are limited neither by, nor to, a field of subject matter. They use a field both as an environmental background for learning activity, and as a *means* of emphasis on learning experiences.

Physical education, through its emphasis on (1) wholesome activity, (2) group participation, (3) skills for self-expression, (4) proficiency and ease in movement, (5) recreational and social tastes and skills, (6) self appraisal and (7) desirable attitudes, furnishes an excellent background and a fruitful means for satisfaction of human needs. There is a psychic and a physical therapy in enjoyable motor activity, and a means of self-expression in sports, the dance, in physically-active fun. The nature of the program makes an increase in biological fitness a concomitant.

Physical education is not a new experience. Man's development has never been dissociated from physical activity. Most of our knowledge of prehistoric man is based upon evidences of what he did—crude tools, drawings, shelters, all a result of physical activity. But, the machine age and its aftermath has brought the new experience which tends to rob man of the very types and intensities of physical activity that helped make him what he is. Physical education in schools is now attempting to help man adjust himself to the conditions that accompany the space age.

To foster the adjustment to modern living, the physical education teacher aids in the selection of those activities that are beneficial in terms of the objectives stated above.   He selects or creates an environment that is healthful.   He adapts the program to individuals. He disseminates knowledge of and promotes desirable attitudes toward vigorous, healthful, and joyous living.

The supervised program of physical education also provides the school child with those tools of participation in recreation that enable him to spend his leisure time pleasurably and beneficially in out-of-school days and after-school years.   Moreover, the games and sports, the team play, the group enterprises are good bases for incorporating social attitudes and understandings and democratic principles of living.

Accomplishing these purposes of physical education is much more difficult than reading or writing about them.   This fact, together with other challenges facing the teacher, causes him to seek the answers to many questions.

SECURING A POSITION

Securing a position often ranks as the uppermost problem in the upperclassman's mind.   Job-getting is so vital to the prospective teacher that it forces itself into this book as a primary consideration. Securing a position in any profession immediately raises the question of the qualities and characteristics demanded of the person desiring such employment.   Some of the traits and abilities that facilitate securing a position as a teacher of physical education are:

Personality.   A first major factor in securing a position is personality.   School superintendents as well as leading teacher-educators rate personality as the *primary* requisite of successful teaching. Personality has been variously defined and described; it is a complexity of many characteristics.   At this point we are interested chiefly in those traits that count most in job-getting.   They are appearance, speech, and carriage.

The aspects of appearance that call for special notation are dress, complexion, hairdress, condition of teeth, cleanliness, and facial expression.   Those aspects of speech that aid most in securing a position are pitch and texture of voice, rate of speech, enunciation, pronunciation, and grammar.   Carriage, although an aspect of appearance, deserves special emphasis.   Its value in securing positions in every vocation is tradition.   The well-poised, well-postured candidate has first call over the slouchy, foot-shuffling, ill-poised candidate.

Persons who hire physical education teachers pay particular attention to the applicant's appearance, speech, and carriage. Boards of education know all too well that the pupil imitates his teacher more than he obeys the precept, "Do as I say, not as I do." The public has come to expect teachers of physical education to be living examples of their profession.

Versatility.   The *first* factor that emphasizes the growing need for teachers of physical education to be versatile is the breaking down of subject-matter lines in the school curriculum. Evidence shows a possibility that the teacher of tomorrow must be prepared to integrate physical education so that it dovetails directly and positively into many other of the pupil's experiences. Integration, the core curriculum, fused teaching, or whatever the new emphasis may be called demands versatility on the part of the physical education teacher.

The *second* condition indicating the need for the development of many abilities is that most beginning teachers secure positions in the smaller communities. The teacher of physical education should be prepared to teach one, two, or three other subjects. Such versatility greatly increases his chances for employment. The teacher prepared to teach in three fields is not only three times more versatile than the teacher with one specialty but has a six-to-one chance of employment over the latter, other factors being equal.

The rapid development of extracurricular activity programs in schools is a *third* factor underlining the importance of versatility. Extracurricular activities have assumed a position of major consideration and importance in the school life. School administrators now look for teachers prepared to direct and guide this program, and the student-in-training who participates in such activities as music, dramatics, debating, publications, student organizations, and athletics is more in demand than the one-line specialist. Rarely does a teacher's application blank from any school district not seek to discover the candidate's versatility in extracurricular activities.

Young men, in particular, should be prepared to coach athletics. Failure to participate in college athletics renders it difficult in many localities for a young man majoring in physical education to be placed. Certainly few beginning teachers who are nonathletes make successful coaches if they secure a position on the strength of having taken a coaching course. Most of the outstanding leaders in physical education consider athletics as the front door into the profession. The same reasons indicate the necessity for young women majoring in physical education to participate in sport and dance activities.

A *fourth* fact pointing up the need for versatility is the variety of duties performed by the teacher. Today's teacher must understand that the "whole child" goes to school, that environment is a force constantly influencing the child and his conduct, that the pupil's system of values is worthy of study and consideration, that education must move out of its academic stronghold and establish harmonious relationships with members of the community. The duties involved in implementing this wider understanding demands a versatile teacher.

Professional aptitude.   The need for versatility does not eliminate the importance of the prospective teacher's possessing special abilities in physical education activities and a knack for teaching them. Activities form the medium through which the physical educator educates the pupil. The teacher of physical education who lacks ability in activities will attain no more teaching success than the teacher of English who does not know how to speak or write correctly.

The prospective teacher should also demonstrate some aptitude in teaching. Merely wanting to be a teacher is not an index of one's fitness for the profession. There are many vocational misfits in the world today. Some of these unhappy persons insisted upon entering a vocation in spite of being advised that their aptitudes pointed toward another type of work.

Teaching physical education is more than merely telling pupils how to perform skills. It is more than showing them how. Unfortunately, the prospective teacher is usually a poor judge of his ability as a teacher. The judgments of one's major professors, supplemented by tests, provide more accurate indices of one's knack for teaching. Such information should be desired by the student-in-training. It provides an answer to the question of one's fitness for the profession.

Scholarship.   School administrators now give close attention to the scholastic records of prospective teachers of physical education. Some time ago, the school administrator's chief consideration was the student's athletic record.   This item may still be an important consideration, but, more and more frequently the opening remark of the school superintendent to the placement officer is, "I would like to see the records of your better students."

Scholarship is a permanent record of the degree to which the candidate applied himself to the more important tasks assigned to him in college.   It indicates the extent to which the student recognizes the chief purpose of his college education, which, in turn, is an index of his maturity, his judgment, and his ability to weigh values.   The scholastic record serves as a guide in determining the candidate's ability to carry through the major responsibilities assigned to him as a student.   Such a record measures the individual's ability to make proper use of his opportunities.

Contacts and references.   Most employers hire applicants they know best, other things being equal.   The well-qualified candidate who is known to some member of the board of education has a tremendous advantage over other well-qualified candidates.   In most instances, however, candidates are not employed by persons who know them well.   It becomes necessary for employers to gather information about the applicant in other ways.   One common method is the reference letter or form.

Prospective teachers should begin in the junior year of college, at the latest, to make contacts with persons who may recommend them and help them to secure positions.   After such contacts are made, they should be renewed from time to time.   The student should be aware that the impressions he makes and the reputation he establishes during his college years will determine the quality of the recommendations he will receive.

School officials are becoming more circumspect in attempting to employ the right teacher.   A photograph and application blank often are inadequate guides.   An interview places the emphasis upon first impressions.   Therefore, boards of education desire to hire a teacher who, if not known to them directly, has the enthusiastic support of his professors or of respected citizens of the community.

Perhaps other factors should be considered in securing a position, but these five are of first importance.   Failure to be prepared in one of them diminishes the chances of employment; these five abilities and characteristics, personality, versatility, professional aptitude, scholarship, and contacts, enable the teacher to be successful on the job.   Chapter 18 is devoted to the details of job-getting.

APPROACHING THE JOB

Helpful sources.   The beginning teacher shows good judgment if he arrives on the scene of his new position several days before school begins.   Particularly if a position is accepted in a smaller community, upon arrival the new teacher should interview the superintendent or supervisor or principal as soon as possible.   In some larger communities this may also be advisable.   A great deal of helpful information and many hints and tips can be secured from these persons.   They know the scope of the work, the major problems, influential community members who may help, equipment needs, and desirable areas in which to live.   These persons may also provide valuable information about community attitudes.   They can refer the teacher to other sources of information.   The school nurse, the school doctor and other teachers may also have worthwhile suggestions.   Office secretaries and school janitors can offer invaluable detailed information if approached in the right manner on appropriate matters.   The superintendent and principal, if approached in the proper manner, can suggest other contacts that might well be made sometime during these preliminary days.   In these ways the new teacher takes his first step in becoming stabilized in the community.

Some schools provide elaborate orientation programs for new teachers to help speed adjustment to the new school and community. In other schools making contacts and gathering information remains largely the individual responsibility of the new teacher.

Surveying the situation.   After interviewing the superintendent and principal and securing living accommodations, the new teacher is ready to survey the facilities and equipment, check on such matters as previous locker-room procedures, enrollment procedures, the type and availability of gymnasium costumes, and policies regarding excused absences from physical education classes.

The new teacher will do well to find out previous practices in his school system and conform to them.   A friendly chat with one of the older teachers usually reveals information that will save the new teacher embarrassment.   In some situations, after a conference with the school administrators, certain changes in routine may be inaugurated. It is important that, before school starts, the new teacher work out plans for all these routines in conformity with administrative policies.

The new teacher is frequently faced with discouraging problems of registration. If the physical education registration is done last, some classes may be too large, many classes may be extremely heterogeneous, and the sizes of classes may not fit the facilities. The new teacher should plan his classes in accordance with equipment and facilities if possible. At registration time he reports that a class should be closed when it is as large as the facilities permit, if this procedure is recognized in the school. If overcrowding does occur, the teacher should, at the earliest possible moment, get the schedule cards of the students in the large classes and work out with the main office suitable changes of schedules. (This statement assumes that such a procedure is practiced in the school.) In general the changes can be made most easily by the teacher himself. The main office then can send out notices of such changes. If there are to be co-educational classes, plan accordingly.

Plans for supervision of halls and locker rooms must be understood. In many schools the teacher cannot expect to await his classes on the field or gymnasium floor. If suitable plans for roll-taking, activity assignment, and issuing of equipment are ready at the opening day, the work will move more smoothly. If the teacher does not make definite plans to keep the pupils interested and busy from the start, he can expect problems in discipline. This preliminary planning will take up much of the new teacher's time before school opens.

Getting acquainted with the community. The school administrator will be helpful in assisting the new teacher in learning to understand the community.

Community attitudes toward religion must be sensed. Any act that might in any way offend the most prudish of the community members must be avoided. One should not disregard the possibility of local prejudices, however unreasonable they may seem. The youthfulness of the newcomer may be held against him. The spelling of his name, his race, religion, political views, manner of dress, or even stature may arouse community prejudices.

Many communities are critical of the new teacher who gives the appearance of being overinterested in adults of the opposite sex. Teachers who are indiscreet in these matters create a delicate problem for the school administrator. Sometimes an otherwise excellent teacher loses his position merely because he fails to appreciate that a community sets up standards of conduct for its teachers that are not applied to others in the community. Although this problem is not as acute as it was some years ago, it still exists in some areas, most notably in the smaller communities. Teachers who run counter to these standards are often dealt with abruptly and severely.

Sometimes a new teacher discovers that an entire community is somewhat prejudiced against physical education, or against teachers of physical education. Such a community attitude has a background of experience. The new teacher confronts a difficult problem here —but not an insurmountable one. His speech, work, and social relationships will be directed toward establishing and stabilizing himself and his field in the community.

Conservatism, competence, and community cooperativeness on the part of the new teacher will do much to prevent unfortunate first impressions. Later modification of extreme circumspection in personal behavior must come only after it is clear that the school administration and community will approve of such changes.

During the days before the beginning of school, the new teacher might also acquaint himself with the press, P.T.A., leaders of youth organizations, and service clubs. Such steps lay the foundation for developing and favorably publicizing one's program.

RELATIONSHIPS WITH PUPILS

Discipline. Most superintendents and principals of schools want to know specifically of an applicant's ability to maintain discipline. This, however, is not the sole reason why beginning teachers give this problem considerable thought. The beginning teacher is aware of his inexperience. He easily recalls his public school years when he or his friends tried out the new teacher—particularly if the new teacher were just out of college. He may recall instances in which parents or neighbors spoke in an uncomplimentary manner of Mr. A or Miss B, who could not keep discipline. In addition, as a beginning teacher he knows the need of being respected. He realizes that without respect a teacher not only has a sorry time but accomplishes little, and he does not gain the confidence of the community.

Many beginning teachers attempt the solution of disciplinary problems through the exercise of authority.   This emphasis by the inexperienced is not surprising.   The typical untrained way of handling individuals and groups is authoritative, dictatorial, autocratic. This fact is particularly true of persons who are on the defensive; and the young teacher is apt to be so because of a lack of self-confidence.   Emphasis upon authoritative methods in maintaining discipline also grows out of confusion regarding what is meant by maintaining discipline.   If the student has in mind the stifled, pin-drop, response-to-command type of discipline, there will be many demands for the use of autocratic methods.   On the other hand, the wise teacher avoids top-sergeant methods.   The teacher is a leader, a guide, an encourager, a stimulator, a challenger, not a dictator. He represents authority but uses it only when necessary.   The effective teacher leads, and seldom orders, compels, or drives the pupil.

Frequently the beginning teacher's grave concern over disciplinary problems is unjustified.   The teacher with a knack for teaching learns early that careful preparation, enthusiasm for and interest in his work, and a consideration of pupils' interests, together with other factors of leadership, eliminate the necessity for disciplinary measures in most situations.   Discipline is best thought of as control measures used by the teacher to accelerate and motivate learning.

Nevertheless, in spite of assurances to the contrary, discipline remains a bugaboo to many beginning and experienced teachers.

Social distance.   Another problem which perplexes the beginning teacher, and one related to discipline, is that of social distance.   Many college students have experienced occasions and situations in which it was necessary to create social distance, even toward their classmates.   For example, as committee chairman, or as class president the student has definite responsibilities to be accomplished within given time limits, which means that he has to lead, guide, and stimulate those who work with him.   The position itself and the recognized responsibility placed upon him automatically create a certain amount of social distance between him and his followers— while he is in the role of leader.   Social distance occurs in such situations whether it is purposely created or not.

Many students have also learned to use varying degrees of social distance according to persons.   We permit a few persons to know us very well, and in such cases the social distance is almost always negligible. We are fairly friendly with many acquaintances but increase the social distance with total strangers. Even with friends we vary the degree of social distance according to time and place, as do they.

Even such a factor as dress has a tendency to increase or decrease social distance, at least temporarily. A newcomer who wishes to be regarded as one of the group adjusts his dress so that it is somewhat similar to that of the group. The city chap adjusts to his country cousin and friends, and vice versa.

Other factors operate in creating social distance, but at this point only one more will be considered. The person who is recognized by a group as being outside and above them often represents prestige. The group expects Mr. Prestige to construct an appropriate degree of social distance and recognizes that he is justified in so doing.

These observations serve to illustrate the practical nature of social distance as a teaching device. It is at once a valuable and dangerous tool. Some students, prior to the period of directed teaching, fully appreciate the necessity of social distance between teacher and pupil. They find it difficult, however, during actual practice-teaching to use it appropriately. They ask such questions as these of their critic teachers: "How can I get the pupils to respect me, yet like me?" "How can I prevent the older girls (or boys) from getting too familiar in the study hall and downtown on the street?" "What can I do to keep the pupils from being overfriendly?"

Popularity with pupils. Most prospective teachers want to be considered regular fellows by their pupils. Yet every experienced teacher knows that this is a secondary consideration. The primary considerations are such accomplishments as gaining the respect of colleagues and pupils, gaining their confidence, cooperating with the administration and with one's fellow teachers. The new or young teacher who is a seeker of popularity is slated for difficulty, disappointment, and perhaps failure. Generally speaking, the physical education teacher need not be concerned about being liked by pupils. He is offering a program which is (or should be) enjoyed by almost every pupil. If he teaches it effectively and interestingly, the pupils naturally associate him with the interesting, enjoyable program.

The beginning teacher is anxious to gain the confidence of pupils.

One way to defeat the accomplishment of his desire is to "kid" pupils before he is well known, respected, and liked by them. "Kidding" invariably leaves the new teacher in the position of having the pupils reply in kind. Embarrassing situations arise, and at best the teacher loses prestige, their respect, and confidence.

The teacher maintains varying degrees of discipline and social distance toward the pupils, fitting as best he can the purpose of his work with the occasion at hand. Under normal circumstances he expects and tries to get along amicably with them.

Understanding the pupil. The proper times for, kinds of, and degrees of discipline or social distance are dependent upon, in large part, an understanding of the pupil, which includes other important factors besides his anatomical structure and physiological functionings. His temperament, home life, outlook on life, interests, associations, dislikes, strengths, weaknesses, and peculiarities are some of the other knowledges basic to an intelligent understanding of him. In short, the teacher must really know the pupil as a person—as a personality. How else can he appeal to, inspire, and guide him? Certainly there are no magic formulae that secure identical results and reactions from all pupils, or from any two, for that matter.

Respect and liking are usually accorded the teacher who can guide pupils with understanding. The excellent teacher is effective in stimulating conscientious efforts and hard work, and at the same time seeming human to the pupils. Pupils feel that such a human teacher understands them. They feel that he will work toward their interests and their welfare.

Relationships with pupils of the opposite sex. Occasionally a beginning teacher inadvertently creates jealousies and brings criticism upon himself. One sure way of accomplishing these two reactions is to hold protracted conferences with pupils of the opposite sex. In such cases the teacher is doubtlessly sincere in believing that such conferences are necessary and accomplish worthwhile professional purposes. But teachers are usually judged in such cases on the basis of adherence to the rules of conventional behavior.

COMMUNITY MEMBERSHIP

Participation in community affairs. "But I was hired to teach, not to waste my time socializing," was the angry retort of a young teacher who had just lost his position. The superintendent had reluctantly dismissed him under community pressure. The crux of the matter was that this young man had refused to take part in community affairs. He was mistaken if he believed he was hired only to teach. He was hired as a teacher in that community. Whether it seems reasonable or not, most communities expect their teachers to participate in and support community projects actively. If, after a reasonable length of time, the teacher is not asked to enter into the affairs of the community, he should engage in some self-analysis. In fact, most physical educators develop into leaders of many community activities.

Most prospective teachers can appreciate these facts by remembering the reactions of the adults of their home communities toward teachers who did or did not participate in the community's affairs. The beginning teacher may be perplexed as to how much he can afford to engage in the life of the community. Usually an older member of the teaching staff or the principal can give sane advice in such matters. Experience has acquainted the older teachers with those types of community projects requiring staff support. They also know which projects can be side-stepped without creating a furor.

No teacher can effectively conduct his school duties and responsibilities and say "yes" to every request for his time and financial support. On the other hand, the teacher of physical education may expect to be called on by the community more often than are the other teachers. He should accept gracefully those responsibilities which are possible for him to carry through with reasonable success.

Common sense, then, tempered by the advice of older teachers with social intelligence and by the knowledge that he has a real obligation in serving the community, is one of the guides.

Loyalty to the community. The new teacher must find his life in the community if he plans to succeed. Beginning teachers, particularly, too often succumb to the temptation to leave town over the week-end. If they are located near their alma mater, they want to return for dances, athletic contests, and other college affairs. This lack of maturity, lack of interest in the community that gave them a job creates barriers between such teachers and the community.

Young teachers sometimes fail to recognize their implicit obligation and responsibility to the community. They fail to appreciate that the community often believes that teachers "think they are too good for us" when they leave the community over week-ends. Such teachers, because of this innocent ignorance, are often surprised when evidence of community antagonism or lack of cooperation is heaped upon their shoulders. Yet they must rapidly get over the college youth complex and assume the role of a member of the profession and a member of the community.

Publicity. The experienced physical education teacher knows that publicity is a two-edged sword. The teacher may receive favorable publicity for his program in the local newspaper. At the same time he may receive unfavorable publicity through the pupil-to-parent, parent-to-parent, teacher-to-teacher routes. Any new teacher of physical education should tactfully arrange contacts with the P.T.A. through the administrator of the school. If the teacher wants to make certain that the parents understand his program, its purposes and values, he should take every advantage of an opportunity to address them. If such a parent-teacher organization is lacking, visits and conferences with parents of pupils provide an avenue by which the teacher may gradually disseminate the correct information about his program and start building proper attitudes.

Articles for the local press should be carefully prepared and checked for accuracy before publication. Too much publicity often becomes a boomerang, particularly as regards creating professional jealousy among the other teachers.

WORKING HOURS

Although teachers may enjoy longer vacations and more extended holidays than persons in other fields, they must expect to work long hours during the months when school is in session. Even so, it is not an uncommon sight to see some teachers, books under their arms, follow the pupils out of the building. But teachers of physical education are often the last to leave the school. If the physical educator has no team to coach or assist, there is the intramural program to conduct, officiate in, or help with; there are informal teams or unorganized groups to prepare for the coming operetta, circus, play day, sports night, or demonstration; there are individuals, such as those who have handicaps, who need and earnestly desire special attention; there is equipment to check for safety factors and repair; or the gymnasium must be put in preparation for a coming event. Something always seems to need doing.

The teacher of physical education should not think of his position in terms of hours. He should think of it rather in terms of service he can render. The clock-watcher has no place in physical education or any other profession. Many first-year teachers of physical education are surprised at how the day's work at school stretches into ten, twelve, or more hours. Fortunately for most, these hours pass all too quickly; the work is interesting and challenging; and teachers are conscious of rendering vital service to pupil, school, and community.

In recent years an increasing number of schools throughout the country have been granting extra pay for extra services. Physical education teachers are among those who usually receive these benefits. This policy may be appropriate if the additional money is for increased service to the students, school, and community. Some teachers in the school actually do provide additional services. The leader of the school band, the conductor of the orchestra, the directors of choral and drama groups, the director of intramurals, the athletic coaches, and sponsors of other student activities all must spend many hours beyond what might be considered the normal school day. The requests for extra compensation for such persons often have been based on the additional hours involved in these special duties—a request for extra pay at an established hourly rate.

The prospective teacher should be aware that pay-by-the-hour departs from the *idea* of a profession. In the professions, *time* is not the criterion for salary. In the trades, *time* is the criterion; the worker is paid by-the-hour at an established rate. In the professions, the *quality of service* becomes the measure of the worth of a professional person.

FITTING INTO THE SCHOOL

Colleagues as judges. Usually, when experienced teachers recognize that a young teacher prepares his work and is devoted to it, they begin to respect him. Conscientious and efficient work is the first step in gaining acceptance by one's fellow teachers. The teacher of physical education who attempts to get by, whose conduct is unbecoming and inappropriate in the eyes of his colleagues, who is obviously a seeker of popularity, and who basks too comfortably in the sunshine of student-approval of physical education can hardly expect to fit amicably into the company of the other teachers of the school—if others are high quality professional persons. Such behavior prevents cooperation and acts as sand in the machinery of staff relationships.

Establishing a common ground. Beginning physical education teachers should appreciate that, superficially, the material and activities they teach place their duties in a different category from that of the teachers of academic subjects. But the general problems, principles, and techniques of teaching are similar, whether the content is algebra or archery. The physical educator is obligated to make this fact evident to his colleagues at appropriate times and places in order to insure the success of his program and its fusion with the rest of the curriculum.

The assumption by some physical educators that their work has little in common with other school subjects encourages the tendency to "ride alone." This attitude, coupled with a certain independence that many teachers of physical education have acquired, makes it doubly difficult for them to be accepted readily and fully by their fellow teachers. One has difficulty in securing cooperation from his colleagues if he is regarded as an outsider.

Selling oneself to one's colleagues. The difficulty of fitting in may be a different problem for the young teacher of physical education than for a beginning teacher of one of the long-established subjects. Physical education is new as a school subject. The acceptance of physical education in some academic quarters has been slow. It has yet to earn its place in the minds of many teachers and some administrators. Every physical educator is a salesman in the broadest interpretation of that word. He must sell himself as a teacher to his colleagues if he expects them to accept him and his program.

Therefore, he must speak their language, discuss their problems understandingly, show the similarity of their problems to his, and by his manner, attitude, speech, and work assure them that he is a teacher. Obviously, this statement means that he usually must go more than halfway to meet them.   This sacrifice is one any salesman is glad to make if he believes in his product.   It is the price that the pioneers in any field have always paid.

Cooperation with the administration.   The new teacher is sometimes surprised to find that something he has done was at cross-purposes with the principal or superintendent.   The teacher's first step is to find out the administrative rules and policies of the school. His next step is to support them.   The new teacher obviously should not join the group who oppose the administration—and every administrator has his opponents.   If certain regulations or policies seem unfair or not understandable, the new teacher might courteously tell the administrator, at the proper time and place, that he would like to know more about them.   Usually some very good reasons are back of most rules and policies.

Athletic problems.   The teacher of physical education is naturally interested in regulations pertaining to athletics.   Schools encounter problems if an athletic program is not provided.   Yet once it is introduced, new problems arise.   Financing such a program, supervision on trips, scholastic difficulties of athletes, eligibility, scheduling, and sportsmanship of spectators and participants are only a few of the problems in the boys' program.   Many schools are faced with the highly controversial question of whether there should be interscholastic athletics for girls.   Those schools that sponsor such a program add further problems to those related to the boys' athletic program.

The beginning teacher is perplexed at the complexity of these many problems and the far-reaching consequences that sometimes result.   He should work closely with the school administrator on all such problems.   He should arrive at each decision circumspectly. Above all other considerations he must regard the welfare of the pupil and the school as basic.   The policies of the school require loyal support even if it means being temporarily misunderstood by townspeople, colleagues, and pupils.

Cooperation with the "other" department.   The boys' physical education department usually is given more favorable consideration and support by the school officials than the girls' department.   One of the chief reasons given for this favoritism is that the former "makes the money" and gains the intense interest of the community through its athletic program.   Too frequently antagonisms spring

up between the two departments.   If physical education is to pros-
per, if it is to become stabilized and deep-rooted, physical educators
must work together.   The allocation of funds, facilities, equipment,
and personnel should be made on the basis of and proportional to
respective needs.   No physical educator can fit into the school if
he fails to cooperate fully with his professional colleague.

DEFERRED RESULTS

The young teacher tends to be enthusiastic, optimistic, and perhaps at times impatient for greater speed in pupil-learning.   He
wants to see accomplishment of great things in a short time.   Enthusiasm and optimism are highly desirable traits of the teacher, but
there must also be understanding of the pupil and of the learning
process or discouragement and skepticism may follow.

Complex habits are not likely to be formed quickly.   The parent
trains the child for years in neatness and cleanliness before the results become apparent as personality traits.   Every year, the coach
trains a group of beginners without expecting them to achieve integration of skills, physiological maturity, or emotional control in
that particular year.   He is looking forward toward future development.   He merely sets up an environment which fosters that development.

The older teacher foresees the awkward, impulsive, shy pubescent
as the socially poised, coordinated leader of the twelfth grade.   Years
of observation have taught the older teacher that *learning takes
time.*   The same years of experience have taught him patience and
a faith in the educative process.   He has seen a generation of irresponsible and impulsive children turn into responsible citizens.

The beginning teacher will grow in his ability to foster student
development.   Such a teacher's self-analysis and self-criticism will
help if it is based on an understanding of his job.   Discouragement
and self-blame for slow pupil-progress are usually unjustified in the
conscientious teacher.   Moreover, they dim the youthful enthusiasm
of the beginning teacher, one of his greatest assets.   This very youthful enthusiasm and energy of the beginning teacher will compensate
for much of his lack of experience.

The beginning teacher must realize that personality change in the
student is a process of slow growth.   Development pauses on pla-

teaus, and it may even pause until a later stage of physiological development. But, the environment fostered by the enthusiastic, helpful and sympathetic teacher is almost a *sine qua non* of pupil development.

All the teachers are trying to mold the pupil into a worthy citizen. The physical education teacher cannot accomplish this feat alone. The significant contributions of the physical education teacher are most effective when synchronized with the total school effort toward pupil development. This fact implies close teacher cooperation. For that matter, the school is not the only force attempting to mold the child. One can hardly ignore the influences of such agencies as church, club, theater, movie, television, camp, playground, vacant lot, street, alley, neighborhood library, newspaper, magazine and the old swimming hole.

SAMPLE TEST ITEMS [1]

True-False

1. School subjects are means to ends.

2. The child understands his own needs.

3. Personality factors that count most in job-getting are those that are seen and heard.

4. The teacher's carriage, speech, and appearance are frequently imitated by pupils.

5. Teachers of today need to be more versatile than the teachers of two decades ago.

6. A prospective teacher of physical education is a good judge of his ability to teach physical education.

7. A teacher of physical education, to succeed, must possess superior abilities in all physical education activities.

8. School administrators recognize that a prospective teacher's scholarship is the best index of his teaching success.

9. Other things being equal, most employers prefer to hire applicants they know best.

10. Arriving in town the night before school opens is early enough for the new teacher to prepare for the school year.

---

[1] The sample test items at the close of each chapter are intended to provoke thought and discussion, form attitudes, test understandings and comprehensions, and create felt needs.

11. Two weeks before the opening of school most school suprintendents are too busy to grant an interview to a new teacher about the local situation.

12. It is a wise policy for a new teacher to find out previous practices in the school system before school begins and to plan to conform to them.

13. Any changes made in previous local practices in physical education should conform to local administrative policies.

14. Registration for physical education classes should take place after all other classes are scheduled.

15. An effective opening-day's plan can circumvent many later disciplinary problems.

16. The prejudices of a community are the concern of the superintendent, not that of the teacher.

17. In order to gain the respect of the pupils the new teacher must show authority at all times.

18. Social distance is a delicate instrument in the hands of the teacher and can be an asset or a liability.

19. The teacher should be more desirous of gaining the pupils' respect than of seeking to be popular with them.

20. There can be no intelligent teaching unless the teacher understands the pupil.

21. Active participation in community affairs is one of the chief obligations of the teacher.

22. Favorable publicity in the press may serve as an obstacle to being accepted by one's colleagues.

23. Most of the fundamental problems of the physical education teacher are similar to those of the academic teacher and are so recognized by them.

24. Being accepted by one's academic colleagues is socially but not professionally important.

25. The new teacher should make up his mind as to whether he is for or against the administration and then have the courage to declare his convictions to others.

26. Other things being equal, physical education progresses best in situations where the men and women physical educators actively cooperate.

Discussion Questions:

1. What are some other vital traits or characteristics instrumental in securing a position?

2. What should the new teacher do during the one or two weeks before school begins?

3. What does the teacher consider in establishing and maintaining proper relationships with pupils?

4. What are the responsibilities and opportunities of the teacher in becoming a member of the community?

5. How might these responsibilities vary in large and small communities?

6. Should the physical education teacher receive a higher salary on the basis of working longer hours than other teachers?

7. If you had the opportunity to vote for either a physical education profession or a physical education trade union, which would you select? Why?

8. What can the teacher of physical education do in order to fit into the school?

9. What do you think will be your chief problems as a teacher?

10. Why did you choose teaching as a career?

11. What traits and abilities do you have indicating success as a teacher?

BIBLIOGRAPHY

Adams, Harold P. and Frank G. Dickey, *Basic Principles of Student Teaching.* New York: American Book Company, 1956.

Douglass, Harl R. and Hubert H. Mills, *Teaching in High School,* 2nd ed. New York: The Ronald Press Company, 1957.

Eye, Glenn G. and Willard R. Lane, *The New Teacher Comes to School.* New York: Harper & Brothers, 1956.

Frank, Guy P., *The Difficulties of Beginning Teachers.* Laramie: The Bureau of Educational Research and Service, College of Education, University of Wyoming. Educational Problems Series, Bulletin No. 6, November, 1952.

Gruhn, William T., *Student Teaching in the Secondary School.* New York: The Ronald Press Company, 1953.

Huggett, Albert J., and T. M. Stinnett, *Professional Problems of Teachers.* New York: The Macmillan Company, 1956.

Knapp, Clyde, *Physical Education: Student and Beginning Teaching.* New York: The McGraw-Hill Book Company, Inc., 1957.

Kozman, Hilda Clute, Rosalind Cassidy, and Chester O. Jackson, *Methods in Physical Education.* Philadelphia: W. B. Saunders Company, 1958.

Murray, Ruth L., and Delia P. Hussey, *From Student to Teacher in Physical Education: A Guidebook for Student Teachers and Beginning Teachers of Physical Education.* Englewood Cliffs, N. J.: Prentice-Hall, Inc., 1959.

Schorling, Raleigh and Howard T., *Student Teaching.* New York: The McGraw-Hill Book Company, 1955.

Van Dalen, Deobold B., and Marcella M. Van Dalen, *The Health, Physical Education and Recreation Teacher, and Introduction to the Profession* Englewood Cliffs, N. J.: Prentice-Hall, Inc., 1956.

2

The nature of teaching

Method is the master of masters.

—Talleyrand

THE PRACTICAL VERSUS THE THEORETICAL

WHAT DOES PRACTICAL MEAN? SOME TEACHERS IN PHYSICAL education assume their work is more practical than that in the academic areas. Pupils actually *do* something in physical education. Many teachers of industrial arts and domestic science believe their work is practical because it is *used* in the daily life. A few teachers of physical education still believe that work is practical only when the emphasis is placed on *how*—that when one asks *why?* he is becoming theoretical. These teachers feel their job is only to show how to do things; they think objectives and purposes are theoretical, that activities should be *assumed* to be worthwhile.

These three concepts of the practical—(1) the higher the degree of activity, the higher is the degree of practicality, (2) the clearer the evidence of specific use in daily living, the more it is practical, and (3) *how* to do an activity is practical, but *why* to do the activity is theoretical, hence less important—serve to illustrate vague, confused, and erroneous thinking.

This type of thinking reveals several weaknesses; for example, in the first concept, reading or computing seem to be less active processes than typewriting or piano playing; yet one hesitates to consider the latter two of more immediate application in life. Baking a

27

cake might be much less useful (practical) than learning the legal requirement of property ownership, of car driving, or of debt payment.   If the physical education teacher bases his instruction only on *how to do,* without regard for *reasons for* doing or not doing, the student will suffer.   If the teacher himself does not consider *why,* he is unlikely to think of community and students' needs.

What does theoretical mean?   The word *theory* means a *generalization based on much past factual experience with similar situations.*   A generalization without many facts is a *guess* or a *hypothesis.*   If great numbers of facts indicate that the guess is correct, the guess becomes a *theory.*   After corroborative facts have accumulated over a long period, or in vast numbers, the theory is called a *law.* One speaks of the *laws* of nature but of the *theories* of electricity or light.   The theories of the nature of matter have changed greatly in recent years.   These *theories* have become *practical problems* because of newer ideas about energy-release.   Theories of what produces fitness often become practical problems in a national emergency.

The term *theoretical* is often used to show disapproval.   Thus, a player says, "That coach is too theoretical," meaning that he cannot carry out the coaching in action.   Perhaps the undergraduate occasionally falls back upon the term *theoretical* as a defense against admitting lack of knowledge or understanding.

These questions suggest answers that serve as guides in studying the following pages in this chapter:

1. May the criticism "too theoretical" be an indication of the critic's lack of experience?   May such a criticism be a type of defense against strenuous mental effort in learning?   May the criticism be a defense against confessing a lack of comprehension?

2. Should new teaching material be associated and interpreted for the learner in terms of his first-hand experience?   Is this usually possible in teaching physical education?   How could this be done in a class of prospective teachers who are learning how to be teachers?

3. What theories do athletic coaches use?   Teachers in physical education?

The theoretical becomes practical.   A twelve-year-old hopes some day to make the All-American football team.   His older brother, a college football player, comes home for a vacation.   The boy expresses a desire for some coaching.   Soon, in the opinion of the twelve-year-old, the older brother becomes highly theoretical.

Some undergraduate professional students in physical education are discussing program-building. The instructor points out that the pupils' needs and interests are basic factors to be considered in curriculum construction. He explains and elaborates his point. The matter becomes highly theoretical to these prospective teachers. Some prospective teachers in physical education consider only the activity courses practical. All other courses are theoretical, excepting perhaps parts of courses in which they are told precisely what to do in stated situations.

Occasionally an experienced teacher conversing with a novice gives this advice, "The first thing to do is to forget all that theory you learned in college. All you have to do is to select some activities and go to it."

We place the label of "practical" on certain things that fit in with what we know, what we have done, seen, and heard. If we can use or can see a use for something, we may be willing to call it "practical." However, as soon as the matter stretches beyond our experience or comprehension, we quickly apply the label "theoretical." The utility of correct theory is succinctly described in the following quotation:

"It's all right in theory, but it won't do in practice, is another popular way of revelling in logical absurdity. The philosopher Schopenhauer said all we need to know about this sophism: "The assertion is based upon an impossibility: what is right in theory *must* work in practice; and if it does not, there is a mistake in the theory; something has been overlooked and not allowed for; and consequently, what is wrong in practice is wrong in theory too." [1]

Some prospective teachers feel that a discussion of the principles of teaching is confusing. They feel it unnecessarily switches their attention from practical aspects of teaching to the theoretical! They may say, "Does not this bringing-in of theories make teaching needlessly more complex than it really is?" "How can one teach when he has to think about all these extraneous things about teaching?" "From where do these theoretical *dicta* come anyway?" "Cannot one become a successful teacher without using them?" "Were there not successful teachers before these theories were constructed?"

Less preliminary work is required for the high school teacher to

---

[1] Max Black, *Critical Thinking: An Introduction to Logic and Scientific Method*, 2nd ed. (Englewood Cliffs, N. J.: Prentice-Hall, Inc., 1952), p. 236.

present the program of physical education that he learned in his undergraduate days. But neither the specific teaching techniques nor the specific activities are likely to fit the new situation. Teaching should be *fitted* to the group to be taught and to the teacher's particular type of personality. Without a background of generalizations (theories) about how to determine specific needs, select appropriate activities, and fit teaching to the particular situation, the teacher must depend upon crude trial-and-error as a means of learning to teach.

At first, principles of teaching get in the way. This condition is not surprising. A beginner in golf has difficulty in following the principles laid down by the pro. The novice wants to start participating! On the other hand, *any beginner* who receives instructions and wants to improve rapidly and to a considerable degree, must do three things: (1) try out, (2) apply, and (3) experiment with the suggestions given him.

Assuming a mature attitude. The student-in-training should not dismiss teaching guides with a scornful wave of the hand because they now seem theoretical. The novice should realize that *the principles of teaching arise from the cumulative experiences of thousands of teachers of physical education, the findings of such sciences as anatomy and physiology, the present findings of psychology, and the best thought of leading educators and physical educators.*

The novice teacher, therefore, might well reason along these lines: "In spite of the fact that these principles seem theoretical to me, I'm going to try them out. Since these theories represent the best that sciences, near-sciences, experience and careful thought of successful teachers can give, there must be something to them. So, I am at least going to keep an open mind, find out all I can about them, and try them out when I begin to teach. Then, after a fair trial over two or three years, I'll accept those that experience proves are okay for me."

Teaching, not simple. The teacher must consider the *how* and *why* of teaching. Merely telling is not teaching. He also must consider the when, where, what, and whom of teaching in these modern times. *How* is method, *why* is purpose, *when* is time, *where* is location, *what* refers to the activities, and *whom* refers to the nature of the pupil. The complexity of teaching astounds some prospective teachers because of their former ideas regarding the sim-

plicity of teaching.   They need to learn to assume a scientific attitude toward each teaching situation.   (The scientific attitude
suggests that we delay judgment until all the evidence has been
gathered.)

The student-in-training should consider the fact that today's principles of teaching are the theories of yesterday which have been made
practical through the experiences of many teachers.   *Experience
turns the theoretical into the practical.*

The point was made in a previous paragraph that prospective and
beginning teachers often agree that activity courses are the only practical ones.   Many persons hold the belief that, if an individual can
do a given thing, he can teach it.   Does it not seem logical that great
performers make the best coaches?   If a student-in-training can
perform the activities in the major curriculum well, will he necessarily make a good teacher?

WHAT IS TEACHING?

Combining the practical and the theoretical.   A high quality of
skills is required in both game performance and in coaching or
teaching.   But they are not the same skills.   The prospective
teacher has to *combine* these two differing sets of skills.

This *combining* of the ability to perform and the ability to teach
is not difficult for the major student who has the knack of performance in sports, dance, or other activities *as well as* the knack of
teaching.   But this combining—this *connecting*—of the two may
prove to be difficult for the athlete who is slow to catch on to the
fact that if he is to coach, he must learn, understand, and apply considerable theory.   Similarly, the major student who wants to concentrate on the theory part and avoid the responsibility for learning
to perform well will also have trouble.

If the musician, the sculptor, the writer, or the painter (or any of
the others whose professions require that they be able to perform)
lacks either the practical or the theoretical, he is *incompletely* prepared.   Some of these people, who begin to work without being
prepared and find out how unprepared they are, then must seek
means to fill the gaps.   State laws and regulations prevent this
happening in the field of teaching.   To make mistakes on a piece

of marble or on a canvas is regrettable. To make mistakes in the lives of tomorrow's citizens is tragic.

Obviously, *both* performance in physical education and performance in teaching require both the practical and the theoretical. Teaching also combines other kinds of practical and theoretical processes.

Learning, a practical-theoretical process. Before we discuss teaching as a process, a glance should be taken at learning and the learner (see Chapters 4, 5, and 6 for more complete details). When one thinks about teaching, he thinks about *whom* he is to teach. That is the height of practicality. You would not teach a sixteen-year-old as you would a six-year-old. You would not teach a sixteen-year-old who knew nothing about tennis as you would a sixteen-year-old who has played in several tennis tournaments.

"But where does the theory come in?" a skeptical student asks. "All you have to do, no matter *who* it is, is to tell 'em what to do." Here we find two of the most commonly-held, mistaken views: *first,* the idea that "telling 'em" is the way that teaching takes place; and *second,* the blind faith that *learning* is *supposed* to take place. Related to that is the inescapable fact that every act of teaching and every moment spent in teaching *assumes* that learning takes place in some *certain* way(s).

Even the "tell 'em" idea of teaching assumes that when the learner *hears* what the teacher tells him, he has *learned* to do whatever it was! Most of us have heard a young teacher or a young coach say (often with considerable impatience), "But I *told* you to . . ." The adjective "young" is used here because it is a characteristic of most beginning teachers (and coaches) that they think telling a learner once or twice how to do something constitutes teaching.

The old saying, "No one has taught unless someone has learned," is not accurate. The acid test is this, "No one has taught unless someone has learned *that which was taught.*" We teachers cannot be satisfied with the boy or girl saying, "Yes, I know it now," or "Yes, now I can do it." We also want to know how firm, how permanent the learnings are. The only way the learner can show that he has learned is to produce, to perform. This is the acme of practicality.

As teachers, our main duty is to *help* learning take place as quickly, as permanently, as easily as possible. Most teachers would also add, "and as interestingly." Once this main duty is understood, the following questions are raised: How does one give this help? How does one influence the girl or boy so that he has or *gains a desire* to learn what is being taught? How does one extend this influence on the learning process so that the girl or boy actually learns what is taught? Some teachers believe that the pupil does not actually learn unless he has *mastered* that which was taught.

These commonplace questions demand that we know all we can about learning. This sends us into courses in psychology and stimulates us to read books about learning. How *does* learning take place? The fact that there still is no final answer to that question is discouraging to teachers. Thus, as in so many things in life, we must use the best we have in the best way that we know. For the beginning teacher this probably means accepting (for the time being) the theory of learning recommended by his major professor or by his psychology professor.

Whatever theory of learning is adopted (for all teaching is based on *some* assumption about how learning takes place), the major student should examine it and *understand* it thoroughly. Then, in trial-teaching and directed (student) teaching he can begin to *apply* the parts of this theory of learning. Here again one must develop the ability to combine theory and practice.

Some other determinants of teaching. A powerful force, if not the most powerful in determining one's ideas of teaching consists of the purposes of teaching, as presented in Chapter 7. *Why* are you teaching *what* you are teaching? Let us say that the activity is basketball. You would teach (or coach) it differently if your main purpose were to prepare the players for competition than to enable them to have a good time in a recreation program. And, you would teach it still differently if your purpose on the one hand were to help beginners in a physical education class, or on the other hand if it were to help a class of major students who wanted to become expert in their trial-teaching of basketball.

Other determinants of your conception of teaching are: your own standards of teaching; your values of physical education; the potential you hold for those you teach; the degree to which you catch, retain, and apply the teachings of your instructors; how well you accept the responsibility for the welfare of your classes, within the policies and jurisdiction of your school; the degree to which you are willing to uncover and bring forth the desirable outcomes of a given activity; and, your philosophy of life.

Ideas of value affect teaching. Let us look briefly at the influence of one's ideas of what is valuable. The teacher's ideas of the values of physical education is such an important determining force that it is discussed at length in Chapter 8.

Should you teach the activities you are most interested in? So many activities in physical education might be taught, the teacher often is confused as to just which ones to teach. The better part of wisdom is to select those of most value to the individual and to society. But all individuals are not the same. What is most valuable to some is not particularly valuable to others.

While in a democracy we consider the greatest good for the greatest number, we also take into consideration the welfare of the individual. A reasonable position is that the physical education selected for a given group should be that which is most valuable to the greatest number of pupils. However, special activities for the physically superior, for the physically inferior, for those with physical handicaps, and for those with other special needs and interests are also needed. Physical education should be made to fit the individual.

We must also determine what objectives of a given activity are most worth while to the pupil at a given time and place. In a game of volleyball, should organic vigor or skill receive chief emphasis? Is enjoyment or meticulous obedience to rules the point of emphasis? Shall we make it the socio-moral attributes such as good sportsmanship, or winning the game? The teacher also must decide which skills of volleyball are most worth while to learn at a particular time. Shall it be spiking, passing, or serving? When seeking an answer, we must reconsider whether we have in mind the individual or the group. And, after this question is answered, we must face the question of whether we were thinking of worth-whileness to the child now, next year, or in postschool years?

For example, the teacher's ideas of teaching volleyball will vary according to his ideas of what is valuable. If he conceives that winning the game is most valuable, he will teach a certain way. If he considers acquirement of socio-moral attributes most worthwhile, obviously he will teach differently. Teaching also will vary if the teacher considers brilliance of individual performance more valuable than the enjoyment that the group gains from volleyball. The fact that the teacher selected volleyball in the first place as the most valuable for the greatest number at the time is a basic value judgment.

The responsibility thus placed upon the teacher's vision and judgment is no small matter. In addition, he may have to discard some of his own personal preferences and biases. More and more we extend our concern about values. The task of the teacher in developing new interests and guiding the pupil to appreciate new or different values is clear. This deepening, broadening, and enriching the experience of the child is a prime factor in making physical education more *educational* and in being an effective teacher.

The teacher also must check each other phase of teaching—the environment, the pupil, the activity, the objectives to be accomplished, and the testing procedures. These must be so controlled that the *sum total* of the resulting experience for the pupil is of most value to him.

A more obvious relationship between teaching and value is seen in the answer to this question: In what ways can I make volleyball most valuable to these pupils? In answering such a question, the teacher takes the first step toward more valuable teaching.

Teaching and content inseparable. The program is another force which influences one's ideas of the nature of teaching. Certainly each activity varies in its complexity, number of participants, rules, facilities and equipment, skills, play and strategy, necessary conditioning, demands for output of energy, and the like. Further, the mental set varies from one type of activity to another. One does not teach swimming as one teaches tennis. Also, consider the expansion of mental content, number of plays, variety of offenses and defenses taught today as compared with a decade ago.

The reasoning behind rule-changes indicates changes in teaching. The performer of tomorrow apparently is expected to possess more skill, be more clever, take on more responsibility, and become more apt at adjusting to rapidly changing situations on field and floor.

In addition, while one activity demands that teaching emphasize the acquirement of strength, for example, another activity requires that teaching stress such psychological factors as emotional control or perhaps such social acquirements as teamplay.

The effective teacher also emphasizes *participation*. Unlike some of the other school subjects, to know, in physical education, is not enough. No amount of sitting around *talking about* (no matter how democratically conducted) how to shoot a basket, make a goal in hockey or how to control one's temper, can possibly substitute for the real experience.

The effective teacher also knows that teaching and content are related in another way. If teaching takes place, there *must* be some instruction. On the other hand, the novice is warned that most of us as novices in anything tend to overcontrol. Few indeed are the novice teachers who do not overteach.

From your personal observation or experience, give an example of this statement: Teaching changes when content changes. The responsibility of the teacher for program-building (content) is discussed at some length in Chapter 9.

Teaching takes place somewhere. "But I was hired to teach, not to compete in a community popularity contest!" These bitter words, much like those of the young man in Chapter 1, came from another teacher, after a year of experience, as he talked to a former major professor. His mistake was that he had not been sold, during his undergraduate years, on the necessity of studying the community. He carried out rather forcefully his idea that the community should have nothing to say about *how* he taught. His manner of teaching was irritating enough to a sufficient number of parents so that he was asked to leave in April, after the principal and superintendent had tried to reason with him. Communities are made up of people. It is not surprising that they, like people, differ. Communities also influence and are influenced by people. Most parents in most communities are more concerned about program content, but community attitudes about the way teaching is conducted are not unusual.

Excellent teaching, uncommon. How many *excellent* teachers are there in the schools, colleges, and universities today? One answer might be, about the same proportion as there are excellent physicians, chemists, and engineers in these respective professions. And yet there is a difference. The standard of excellence for practice in these three professions has been raised considerably in the past two or more thousand years. The methods and practices of the medicine man, the alchemist, or the early engineer of Egypt are hardly comparable to the work of men today in these professions.

What kind of teacher will the prospective teacher make of himself? Will his students remember him as a good teacher, or will he be forgotten—one of those teachers who never made a lasting, commendable impression upon even one pupil? Will he be satisfied with being a mediocre or poor teacher, or will he strive toward excellency in his profession? These are questions that continually face prospective, beginning, and experienced teachers. Most teachers desire excellence. Some work hard enough to attain it.

Teaching perspectives. One set of perspectives on teaching is formed by considering who most frequently looks at teaching. Immediately above, there is the *teacher* looking at teaching. He looks at it with the thought of quality of service. Previous to that, in this chapter the teacher has been looking at his work from still other viewpoints.

The *pupil* also looks at teaching. He seldom separates teaching from the teacher. He seldom separates these two from school. A few seniors and juniors in high school develop ability to recognize good teaching. The average senior high school student expects a good deal of his teachers. Fairness, objectivity, carefulness, sympathy, sportsmanship, maturity, thorough mastery of his subject, an interest in young persons, and a host of other fine traits. The pupil's vehement condemnation of a teacher who errs springs largely from the high place which he occupies in the teenager's mind. There are exceptions to this rather roseate picture, unfortunately. On the other hand, many students have higher expectations of their teachers.

Parents look at teaching in quite other ways. There are, of course, parents who have attitudes toward the school which can best be described as negative. Some of them look at teaching with an emotional chip on their sensitive shoulders. Others must be labelled negative or worse because they seem to care little about what happens to Jack or Jill. Yet, there are many who look at teaching with admiration, with gratitude, with respect. Think of the near-miraculous things which teachers have been able to do with some of their children! Awkwardness turned to grace. Clumsiness turned to coordination. Fear transplanted by courage. Self-centeredness changed to self-subordination-for-the-good-of-the-group. Weakness and fatigue replaced by strength and endurance. And so on through the long list of accomplishments which any effective physical education teacher could remember if he were urged. The parent's way of looking at teaching should be kept firmly in mind. If there were time, we could consider what others see when they look at teaching—one's academic colleagues, the administration, the tax-payers, the board of education, the alumni who did not go to college as well as those who did, and so on.

A *second* teaching perspective emerges from thinking about some of the larger concerns of teaching. The *philosophical* way of look-ing at teaching is not interested in the question of how to play basketball, for instance. It is interested in the values in basketball now and later on for the participant, for the spectators, for the com-munity as a whole. It is interested in the larger purposes of basket-ball and whether these purposes are valuable to the player and to society.

The *scientific* way of looking at teaching sees the use by the teacher of scientifically-determined facts about the child and the environ-ment. Some of these facts relate to the biological nature of man, others to the child's physiology, anatomy, behavior, and reactions. Still others of these facts relate to geography, temperature, humidity, lighting, sanitation, and additional environmental factors. The teacher not only discovers these facts but applies them.

The *psychological* look at teaching is one in which the facts men-tioned above are manipulated and adjusted to the uniqueness of the individual child. The psychological approach is interested in con-trolling the child and his environment so that learning is made easier, more rapid, more permanent, or more interesting. The selec-tion, use, and effects of certain principles and techniques of instruc-tion are also a part of the psychological approach.

The *sociological* phase of controlling pupil experience shifts atten-tion to the social outcomes and social implications of teaching. The emphasis here is upon teaching as it develops desirable social traits within the individual and the effects of teaching upon a particular group and society in general. Environment is controlled, activities are selected, and techniques of instruction are used so that such traits as friendliness, respect for the rights of others, unselfishness, cooperation, and sociability can be learned by and developed in the child.

If these four ways of looking at teaching—philosophical, scientific, psychological and sociological—are combined and fused, we are apt to have effective teaching.   Thus, we say, "Teaching is that process taken to direct and control the experience of the learner."   Whenever you do anything to direct or control the experience of the pupil, you are taking a step of some kind in the teaching process. Figure 2-1 illustrates this general pattern of teaching.

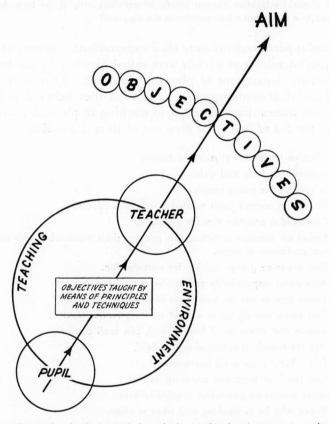

Fig. 2-1. The teacher leads a pupil through the teaching environment toward an aim.

This simple diagram does not show that throughout the entire process the teacher may emphasize one or all of the four kinds of controls of the child's experiences and that all four controls are to be considered.   The sketch is neither a set procedure nor a comprehensive picture.   It merely illustrates the point that the program as well as the principles and techniques of instruction are the *means* by which the pupil is guided and led by the teacher toward the accomplishment of certain outcomes.

1. In the diagrammatic sketch, why are both the pupil and the teacher placed partly inside and partly outside of the Teaching Environment?

2. If physical education consists chiefly of activities, why is the term Activities relegated to a somewhat minor position in the diagram?

School superintendents state their expectations. Some outstanding superintendents of schools were called together by the head of a university department of physical education. They were asked to express their frank opinions as to what they believed were the important things that typified good teaching in physical education. Here is the list of items that grew out of their discussion.

The *effective* teacher in physical education:

1. Understands boys and girls.
2. Is interested in young people.
3. Knows the content fields related to physical education.
4. Can build a program that fits all pupils.
5. Knows all common activities, can perform them reasonably well and is a top performer in some.
6. Can organize groups quickly for participation.
7. Anticipates responsibility and carries out all assignments.
8. Knows how to get the values out of physical education.
9. Can administer discipline without creating further trouble.
10. Speaks and writes good English; and, can spell correctly.
11. Has the broad viewpoint about his field.
12. Fills cultural gaps in his background.
13. Can teach at least one academic subject.
14. Bases grades on justifiable, sensible criteria.
15. Knows why he is teaching and what to stress.
16. Can carry out a program planned by someone else.
17. Is well-balanced, adjustable, and energetic.
18. Possesses ingenuity.
19. Uses good judgment as a staff and a community member.
20. Realizes the great influence he has over his pupils.
21. Takes part in the whole school program.
22. Does not have the "I-am-the-coach" complex.

23. Does not look *down* at the elementary and junior high schools.

24. Is highly professional in thought, word, and act.

25. Takes praise and blame with equanimity.

26. Has unbounded enthusiasm, vitality, and vigor.

27. Is youthful in mind and spirit.

28. Likes people and people like him.

29. Gives more of self than is asked or expected.

30. Makes his teaching stick.

31. Is a natural in guidance.

Experienced school administrators, generally, have learned that they can have such expectations as these—and, of course this would be only a partial list if all good administrators expressed themselves.

One of the most difficult responsibilities for the beginning teacher to carry through in the departments consisting of one woman and one man, or perhaps two, is to demonstrate good judgment in the selection of the program.   The importance of this duty appears several times in the above list.   Young men and women preparing to teach in this field enjoy physical activity.   Almost all of them have several favorites, and sometimes there may be one or two activities they dislike.   The difficulty comes when one suddenly finds himself with the responsibility of planning or helping to plan an *entire* program.   This task is so important that it occupies all of Chapter 11.

Teaching demands the "touch" of the artist.   Sometimes there is discussion about whether teaching is an art or a science.   Teaching is largely an *applied* field, as suggested by the philosophical, scientific, psychological, and sociological ways of looking at teaching.

On the other hand, teaching joins medicine, engineering, theology, and such sciences as chemistry and physics in the qualities it demands of its members.   These special qualities have to be developed and used with artistry, human beings being what they are.   Some of these qualities are:

1. A creative and courageous imagination.   Creative imagination is useful in solving problems.   It occurs frequently in a mind saturated with information; in a mind full of knowledge based upon ability in skills and a thorough acquaintance with previous studies in the field.   In periods of relaxation, various ideas from this wealth of background pop into the mind in new arrangements.   Often

these new arrangements solve the problem.   The individual is said to have created a new idea.   Courageous imagination allows the individual to rearrange these bits in ways contrary to custom and tradition.   Consider the courage of Thomas D. Wood and others in thinking out the natural program of physical education in a field dominated by the tradition and authority.

A creative imagination is basic to ingenuity in the physcal education teacher faced with such practical problems as having inadequate facilities and equipment, making the most of limited material for athletic teams, or educating a backward community to the newer ideas in physical education.

2. A mastery of information, skills, and previous work.   Authorities consider this mastery as one of the most pertinent factors in teaching success.   Without such mastery, a teacher cannot properly build a program, select effective techniques of instruction, set up desirable goals of accomplishment, or adjust all of this to the learner.

A teacher cannot know enough about his field.   A teacher is never completely prepared for his profession.   He must continually be on the alert for new information, new ideas.   He must continually master the new and remain master of the old.

3. Enthusiasm.

4. High standards and ideals of work.

5. Ability to project his personality.   In addition to these qualities that apply to the professions in general, teaching demands the projection of the teacher's personality into what is being taught and into those being taught.   The teacher makes his subject live and alive.   How?   Through energy and the zest of his presentation; through his dramatic ability as expressed in demonstration, facial expression, and voice intonations.   He senses and associates the individuals' vivid experiences and their systems of values with what is being taught.   The teaching of an excellent teacher, therefore, sticks.

The science of teaching.   Teaching as an art is almost ageless. Teaching as a kind of applied science is in its infancy.   In a sense, the term "science of teaching" is inaccurate.   Teaching deals with human beings who are variable and largely unpredictable.   They have age-old emotions and resistant nervous systems, and they have a way of refusing to be placed into compartments and categories.

In spite of this non-objectivity of human beings, we need more scientific teaching.   Teachers should formulate *principles* and use them in their work; they should *experiment* in order to find out which principles and techniques bring the best results; they should formulate *tests* and use more *theories,* with the intent of verifying them and developing them into *laws;* they should *formulate theories* and *hypotheses* as to how persons in general may be expected to behave in certain specific situations; they should invent *devices* to make teaching more exact, more objective; and they should *use* more *tests* to evaluate and measure the outcomes of teaching.

The beginning teacher will find that to follow "best guess" is easier than to apply the principles of teaching.   He will also find it more convenient to use specific techniques recommended for each detailed teaching situation.   Nevertheless, when the teacher uses scientific teaching principles, he is taking a step toward better teaching.   And, as he gains skill in their use and learns to coordinate the art and science of teaching, he will move toward that goal of being effective.

Which do you think will take the longest to master, the art of teaching or the science of teaching?   Why?

What is teaching?   We have been saying, directly and indirectly, that teaching includes controlling and guiding the experiences of the learner and providing the most suitable environment possible for learning to take place.

The teaching process thus includes anticipating, planning, and preparing.   It includes selecting and using the right principles, methods, and techniques of teaching; it means presenting that which is to be learned, explaining, organizing and managing classes, establishing and maintaining routines, using sensory aids including the familiar demonstration, observing the pupil as he performs, and providing suitable opportunities for pupil participation.   In addition, teaching includes motivating, administering discipline, analyzing, directing, generalizing, diagnosing, individualizing instruction and taking steps to help the pupil become more acceptably socialized. Furthermore, the physical education teacher usually is expected to conduct an evaluation program to find out to what degree pupils accomplish the objectives toward which they have been striving. His responsibility in guidance was referred to above.   The modern teacher also tries to enhance the public relations status of the schools, and, above all, to render high-quality professional service. Chapters 11 through 17 discuss these matters in detail.

In summary, teaching is concerned with:

1. Helping the pupil to have *worthwhile* experiences.
2. Helping him learn to *react* better.
3. Helping him *find and develop his talents,* his potentials.
4. Providing chances for the student to *perform better.*
5. Helping him find *better ways of thinking, acting and being.*
6. Discovering the *best reasons for teaching* each activity.
7. Finding the *best ways of teaching.*
8. Teaching the *best of that which we know.*
9. Going higher than competency, *going beyond the call of duty.*
10. Learning and striving to become an ever-better teacher.

It should now be clear that we are suggesting that the effective teacher does far more than teach pupils by means of activities. On the other hand, a few teachers in the field may still take the view, "I was hired to teach physical education activities. I teach 'em to the kids that come to class. They also gave me some additional chores, such as being a policeman, a bookkeeper, and a health knowledge disseminator. They heaped still more work on me in the form of school committees, an after-school activity, and pushed me into some community-service work. Now, don't tell me you're going to *expand* my work responsibilities for the salary that *I* get!"

What is the "size" of teaching? Our concepts not only limit what we believe, they also limit what we do! Experiments indicate that when a person's concept of his ability is changed, his performance changes also. He didn't think he could, so he didn't. He thought he could, so he did. There are limits in applying the psychology of self-actualization. Yet, the quality of professional teaching differs chiefly in one thing, the "size" of teachers' thinking, of their estimates. Would you hire a teacher who had a low estimate of himself, a small estimate of his profession, a limited estimate of the potential in young persons, of what teaching can do for, with, and to pupils and of education in general? One reason that the physical education teacher usually is so highly valued by school administrators is because they see beyond the subject. They believe there is great good in girls and boys. On one occasion, the chairman of the American Council on Education said to a physical educator who had been called in as a consultant, "We think you people are the most enthusiastic professional persons in all of education, and, you believe more definitely in what can be done through this field."

He who has a great belief in his life's work must have a high aim, together with high-level major objectives. Let us turn now to a consideration of this Golden Key of one's profession.

TEACHING DEPENDS ON AN AIM AND OBJECTIVES

Teaching and an aim.   Ask a man his aim in life and you will receive a concentrated form of his philosophy of life. Ask a man his aim of physical education, and he gives you a pellet form of his philosophy of physical education.   ,

An aim may be defined as a *general and high ideal or remote end toward which one is striving.*   The statement of the aim is so worded that it seems possible to attain. If one constructs an aim that is accomplishable *now,* it is not an aim; rather, it is an objective. It is not remote enough to serve as a guiding star and a challenge for future striving.   If it is accomplished, what guide remains for further progress and improvement?   An acceptable aim of physical education obviously must lead the teacher to teach in such a way that the pupil will fit into society and add to its advancement.

Some stated aims.   Several leaders in physical education have constructed aims of physical education.   Let us see how they compare:

> Physical education is that phase of education which is concerned, first, with the organization and the leadership of children in big-muscle activities, to gain the development and the adjustment inherent in the activities according to social standards; and second, with the control of health or growth conditions naturally associated with the leadership of the activities so that the educational process may go on without growth handicaps.[2]

> . . . .

> It must be clear, therefore, that a naturalized program of physical education definitely aims to obtain, as physiological results from its activity program, normal growth and function, vigor, hardihood, and endurance. In a natural program much emphasis is put upon the social and mental qualities which hitherto have been largely neglected and underestimated in connection with physical education activities, but such emphasis is made

[2] Clark W. Hetherington, *School Programs in Physical Education* (Yonkers-on-the-Hudson, New York: World Book Company, 1922), p. 45.

with a full understanding of the needs of normal physical growth and development, and with a confirmed belief that, if the environment is hygienic and the child is unhampered by abnormal physical conditions, a naturalized program will secure the essential physiological and hygienic values within its sphere of influence as by-products. The possibilities are limitless in such a program to produce citizens who are physically normal, mentally alert and progressive, socially unselfish and cooperative, and morally sensitive and contribute to the group good.[3]

. . . .

Physical education should aim to provide skilled leadership and adequate facilities which will afford an opportunity for the individual or group to act in situations which are physically wholesome, mentally stimulating and satisfying, and socially sound.[4]

. . . .

The aim is social efficiency. The final aim should be an individual better equipped to meet the demands of the society in which he lives and to make contributions to that society.[5]

. . . .

Physical education, as one part of education, aims to aid the individual to attain his fullest development in meeting the demands of living in a democracy and in an interdependent world. It achieves this through the selection and guidance of experiences appropriate to the field directed toward the total fitness of the individual.[6]

. . . .

The aim of physical education is to advance the quality of living by providing the opportunity and encouragement for the development of the individual's social effectiveness and personal well-being through controlled participation in a program of physical activities conducted with effective guidance, ample equipment, and excellent facilities.[7]

. . . .

Organized physical education should aim to make the maximum contribution to the optimum development of the individual's potentialities in all phases of life, by placing him in an environment as favorable as possible to the promotion of such muscular and related responses or activities as will best contribute to this purpose.[8]

. . . .

[3] Thomas D. Wood and Rosalind Cassidy, *The New Physical Education* (New York: The Macmillan Company, 1927), pp. 69–70.

[4] Jesse F. Williams, *Principles of Physical Education* (Philadelphia: W. B. Saunders Company, 1959), p. 237.

[5] Agnes Wayman, *A Modern Philsophy of Physical Education* (Philadelphia: W. B. Saunders Company, 1938), p. 85.

[6] Hilda Clute Kozman, Rosalind Cassidy, and Chester O. Jackson, *Methods in Physical Education* (Philadelphia-London: W. B. Saunders Company, 1958), pp. 108–109.

[7] The Authors.

[8] Eugene W. Nixon and Frederick W. Cozens, *An Introduction to Physical Education*, 5th ed., Revised by John E. Nixon and Florence Stumpf Frederickson (Philadelphia: W. B. Saunders Company, 1959), p. 56.

Physical education serves as a medium for the total education of the being, intellectually, emotionally, developmentally, by the use of experiences having their center in movement.[9]

.   .   .   .

Should leaders agree on a general aim?   A good deal has been made of the progress which this nation has made through diversity of approach and method.   The same might be said of education.   Surely no other nation could display the variety of programs and methods of teaching that one might find in one of our *states!*   But, with it all, there is a magnetic lodestone that draws us on.   We hold to, and work toward a common, general aim.   When we reach toward the mutual ever-receding *summum bonum,* differences in how to try to get there may be acceptably different.

Singleness in the over-all aim is important for professional progress.   Some of the aims listed above came from old-timers, some came from younger persons in the profession, some came from women leaders and some from men.   In spite of this, there is a *focus* of thinking expressed that reflects a general agreement as to the aim of physical education.   And, when the time comes for a change in that aim, in spite of a period of spirited disputes and perhaps some harsh accusations, there will be a rallying of belief in and support of the new aim—if the field is to continue to progress and suvive.

Any teacher's aim of physical education should be compatible with the aim of all education.   Children are taught physical education in an educational environment.   Furthermore, teaching must be compatible with the principles of education.   These emphases upon the necessity of physical education aligning itself with general education have appeared in literature repeatedly.   Yet the actual practice lags.   This lagging, this failure is a force that retards physical education.   The profession needs to align itself with the aims of other *related* fields such as psychology, physiology, and medicine.   And the ties and connections with these and other areas are distinctive and essential.   What we are saying is that the aim of physical education need not be, it cannot honestly be, only and *merely* a duplication of the aim of education.

Should the aim of physical education differ in wartime from that which it is in peacetime?

[9] Delbert Oberteuffer, *Physical Education,* Revised ed. (New York: Harper & Brothers, 1956) p. 5.

Relationships between an aim and objectives. While an aim denotes a remote end which beckons, objectives are reasonably-reached goals. They are concrete. They are definite. Often, for the sake of pinpointing effort and thought, the major objectives are broken down into still more definite steps. While the attainment of major objectives do not lead *to* the aim, like stairsteps leading to the next floor, they are in agreement with the aim and lead *toward* it. That is, an aim sanctions the objectives. Objectives are never in contradiction to an aim. (See Figure 2-2.)

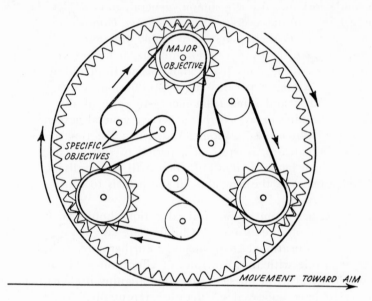

Fig. 2-2. *The mechanics of leading the student toward the aim. As the teacher and pupils work on objectives, movement is generated toward the aim.*

Stated major objectives. Quoting again from various leaders, here are some sets of major objectives. One of the finest statements is that of Clark Hetherington. A number of today's leaders regard this as one of the best statements made to date, even though it is not up-to-date:

1. The immediate objectives in the organization and the leadership of child life as expressed in big-muscle activities.
2. The remote objectives in adult social adjustment or efficiency.

3. The objectives in development—
   a. The development of the instinct mechanisms.
   b. The development of the intellectual mechanisms.
   c. The development of neuro-muscular mechanisms and nervous power.
4. The objectives in control of health conditions.[10]

. . . .

1. Physical education should provide physiological results, scientifically determined, indicative of wholesome, functional activity of organic systems, and sufficient for the needs of the growing organism.

2. Physical education practice should have meaning and significance for the individual and should provide a carry-over interest.

3. Physical education practice should provide opportunity for the individual to satisfy those socially desirable urges and impulses of nature through engagement in motor activities appropriate to age, sex, condition, and stage of development.

4. Physical education practice should offer opportunity to the individual under wise leadership to meet educative situations as one of a social group.[11]

. . . .

1. To develop organic power and stimulate bodily development through participation in beneficial physical education activities.

2. To develop recreational and utility-in-life skills, useful or pleasurable in the present or in out-of-school life, through participation in selected physical education activities.

3. To develop habits of and attitudes toward healthful living related to participation in physical education activities.

4. To develop desirable attitudes toward physical education, and desirable attitudes through participating in physical education activities.

5. To develop desirable social traits that are related, directly or indirectly, to participation in physical education activities.

6. To provide opportunities for the individual to satisfy his need for self-realization through individualized teaching and suitable organization of the program of physical education activities.[12]

. . . .

1. The development of organic power and vigor.
2. The development of specific skills in physical education activities.
3. The development of desirable social habits and attitudes.
4. The development of enjoyment of recreation.[13]

[10] Clark W. Hetherington, *School Program in Physical Education* (Yonkers-on-the-Hudson, New York: World Book Company, 1922) p. 20.

[11] Jesse F. Williams, *Principles of Physical Education* (Philadelphia: W. B. Saunders Company, 1959) pp. 351–356.

[12] The Authors.

[13] Eugene W. Nixon and Frederick W. Cozens, *An Introduction to Physical Education*, 5th ed., Revised by John E. Nixon and Florence Stumpf Frederickson (Philadelphia: W. B. Saunders Company, 1959), p. 67.

. . . .

In the area of body education:
To understand and accept the body as an instrument for the expression of the self.

To grow in understandings and skills in maintaining fitness for living;
In the area of social education:
To develop socially acceptable and personally rewarding behaviors in and through relationships with others in physical education activities.

To acquire enthusiasms, skills, and rich resources for leisure time activities.[14]

Major objectives may be set up as general criteria or general standards for judging whether a given physical education program is measuring up to what it is supposed to do. Williams[15] regards major objectives as "standards for judging physical education." Some writers prefer the term "general purposes" to the term "major objectives."

The reader should not be confused by differences in terminology. The point is that, regardless of the name given to major objectives, they are the major attainable ends toward which physical education is being directed.

LaPorte has compiled a list of ten comprehensive objectives. These are less general and more concrete than any of the sets of major objectives mentioned above. They are presented here to illustrate further that, just as an aim is broken down into major objectives and thus definiteness accomplished, so major objectives may be broken down progressively. LaPorte's ten comprehensive objectives are:

1. Developing useful and desirable *skills* in aquatic, gymnastic, rhythmic, and athletic activities for both developmental and avocational (hobby or carry-over) purposes.

2. Acquiring comprehensive *knowledge* of rules and techniques and strategy of above activities suitably adapted to the given age level.

3. Developing acceptable social *standards, appreciations,* and attitudes as a result of intensive participation in above activities in good environment, and under leadership that is capable and inspired.

4. Developing essential *safety skills* for self and others.

5. Effecting the removal or modification of *remediable* defects, based on adequate physical and health diagnosis.

[14] Hlida Clute Kozman, Rosalind Cassidy, and Chester O. Jackson, *Methods in Physical Education* (Philadelphia-London: W. B. Saunders Company, 1958), p. 109.
[15] Jesse F. Williams, *Principles of Physical Education* (Philadelphia: W. B. Saunders Company, 1959), p. 351.

6. Developing normal conditions of the body organs and *functions* including postural mechanics.

7. Developing power of *self-expression* and *reasonable self-confidence* and emotional control (poise) by mastery of difficult physical and social problems in activity.

8. Developing *leadership capacity* through the medium of actual responsibility for activities under careful supervision.

9. Developing powers of *observation, analysis, judgment,* and *decision* in complex mental-physical situations.

10. Developing essential *health habits, health knowledge,* and *health attitudes* as results of specific instruction and supervision.

The point is again emphasized that a teacher must set up an aim and select major objectives. In this way his teaching becomes purposeful, stable, and free from aimless wandering.

Which set of objectives do you consider most comprehensive? Most attainable?

Earlier in the chapter we discussed the acid test of teaching. A companion criterion must be added to that acid test: "Teaching must uncover the best possible opportunities for growth, and it must help in the realization of the opportunities by all possible students."

This double-barrel test *denies* that knowledge about and skill in what is taught is all that is needed to be an effective teacher. For, the teacher must put to work all the ingenuity he has and can develop in order to find the pupil's talents and his own; in order to establish rapport with the youngsters so that well-intended help will be accepted; in order to become just enough involved in their experiences to show that he understands; and, in order to make his teaching stick. It will also take patience as well as ingenuity to stay with the pupil when he fumbles and falters; to keep some atttractive lure before him so that he continues to develop his better self.

We have been seeking the nature of teaching by *first* recognizing that it is a combination of the practical and the theoretical. *Second,* we have examined teaching as a process. Some of the functions, obligations and responsibilities of the teacher have been briefly noted with references given to later chapters for fuller discussions. Here, we remind ourselves that we *teach someone,* we teach in ways that better ensure that *he learns,* we teach him *something,* for certain *reasons,* and this is done in *certain ways* and at some *certain place. Third,* the Golden Key to teaching, an aim and major objectives, has been considered. For, without the key the door to learning opens with difficulty, if at all.

A word about the following questions. Some of the test items that follow refer directly to the present chapter. Other questions refer to knowledge about teaching which the student should have acquired by this time, and remembered. Still other items point up how well the student knows the information that will be discussed in the chapters that follow.

SAMPLE TEST ITEMS

True-False

1. Physical education is more practical than any other school experience.

2. Everyone understands that a theory is based upon known facts.

3. Many laymen consider as theoretical that which does not seem to be manifested in practice.

4. Broadening one's pertinent experiences usually results in broadening one's concept of that which is practical.

5. Those proposals seem practical that are related to one's first-hand experiences.

6. Athletic coaches are more practical than academic teachers because the former avoid theories.

7. Principles of teaching are cumbersome to most beginning teachers.

8. The prospective teacher should accept principles of teaching as permanent rules.

9. The more one knows about teaching, the more complex it becomes.

10. A valid rule of teaching physical education is that he who performs best in activities makes the best teacher.

11. The principles of teaching and the principles of performance in an activity are synonymous.

12. In the performance of activities, the teacher and the participant should be equally adept in self-analysis.

13. One can effectively teach physical education through good demonstration alone.

14. There are several good ways of demonstrating proper performance in an activity.

15. A teacher might be able to analyze a pupil's movements in activity but fail to reach the proper conclusion regarding why poor performance results.

16. In arriving at conclusions, most beginning teachers postpone judgment too long.

17. A teacher who draws proper conclusions regarding a pupil's failure to perform effectively in an activity is certain to explain clearly the pupil's difficulties to him.

18. When a teacher has effectively explained to a pupil his performance difficulties, the teaching process is complete.

19. Failure to perform an activity properly in itself always motivates a pupil to try again.

20. Length of years of experience is related directly to improved teaching.

21. The art of teaching is related to a teacher's inherited characteristics.

22. Teaching can become scientific in the same sense that the chemist is scientific.

23. It is easier for the beginning teacher to rely upon recommended techniques of teaching than upon recommended principles of teaching.

24. The philosophical look at teaching is certain to seem impractical to most prospective teachers.

25. The sociological look at teaching is of recognized value and is related to a nation's basic political beliefs.

26. Equal emphasis always is given to the philosophical, scientific, psychological, and sociological approaches to good teaching.

27. The teaching environment includes both teacher and the pupil.

28. The aim of physical education of a people is related to its social and political beliefs.

29. The aim of physical education in the United States has never changed and probably never will change.

30. There is a fundamental similarity in the opinions of most leaders as to the aim of physical education.

31. An aim is a general and remote end and is consequently unrelated to everyday teaching.

32. Objectives of physical education invariably lead to the aim of physical education.

33. Leaders in physical education are agreed in their statements of the specific attainable ends of physical education.

34. A given activity, to be well taught, demands the use of certain specific techniques of teaching.

35. Good teachers are agreed as to the sequences of skills in learning a given activity.

36. Teaching is practical and theoretical.

37. Principles of teaching are valuable because they represent the beliefs of college professors.

38. Principles of teaching, if intelligently applied, are apt to help the teacher avoid serious blunders.

39. The teacher is thoroughly qualified to determine those activities of most value to all members of a class.

40. The attainment of a given objective is equally valuable to all class members at a given time.

41. A teacher's system of values regarding an activity is important but unrelated to his teaching.

42. Increased teaching ingenuity often results if a teacher strives to make physical education as valuable as possible to a pupil and to the class.

43. While the principles of teaching physical education are fairly stable, the techniques of teaching change to fit the activity.

44. All of the content of a given activity is similar.

45. Two teachers could use different sets of techniques in teaching the same activity to a given group and both be judged as excellent teachers.

46. One may have the knack of motor performance without having the knack of teaching that which one can do.

47. Teaching is based on many theoretical aspects of learning.

48. Teaching is best described as telling pupils how to do something.

49. Teachers, pupils, and parents have the same ideas of what constitute good teaching.

50. Anybody who can teach one thing well can teach anything well simply by using the same methods.

BIBLIOGRAPHY

Alexander, William N., and J. Galen Saylor, *Secondary Education.* New York: Rinehart & Company, Inc., 1950.

Bossing, Nelson L., *Principles of Secondary Education,* 2nd ed. Englewood Cliffs, N. J.: Prentice-Hall Inc., 1955.

Brownell, Clifford Lee, and E. Patricia Hagman, *Physical Education—Foundations and Principles.* New York: The McGraw-Hill Book Company, Inc., 1951.

Bucher, Charles A., *Foundations of Physical Education.* St. Louis: Mosby, 1956.

Chase, Francis S., and Harold A. Anderson, eds., *The High School in A New Era.* Chicago: The University of Chicago Press, 1958.

Chisholm, Leslie L., *The Work of the Modern High School.* New York: The Macmillan Company, 1953.

Cowell, Charles C., "Some Beliefs Concerning Physical Education, An Educational Credo," *The Physical Educator,* December 1954, 99.

Cozens, Frederick W., and Florence S. Stumpf, *Sports in American Life.* Chicago: University of Chicago Press, 1954.

Douglass, Harl, *Education for Life Adjustment.* New York: The Ronald Press Company, 1950.

Duncan, Margaret M., and Ralph H. Johnson, *Introduction to Physical Education, Health Education and Recreation.* Englewood Cliffs, N. J.: Prentice-Hall, 1954.

Educational Policies Commission, *Education for all American Youth: A Further Look,* Revised. Washington, D. C.: The National Education Association, 1952.

Kozman, Hilda Clute, Rosalind Cassidy and Chester O. Jackson, *Methods in Physical Education.* Philadelphia: W. B. Saunders Company, 1958.

Lieberman, Myron, *Education as a Profession.* New York: Henry Holt & Co., 1956.

Macomber, Freeman G., *Teaching in the Modern Secondary School.* New York: The McGraw-Hill Book Company, Inc., 1952.

Mendenhall, C. B., and K. J. Arisman, *Secondary Education.* New York: William Sloane Associates, Inc., 1951.

Morrison, H. C., *Basic Principles in Education.* Boston: Houghton Mifflin Company, 1934.

Nash, Jay Bryan, *Physical Education: Interpretations and Objectives.* New York: Ronald Press, 1948.

Oberteuffer, Delbert, *Physical Education. A Textbook of Principles for Professional Students.* New York: Harper & Brothers, 1956.

O'Keefe, Patricia R., and Helen Fahey, *Education Through Physical Activities.* St. Louis: The C. V. Mosby Company, 1955.

Rice, Emmett Ainsworth, John L. Hutchinson, and Mabel Lee, *A Brief History of Physical Education.* New York: Ronald Press Co., 1958.

Risk, Thomas M., *Principles and Practices of Teaching in Secondary Schools.* New York: American Book Company, 1958.

Van Dalen, Deobold B., Elmer D. Mitchell, and Bruce L. Bennett, *A World History of Physical Education.* Englewood Cliffs, N. J.: Prentice-Hall, Inc., 1953.

Williams, Jesse Feiring, "A Fundamental Point of View in Physical Education," *Journal of Health and Physical Education,* January 1930, 10.

Williams, Jesse Feiring, "Education Through the Physical," *Journal of Higher Education,* May 1930, 279.

Williams, Jesse Feiring, *The Principles of Physical Education.* Philadelphia: W. B. Saunders Company, 1958.

OF SPECIAL INTEREST

Anderson, William Gilbert, *Methods of Teaching Gymnastics.*   New York: Hinds, Noble and Eldredge, 1896.   (Out of print.)

Bagley, William C. and John A. H. Kieth, *An Introduction to Teaching.* New York: The Macmillan Company, 1924.   (Out of print.)

Hughes, James L., *Dickens As An Educator.*   New York: D. Appleton and Company, 1913.   (Out of print.)

James, William, *Talks to Teachers.*   New York: Henry Holt and Company, 1925.

Parker, Samuel Chester, *Methods of Teaching in High School.*   Boston: Ginn and Company, 1915.   (Out of Print.)

Roark, Ruric N., *Method in Education.*   New York: American Book Company, 1899.   (Out of print.)

Skarstrom, William, *Gymnastic Teaching.*   Springfield, Massachusetts: American Physical Education Association, 1921.   (Out of print.)

3

Self-analysis and improvement

Know thyself.

—Thales

"How good will I be?" "I wonder how well I really did?" "Where did I make my mistake?" "Am I fitted for this work?" A thousand questions like these challenge us. Every day we engage in momentary self-appraisals. Sometimes we are curious. More often, anxious. Still more frequently we ask ourselves such questions so that answers will lead to improvement. In fact, continued improvement of oneself is based on continued self-appraisal.

A related but different advantage of self-appraisal is: when we know our assets and liabilities, we are more apt to know where to concentrate our efforts. Sentimentally, it may be nice to want to be a physical education teacher because our favorite high school teacher or coach was. But, what if one cannot handle groups, does not enjoy young people, and has a poor personality!

Analysis and improvement through student teaching. Related to the importance of knowing one's strengths and weaknesses are the benefits of knowing the kind of work one would like to do, the type of position in that vocation, and even one's preference of places to live and work.

The prospective teachers using this book will, in all probability, very soon be involved in student (directed, practice) teaching; perhaps they may already have had some experience in student or even trial teaching. Student teaching may be thought of as one culminating experience of professional preparation. Student teaching makes it possible to put philosophy and objectives into action. The student teacher *is* a teacher as much as he is a student. He has a continuing responsibility for pupils; he guides them through learning experiences; if he fails to function effectively, his students are the losers.

Student teaching provides an opportunity to try out various methods and techniques. Ideally, student teaching takes place in a typical school situation where the student teacher *conducts himself* more as a teacher than as a student. He should be self-directing and not just follow the directions of his supervising teacher. But his methods cannot be haphazard or purely experimental. He must be able to predict, to some degree, what the results of his efforts will be. And through these efforts, he learns to make the most of his strengths and to discover the weaknesses which he should eliminate or lessen. Student teaching makes it possible to find out how good a teacher one is.

The student teacher is carefully and comprehensively evaluated. This evaluation is very important, for the record established in the student teaching experience is probably *the most important single criterion for future placement in a teaching position.* No matter how much the teacher knows, how fine his scholastic record, or even which methods he uses, he is not an effective teacher if he cannot *put into action what he knows and get sound, beneficial results.*

Students rather commonly report that their student teaching situations are unsatisfactory. Some claim that they are overdominated by their supervising teachers and that they do not have the opportunity or freedom to implement ideas and methods that are their own. Other student teachers indicate that their supervising teachers are not of sufficient help; that they are not given the guidance and criticism necessary for improvement. Perhaps some of these complaints are justified, but frequently these criticisms are made by *weak* student teachers.

Upon what bases are student teachers evaluated? What abilities are teachers expected to have? What personal qualities should teachers possess? Rather than postpone the answer, the student teacher should now make a self-analysis of those characteristics and abilities that appear to be important in successful teaching. For this reason several self-rating devices are presented in this chapter. These approaches to self-analysis will help the student determine important shortcomings and speed his self-improvement.

The chief factor of the many necessary for effective teaching is *personality*. Personality is *not* an intangible enveloping aura; neither is it a rigid pattern which persists through life; nor is it a cataloguing of the individual as dull, neutral, colorful, or dynamic, irrespective of personal efforts or environmental influence toward change.

Actually, personality is the impression one's behavior makes on others. Certain phases of behavior influence this impression more than others. People like a ready smile and an amiable disposition. They like a sense of humor, kindliness and sympathy toward others, fairness, cooperativeness, dependability, and responsibility. They like an energetic individual with socially worth-while enthusiasms. Personal habits of neatness and cleanliness, appropriate and tasteful dress, and cultivation of pleasant and expressive voice pitch and intonations are three factors that add to the attractiveness of personality. Look over these aspects and note that almost all can be adopted as a part of your behavior.

A maladjusted person is one who cannot get along with other people. Getting along with other people is one of the big jobs of the school teacher. Studies of teacher failure list *inability to discipline* and *inadequate personality* as major causes. The teacher must guide, direct, and control others and at the same time maintain the respect of his students and of the citizens of the employing community.

A conscious first step to improve your personality and, thus, your teaching ability is *self-analysis*. You must know your weaknesses before you can intelligently undertake self-improvement.

How good a prospective teacher are you?   The factors in the rating scale (see pp. 60–76) are associated with teaching success. *Not all are equally important,* but a high general rating is somewhat indicative of success in teaching. This scale is intended to help you appraise yourself on attitudes, interests, understandings, abilities, and plans. Rate yourself as carefully as you can. Keep in mind

SELF-RATING SCALE

Length and Continuity of Interest in the Profession

Have had long and continued interest in becoming a teacher. Possess deep interest in community, pupils, profession, learning.	Decided in college to be a teacher; have grown interested in the field since I took it up.	Am using teaching as a stepping stone; just a temporary interest.	Forced into teaching by circumstances; it has little interest for me.

Professional Direction and Plans

Have clearly defined personal-professional objectives. Tentatively determined what I want to be doing upon graduation; three years afterward; and in ten years. Have made plans for graduate study; looking forward to teaching.	Have tentative plans and purposes but am not too sure. Plan to do graduate work, but not sure where or when. Know what I want to do after graduation but not beyond.	Quite unsure of personal-professional objectives. Unsure of type of position, location, and other factors.	Professional plans are lacking. Do not know what I prefer to do upon graduation. No plans on graduate study.

Professional Understanding

Understand the need for professional standards. Know ethical relationships with pupils, other teachers, administrators, profession, and public. Intend to adhere to a professional code of ethics.

Have some understanding of professional ethics, standards and relationships. Have not carefully examined or developed a professional code of ethics.

Have limited understanding of these aspects of the profession. Exhibit milder degrees of statements at the left.

Have not been concerned with professional standards or ethics. Know little of ethical relationships.

Professional Activities

Member of student professional organizations. Seek professional growth by taking time and effort to attend professional meetings and conferences. Have formulated plans for membership and contributions to professional organizations in the future.

Rather inactive member of professional associations. Occasionally attend professional meetings. No plans for future membership, participation, and contributions.

Belong to professional organization but have little interest. Make no contribution. Do not attend meetings or conferences.

Do not belong to professional organizations. Have not attended professional meetings or conferences.

SELF-RATING SCALE (Continued)

Interest in Professional Growth

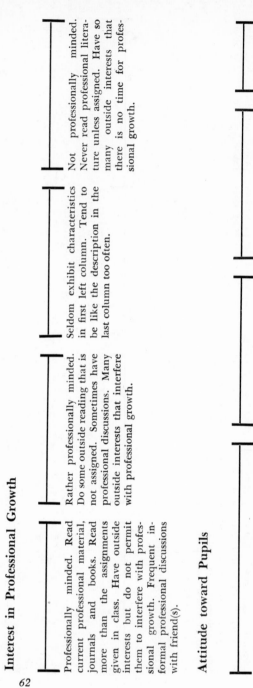

Professionally minded. **Read** current professional material, journals and books. Read more than the assignments given in class. Have outside interests but do not permit them to interfere with professional growth. Frequent informal professional discussions with friend(s).

Rather professionally minded. Do some outside reading that is not assigned. Sometimes have professional discussions. Many outside interests that interfere with professional growth.

Seldom exhibit characteristics in first left column. Tend to be like the description in the last column too often.

Not professionally minded. Never read professional literature unless assigned. Have so many outside interests that there is no time for professional growth.

Attitude toward Pupils

Appreciative
pleasant
sympathetic
patient
impartial
human
friendly
companionable
helpful

Adjectives at left describe me in general, but I have occasional moods when I veer toward the other end of the scale.

Tend to be midway between these extremes.

General pattern of my behavior described by adjectives to right but in a mild degree only.

Not helpful
overbearing
"hard-boiled"
stubborn
impatient
discourteous
partial
grouchy
cross

SELF-RATING SCALE (Continued)

Extracurricular Experience

Spend all possible spare time in wide variety of extracurricular activities, such as: fraternity or club activities; leader or participant in group organizations for music, journalism, athletics, or other activities.

Allot time to extracurriculars. Am an important cog in a few and an occasional leader.

Belong only to a particular group and am not a leader. Seldom take part in extracurriculars. Have some informal group associations.

Participate in no club life. Am a member of no fraternity, athletic, music, forensic, or other group organizations.

Intelligence

Am high in intelligence, learn new things easily, remember what I have learned, see the significance of facts and experiences; possess good common sense, get along well with people.

Work hard to learn but remember what I have learned; friends think I have good common sense and judgment; am neither friendly nor unfriendly; kindly but not very tactful.

Have to work hard for everything I learn; about average judgment; make few friends.

Slow learner, impetuous, not appreciated by my associates; rarely make friends; frank and outspoken.

63

SELF-RATING SCALE (Continued)

Academic Attainment

Have always rated high in class and examinations; have carried extra work; have taken more than required number of hours of professional courses; am planning to continue graduate work in summer schools.

Am average student; made above average grades in professional subjects; carried extra hours occasionally; may go to summer schools.

Below average in other subjects but average in professional courses; will take what graduate work seems necessary to hold job; had difficulty carrying enough hours to be certified in minor fields.

Most of grades below average; carried no extra hours; have no additional units above requirement for certification in professional courses; plan to enjoy a vacation, not go to school in summer; have only one minor on my certificate.

Stamina and Persistence in Academic Work

Hard courses have always challenged me. I took more than two years of foreign language or science. Never have changed to another course just because it was easier.

Dropped some difficult courses because they did not interest me. Am inclined to change courses rather than work laboriously at a subject.

Work hard by spells but not continuously through a course. Do not believe in doing much homework.

Have refused to let my studies interfere with my education!

Plans for Self-Improvement

Intentionally planning and seeking to improve personality, abilities, and understandings. Set goals for self-improvement. Seek criticisms from others and accept them agreeably.	Make some plans for self-improvement but do not set definite goals. Interested in constructive criticism but do not seek it. Can accept criticism satisfactorily.	Tend to be rather self-satisfied. Seldom set any goals for self-improvement. Avoid criticism. Am often annoyed by criticism.	Exhibit more extreme degrees of characteristics described at left.

Attitudes toward Others

Am considerate and sympathetic. Can work with other adults and pupils without allowing prejudice of race, religion, or any other factor to reduce effectiveness.	Some limitations in characteristics described at left.	Milder degrees of characteristics at right.	Not too considerate or sympathetic with others. I have some prejudices toward groups and individuals.

SELF-RATING SCALE (Continued)

Self-Direction, Personal Security, Maturity

Self-reliant, enterprising, capable of thinking independently, need not rely on judgment of others. Can work well anonymously. Capable of frankly admitting mistakes.	Usually self-reliant and somewhat enterprising. Think independently sometimes but feel more secure referring to others. Some difficulty in admitting mistakes but do it sometimes.	Exhibit milder degrees of characteristics at right.	Dependent upon others, have not done much independent thinking. Usually need recognition for doing a good turn. Seldom admit mistakes—particularly in public.

Ability to Work With Others

A very sociable person. Enjoy relationships with people of various ages and both sexes. Compliment others. Can make criticisms *constructive* suggestions. Human and approachable. Can pool and share ideas.	Fairly sociable. Fairly good relationships with persons of various ages. Can tactfully criticize. Work in groups fairly well.	Am not too comfortable with persons of different age groups. Can give compliments but not my nature. Not good at working in groups. Often become annoyed with thinking and actions of others.	Not sociable. Do not enjoy people of different ages. Seldom give compliments. My criticisms are negative, resemble complaining. Have problems when working in groups. Tend to be dissatisfied with others and tend to withdraw myself.

Establishing Good Human Relationships

Always patient and understanding. Always optimistic and pleasant. Look for the best in people. Like to make new friends.	Usually patient, understanding, optimistic and pleasant, seldom critical. Sometimes become disgusted wtih others when they don't respond quickly.	Tend to be impatient, and somewhat pessimistic. Exhibit characteristics at right but in milder form.	Quite impatient and pessimistic. Very critical of others. Become disgusted with others readily. Frequently act like a know-it-all.

Response of Others

Many people seem to enjoy being in my company—especially young people. They like my stories. Like to do what I suggest.	People usually seem to enjoy my company. Fair rapport with young people. Occasionally am aware people avoid me or condemn my actions.	Milder form of pattern described by statements at right. Young people do not respond to me quickly or warmly.	Have limited number of friends. Few people enjoy being in my company. Young people do not gravitate toward me. Others think I have no sense of humor.

SELF-RATING SCALE (Continued)

Enthusiasm and Interest

Like to work with young people. Usually generous with time and willing to help individuals. Want to assume duties beyond classes taught and teams coached. Will *voluntarily* work on improvement of needful situations.

Usually interested in young people and willing to give some time to help others. Willing to do extra work if it is required. Sometimes volunteer.

Not too interested in helping others. Tend to exhibit milder forms of characteristics listed at right.

Usually not generous with my own time. Prefer not to help others. Not particularly interested in young people or what they do. Almost never volunteer for additional work or responsibility.

Effectiveness in Organization

Good organizer. Always plan carefully. Think through projects and situations before action is initiated. Attempt to anticipate consequences before acting. Usually enjoy success in carrying out plans.

Fairly good organizer. Sometimes fail to plan and anticipate. However, seldom waste much effort because of poor planning.

Rather poor organizer. Have characteristics described on right more than those at extreme left.

Poor organizer. Must often give up and change goals. Much wasted effort because of poor planning. Tend to act on first impulse without considering consequences.

Personal Standards

Dependable, keep word when agreement is made with adult or child. **Show** punctuality. Have high moral and social standards.	Fairly dependable and punctual. Good moral standards.	Rather undependable at times. Moral standards not always worthy of being an example to younger persons.	Frequently undependable. Questionable moral standards. Am not a good example to young people.

Flexibility and Open-Mindedness

Adaptable and open-minded concerning new ideas and different ways of accomplishing purposes. Can adapt effectively to changing or unexpected situations. Can remain cheerful when things are not going my way.	Usually adaptable and open-minded but sometimes upset by changed plans or situations. Find it difficult to do things in ways other than my own but attempt to make best of situation and remain cheerful.	Not as flexible and open-minded as should be. Seldom adapt to changes easily. Difficulty remaining cheerful **un-** der such circumstances.	Difficulty adapting to changes, changing mind, or giving in. Disagreeable when things not going my way.

69

SELF-RATING SCALE (Continued)

Accepting Responsibility

Can face responsibilities squarely and avoid shifting them onto others or explaining them away. Can respond to demands promptly and cheerfully—in spirit as well as letter. Can do assigned tasks without fret or worry. Can do disagreeable work without expecting recognition or praise.	Usually can accept responsibility and respond promptly. Sometimes complain about disagreeable work and sometimes feel sorry for myself.	Often attempt to avoid responsibility. Expect recognition and praise when difficult or disagreeable work is undertaken.	Often alibi and shift responsibility. Blame others, the situation, the equipment, etc. If forced to carry out responsibilities, fret and worry.

Dress and Grooming

Make the effort to dress neatly and appropriately at all times. Realize the importance of this in influencing others.	Pay some attention to dress and grooming but occasionally veer to right column. Usually am appropriately dressed.	Do what is necessary with dress and grooming. Often attempt to get by with minimum standards. Am occasionally lax.	Pay little attention to dress and grooming. Consider these concerns pretentious, superficial affectations which have little to do with person's worth. Poor example to pupils in this respect.

Dignity, Poise, Self-Control

My manner is dignified; possess unusual poise and self-control.

Usually dignified; average in poise and self-control.

Tend to be undignified, impulsive and careless about manner and physical aspects but can assume dignified social manner and poise when it seems necessary.

Avoid appearance of dignity and poise; feel that such appearance stamps one as a pedagogue. Feel dignity belongs to old age.

Force, Color, Temperament

Am magnetic, forceful, stimulating, full of energy and enthusiasm; tend to be witty and optimistic.

Have forcefulness and energy but little color; my wit tends to be dry and my optimism tempered with cynicism.

Have spells of energy, forcefulness, enthusiasm; fluctuate from optimism to pessimism, from good humor to bad; have spells of boredom and discouragement which reflect in my work.

Tend to be neutral in personality; have little forcefulness and enthusiasm; am inclined to be serious and pessimistic.

SELF-RATING SCALE (Continued)

Leadership and Control

Can maintain balance between freedom and security with a group. Can be forceful and firm, yet not establish barriers between self and pupils. Can maintain discipline. Activities and routines progress in orderly manner without confusion, mischief, and horseplay. Can gain attention with little noticeable effort.

Fairly effective in leadership and control skills. Able to keep a fairly even temper in all situations.

Have problems in leading pupils to hard work—often must drive them. Frequent behavior problems. Sometimes lose emotional control before groups of troublesome pupils.

Have many behavior problems in a group. Difficulty in administering discipline effectively and fairly. Have difficulty in distinguishing between petty, annoying behavior, and genuine difficulties. Often lose emotional control before groups.

SELF-RATING SCALE (Continued)

Understanding of Pupils

Can communicate with young people in many areas of their interests. Make an effort to keep up with things that interest young people. Young people working under my guidance appear happy and enjoy success. Can quickly make the necessary contact with individual pupils.

Can usually communicate with pupils in some areas of their interests. Make some effort to keep up with what interests them. Have difficulty in making contact with some.

Often have difficulty in communicating with pupils. Occasionally veer to characteristics described at right.

Have difficulty in communicating with young people. Do not understand or see reasons for many of their actions and interests. Have difficulty in making close personal contact with many pupils. Young people do not usually seem happy working under my guidance.

SELF-RATING SCALE (Continued)

Understanding of Evaluation

Understand methods of evaluating pupil progress and accomplishment. Can be unbiased, fair, impartial in evaluating pupils. Can use findings from standardized tests of achievement and ability. Skilled in constructing informal tests and measuring devices. Capable of effectively marking pupils.

Qualified to do most operations at left. Unsure about some. Have the ability to be impartial in evaluating pupils.

Limited understanding of evaluating procedures. Not familiar with measuring devices. Would have difficulty in fairly marking pupils.

Little understanding concerning the abilities at far left. Difficulty being unbiased.

SELF-RATING SCALE (Continued)

Understanding of the Learning Process

Have a workable understanding of the principles of learning and of motor learning. Know and am able to practice sound learning theory. Keep informed on current research on the psychology of learning.

Know something of learning theory, but not aware of latest research and recommended practice.

Do not have workable understanding of latest research, but know something of the psychology of learning. Understanding somewhat limited.

Limited understanding of learning. Must rely, for the most part, on teaching the way I have been taught.

Understanding of Teaching

Know a variety of devices, methods, and techniques of teaching each particular activity. Can adjust teaching to individuality and difficulty. Can use all available teaching material in physical education. Can use supplementary and enriching material. Know the principles of teaching.

Know some devices and techniques, but weak in some activities. Can use more than one method and some supplementary material.

Strong in a few activities but weak in many. Skill in these is described by characteristics at right.

Must rely chiefly on the one method used by the teacher who taught me the activities. Do not know many principles of teaching.

75

SELF-RATING SCALE (Continued)

Interests and Abilities in Guidance

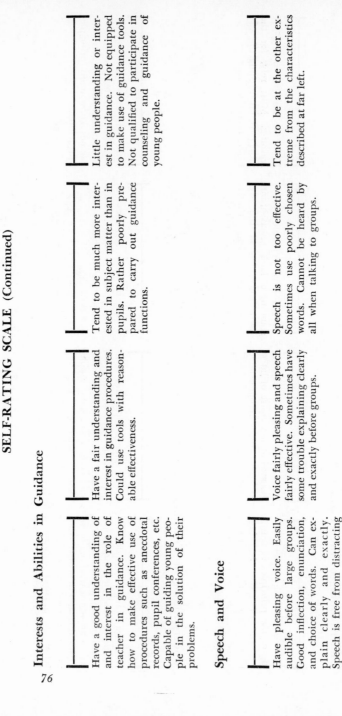

Have a good understanding of and interest in the role of teacher in guidance. Know how to make effective use of procedures such as anecdotal records, pupil conferences, etc. Capable of guiding young people in the solution of their problems.

Have a fair understanding and interest in guidance procedures. Could use tools with reasonable effectiveness.

Tend to be much more interested in subject matter than in pupils. Rather poorly prepared to carry out guidance functions.

Little understanding or interest in guidance. Not equipped to make use of guidance tools. Not qualified to participate in counseling and guidance of young people.

Speech and Voice

Have pleasing voice. Easily audible before large groups. Good inflection, enunciation, and choice of words. Can explain clearly and exactly. Speech is free from distracting mannerisms. Also capable of listening and not dominating conversations or discussions.

Voice fairly pleasing and speech fairly effective. Sometimes have some trouble explaining clearly and exactly before groups.

Speech is not too effective. Sometimes use poorly chosen words. Cannot be heard by all when talking to groups.

Tend to be at the other extreme from the characteristics described at far left.

that there is a tendency for most people to overrate themselves. Check the approximate point on the line that seems most nearly to describe you. Items are intentionally interspersed to give you the opportunity to look at yourself from various aspects. It may be valuable to have a friend rate you on these same factors. This may help you see more clearly both assets and liabilities that you may have exaggerated in your self-rating.

In addition to the traits listed in the rating scale, the physical education teacher should also have a thorough understanding of the specific tools of his profession. The well-qualified teacher should not have to teach with the activity book *in hand!* He should be able to demonstrate and teach effectively a wide range of activities with assurance. The following is a rather comprehensive list of activities which might be included in physical education programs at various levels and in various localities. Check the breadth and depth of your qualifications to teach these activities.

HOW WELL DO I TEACH?

Activities	Confident and well qualified to teach	Able to teach but not too confidently	Limited confidence and ability	Unable to teach with any degree of confidence at present
1. Adapted Exercise				
2. Archery				
3. Badminton				
4. Bait Casting				
5. Basketball (Men)				
6. Basketball (Women)				
7. Bowling				
8. Dancing, Folk				
9. Dancing, Social				
10. Dancing, Square				
11. Deck Tennis				
12. Diving				
13. Fencing				
14. Field Hockey				
15. Football				

HOW WELL DO I TEACH? (Continued)

Activities	Confident and well qualified to teach	Able to teach but not too confidently	Limited confidence and ability	Unable to teach with any degree of confidence at present
16. Fly Casting				
17. Golf				
18. Gymnastics				
19. Handball				
20. Home Games				
21. Horseshoe Pitching				
22. Ice Hockey				
23. Life Saving and Water Safety				
24. Paddle Tennis				
25. Shuffleboard				
26. Skating				
27. Skiing				
28. Soccer				
29. Softball				
30. Speed Ball				
31. Squash				
32. Swimming				
33. Table Tennis				
34. Tennis				
35. Touch Football				
36. Track and Field Events				
37. Trampoline				
38. Tumbling				
39. Volleyball				
40. Water Polo				
41. Weight Training and Lifting				
42. Wrestling				

SELF-IMPROVEMENT

Ways to improve.   Self-analysis is only a first step.   It becomes just rating gymnastics unless it is followed up by efforts toward self-improvement.   After particular weaknesses are discovered, standards of improvement can be set up.   These standards need careful consideration.   The serious student might ask himself these questions: Am I willing to perform the tasks and *pay the price* for suc-

cess in this profession—*day in day out, year after year?*   Does physical education challenge me to use my best talents in the best ways?
Or, is this vocation merely a way to earn a living?   Have I studied
and weighed all the important aspects of this vocation—both pro
and con?   (It is better to find out in the last year in college that
one's chosen vocation is incompatible, and change, than to go
through life a misfit.)   Am I willing to go through much more professional preparation for the type of position I plan to hold at the
peak of my career?   Do my self-analysis and the judgments of qualified persons indicate another vocation for which I may be better
suited?   If so, why have I remained in physical education up to
now?   After consideration is given to such questions, ways to improve and attainment levels may be established.

The student may proceed to formulate plans for achievement of
the goals set up.   He may wish to list his assets and liabilities using
the rating devices presented in this chapter as a guide.   In attempting to overcome weaknesses and increase strengths, he may seek help
from respected individuals who know him and may purposely plan
a program of independent reading and study.   He also may take
specific courses and plan definite experiences for himself, realizing
that *self-improvement is largely a matter of self-determination.*
Simply stated, the steps are: (1) identify weaknesses, (2) set standards
for improvement, (3) plan ways of accomplishing goals, and (4) now
go to work!

Capitalizing on professional preparation.   Certainly one of the
best means of self-improvement is to take full advantage of what remains of professional courses.   The person who is interested in self-
improvement must capitalize on opportunities for learning, must
seek criticism, and must *plan* for improvement.

Some of the difficulties of the young teacher arise because as a
student majoring in physical education he failed to apply himself
fully; or he failed to be circumspect in his choices and plans.

For example, some prospective teachers want to *overspecialize.*
Even a person with great potentialities needs breadth of education,
or he is likely to see great importance in anthill minutiae.   Too
frequently, early specialization at the undergraduate level results
in the teacher who lacks perspective, whose view is myopic.   Occasionally one finds professional persons who encourage early specialization.   But, more and more professions are beginning to realize

the value of a broad type of background as a preparation for specialization.

Fredericks,[1] in a nation-wide study, found that several hundred experienced physical education teachers felt that their professional preparation had many limitations. Many complained of unnecessary overlapping and repetitions in professional courses. Others complained that two or three *closely* related courses were taught one, two, or three terms apart. Some felt that at no time was the professional job pulled together into a meaningful whole. Some teachers believed that the various practical tasks to be performed on the job either were not covered or were scattered piecemeal throughout the undergraduate years. Some thought that the fifth year of professional preparation now being required in some institutions is merely a multiplication of these limitations. Among the many who went on for graduate work were those who sensed an attempt "to make whipped cream out of skimmed milk." Even though Fredericks' study was made some years ago, some of the bases for these reactions still exist. Appropriate changes must be made—perhaps by the very ones who now complain. But, the prospective teacher might well check with himself to see if some of these complaints do not arise from *lack of application, lack of study, lack of imagination and initiative.*

No magician-professors can bring forth rabbit-solutions from their black hats of experience and preparation. No one can learn for another. What is needed today, more than anything else, is the teacher who, *on his own initiative,* fills the gaps which he feels his professional preparation may have. As a rule, the students who complain most loudly as undergraduates are the ones who as young teachers want to use their alma maters as a crutch. They are hesitant about learning to walk professionally on their own two feet.

Prospective teachers should supplement their formal courses by placing themselves in situations where they must make decisions, carry responsibility, be ingenious and imaginative, be self-reliant and adjustable, practice leadership and cooperation, and develop their personalities. Any major professor can suggest activities and

[1] John Wynn Fredericks, "Gaps, Overlappings, and Other Weaknesses in Undergraduate Professional Training in Physical Education as Experienced in Practical Situations" (Unpublished Doctor's Dissertation, The Pennsylvania State College, June, 1940).

projects through which such qualities *can* be developed.   But, all too frequently, the prospective teacher begins thinking about these vital matters in the *last* semester of the senior year!   These tools of success are too intricate for one to become adept in their use overnight.   Practice in their use should begin in the freshman year or, better yet, in high school.

The school as a force needs strong teachers.   Here is the statement of one of the country's outstanding administrators: "The physical education program is my most useful tool in running the entire school, *if* it is conducted by effective teachers.   If physical education is handled by weak teachers, it then becomes not only the most useless but most troublesome instrument in the whole school."

Observation as a means of self-improvement.   Let us assume that in the next few months the prospective teacher will have the opportunity to watch high school physical education teachers and their classes in action.   Perhaps in the past he has had opportunities to observe physical education teaching in various settings.   Such observation can be extremely valuable to the student-in-training provided he knows what to look for and is able to see it.   Careful observation goes far beyond mere looking.   After the student begins full-time teaching, opportunities to observe teaching in various settings are seldom possible; and, he is not free to evaluate and learn from watching the conduct of other classes in the schools.

The student's first continuing responsibility as a full-fledged teacher may be near at hand, but he may still have time during the months that lie ahead to gain from the experience of others.   One way to do this is to take advantage of opportunities to observe physical education being taught in various settings.   To assist in making observations valuable for self-improvement, the following suggestions of what to look for while observing are offered.   Many more of the thousands of details performed by teachers could be included. These suggestions merely direct attention to some important aspects of teaching.

KEYS TO OBSERVATION

1. What precise evidences are there that the teacher recognizes different abilities of pupils, varied interests of the class, and the physical, mental, and social characteristics of the class members?

2. If the teacher seems to have some goal in mind besides mere exercise, can you tell what it is?

3. Is there maximum pupil activity and minimum teacher activity?

4. What principles, methods, and techniques of teaching does he use? Do they seem suitable?

5. What of his dress? General appearance? Carriage? Manner?

6. What seems to be his attitude toward the class? Toward individual members?

7. What concrete evidences are there that he likes or dislikes his subject?

8. Is he prompt? Does he require promptness on the part of pupils? How does he require this?

9. Do pupils follow his suggestions cooperatively? How is this accomplished? If the teacher must secure cooperation of the group, how does he do it?

10. Does he know his subject thoroughly? What evidences of this are shown?

11. Do the students like the subject? Is this because of the subject-matter or the way it is taught? Is the lesson satisfying to pupils?

12. What seems to be his idea of discipline? Does he have to get discipline? How often? If not, why not?

13. What evidences are there that he is considering the particular locality, as he teaches?

14. Does he enter into the spirit of the class or is he detached?

15. Does he have all necessary equipment on hand in suitable places before the class starts?

16. If the lesson is clearly directed toward a certain goal, does the class know what it is? If so, do they approve of it? Does he accomplish it? If not, why?

17. Is today's lesson related in any way to yesterday's lesson? Tomorrow's? How is this made known?

18. Does he correlate his subject with any other subjects in the curriculum? How is this accomplished?

19. Does he present the lesson effectively or does it follow a hit and miss scheme? If it is well organized, is it organized with a view to accomplishing some goal(s) or according to some other plan?

20. Does he explain and describe well? Does he talk too much? Voice? Diction?

21. Are the activities well adapted to the class?

22. What concrete opportunities does he provide for developing individual initiative?

23. Do all pupils participate voluntarily?   Under compulsion? Spontaneously?

24. What do you think is the weakest feature of the lesson?   The strongest?

25. Are students permitted some self-direction?   Do they avail themselves of the opportunity?   How much?   How is this accomplished?

26. How much demonstrating is done by the teacher or by someone he selects?   Is there enough of this?   Too much?   Is it of high quality?

27. Is the teacher tactful?   Patient?   Sympathetic?   Humorous? Courteous?   Imaginative?   Energetic?   A well-organized person? In what ways are these characteristics evidenced?

28. Are his standards of teaching high?   How do you know?

29. What concrete evidences are there that the needs of the individuals are considered and efforts made to meet them?

30. Does he use his time advantageously?   How many minutes are wasted?   Doing what?

Well-planned observation of another's teaching may enable the prospective teacher to take further steps toward self-improvement. This can be accomplished through learning and profiting from the experience of others.   The following suggestions may increase the value of observation experiences:

1. Carefully appraise the personal qualities of the teacher you observe.   If you were hiring a teacher and had the pick of the field, would you hire this teacher?   Determine specific reasons for your answer and apply the same measures to your own characteristics.

2. Note every single trick, method, technique, principle, and procedure that the teacher uses throughout the entire lesson (what he has done to prepare for the lesson, what he says, what he does).

3. Determine what experiences you would have selected for the lesson which the teacher did not, justifying each selection.

4. Formulate the specific principles and methods you would have tried which the teacher did not.

5. Note all methods and techniques which obviously did not work. Examine precisely why you think each of these tricks did not accomplish the result expected by the teacher.

Student teaching as a means of self-improvement.   Student
teaching is so valuable that most experts are recommending that
more time be devoted to it and that it begin earlier in the sequence
of professional experiences.   As described at the beginning of this
chapter, one of the chief means of self-improvement is through profiting by this student teaching experience.   Here theory and experiences are applied.   What must one know to be an *effective* student
teacher?   Everything!   This answer is absurd but true.   If the student teacher were so gifted that he had reached perfection, he would
not need the experience.   But teaching is never so effective that it
cannot be improved.   While one is engaged in student teaching, the
school becomes a laboratory.   The student teacher plans, manages,
directs, evaluates, and performs all of the tasks of teaching.   In student teaching he has an opportunity to use almost all that he
knows.

The chapter titles of this book outline only partially the scope
of a teacher's necessary understandings and abilities.   A careful examination, understanding, and evaluation of the material in the
remaining chapters of this book is related to improved teaching and
hence to self-improvement.   But, no book can contain all of the
answers or be completely helpful on all issues for all persons.   However, the students' application of the information, principles, and
procedures described in this volume should be an aid to the self-
improvement needed for successful teaching.

Student teachers often miss one of their best opportunities for
self-improvement.   They fail to *seek* advice from their supervising
teachers and from others who are in a position to help them.   They
fail to realize that they have the opportunity to take advantage of
private consulting service.   They avoid seeking help from the people who are in a position to know them best and who know the most
about the problems at hand.   Perhaps they want to give the appearance of being self-assured.   They may have inferiority feelings
which they do not want to admit to others, especially those under
whose supervision they are working.   Sometimes they are overcon-
fident and think that they cannot profit from the advice of others.
In other cases they lack confidence in the ability of others to help
them.   Often they feel that asking for help is an admission of weakness; they are fearful that they will get a lower rating if a weakness
is discovered.   Still other student teachers fail to seek help because

they want to avoid the appearance of being "apple polishers." A beginning teacher should realize that he is not expected to be so expert that he does not need some help and helpful criticism. A beginning teacher is not a finished product and should not be embarrassed about his need to supplement his own best efforts. He should be straightforward in asking for assistance when it is truly needed.

Sometimes self-improvement in student teaching is limited because the attention of the student teacher is directed toward the wrong end. Too often the student teacher, overanxious to please his supervising teacher, directs his efforts toward satisfying the supervising teacher *more than* the young people he is teaching! This is one disadvantage that may arise when working under very close supervision. The student teacher's primary focus of attention may be directed to that which the supervising teacher wants, gives the best rating for, approves of and encourages. The relationship of the student teacher to the supervising teacher in some cases may be delicate. The student teacher must learn to be a better teacher; he needs a superior rating for future placement; and, at the same time, he must be concerned about meeting the needs of the young people whose lives he is influencing. At times, all of these purposes may not harmonize. The student teacher may be helped with problems of planning and human relationships in student teaching if he takes the opportunity to talk over difficulties with his major professor.

Self-improvement through help from fellow students. No prospective teacher can expect to be expert in performing and demonstrating all of the sport and dance skills needed. There is simply not enough time to become proficient in everything. But he should not expect that the *minimum* skills and understandings acquired through class work are sufficient. One way that the purposeful major student can overcome some of these weaknesses is to profit from his fellow students who have particular skill specialties, just as he may help them. The expert performer has the opportunity to clarify his *thinking* about the skills he knows best as a *teacher,* while the unskilled person profits from competent assistance. Some student professional organizations or major student clubs organize a series of clinics to study various activities. These are conducted by those students who have exceptional abilities. Such help from fellow students, coupled with additional independent study and practice, help to overcome weaknesses.

BIBLIOGRAPHY

American Association for Health, Physical Education and Recreation, *1957 Yearbook, Fit To Teach.* Washington, D. C.: The Association, 1957.

Grim, Paul R., John U. Michaelis, *et al., The Student Teacher in the Secondary School.* Englewood Cliffs, N. J.: Prentice-Hall, Inc., 1953.

Knapp, Clyde, and Ann E. Jewett, *Physical Education Student and Beginning Teaching.* New York: The McGraw-Hill Book Company, Inc., 1957.

Kozman, Hilda Clute, Rosalind Cassidy, and Chester O. Jackson, *Methods in Physical Education.* Philadelphia: W. B. Saunders Company, 1958.

Schorling, Raleigh, and Howard T. Batchelder, *Student Teaching in Secondary Schools.* New York: The McGraw-Hill Book Company, Inc., 1956.

Part Two

YOUR STUDENTS
AND LEARNING:
characteristics and implications

4

What is the nature of
the learner?

Effective teaching is forever concerned first with the learner.

HUMAN LIKENESS. THE PROVINCIAL AMERICAN IS HEARD TO say, "All Chinese look alike." The same statement may be applied to Indians, Japanese, Frenchmen, and other nationalities with which the speaker is relatively unfamiliar. The Midwesterner may say the same similarity applies to New York City residents. Probably the average Russian thinks all Americans look much alike. Some facts stimulate the above generalization. Groups reared in the same environment take on the same large behavior patterns, whether they be in speech, manners, style of dress, or postural and movement patterns.

Human similarities go deeper than external appearance and overt behavior. They include basic needs and basic drives to action. Kipling says, "The Colonel's Lady and Judy O'Grady are sisters under the skin." Such expressions as the common man, the ordinary mortal, or just an average American are recognitions of similar needs, similar desires, and similar life experiences.

Differences only in degree. Scientific study has indicated that normal human beings all possess the same traits. They merely possess different degrees of the various traits. One individual may seem to possess a higher degree of academic aptness; another may seem to possess greater social intelligence; a third may rate high in mechanical abilities or motor skills; a fourth may be highly sensitive to emotional stimuli and to the esthetic aspects of our culture. Each has some degree of the above aspects of human personality. The *quantitative* differences in the various aspects, when blended into that dynamic whole called personality, result in human individuality. But the separate individuals differ only in degree. They have the same basic drives and the same general developmental patterns. All normal persons want food, comfort, security, affection, respect, and opportunity for self-expression.

Specific trait variation often measured. In physical education many measures have been made of specific aspects or traits of individuals. The maximum contractile pull of a muscle or set of muscles has been registered on various types of dynamometers. This aspect, called strength, has been measured for hand grip, back and leg lift, and so forth. Various types of speed have been measured. Speed of perception has received emphasis in pilot training. Speed of simple response has been measured many times and compared with speed of response after choosing between stimuli. Accuracy, both in reference to precision of movement and in projection of an object toward a target has been frequently measured. The ability to persist at an activity, called endurance, is frequently measured.

Man tends to be average. Any particular individual may vary markedly from the average in a particular trait. His scores on various other aspects or traits are very likely to be closer to the average. In other words, extreme variation in many aspects of one's personality is very unusual. This is just another way of reiterating the earlier statement that human beings are much alike.

Education attempts to produce some basic similarities. Education attempts to adapt varying human traits to civilized customs and conventions. Health rules and behavior are relatively standardized. Approved social and ethical behavior is the educational aim for all normal humans. Each normal individual is expected to take on basic skills and knowledges that are a common social inheritance from the past experience and improvement of man. Individual ability and the time available to learn are limiting factors in this education process. But as teaching improves, man may be able to adapt more and more of this vicarious past experience to his own needs.

Trait emphasis obscures human likenesses. Classification of individuals according to variation in exceptional traits has caused us to overlook the great similarity in individuals when all traits are considered. In the field of physical education, clumsiness and awkwardness indicate lack of suitable activity-experience rather than inability to learn. But, most motor tests merely measure *acquirement to date.* With a fostered environment, adjusted teaching techniques, strong motivation, and adequate time, most individuals could acquire such basic body-control skills as are essential for ease, grace, and efficiency of movement in the ordinary activities of life.

In the psychological field, various attempts have been made to classify individuals into groups according to a particular variation in some single trait of personality; for example, athletic types, research types, social types, and the like. Studies aimed at type classification are valuable in that they call attention to important aspects of personality. But, they may be misleading in their inference that humanity is classifiable into types and in their overemphasis upon a certain aspect of personality. Personality is not a summation of traits but a blended whole. Each component part modifies the other parts and is itself modified by its inclusion in the unity of the individual's personality.

Individuals differ in their reactions to stimuli. Some tend to act immediately on impulse or on reception of perceptive cue. Others tend to reflect, to hesitate, or to inhibit overt activity. More than average variations of the first type appear in the athlete, the business executive, the soldier, the social leader, and the intruding salesman. Variations of the second type occur in the research man, the poet or novelist, the scholar, and the hesitant, lonely, seclusive individual. The extremes in either case are unusual, almost atypical. The typical human is not extreme but manifests many responses in each direction.

The active types are called *extroverts,* and the studious, hesitant, or reflective types *introverts.* The great central group has been well named *ambiverts.* Most of us have our periods of activity and our periods of reflection, our periods of sociability and our periods of seclusiveness. The central type is the rule. This boy dominates in his fraternity but submits on the athletic squad; or he leads on the athletic field and follows in social activities. More likely, he leads occasionally and follows at other times in most situations. He adjusts his behavior to the exigencies of the situation.

Adjustment to society in relation to academic aptness. Opinion differs about individual differences in ability to learn. Much of the controversy is over the relative influence of inborn ability and of environmental factors as determiners of the use of intelligence. One view is that inborn intelligence determines almost entirely one's degree of success or failure in schoolwork and life. The opposing view is that environment is the controlling factor. Evidence points to education as a highly effective influence on intelligence. Though, of course, training cannot overcome all of one's individual limitations. However, better teaching techniques and more learning time may adjust many of the more limited—adjust them in the personality attributes necessary for adaptation to highly civilized society.

Biological factors. Man's form, structure, and organic specialization of parts are largely predetermined by the genes of the chromosomes in the germinal material that initiates him. The fact that chimpanzees cannot acquire language no matter how carefully they are taught, indicates the importance of certain preconditions in the germinal material. The fact that the deaf person with no defect in vocal equipment does not acquire speech without very special training illustrates the importance of environmental stimuli.

Environment influences growth. The above illustration does not clarify the whole picture. Growth itself is both fostered and directed by environment. Environmental stimuli cause activity in human protoplasm, known as growth activity, which resembles to a great degree the change we refer to when we speak of learning. The evidence that environment may affect the growth of some traits more than others is abundant. A rural atmosphere of outdoor exercise, sunshine, and good food fosters physiological development; yet it may, at the same time, not provide the experience necessary for developing social maturity.

The beginning of motor adjustment to environment. Human cell stuff is sensitive to stimuli (irritable) and responds to stimuli by electro-chemical activity, by conductance away from the excited (chemically active) area to other areas. In the earlier stages this excitation is transmitted throughout the organism with decrease of activity in parts less related by structure. The innumerable random motor responses of the infant to chance stimuli illustrate this diffuse excitation.

Adjustment by reflexes. Conditioned reflex learning characteristic of infant adjustment is an adjustment in which general and diffuse response is narrowed down to a specific response to a specific stimulus. More complex behavior develops by a recombination of these preliminary reflex units. First, the general diffuse excitation and random motor activity grows into a variety of small adjustment units. Later, these small units combine into the larger behavior patterns. The behavior patterns of the human organism will be whatever environment has fostered. Thus, similarity in the major environmental stimuli produce similarities in the major traits and characteristics of the human organism.

Growth a developing continuity. Because physiological growth is more apparent in childhood and adolescense and is prerequisite for the complexities and niceties of school and life development, one tends to think of education and adjustment as processes differing from this earlier development. All are, however, the changes in the organism resulting from environmental nurture. Each successive change of the growth process is dependent on all preceding growth.

Doctrine of "natural activities." The preceding viewpoints of development are of particular interest to the physical education student because of certain advocated procedures in program building. The hypothesis has been advanced that physical education programs should be based on the so-called "natural activities" of hanging, climbing, carrying, lifting, throwing, running, and jumping. Perhaps a physical education program based on the skills of the Pithecanthropus might be to a considerable degree inappropriate for the needs of modern society. Such scientific studies as are available indicate that the physical education program should be determined by man's needs in the world today. In the first place, heredity does not seem to foster specific neural patterns; hence, it does not seem to make any *specific* motor patterns easier to learn. In the second place, both interest in activity and acquirement of motor skill seem to depend on environmental stimuli. Swiss children have demonstrated that skiing skill may be acquired in mere infancy. Hawaiian children, among others, have shown that the swimming skill can develop at least as rapidly and as perfectly as the so-called "natural" activities.

Activities for success, respect, and joyous self-expression. Man seems to be limited in his development to whatever outcomes the environment fosters. The responsibility of the physical education teacher is to see that activities of the environment foster growth, develop body-control skills, and generate energy supplies. If possible, he should also see that these activities furnish opportunities for success and for gaining self-respect and the respect of others. Moreover, they should furnish a means of joyous self-expression.

Growth, body control, and energy are mere supplements to the other objectives and may be developed through many types of activities. The focus in activity-selection should be on whatever will bring the child success, respect, and joyous self-expression. The child must have guidance and help, with freedom to select from an environment rich in a variety of activities.

Such is the nature-nurture process. The worm may turn into the butterfly, the egg into a hen, and the damp squirming infant, with its much greater susceptibility to environmental influence, into a human adult—an organism with potentialities beyond its own imagination.

Common emotional patterns.   Emotions seem to originate from stimuli which initiate a state of hypertonicity in the smooth muscles and a general diffusion of excitation. They grow into specific patterns, both as to motor expression and as to neural association. Environment encourages specific adjustments. Emotional maturity is evidently highly dependent on training. We find childish impulsiveness, sullenness, pouting, ridiculous fears and worries, anger outbursts in adults of various ages. Frequent display of such behavior points to very definite inadequacies in the general pattern of social environment.

Pre-adolescent development is characterized by the preponderance of sense experience. The child at this age is interested in things. He likes to handle objects, to explore, to discover, and to manipulate things. As the healthy individual approaches the adolescent stage, he tends to be an exuberantly joyful, sensorimotor organism. He eats ravenously, sleeps soundly, and plays vigorously. His play is only half socialized, his mental activity nonreflective, and his morals opportune.

The changes of the adolescent.   Physiological changes make the adolescent less vigorous, more awkward, more social, and more serious. He experiences accelerated growth—an increase in height and weight and an overall increase in muscular strength and endurance. Growth proceeds at different rates in different parts and organs of the body with some consequent maladjustment. Sex development adds its problems. The individual becomes conscious of his increased size and change in appearance, thinks of himself as an adult, and becomes less submissive to authoritative dominance. He becomes more introspective, self-conscious, and inclined toward greater inferiority feelings. He is frequently embarrassed. He is more sensitive to criticism—at times he is hypersensitive. He tends to alibi. Personal appearance becomes important. He is ambitious, inclined to be spectacular, and romantic. He is easily interested or bored. People begin to replace objects in primary interest. He has a great desire to gain independence. The integrating of changing organic and glandular patterns into unified and balanced function comes slowly with accompanying emotional stress and instability. Increased emotional tensions tend to express themselves in impulsiveness, anger or moodiness, religious zeal, daydreaming, idealism, hero worship, or delinquency. Greater content and happiness tend to appear only with physiological and emotional maturity.

Similarities in the post-adolescent and adult. Conformity to customs, conventions, manners, and even style is so universal as to tinge man with monotony. Physically, he typically possesses minor in-coordinations of posture and body control. He has his car accidents, hits his thumb with a hammer, or steps on his partner's feet. He is unlikely to be completely mature mentally, emotionally, or socially. He believes in courting luck, in accepting printed material as true, particularly if it agrees with what he believes, and in reducing mental activity to beliefs, habits, and slogans. He succumbs to flattery and dislikes truth which pricks his ego. He resents orders except from his admitted superiors, glosses over irritation with thin, almost transparent, courtesy, but gets along and is frequently happy. He maintains a reasonable degree of self-reliance and independence. And, in the light of his own mistakes, he plans an environment which he hopes will make his progeny superior to him.

Differences in pupils. Attention was called to the importance of environmental stimuli on rate and direction of growth. The growth processes are much the same in all individuals. However, individuals do not grow at the same rate, nor do the separate traits within any one individual develop at the same rate.

Varying environments, both internal and external, different gene influences, and variation in growth rates of the various traits of each single individual are some of the factors which account for the uniqueness of any human organism. This uniqueness is a functional variation, a distinctiveness noted in the person's individuality. A trait or aspect of a personality is meaningless unless considered in its fusion with other traits. Just as oxygen combines with hydrogen to form a variety of compounds, so do the degrees of various traits combine in various individuals to form a variety of personalities.

Growth varies in rate and in length of time it continues. Studies of individual differences indicate that traits do not reach their maximal growth at the same time; for example, one's height may reach almost its ultimate attainment before the rest of the body has gone through its later adolescent development period. One boy excels the average in strength in the developing period but tapers off sooner in his strength development. At adulthood he may even be below average in strength. The rate of growth is not a sure index of the final peak achievement.

Examples of growth variation. Some of these eccentricities in growth patterns may be made more clear by example. One's feet may grow faster than the rest of his body and reach their approximate maximum quite a while before growth in height is completed. Some persons' legs grow faster than their trunks and vice versa. People of the same height have different lengths of legs, trunk, size of feet, length of neck, *ad infinitum.* The rates that the various parts grow vary from individual to individual, and the parts stop growing at different ages. These characteristics of growth difference apply to traits of personality, intellect, and organic development as well as to physique. The inability of the body metabolism to keep up with physical and organic growth may account for cases of malnutrition, skin irregularities, lack of endurance, and the like, in rapidly growing adolescents.

Urban environments tend to lack maximum stimuli toward physiological development. In any area, economic status may affect the nutrition, hence the physiological development. Home conditions and the neighborhood associations will have accelerating or retarding effects on desirable trait development, depending on their specific nature.

Relative rank maintained by many. In measuring groups, the majority tend to retain the same relative rank in regard to each other as development progresses. The stronger boys tend to continue to be relatively stronger even though the lower levels are steadily increasing in strength. The faster runners tend to remain in their relatively high rank even after the lower ranks increase in speed. The same statement about relative group development applies to almost all human traits and characteristics. The relative rank varies with the trait selected, however. The individuals in the group who rated high in strengths might be in a large part different individuals from those in the group who rate high in speeds.

The value of such statements about group studies, group curves, and group averages is questionable if the teacher is concerned with the improvement of each individual. In attempting to classify high school students for competitive sport participation, the problem of the large, heavy, and relatively strong boy who is physiologically immature, is well known. If we gather together pupils who are much alike in one trait, they tend to be dissimilar in other traits. We must remember that mathematical descriptions of group averages are purely mental concepts. The groups are made up of individuals. Individuals are not made in identical molds.

Effects of similar school experience. American education attempts to produce in all normal individuals certain desirable changes. That this pursuit of the same basic curriculum produces greater likeness in individuals is not assured. Certainly all will be familiar with many facts in the same fields. But the brighter individuals learn faster than the duller, transfer more learning from one situation to another, and may display a greater absolute difference after like practice. Similar amounts of time spent in activity in a given field seem to increase the absolute difference range of the individuals participating, unless the field is relatively simple.

Differences in aptness for learning manifest themselves in innumerable ways. Individuals learn at different rates.[1] They begin at different levels and acquire skill or knowledge at different rates. The duller seem to vary less than the brighter. Those progressing at approximately the same rate may vary in the final level they can attain. There seems to be a hereditary upper limit. This hereditary limit may be overemphasized. The student of individual differences needs to note that *variation results from varying environment* and that *environment is never the same for two individuals.*

Sex differences. Certain differences in the sexes are due to bi-

[1] The rate of learning must not be confused with the speed of performance on such a type of activity as taking a test. Studies have thrown considerable doubt on the old hypothesis that speed of intellectual performance (on an I.Q. test, for example) is highly related to level of intelligence.

ological nature and function and to differences in environment. Girls mature somewhat earlier than boys, on the average. In general, the average man is superior to the average woman in motor capacity. Women excel men in sensory capacities except in the kinesthetic sense. The average woman has better memory, particularly rote. Men tend to do better in tests of originality. All these differences are small and are differences in *averages*. Men show slight superiority, on the average, in reasoning tests, arithmetic computation, and mechanical tests. Women tend to show superiority in aesthetic comparisons, drawing designs from memory, and in linguistic ability. These differences are very slight compared to the differences *within* each sex.

Feeling and emotion. Pupils differ in their susceptibility to emotional stimuli. This difference is what we mean by temperament. Temperament refers to the individual's sensitivity and characteristic reaction patterns to emotional stimuli. Some are very sensitive and deeply hurt by mild disapproval; at the other extreme one finds the boy who seems impervious to ordinary criticism.

The feeling tone which accompanies genuine interest (or perhaps is genuine interest) deviates widely from individual to individual. Interest fluctuates in any single individual. It seems to be affected by all types of environmental factors.

Volition is a general word to describe one's decision upon a course of action and the initiation of the course of action. Innumerable words describe the wide variations in this trait. Individuals are classified volitionally as lazy, lethargic, impulsive, extroverted, determined, persistent, negativistic, suggestible, strong-willed, stubborn, bullheaded, vacillating, and so forth.

Character is another general classification of traits with feeling or emotional toning. It refers to patterns and urges of response to social and ethical situations. One's social behavior can be analyzed as to various social and ethical traits. For example, individuals differ in *degree* of honesty, selfishness, decency, responsibility, amicability, idealism, and so on.

Motor movements. Individuals vary widely in their variety and type of motor reactions. Experimentation has shown individual differences in reaction time. Individuals seem to vary widely also in maximum speed of movement after starting to react. Reaction time refers to the time elapsing *between the occurrence of the stimulus* *and the beginning of the response.* In running, slow reaction time is evidenced by slow starting. Speed of muscular contraction, *after the muscle is stimulated,* seems to appear in fast dash men in track who are slow starters.

Speed is not at all a unitary trait in man. The relative speed of an individual in comparison with any other individual varies with the task he is performing. One does not have speed but speeds. One may rank high in speed among his fellows in certain types of coordinated activity and low in others. Some persons can run fast but change direction slowly. Others start quickly, cannot run so fast as many slower starters, but can change direction rapidly. Some people are quick with their hands but not with their feet, and vice versa. A person may climb a rope in near record time but trail the group in a sprint around the block. Some of these performance speeds seem to have been modified significantly by training.

Accuracy of performance is an important factor in many motor skills. The variation between individuals and the fluctuation in any one individual in accuracy are well known. Practice improves accuracy, but individuals vary widely in final attainment when the preliminary movements required are at all complex. Steadiness, automaticity of pattern, sense keenness, and physiological condition are some of the factors affecting variation.

Coordination in muscular movement refers to skilled movement. Coordination implies that muscles function in a harmonious action pattern. The individual movements are exact and are varied in strength to suit the total pattern. There is a nice balance between inhibited and released movements, and each muscle movement occurs in the right temporal sequence. The parts are synchronized into a functioning unit of motor behavior.

Individuals differ in degree of movement coordination. Probably no two individuals use exactly the same muscle groups for a complex action pattern. Persons vary in the timing of the part movements, in the relative strength exerted by the muscles reacting, in the tension of the inhibited muscles, and in the sequential order of the individual muscle movements. In such a relatively simple movement as striking a pitched ball with a bat, individuality of style characterizes even the experts. Professional basketball teams vary widely in foul shooting stance and in the muscular movements of the act. Yet all are tossing a ball of little weight a short and constant distance, and almost all are highly successful in throwing the ball where they intend it to go. Individual differences are so great in motor skills that a recommendation of the *correct form* for any complex motor skill is a questionable procedure.

Individuality. Individual differences allow for a uniqueness, an individuality, a personality in the individual which distinguishes him. His face, his form, his handwriting, and his unique movement pattern identify him as an *individual.* His voice, his stride, and even the sound of his footsteps identify him to his intimates. His footprints identify him in the maternity ward and his fingerprints in the police station. He copyrights *his own* mechanical contrivances. He is an individual entity with his own peculiar sets of habits, ideals, attitudes, and beliefs. His very individuality can foster itself by its interaction with environment. His counterpart is impossible even in his offspring. Hybrid as he is with interacting traits and characteristics of all degrees, his progeny must be more so. They will also differ from all other human beings, but not by identical differences.

SAMPLE TEST ITEMS

Yes-No

1. In almost all cases, will the measures of a single trait of large numbers of individuals be found to be distributed according to the normal curve?

2. Is an individual likely to be closer to the average on measures of combinations of related traits than he is on a measure of one trait?

3. Can humans be divided into distinct types in traits of personality?

4. Does it seem probable that man today is a superior organism at birth to that which he was ten centuries ago?

5. Does one's inborn intelligence determine almost entirely one's degree of success or failure in schoolwork and life?

6. Is the degree of attainment of body-control skills, such as we imply when we speak of grace, poise, and coordination, largely dependent on a factor of innate "motor intelligence"?

7. Are learning and growth much the same sort of physiological processes?

8. Is there some innate condition in man which makes the "natural activities" more attractive to him than other forms of motor activity?

9. Do all normal individuals possess, to some degree, the same traits?

10. Can one assume that modern education has developed many individuals to the limit of their potentialities?

11. Does the nature of the activity itself determine whether it is work or play to the individual?

12. Is the only difference between work and play a difference in attitude?

13. Is rate of growth of the various body parts uniform during adolescence?

14. In general, does adolescent moodiness have a physiological basis?

15. Does the average adult typically possess minor in-coordinations of posture and body control?

16. Does the typical adult attempt to govern his own behavior by careful use of his reasoning abilities?

17. Do human traits reach their maximal growth at the same time in the individual?

18. Do individuals tend to maintain the same relative rank, in regard to each other, in any one trait as growth progresses?

19. As a general rule, do one's legs grow at the same rate as his trunk?

20. Do specific body parts stop growing at approximately the same chronological age in different individuals?

21. Do excellencies in mental traits as determined in studies of large groups show a high degree of covariance; i.e., is a person who rates excellent in some traits more likely to rate excellent in other traits?

22. Do similar amounts of time spent in learning activity in a given field tend to decrease, in the individuals' participating, their absolute differences in that field?

23. Do individuals with the same degree of interest learn at the same rate?

24. Do those who learn at the same rate tend to be the same in the final level that they can attain?

25. Do excellencies in motor traits tend to show a high correlation with excellencies in mental traits?

BIBLIOGRAPHY

Allport, Gordon W., *Becoming: Basic Considerations for a Psychology of Personality*. New Haven: Yale University Press, 1955.

American Association for Supervision and Curriculum Development, *1952 Yearbook, Growing Up In An Anxious Age*. Washington, D. C.: National Education Association, 1952.

Anderson, John E., "Present Levels of Understanding Regarding Child Growth and Development," *American Academy of Physical Education, Professional Contributions No. 6*, (1958), 1–12.

Ausubel, David P., *Theory and Problems of Adolescent Development*. New York: Grune and Stratton, 1954.

———, "Viewpoints from Related Disciplines: Human Growth and Development," *Teachers College Record*, 60:245–54 (Fall, 1959).

Bernard, Harold W., *Adolescent Development in American Culture.* New York: World Book Company, 1957.

Blair, A. W., and W. H. Burton, *Growth and Development of the Pre-Adolescent.* New York: Appleton-Century-Crofts Company, Inc., 1951.

Bossard, James H. S., *The Sociology of Child Development.* New York: Harper & Brothers, 1954.

Bugelski, B. R., *The Psychology of Learning.* New York: Henry Holt and Company, 1956.

Clarke, H. Harrison, "Relation of Physical Structure of Motor Performance of the Male," *American Academy of Physical Education, Professional Contributions, No. 6,* (1958) 63.

Espenschade, Anna, "Growth and Development of the Junior High School Student," *Journal of Health, Physical Education and Recreation,* 30:22 (1959).

Gesell, Arnold, Frances L. Ilg, and Louise B. Ames, *Youth: The Years from Ten to Sixteen.* New York: Harper & Brothers, 1956.

Harris, Dale B., ed., *The Concept of Development: An Issue in The Study of Human Behavior.* Minneapolis: University of Minnesota Press, 1957.

Havighurst, Robert, *Adolescent Character and Personality.* New York: John Wiley & Sons, Inc., 1949.

Horrocks, John E., *The Psychology of Adolescence.* Boston: Houghton Mifflin Company, 1951.

Hurlock, Elizabeth B., *Adolescent Development.* New York: The McGraw-Hill Book Company, Inc., 1955.

Jersild, Arthur T., *The Psychology of Adolescence.* New York: The Macmillan Company, 1957.

Landis, Paul H., *Adolescence and Youth.* New York: The McGraw-Hill Book Company, Inc., 1952.

Malm, Marguerite, and Olis G. Jamison, *Adolescence.* New York: The McGraw-Hill Book Company, Inc., 1952.

Moser, Clarence G., *Understanding Boys.* New York: Association Press, 1953.

Remmers, H. H., and D. H. Radler, *The American Teenager.* New York: The Bobbs-Merrill Company, Inc., 1957.

Seidman, Jerome M., ed., *The Adolescent: A Book of Readings.* New York: The Dryden Press, Inc., 1953.

Stolz, Herbert R., *Somatic Development of Adolescent Boys.* New York: The Macmillan Company, 1955.

Wattenberg, William W., *The Adolescent Years.* New York: Harcourt, Brace and Company, Inc., 1955.

5

What is the nature of
motor learning?

*. . . men become builders by building
and lyre-players by playing the lyre. . . .*

—Aristotle

A<small>N IMPORTANT, AND VERY SPECIAL CONCERN OF THE PHYS-</small>ical educator, is how and under what conditions bodily movements are best learned. Our society has a universality of interest in learning. All of the nearly 40,000 vocations *assume* that learning takes place in certain ways. Each vocational field requires some training for specialists; workers must be skilled and able to perform their tasks. Educators too *assume* that learning takes place in certain ways. The home, the church, the state, advertising agencies, propogandists, and all assume that learning takes place in certain ways. What, then, should the intending teacher of physical education understand about learning in general and about motor learning in particular?

Learning is changing. Yesterday the child touched the hot radiator and burned his hand. Some change, in addition to the tissue injury, occurred in him. We know that a change occurred because today we see him avoiding the radiator. Some connection between sense organs and muscles has been changed. The sight of the radiator, its nearness, and the warmth coming from it form a pattern of stimuli which arouse a motor response of avoidance. We might say that learning is a change in behavior due to stimuli. Learning involves profiting from experience.

The study of learning is an important concern of contemporary psychology and education. Findings about learning in educational psychology have influenced not only methods of instruction but the curriculum as well. Yet, no one is *sure* about most of psychology. Our better psychologists speak of *theories* not *laws* of psychology. Evidence is still being accumulated. As many research papers are published in psychology as in all other fields combined; and *over half* of these studies deal with learning. The uncertainty and lack of finality of our understanding is indicated by this preponderance of research. All of the facts are not in. No one has all of the answers—for sure—once and for all. And yet, we must assume things about how learning and performance take place, or we would not know when or what or how to teach or coach.

Motor learning is usually defined as learning in which bodily movements play a major part. These movements are patterns of responses to recognized stimuli; i.e., they are perceptual-motor responses. The recognized (perceived) stimuli may be visual, kinesthetic, auditory, or any other sense stimuli or a combination of the stimuli of several senses. The learned response may be simple or complex, persisting over a time or relatively momentary. Much of the motor response may be inhibitory response. Think of the inhibited movement essential for marksmanship, balancing acts, or any skill requiring steadiness and fineness of control.

Highly skilled motor performance seems to be, to a large degree, automatic habit-performance. The sports and games themselves demand almost constant variation in skill sequences and combinations. The performer keeps his attention focused on the perception of cues for the next appropriate behavior while he is responding automatically to cues already received.

He gets the cue for the next appropriate act, shunts it into the custody of automatic performance, and watches the changing panorama of the game for the next cue. Probably the level of diffused attention over the general pattern of the movements is low, although the details are, for the most part, completely absent from his consciousness.

The motor patterns used by the performer are not exact repetitions even when they comprise the same general act. In other

words, his automatic performance is adjustable in details; it is somewhat generalized to fit slight variations in the total situation. For
example, his batting pattern adjusts while he concentrates intently
on the rapidly approaching ball. His feet, body stance, and racket
stroke adjust while he focuses intently on the tennis ball. He drib-
bles the basketball and changes rate or direction while he is centering his attention on teammates down the floor ahead of him, estimating their speeds and their distances from opponents. Consider
learning to strike a handball one hundred successive times. It is
improbable that the ball will ever rebound to exactly the same position on the court, and if it did, it would undoubtedly not be approached by the learner in the same way. Each time the stimulus
(the handball) is in a different position, and each time the response
necessary to strike the ball must vary. What must be learned, then,
is a *general* pattern, not specific responses to exact repetitious stimuli.

Motor learning is generalized. Motor learning is a change in
general form of behavior; for example, the boy learns to throw a
basketball into a basket in a variety of situations, none of which are
identical with his original learning situation. Distances vary, backgrounds vary, baskets and backboards vary, techniques of opponents
vary, the basketballs vary, and the learner varies in physiological
functioning. True, efficiency of performance varies somewhat with
variation in the above factors, but the variation decreases with thorough learning.

The act of shooting a basketball into a basket is capable of becoming a generalized habit set off by a very few cues in a total stimulus pattern. The set of the competitive game, the possession of
the ball, and the momentary relaxation of an opponent may set off
the pattern of shooting. The form of the movement, its rate, relative strength, and complexity vary with the situation.

Let us follow up this statement of generalized motor habit with
other examples. We learn to walk and then adjust our walking to
the terrain. We learn to ride and then adjust our riding to the
horse, pony, mule, or other animal. We learn to hit a tennis ball
with a racket, and adjust much of the habit to table tennis, badminton, or handball. The baseball player must hit the ball in spite
of the variety of pitchers and the eccentricity of their deliveries.
All forming of motor patterns seems to be of this *generalized* nature

—not a specific chain response to an exact stimulus pattern. Just as the arabic numeral "2" applies to twins or parents, dice or double fouls, so does a throwing movement adapt itself to a ball or a stone, a javelin or a trout line.

Motor learning is pattern learning. Ability to make almost all of the specific movements one performs is attained during the pre-school and primary school development. When, for example, a secondary school student tries to acquire the skill of curving a base-ball, he does not need to learn new individual movements. He al-ready possesses the needed movements, but he does not know which of his available repertoire of movements should be selected and fused into the new pattern. He can grip the ball with his fingers; he can make the throwing movement with his arm; he can draw his body back and thrust it forward; he can snap his wrist. He resorts to trial and error in an attempt to determine exactly which move-ments are needed. And he does not know how to put together the movements until he finally hits upon one as best fitting. The exact timing of each movement in the pattern, the amount of strength per movement, and the fusion of these movements with the requisite strength and correct timing into the *unity* essential for skilled execu-tion—these are further problems. Wrong selection of movements may throw too great strain on his arm. Correct selection may de-pend upon careful development of needed strength in part move-ments. No one can tell the individual exactly how *he* should throw a baseball. If major league baseball managers could give such ex-plicit directions, they could save themselves great economic loss.

Characteristics of beginners. The learning process of the in-dividual in the early stages of acquiring any particular skill pattern is characterized by variety and diversity of response. The entire body tends to increase in muscular tension. The energy released by the stimuli flows out into innumerable movements of the individ-ual. Random and inappropriate movements are frequent. Emo-tional intensity is likely to accompany the learning. Much move-ment is nonapplicable, and, in its extremes, may inhibit applicable movements. The hesitancy and timidity of the beginner may be so great as to interfere seriously with his learning. The difference be-tween the mild amount of emotional energy that drives an individ-ual to surpass his previous performance and the amount that causes him to "choke up" or seriously interfere with his performance may be very little. The beginner is apt to make excuses, become annoyed, find fault with the quality and utility of the equipment; he may become embarrassed and laugh at himself; he may project the blame on others for his own errors or exhibit extraneous gestures and facial expressions. He may go so far as to renounce the activity and express preference to engage in activities which are already mastered. Such behavior is human and typical and has been observed by experienced teachers countless times.

The teacher is well aware of how visitors may upset pupil performance. If, however, the pupils are in a more advanced stage and have had previous experience in performing before strangers, the smaller amount of emotional stimulus may actually improve performance.

Teachers must keep in mind the greater fatigue accompanying the early stages of learning. This fatigue is due to: (1) greater number of actual movements made in performing the act; (2) additional emotional tensions and consequent sapping of energy; and (3) greater physiological fatigability of the untrained body. The beginner has not yet learned to eliminate the unnecessary movements. His tensions prevent the relaxations of body parts not in use.

In the beginning stages of learning, the learning environment should be as free from pressures as possible. New responses not yet thoroughly automatized may be released by a variety of stimuli. The response is not yet limited to the appropriate stimulus pattern. Overtensity may inhibit action or cause action to spill over into extremely erroneous performance. Long training will limit the response to stimulus cues that fit the immediate purpose. The emotional accompaniment of early performance in a social situation may become too intense if the distractions are too great. Inappropriate emotional responses are common. Stage fright, general tension, and resulting awkward and fumbling movements are such nonapplicable responses. The individual should be inured gradually to such stimuli. This process of *negative adaptation* is a learning process and is subject to the same principles of learning as positive learning. The earlier lessons must not be too complex and difficult. If they are too difficult, failure may bring on discouragement, and greatly retard learning. The beginner who "blows up under fire" suffers an emotional shock, which may result in even greater sensitivity to these emotional stimuli to inappropriate responses.

The general idea. One must have the overall pattern of movement as clearly in mind as possible. Observation of skilled performance by others, of demonstrations by a well-trained teacher, of movies of the skill performance, plus verbal guides, illustrations, and the like, all help in this general orientation. With this directional set, *one proceeds* with a rather slow, continuous action in conformity with the mental construct of the movement pattern. This unit of action should be as large as can be carried through as a continuity. The early attempts will of necessity be slowly performed. But the learner should be hastened to more rapid practice as soon as practicable. This initial slow rate gives time for the attention to be diffused over the total design of the movement pattern and for the general framework consciously to be visualized. The focal point of attention even in the beginning stages is directed toward perception of cues for action rather than toward body movements. A *gross* error will stand out (or should be pointed out by the teacher).

There are various other methods of motor learning, such as the detailed drill-on-parts method—an analytical approach with the knitting together of the parts occurring later. However, the technique discussed above, *of beginning with a total unified pattern, or the largest manageable part,* is the way children usually learn in their free play and in their imitative attempts of experts. This *unit approach* is recommended as the most rapid way to acquire an automatic habit-performance. The child was correct in his unawareness of, and little concern for, detailed errors. The detailed errors can be left to drop out unconsciously. Or, they can be eradicated by careful polish in the advanced stages—the stages wherein the whole is so unified that any part-practice is really whole-unit practice because the rest of the pattern is continually filled in by memory. The part has become undetachable from the whole in significance and meaning.

The child's learning is the key to early teaching techniques. The child does not speed up his performance rate so fast that performance is upset. He plays at an easy rate with completed patterns, no self-analysis, and without great emotional pressure for perfection. He plays at the rate at which he can succeed with others whose rate is comparable.

Playmates improve together. Their movements change and readjust as their speed of performance increases. In time they are far enough along in making responses automatic to endure the techniques of the part-learning specialist without retarding their learning. Then they are at the stage where polish of their weak spots is an advantage. They are far enough along to stand the pressures of survival of the fittest coaching for the varsity without letting the accompanying emotional strain upset their automatized patterns and their rate of progress.

Great emotional concern for perfection of performance, if applied too early in the learning process, tends to retard learning. Putting the boy under fire too soon may do almost irreparable damage to his learning of that activity. However, such experience is invaluable in the later stages. It seems to set the patterns, generalize them for wider application by appropriately readjusting details, accelerate the fusion of skills into even larger units, and produce higher peaks of performance.

Insight learning in motor skills refers to a sudden shift in method. The individual may have practiced for a long time in a particular method and may have approached his physiological limit by that method. Adoption of a better method then results in higher proficiency. Adding the final snap of the wrists in batting or pitching a baseball, substituting finger and wrist control for grosser movements in shooting or passing a basketball, adding body momentum to arm movement in weight throwing in track, all are improved techniques which one may hit upon as partial insights. Teacher demonstration, direction, and encouragement should increase the number of partial insights and short cut the *trial and error* process. To gain insight from verbal directions, one must execute the improved method and make its value meaningful through *personally experiencing* superior performance.

Awareness of exact change is not an essential part of motor learning. One must be very cautious about concluding that a sudden improvement in motor learning is the result of a conscious insight and the subsequent modification of the motor pattern. Frequently, the individual hits upon devices which are successful, adopts them, and performs them in the future without ever having any conscious awareness of just what change took place. Many an individual who can perform a skill well not only cannot tell others how to do it, but actually does not know exactly how he does himself.

Errors may be unconscious. Just as one may unconsciously fall into improved methods, so may he fall into performance errors. A little variation that lowers efficiency may creep into one's activity without his being conscious of it. His consequent lower performance level is likely to cause him to perform more carefully and attempt to eliminate interfering movements. Some of these errors are difficult to discover.

One teaching technique is to have the learner briefly practice the movements of a major error with focus of attention on that error. This practice serves the purpose of bringing to conscious attention that part of the pattern which must be eliminated. If the error has been unconsciously performed, the actual *practice of the error* with attention upon it may help to eliminate the error from the total pattern in later performances.

An illustration from basketball may clarify this point. In a certain play pattern, one forward had fallen into the habit of running in an arc around the screen set up by his teammate. The path of the forward was a longer distance than the chord across the same arc (the correct path), and the forward could not run as fast around the curved path as he could along a straight line. These two erroneous factors, greater distance and a more difficult path to traverse at top speed, spoiled the timing of the whole play pattern. In addition, the incorrect path neutralized the screen by allowing room for the defensive guard to pass between the forward and his teammate posted as a screen. The coach explained the error verbally and then had the forward run through his part of the play several times using the incorrect path. The coach's comment and the focus of attention on the exact error by such practice made the forward realize the movement that had caused the play to fail. Sometimes the most difficult problem is to find the error which is upsetting the total pattern.

The effects of practice. Motor learning does not seem to be a process of repetition until habit is formed. In mental learning we may repeat associations until the response to stimulus is almost instantaneous and involuntary. "The sum of five and five is ____" is an example of association repeated until the reader involuntarily fills in the blank space mentally. The spelling of these words as they are written is a similar example. In motor learning, however, we repeat *wrong* responses (although they are not exactly the same successive wrong responses) in order to learn correct responses. One shoots a basketball in an attempt to make a basket. As a beginner, he shoots unsuccessfully a great many more times than he shoots successfully. Let us assume that, at a medium range, the beginner is unlikely to make a basket more than 10 per cent of the time. He obtains nine times as much practice in missing the basket as he does in making it. Can we conclude, therefore, that he learns by repetition and will increasingly improve in missing the basket while trying to make it?

Very apparently such a conclusion is absurd. What we seem to do in learning a motor skill is to try and fail, change our movements a little, try again, and so on. Motor learners continually revise their methods of performance and gradually seem to hit upon procedures that are successful a greater percentage of the time, or that more nearly approximate the goal they have in mind.

Repetition of a motor movement normally brings about progressive habituation. Everyone has heard that practice makes perfect. For the most part the experimentation that has been done in investigating the conditions of motor learning has involved fine motor activities. Usually these experiments involve simple performances that are novel to the subjects. Card sorting, mirror drawing, maze tracing, dart throwing, rotor pursuit, and several other manipulative tasks have been studied to determine the nature of motor learning. These are examples of *fine motor learning*. Most of these studies have been concerned with the changes in speed and accuracy of performance while other factors have been held constant. Until quite recently, however, few attempts have been made to compile a description of the progressive changes that take place in the learning of *gross motor skills*. (Gross motor skills are the skills which involve the movement of large muscle groups and usually result in the whole body being moved.) Several investigators have established that the learning of gross motor skills and fine motor skills may take place in a somewhat different fashion. A person's ability to learn and the way in which he learns best probably depend upon the abilities he has. No general relationship exists between fine and gross motor abilities; motor abilities are highly specific. There appears to be no *general motor ability*.   There seem to be various motor *abilities,* qualities which are possessed by individuals in varying amounts and in varying clusters.   Some individuals, highly gifted in some abilities, may be lacking in others.

Practice is needed to become accomplished in a complex motor skill.   Unfortunately, we do not know precisely the best practice patterns for the most effective learning of motor skills.   How long practice periods should be and how much rest should be provided between practices is not clearly understood.   Also, the manner in which practice and rest periods are distributed is important.   We have known for many years that spaced or distributed practice is superior to massed practice, but exactly how to distribute the practice for maximum efficiency in acquiring skills of varying complexity by learners at varying levels of maturity has yet to be determined.   Experimental evidence continues to indicate what has been known for many years:

> There is serious doubt concerning the doctrine which insists upon "two hours faithful daily practice" as the best tuitional procedure for beginners on a musical instrument, for the novice golfer, etc.   If we were able to limit practice periods to an optimal length, and to separate them by appropriate rest periods at every state of learning, improvement would be considerably more rapid and effective.[1]

In physical education teaching and athletic coaching we are interested in bringing about maximum learning and retention in limited periods of time.   If practice can be arranged so that maximum learning accrues, more material can obviously be taught and learned in a given period of time.   The following are some generalizations concerning practice:

1. The superiority of distributed over massed effort varies with the material to be learned.   If the material is meaningful and satisfying to the learner, and if the learner is highly motivated, long periods of practice may be efficient and provide good retention. This means that massed effort is *not much poorer* on meaningful material.   The conditions for best distribution depend on the task and the learner.

[1] Samuel Renshaw and William Schwarzbek, "The Dependence of the Form of the Pursuitmeter Learning Function on the Length of Interpractice Rests," *Journal of General Psychology,* 18:3–16 (1938).

2. Practice should be satisfying, and the learner should experience some success. If the results are annoying they tend to be replaced by other more satisfying behavior. Mere repetition does not help learning. For repetition to be effective the learner must in some way be rewarded or reinforced, or his drives will be reduced.

3. Repetition in a learning situation can alter the learning in an unwanted way (provided the conditions in No. 2 above are satisfied).

4. The effect of equal practice on increasing or decreasing the differences among learners is inconsistent. Generally differences *increase* with practice.

5. The more highly developed the individual is, the fewer breaks are needed. In early learning periods breaks should be more frequent. Later, practice may be more massed.

6. Short periods of intense purposeful practice are best. The learner should concentrate on what he is attempting to accomplish rather than just going through the motions.

7. Practice of his skill is most effective if it is done in the way—or as nearly as possible in the way—that the skill will ultimately be used.

Habit levels of performance. Learning is faster and retention of things learned is greater if the learning experience results in satisfaction. If the results are annoying, they tend to be replaced by other more satisfying behavior. The desirability in competitive athletics of a reasonable amount of winning becomes apparent if one considers the effect of such satisfactions of learning. Likewise, for motivation purposes, a few losses in competitive athletics are desirable. Occasional losses eliminate the tendency to be satisfied with the present level of achievement, encourage greater effort toward higher levels, and focus attention on correction of present weaknesses. When the teacher is using competition for motivating purposes, he must equate his competitors. Succeeding too easily is just as harmful to the individual as failing too frequently. If mediocrity of attainment (as compared to one's potentialities of attainment) is followed by satisfaction, mediocrity becomes the habit performance. However, if the competition makes one's mediocre performance appear inferior, he is dissatisfied and tries harder to improve. One's mistakes are more apparent in stiff competition. Analyzing weakness in performance of a competitive skill is extremely difficult if the opposition is inferior.

Learning during rest.   One advantage of distributed practice over massed practice is that improvement takes place during the interval between practice sessions.   Exactly how or why this occurs is not clearly understood.   Chance errors which crop up in practice are thought to be less firmly established than the more appropriate responses and hence forgotten sooner.   In this way the intervals between practices seem to aid in the elimination of errors.   Adaptable performance, recalled and reapplied after an interval of no practice, seems to gain greater permanence than the same adaptable performance successively reapplied on continuous practice.   Short bouts of practice alternated with periods of rest during which learning continues to take place appears to be the process that establishes the most effective learning.   Learning takes time and rest as well as work.   It apparently has to sink in.   Cramming is not an efficient way of learning.

To appreciate the dilemma the teacher may experience in designing the practice pattern to promote maximum learning, consider the following situation: A physical education class meets for 40 minutes daily five days a week.   If supervision, equipment, and instruction are to be excluded as concerns, how can you distribute the 200 minutes of practice on the following five fundamental skill elements of touch football: (1) place kicking, (2) passing, (3) pass receiving, (4) centering, and (5) punting?

The following are a few possibilities:

1. 8 minutes on each of the skills daily.
2. 20 minutes on each of two skills daily.
3. 13 minutes on each of three skills daily.
4. 20 minutes on one skill each day and 5 minutes on each of the other four.
5. 15 minutes on one skill each day and 6 minutes on each of the other four.

There are almost unlimited possible combinations of skill elements and period of practice.   Realizing that learning takes place during rest and that all of the skills are meaningful to pupils, what distribution of practice would be most recommended?

Speed and accuracy in learning movements.   Many motor skills, and most sports skills to be executed properly, require both rapid and accurate bodily movements.   Until rather recently the best results in motor learning were thought to be obtained when actions were slowed down in the early stages of learning. If speed were retarded until a reasonable level of accuracy was developed, then speed could be increased gradually until the skill was executed as rapidly as needed.

Contrary to this view, more recent studies indicate that placing emphasis on speed in the initial phases of learning may produce best results if *both* speed and accuracy are to be involved in the finished performance. For example, the learner attempting to become a skilled batter in baseball, desires to meet the rapidly pitched baseball with the bat and to have the bat in rapid swinging motion at the time that it contacts the ball. Under the older procedure, the ball would be delivered slowly and the batter would take a moderate swing at it in the early learning process. Emphasis on speed from the outset, however, would require that the ball be pitched at greater speed and that the batter take a full cut at it. Obviously this procedure could be carried to the extreme. To pitch a series of balls at 100 miles an hour past a beginner would not allow him to enjoy any satisfaction or success, and the learning process would be seriously hindered. On the other hand, to presume that batting skill at the plate will be greatly increased by almost endless practice of pepper in which the ball is thrown at a relatively low speed and struck with but half a swing is a questionable procedure in light of what is now known.

When practicing at low speeds, the learner is developing habits of coordination which might be quite different from those needed at high speeds in actual performance. Not only are the learned coordinations different but they may actually interfere with the proper performance of the skill as it must ultimately be used. The principle of motor learning is that *practice should be done as nearly as possible approximating the speed and the method in which the skill is to be employed.* To practice one movement in the hope of developing another is ineffective.

In the field of sports, no kind of practice seems to replace in value actual competitive game experience. If the coach is forced by lack of seasoned material to play some lowly substitute, the boy seems to learn the game much more rapidly. Three or four games of varsity experience advance such an individual beyond what he would have been after a whole season of practice and practice scrimmage without varsity game competition. High school coaches prefer boys who have had experience as competitors. In some sports, some college coaches prefer the boy who has had experience on independent teams after graduating from high school. The average college coach wants his freshmen to play a relatively large number of games. Game experience does not seem to be equaled in value by many times as much practice drill and scrimmage.

Transfer of learning. The principle stated above relating to speed in practice applies equally to the concept of transfer of learning. Transfer implies the degree of gain or loss on the performance of one skill as a result of the performance or learning of some other skill. The degree of similarity of one skill to another is the important aspect in the phenomenon of transfer. The more identity one skill has with another, the more elements that it has in common, the more transfer might be expected. Actually the transfer of learning from one motor skill to another is highly specific. For example, the throwing motion in softball and baseball are almost identical and a great deal of transfer occurs. However, a learner accustomed to throwing a basketball with his hand squarely behind the larger ball experiences difficulty in throwing a football in a spiraling pass because the hand cannot be directly behind the ball. This is an example of negative transfer; a situation in which the prior learning interferes with rather than aids performance.

Another example demonstrates how both positive and negative transfer might be involved. The learner who has developed some skill in tennis undertakes the learning of badminton. Many of the elements of footwork, of court position, of general strategy, of keeping the eyes focused on the projectile, and of striking with a racket are very similar if not identical. These elements can be expected to transfer positively. However, in tennis the firm, almost locked wrist is essential because of the weight of the racket, the pace of the heavier ball, and the accepted method of properly executed tennis stroke. Conversely, in badminton great wrist snap is needed to properly accelerate the racket head prior to contacting the shuttlecock. In this latter case, negative transfer is experienced.

More transfer can be expected in the gross or major elements of movements than in the important but specific movements. Transfer occurs in the gross features of throwing, running, weight shifting, catching, and the *general features* of movement patterns.

Transfer of *broad understanding* also occurs. Since most sports activities are quite different in fine specific elements, transfer of these are negligible.

The learner need not be concerned with transfer. In fact, he is probably better off if he concentrates on the present task and makes no effort to remember past experiences. If he concentrates on what he is attempting to do *now*, his nervous system will drag into the present what is useful and appropriate from past experience automatically. Attempting to gain from the *memory* of past performance may be distracting. Analysis is helpful to the teacher, but the beginning teacher may fail to realize that such detailed analysis is not an aid to the learner. In his eagerness to help the pupil he may unnecessarily complicate the task.

Analysis of one's own activity is very difficult in motor skills. Self-analysis is not always a help in motor learning and may be a hindrance. Many motor skills are so complex that exact self-analysis merely confuses the learner. The best method of motor learning, once the general orientation toward the goal is accomplished, is that type of *trial and error* in which the individual is continually revising his procedure in an attempt to improve. Trial and error implies that the learner knows what he is trying to do but does not know how to do it. The learner focuses his attention on the results of his movements. The prospective hockey player knows that he must learn great exactness in body control and balance on skates, but he learns it only by practice. The taxicab driver drives through space with scarcely room for an extra coat of paint and has no idea what movement variations he took on in acquiring this skill.

Analysis through cinematography. Study of motion pictures of oneself may bring to light performance errors undiscovered by ordinary observation and self-analysis. Athletic coaches and players now make wide use of moving pictures of skill performance. These pictures are particularly valuable to teachers because they allow a projection of the performer's movement again and again until the analysis is complete. The performer's individual movements can be compared with movements of specialists in the same skill. Variations may suggest possible ways of improvement, and fine movement analyses are possible. Comparison of the movies of an individual's movement patterns with movies of experts, or comparison with the movies of accepted performance techniques, may reveal errors not noticed in even the most careful and painstaking practice.

Intelligence and motor learning.   The relationships between I.Q. and athletic ability are low.   The ability to be an expert performer in motor skills is not dependent upon high levels of intellectual ability or on excellence in academic intelligence.   Every teacher of physical education knows that this is correct.   The difficulties that some athletic coaches experience when their star performers are declared ineligible in midseason because of scholastic difficulties is testimony to this fact.   The notoriety over such happenings has fortified the nonathletes' preconceived notion that all athletes are dumb.   Nothing could be farther from the truth. Neither is the reverse of this true.   The possession of a high I.Q. is certainly not a hindrance.   In the early stages of the acquisition of a complex motor skill intellectual ability probably has a great beneficial effect.

Intelligence helps the learner to quickly grasp instruction.   It helps him to see the point rapidly.   The bright person is able to sustain his concentration.   The intelligent learner is able to follow directions, to get a notion of what it is that he is supposed to do, to think it through, to formulate the concept, and, if other abilities are efficacious, to perform it quickly and correctly.   Brightness helps the learner to see the relationship of the skill to other movements that are already learned.

Many of the motor skills learned in physical education are game elements.   Although most of these are rather easily understood, the success of the learning of these skills is measured in terms of how effectively they are employed in the game.   In the strategy surrounding the game situations, one's ability to think quickly, correctly, and imaginatively largely determines the success of performance. Brightness enables the performer to capitalize on opportunities. Fielding the ground ball at shortstop is not enough.   The rapid on-the-spot decision of what to do next is equally important.

Intelligence is a definite factor in the acquisition of some kinds of motor skills.   Acquiring very complex movements probably involves more mental learning than motor learning.   Overall, intelligence appears to be more important in influencing rapid *learning* than in having marked effect on ultimate *performance*.

The kinesthetic sense and motor learning.   Learning, as it is customarily thought of, is concerned with mental impressions and meanings. These meanings and impressions are the final objectives of mental learning. On the other hand, perceptual-motor learning uses these meanings and impressions as a means of changing performance. Such movement changes are the object of motor learning. To accomplish this change the learner must perceive cues. This perception is, of course, through the senses. Along with the visual sense the type of perception used most in motor learning is the kinesthetic. Through the kinesthetic sense the learner is aware of the position of various parts of his body and the effects of muscular effort in changing his bodily position. Consequently, motor learning is kinesthetic as well as mental. Kinesthesis is an important element in motor learning, but it is a difficult characteristic to measure. Individuals differ in kinesthetic acuity, and this variability influences ability to learn motor skills. The learner must "get the feel" of particular muscular responses before he can make progress. Having experienced the kinesthetic awareness of what he is trying to do, he can then practice by trying to recreate or modify the feeling.

The kinesthetic sense is of particular importance when the visual sense cannot be used as a guide to the positioning of body parts. For example, when learning to swim the pupil cannot see the position of his legs; he must depend upon feel so that he may fashion the movements that he has in mind. Awareness of the position of the bat while intently watching the approaching pitched ball and knowing how far the tennis racket is drawn back in preparation for a smash when the eyes must be focused on the descending ball are other examples of the need for kinesthetic cues.

The wise policy is to train as many of the senses as possible. Of course, illusions in the kinesthetic sense can be created. Practice shoes are often heavier than game shoes. The lighter game shoes give one the feeling of being light on his feet and agile. The baseball bat seems light and easy to swing after having swung two or three bats together while awaiting one's turn at bat. Other sport illusions are common. Placing the standards farther apart in the high jump or pole vault makes the cross bar seem lower and easier to clear. Spinner plays in football, screens away from the ball in basketball, feints and fakes in all sports are based on the principle that the visual sense is easy to trick.

One may learn to use the kinesthetic sense through practice. One investigation indicates that early phases of learning using lighter objects may be advantageous.[2] Two groups of subjects practiced throwing balls over a barrier at a target while using their nondominant hands. Both groups used balls of the same size, but one group used a light plastic ball and the other group used a heavier softball. Five hundred trials were made by the subjects in each group, and each group significantly increased accuracy in throwing during the course of the experiment. However, the group practicing with the light ball scored higher than the group that practiced with the heavier ball. At the conclusion of the experiment the group that had used the light ball in the learning period attempted 50 trials with the heavier ball and the group that had used the heavier ball had 50 trials with the light ball. This exchange of tasks revealed a remarkable finding. The group that learned with the light ball performed better with the heavy ball than they had ever done with the light ball. In addition their accuracy was superior to the group that had practiced with the heavy ball throughout the learning period. The group that had trained with the heavy ball, when changing over to the light ball, decreased in accuracy to a marked degree. These results *might* be explained by the fact that the group which practiced with the light ball developed greater sensitivity in such practice and when they transferred to the heavier ball this sensitivity was an asset. On the other hand, the group that practiced with the heavy ball was not forced to develop corresponding sensitivity, and when this ability was necessary in the task of throwing the lighter ball accurately, their efficiency diminished.

Perhaps the findings of this study could be applied to the early stages of some sports learning. For if lighter balls or clubs or bats or rackets are capable of developing sensitivity sooner, such practices might be indicated to hasten the earlier stages of learning. More evidence, however, is needed to varify this hypothesis.

The use of cues. Focus of attention on response produces a faster reaction than focus of attention on perceiving the stimulus for the response. Track coaches know that the dash man should focus his attention on shoving out from the starting blocks when he hears the gun. If he focuses his attention on hearing the gun, he will start a

[2] Glen H. Egstrom, Gene A. Logan, and Earl L. Wallis, "Acquisition of Throwing Skill Involving Projectiles of Varying Weights," *The Research Quarterly*, Vol. 31, No. 3 (1960), 420–425.

little later. Football men will charge faster if they learn to focus attention on the initial starting movement and hear or see the starting signal incidentally.

Signals are stimuli to which we supposedly have relatively automatized responses. In continuous team games such as basketball, lacrosse, or soccer, signals are not so common. Perhaps the best signal system for use in these games is that of having the ball as the *cue*. Offensive floor or field formations are quickly assumed upon recovery of the ball. The movement of the ball is the signal for the play. If it is passed to a certain man, that pass is the signal for one play; if to another, a different play. A dribble toward a certain man constitutes a third play, and so on. A sudden exchange of men covered by the defensive team may be an understood signal for a certain maneuver by the offense. Such previously understood cues to appropriate play permit the offensive attack to be made up of all the offensive players, with perfect understanding by each of individual duties and responsibilities. The concerted attack is more rapid because the number of necessary decisions as to appropriate action is decreased.

Teams that have played together for a long while hit upon some signal system, a system which may not be consciously recognized by the players themselves. Players seem to know just what teammates are going to do. Characteristic movements, body positions, or habit patterns are the cues. Teachers are to be criticized because they have not given youngsters methods of speeding up the learning of signal systems (mutually understood cues) in rapid-action team games. Occasionally a boy with more ability than those playing is left on the bench because he does not fit into the combination. If the teacher depends entirely on the trial and error learning of competition itself to develop a set of relatively subliminal cues (signals responded to without conscious awareness of the exact stimulus), he is not fair to the newer group members. Neither is he carrying out his real purpose as a teacher—that of speeding up the learning process.

Some of the smaller patterns that make up the panorama of the game become automatized in a specific movement pattern. Change in timing or in any movement will upset the habit continuum. A boy who learns to take his time on long shots in basketball will be ineffective against a defense which hurries him. A football punter is sometimes less effective if his kicking is hurried.   Golf players have their habitual speeds and may be upset by being hurried. Many of the relatively automatized movement patterns of daily life have a specific performance speed.   This speed is rarely the individual's maximum potential speed for that specific series of movements. It is merely the speed that the exigencies of circumstances induced in him at the time he was automatizing the pattern.   Patterns of sports, established after long practice sessions, may fail to function in games because the established timing of the patterns is too slow for the game, and change in timing upsets the automatic performance.

The effect of sudden change in movements of a team pattern is equally great.   Collegiate football defenses stress this method of upsetting offensive patterns.   Teams trained to play against a five, six, or seven man line are at a loss when first opposed by the sliding line.   Coaches are now faced with the problem of making certain major plays automatic against many types of defensive line play.

Mental activity and motor learning.   Evidence has been recently accumulating to verify the contention that *how* and *what* one thinks has an influence on performance.   One aspect might be called mental practice and the other state of mind.

Motor skills can be learned without actually doing the movements. That is, one may think through, plan, reflect, contemplate, and this application can in some way improve performance.   Some learning can evidently take place without actually going through the movements.   Investigations have shown that regular mental practice is superior to irregular actual practice in the learning of some motor skills.   Although, sitting down and thinking about a skill is not as efficient as actually going through it, thinking through in combination with actual practice is probably the most effective.   Close study, planning, and mentally rehearsing during the inter-practice rest period is helpful.

As the learner turns over in his mind the movements he plans to make, nervous impulses at a sub-threshold level can be measured in the muscles that will be involved in the performance of the skill. Such nervous activity probably helps to organize the learner's understanding and approach to the task and to better later performance. In some instances there seems to be involuntary muscle contraction during mental work when learners imagine that they are performing motor skills.   Gymnasts often feel themselves, and see themselves go through complex patterns of movement prior to mounting the appa-ratus to perform the skills.   Spectators often make partial involun-tary movements along with athletes almost as if they were helping the performer to accomplish the task.   They rotate their trunks as the shotputter uncoils; they elevate one leg as the high jumper makes his kick up to the cross bar.   Such observation of performance is actually a kind of mental practice in which the learner goes through the experience without actually moving through it himself.   Part of the learning that takes place through watching demonstrations or through viewing motion pictures of expert performance may be thought of as this kind of mental practice.

The learner's state of mind also affects the efficiency with which he learns and performs motor skills.   One characteristic that cham-pion athletes have in common is *the ability to concentrate com-pletely on the task at hand.*   They give their complete attention to the performance at the moment and rule out all extraneous environ-mental stimuli.   This intensity of application is just as important in the learning of a motor skill as it is in the effective performance of the movement once it has been learned.   Such singleness of pur-pose is, of course, influenced by the degree of motivation felt by the learner.   Such intensive motivation not only influences the speed in which the skill is acquired, but affects how well the skill is re-tained.   If the learner practices with intent to learn, if he is con-fident of his ability to accomplish the skill, if he believes in his capacity to perform effectively and can see no reason why he should not be successful, his accomplishment may be almost limitless. Great performers in track and field events have demonstrated the effectiveness of proper state of mind.   They talk themselves into a competitive frame of mind.   They intentionally attempt to get themselves worked up or "psyched up" so that all of their efforts and concentration can be focused on the task at hand.   This is not to suggest that the beginning learner should be overtense or over-stimulated.   Usually the beginner has too much tension and is over-anxious.   But, for most efficient learning, he must be purposeful and must concentrate on what he is trying to accomplish.

The effects of fatigue on learning.   One unique feature of motor learning is that the learner is undergoing rapid physiological im-pairment as he attempts to acquire skills.   He cannot practice a motor skill demanding vigorous muscular contractions for several consecutive hours.   This is not the case in other types of learning; the student of mathematics, if sufficiently motivated, could spend all of his waking hours on the solution of problems.   The ambitious drama student may spend a large portion of the day in memorizing a part for the school play.   But a learner of sports skills must often terminate his practice before his interest begins to wane because he cannot function effectively owing to physiological fatigue.   This onset of fatigue can be noted in the slower rate of muscular contractions and a greater frequency of inaccurate movements.   In general, when performance reveals this slower rate, further practice is uneconomical in terms of learning time expended.   Experimental data indicate that when practice periods are too long, the student loses that exuberance of energy and vitality, usually conceded to be essential to progressive learning.   This does not mean that the practice should not be intense.

The question is often raised as to whether the somewhat fatigued pupil may be in a condition for faster learning.   Two hypotheses are: (1) cleverness and finesse are more likely to be practiced in an attempt to save energy; and (2) the pupil will try harder for successful effort in order to save himself from further laborious effort. Both of these possibilities might operate in some circumstances, but recent evidence supports the carrying of highly motivated practice to the point of fatigue and a little beyond.

When attempting to perform a motor skill while fatigued, if the muscles that would normally cause the action are unable to operate effectively, other muscles and coordinations take over.   This adaptation mechanism operates automatically—with sub-cortical control—without consciousness.   The nervous system in the cortical and sub-cortical areas is forced to respond when the situation is made more difficult.   Such a response tends to spread or scatter the responsibility to other muscle groups needed to accomplish the skill if it must be done under fatigue in the future.   Performing under fatigue makes possible new ways of getting the job done.

In the course of the game when he is fatigued, the basketball player must be able to shoot free throws accurately.   His learning of free-throw shooting might be most effective if it is practiced when he is fatigued rather than at the beginning of practice when he is fresh.   The same principle might be applied to passing or kicking a football, executing a racing turn in swimming, or to any other sport skill that must be accomplished when the performer is fatigued. Again, practice and learning should take place in a manner closely approximating the way the skill will be used. The additional stress applied to the nervous system, forcing it to find ways of responding, tends to reinforce the learning process. Even the additional movements and extra tension that the beginning learner exhibits and the extra fatigue he experiences are probably valuable and functional; for this contributes to the effectiveness of the learning process by overloading the nervous system and thereby opening new pathways for coordinations.

If the learner knows what to do and diligently attempts to accomplish his purpose, the body learns new adaptations under the additional stress. It becomes increasingly important that the learner attempt to *accomplish* the task and that he not be too concerned as to the fine details of how he does it.

There seems to be an overlapping in the nervous system. The body will attempt to get the job done in any way that it can manage to do so. If one group of muscles is ineffective in accomplishing the purpose, other available muscle groups are marshalled to assist through the sub-cortical automatic adaptation mechanism.

Recent findings indicate that even muscular strength may be learned through the ability the body has to automatically adapt to stress. Such strength development may be due to a type of learning which results from neurological, sub-cortical adaptation to imposed demands. Logan [3] found that strength was developed most at the point in the range of motion where the greatest resistance was applied. The tentative explanation for this type of learning was that proprioceptive facilitation takes place, e.g., when the body meets greater resistance in a portion of the range of motion, the nervous system automatically feeds back additional bombardments of impulses to overcome the resistance. Upon meeting additional resistance at the same point in the range of motion repeatedly, the body facilitates powerful contractions at that specific point, but the same muscle shows relatively little gain in other areas of the range of motion. Again, this takes place unconsciously. These findings

[3] Gene A. Logan, "Differential Applications of Resistance and Resulting Strength Measured at Varying Degrees of Knee Extension" (Unpublished Doctoral Dissertation, University of Southern California, Los Angeles, 1959).

give further support to the principle of practicing what it is that we are going to do—not something else, for the body makes rather specific adaptations.

The above description of how learning and performance may be improved without conscious awareness does not imply that the voluntary intensive application of the will of the learner is not needed. Nothing could be farther from fact. It is necessary, in fact vital, that the learner vigorously and enthusiastically attempt to accomplish his purposes. That is, he must earnestly try to make the basket, catch the pass, or lift the weight. In so doing, he sets off the automatic adaptations. Neither does the above description imply that the learner should just go at it without instruction or coaching. He must be helped to understand what it is he is trying to accomplish in learning a complex skill. Adequate guidance is essential to define the task and to help the learner reinforce the correct responses.

Some factors in choice of form.   The individual often adopts a form by imitation.   However, wide diversity of forms exists among the experts to whom one might look for a model, particularly in the details of their work method.   A particular work method may even change with the onset of fatigue as described above.   Performance in the later stages of the bout of activity, though remaining effective, might be quite different because of modifications of co-ordinations under fatigue.   Novices are apt to imitate the mannerisms of an expert rather than his performance of fundamentals. The teacher may study the individual pupil, impose a form for the activity on him, and then permit certain individual adjustments as practice progresses.   Any individual's purpose will change his preferred form.   If he wants beauty, grace, and apparent ease, he adopts a certain design of performance.   If he is chiefly concerned with the end result (say scoring in basketball), he is likely to use a somewhat different form.   If he is greatly concerned about economy of motion and energy, perhaps because of advanced age, individual lack of endurance, or even the extreme strenuousness of the type of activity, he will make suitable variations in the form used.

Smooth flowing, graceful movement is not necessarily the most economical use of energy.   Let a human attempt to emulate the graceful walk of any member of the cat family, and he will find that considerable additional movement is entailed.   The feet are picked up and set down with a graceful, sinuous continuity of movement that requires extra effort.   Contrast the energy output of the jump into the water with that of the graceful swan dive.   The balance, the poise, the control, the exactness in tension in both the contracting and the antagonist muscles of the expert dancer require great amounts of energy.

The most economical ways to learn.   Economical ways to learn begin with interest in learning.   The interest in learning is related to the speed and efficiency of learning.   If the student is eager to learn, he will tend to progress toward the desired learning goal more rapidly.   Indifferent attitudes must be eliminated before any marked progress can take place.   Learning experiments indicate that determination to learn has a real effect on the permanence of learning.   This determination manifests itself much more in delayed recall than in immediate recall.   This finding offers some encouragement to the individual who wants very much to succeed but progresses slowly.

Learning is progressive.   Present learning depends upon what has preceded it.   Environment also affects the rate and amount of learning.   The teacher fosters an environment that will focus the pupils' energies in the direction of the desired development.   The question arises as to how these energies can be directed so that a maximum amount of learning will result from the pupil time expended.

Energy and health.   The general health of the student is closely related to the amount of energy he will have available to expend in learning experiences.   The value of correct health habits and sane training regimens becomes apparent.   Learning is an active process, and activity takes energy.

Variability in effective techniques.   The most effective methods of learning will differ with the pupil.   As was mentioned earlier, one's quickness to learn seems to be an individual matter.   In motor skills the more apt individuals can rely to a greater degree on verbal cues and guides.   They can profit more from visual presentation of the desired pattern.   They tend to rely more on verbal guides and visual imagery than does the slow learner.   The slow learner relies to a great extent on kinesthetic cues.   Previous background of an individual and his aptness are what determine the meaningfulness of new material.   The more meaningful it is, the faster he learns.   The more intelligent individuals may make a more effective transfer of previous learnings to present situations than do the less intelligent. Pupils vary in the amount of profit from verbal explanation and description, and from motor demonstration.

In teaching motor skills, concrete verbal directions are, in general, superior to mechanical guidance. Visual guidance from demonstration should include only small units of a complex pattern at any one demonstration. These demonstrations are usually more valuable to the pupil when carried on in slow motion. The beneficial effects of verbal directions decrease rapidly as the amount of such direction, per unit of practice, increases. Mechanical guidance is the least valuable of these three types and should be given only after some preliminary orientation, and then in small amounts. Thus, if the teacher uses the method of taking hold of the hand or arm of the student and thereby guiding him exactly through the desired movement, he should use this mechanical guidance only after the student has a definite (though perhaps somewhat general) idea of what movement he is trying to learn. More than two or three repetitions of this exact manual guidance is probably an unwise expenditure of practice time.

For a few individuals, meaning in motor learning seems to depend almost entirely on kinesthetic sense experience. Meaning to them is expressed in vague feelings and results of activity. They must learn motor skill games by playing them. The final level of attainment of the slow-learning individual who relies to a great extent on trial and error and kinesthetic feel, may be very high. Some learners object to trying new ways of performing skills because the feel is not right. The old—and perhaps incorrect—way, of course, has the right (or familiar) feel. Physique, speed vitality, motor aptness, and great interest may make a professional star out of a boy whose verbal guide and visual image accompaniment to motor learning are practically nil.

Early correction of major error. The teacher should be alert to prevent repetition of major performance errors. Failure to correct major errors early retards learning; replacement by correct forms is much more difficult after longer erroneous performance. This statement does not apply to minor errors—only to errors in gross framework.

Specific directions or none. The teacher should be cautioned against trying to correct unsuccessful performance before he, himself, has determined correctly by careful analysis the specific error in the total pattern. Directions for correction of error must be exact. Exhorting the pupil to try to improve and abusing him for inefficient performance, without specific and constructive criticism, does not foster learning. The learner may even proceed to carry out the incorrect method with greater effort.

Plateaus. The teacher should recognize and adjust teaching methods to learning plateaus when they occur. Periods of no apparent progress will appear in learning. Loss of interest, discouragement, fatigue, and unconscious adoption of error may be contributing factors. Overconfidence and satisfaction with present level of accomplishment impede progress and result in plateaus.

Freedom for individuality. A reasonable amount of freedom for individuality of development is more effective in the heights attained and more economical in terms of progress per unit of time. The individual learner may have approached the physiological limit of improvement by the methods he is using. Further improvement may be possible by the adoption of new methods. He may hit upon these better methods by trial and continual revision with an accompaniment of intense zeal and by experiment with methods that have proved efficient for other individuals. The experienced teacher can make suggestions for such experimenting. As a general rule, the teacher should try to avoid arbitrarily requiring long experiment with a method if the student prefers some other method at which he is reasonably successful. The teacher cannot be certain that a specific method fits exactly the needs of the individual; nor can he be sure that further experiment will prove the method superior. Experts in most of the fields of sports have their eccentricities of performance, eccentricities which seem to be particularly effective for those individuals. Unfortunate but typically true, beginners often imitate the eccentricities of champions. Mannerisms and stylized aspects of the movements seem more important to the immature learner than the actual results of his efforts.

Helping pupils understand motor learning. Since many of the action skills needed for daily living and for recreational pursuits must be partially or totally self-taught, pupils should learn how to acquire these skills in an efficient manner. Young people should be helped to understand that an important factor in enjoying participation in physical skills is to perform well. Performing well is, to a large degree, a problem of *learning* to perform well. Young people should learn that successfully acquiring motor skills depends on a large number of specific abilities unrelated to skills in any other area. One may or may not have these abilities. But despite possession of great or small potentiality in motor skills, some approaches can help most everyone learn motor skills more effectively. An understanding and application of the following principles may help pupils acquire movement skills more readily. High school pupils could easily grasp the following concepts:

1. To save time, have the skill to be learned clearly in mind when you begin to learn. *Get some instruction in some way.* Use a teacher, a friend, a book, or observe others, and instruct yourself. This reduces the development of bad habits.

2. *Pay close attention to what you are attempting to accomplish.* Practice with a purpose. Try to make the performance of the skill a matter of habit. As you learned to drive a car, or ride a bicycle, you noticed that you had to pay little attention to the details of performing the skill after a while. The same thing occurs as you attempt to develop any motor skill. With practice you form habits, and as these habits are formed perception of what you are doing is no longer important and so perception diminishes. The sooner you can form good habits, the better your performance will be for your attention can be freed from the details of the skill and you can begin to concentrate on perfecting the fine points.

3. *Relax and be free of tensions.* Just as important as contracting the correct muscles, is the skill of relaxing the proper muscles so that the movement can take place smoothly. If muscles do not relax and lengthen when they should, the movement cannot be effective, the performer tightens up. Relaxation is one key to effective movement. Relaxation is a neuro-muscular skill and can be learned.

4. *Try to get the feel of the movement.* You should take advantage of all of your senses when learning a motor skill, but especially be aware of the feel of the movement as you perform effectively. If you can become aware of the feeling of the movement when it is done effectively, subsequent efforts can be judged not only by the results but by how nearly the desired movement was repeated as judged by the sensation of feel.

5. *Don't become impatient or annoyed.* When any one begins to master a new physical skill, it is usually unpleasant and disagreeable.

Often beginners, especially those who have a great deal of natural ability, become discouraged, explain their mistakes, alibi for their assumed shortcomings, complain about the equipment, and denounce the activity during the first few practice sessions. First efforts are sometimes exhausting, but with practice energy is expended more economically and with less emotion.

6. *Practice in the way the skill will be used.* Unless you are just trying to think about and rehearse a skill, don't do it in slow motion. If speed is most important, practice speed. If both speed and accuracy are important, emphasize speed from the beginning. Attempt to have practice and learning conditions as much like the situation in which you will perform as possible.

7. *If possible, practice the whole skill from the beginning.* The successive parts of a skill are learned more efficiently if they are practiced in the same relationship with other parts as they will be used when the skill is mastered. In many activities the performance of the first phases of the movement prepares the body to function more efficiently in subsequent movements.

8. *If the whole skill is too complex, get the idea of the whole skill, and then break the skill down into smaller parts,* but keep the parts as large as possible. Try to form habits of performing these parts well; then progressively put the parts together to form larger habit patterns; then put them all together to perform the whole skill.

9. *Rather short periods of intense practice yield the greatest gains.* Practice most skills at least three times weekly during rather short practice periods. Practice once a week is not often enough for the efficient development of most skills. Long practice periods are usually not beneficial.

10. *Rehearse the skill mentally.* Performance in many physical skills can be improved without practicing at all. Many men play better golf after a period of several months without practice. Experiments have shown that this is true in other skills as well. Some experiments have shown that people who do regular mental practice perform better than others who actually practice the skill irregularly.

11. *Practice under pleasant conditions.* Learn with agreeable people in pleasant surroundings. You will be much more apt to enjoy participation and as a result perfect your skill if the total learning situation is agreeable and pleasant.

SAMPLE TEST ITEMS

Yes-No

1. Is motor learning the learning of specific and exact responses to specific and exact stimuli?

2. Do variety and diversity of response characterize the early stages of motor skill learning?

3. Should a general orientation toward the skill patterns to be acquired precede specific drills?

4. Do most of our improvements in motor performance follow insights, i.e., result from insight learning?

5. Can one learn and adopt improved techniques in motor skill performance without being aware of exactly what change in behavior took place?

6. Is self-analysis always a help in motor learning?

7. In motor skill practice, should the individual practicing focus on the results of his movements?

8. Have teachers perhaps placed too great emphasis on verbal and visual cues in motor learning?

9. Is the chief emphasis of the advocates of whole learning techniques on functional meaningfulness?

10. Should mechanical guidance be given major emphasis as a technique of teaching motor skills?

11. Must the individual possess a high I.Q. in order to become a great performer in motor skills?

12. Are general directions to try harder, to fight harder, to expend all one's energy, and the like, of great value in teaching specific motor patterns?

13. Can one improve in an activity during the intervals between practices of that activity?

14. Is specific attention to improvement of *parts* of motor pattern activities more productive of improvement while the *whole* activity is being practiced?

15. May certain transfers of training from one activity to another result in greater learning difficulties?

16. Is it psychologically sound to give more praise to the inferior students than to the superior?

17. Other things being equal, is the teacher justified in planning activity so that the pupil may acquire the desired learning in the shortest time, and in the easiest way possible?

True-False

1. Learning is both a process and a result.
2. Motor learning as a process seems to be greatly facilitated by repetition.
3. Motor habits tend to remain exact and specific.
4. Motor pattern formation consists of establishing specific chain responses to exact stimulus patterns.
5. In motor skills, one practices wrong responses in order to learn correct responses.
6. Timing is inborn and cannot be learned.
7. The experienced baseball coach can tell the novice pitcher exactly what form he should use to throw a baseball.
8. Variety and diversity of response characterize the beginner.
9. Emotional intensity and muscular tension are likely to accompany the early stages of motor pattern learning.
10. Emotional intensity may facilitate learning of motor skills.
11. Emotional intensity may be deleterious to learning.
12. Getting oriented toward the goal is the proper initial step of the motor skill learning process.
13. Insight learning in motor skills refers to a sudden shift in method.
14. Awareness of exact change is an essential part of motor learning.
15. Superior performance of motor skills is usually characterized by accurate self-analytical knowledge.
16. It may be advisable to have the student repeat, in slow motion, erroneous movements that he has been making.
17. Moving pictures have little value as a means of motor skill analysis.
18. The visual sense is the only important sense in motor pattern learning.
19. Individuals assume different relative ranks in performance.
20. Timing is an automatic part of habit patterns of movements, and, when the situation requires a different timing, the habit performance is upset.
21. Determination to learn has no effect on permanence of learning.
22. The student's immediate objective should be set considerably higher than he can achieve.
23. Not more than one incentive should be brought to bear on any one learning problem.
24. In general, the easier the task the greater the interest.
25. At the present stage of experiment, the whole-part method appears superior to either the whole or the part method.
26. In general, whole learning achieves an integration which part learning can achieve only by extra effort in connecting the parts together.

27. In general, part learning seems to offer easier units to adjust to the capacity of the learner.

28. Is present learning indepent of what preceded it?

29. Does environment affect the rate and amount of learning?

30. Is manual guidance (taking hold of and guiding the student's hand and arm, for example) superior to verbal guidance?

31. Is the motor skill learner who depends chiefly on the kinesthetic sense experience greatly limited as to the final level he may attain?

32. In general, are special drills on weaknesses uneconomical of learning time?

33. Is the onset of fatigue characterized by a slower rate of muscular contraction?

34. Is it advantageous in learning to exert oneself occasionally with an intensity that approaches one's maximum?

35. Does adaptable performance, successively reapplied in continuous practice, gain greater permanence than the same adaptable performance recalled and reapplied after an interval of no practice (same total number of applications in each case)?

36. Does best form in motor skills vary with the individual?

37. Is the transfer negative if the stimulus remains the same but the response changes?

38. Does Thorndike's transfer theory of identical elements explain negative transfer?

The following test items are added to stimulate the thinking of those students primarily interested in the coaching of athletic sports.

True-False

1. The first lessons for beginners in a sport should be lessons in detailed analysis of part movements.

2. The skilled sports performer when performing at his best focuses his attention on how he, himself, is performing.

3. Attention should be called to minor errors in the early stages of motor learning.

4. Sports skills should be learned from the beginning under conditions of exacting competitive pressure.

5. In the early practices of a sport, the beginner should practice meaningful units of the sport, not isolated movements.

6. Coordination is a general trait and is acquired.

7. One can learn to relax adequately the muscles in use in the sports skill even though intensely concerned about the outcome of the performance.

8. Sports skills are best performed with chief focus of attention on cues for action, and on results, with only a diffused amount of attention on the major features of the movement patterns.

9. The learner may need to be rehearsed in his own error in order to become aware of just what error he is making.

10. *Parts* of a skill seem to take on polish more rapidly when the learner sees them in the light of the total game background.

11. In no sport is the external appearance of the form used as its measure of efficiency in performing the skilled art.

12. Grace and beauty of appearance of a form are excellent criteria to use in judging the case, efficiency, and success of form.

13. The needs of the next appropriate act should partially determine the advisability of a smooth follow through.

14. The player has neither time nor opportunity, while the game is going on, for genuine thought (in the sense of reasoning).

15. Fatigue comes more quickly in nonhabituated work than in habituated work.

16. Correcting every error the beginner makes in trying to play a game is unwise.

17. A team should be uniform in technique of motor skill behavior, i.e., same batting stance, shooting form, and so forth, for each team member.

BIBLIOGRAPHY

American Association for Health, Physical Education, and Recreation, *Motor Learning and Motor Performance*. The Association, 1960.

Bunn, John William, *Scientific Principles of Coaching*. Englewood Cliffs, N. J.: Prentice-Hall Inc., 1955.

Deese, James, *The Psychology of Learning*. The McGraw-Hill Book Company, Inc., 1952.

Duncan, Carl P., "Effect of Unequal Amounts of Practice on Motor Learning Before and After Rest," *Journal of Experimental Psychology*, 42:257–64 (1951).

Fulton, Ruth E., "Speed and Accuracy in Learning a Ballistic Movement," *Research Quarterly*, 13:30 (1942).

Harmon, John M., and Arthur G. Miller, "Time Patterns in Motor Learning," *Research Quarterly*, 21:182 (1950).

Hellebrandt, F. A. "The Physiology of Motor Learning," *Cerebral Palsy Review*, July–August, 1958, 8–14.

Hilgard, Ernest R., *Theories of Learning*. New York: Appleton-Century-Crofts Inc., 1956.

Kahn, Joel S., "A Comparison of Various Patterns of Practice in Bowling Achievement" (Unpublished Master's Thesis, University of California, Los Angeles, June 1959).

Kingsley, H. L., *The Nature and Conditions of Learning*, 1946, rev. by Ralph Garry. Englewood Cliffs, N. J.: Prentice-Hall, Inc., 1957.

Knapp, Clyde G., and W. Robert Dixon, "Learning to Juggle: I. A Study to Determine the Effects of Two Different Distributions of Practice," *Research Quarterly*, 21:331–336 (1950).

Kretchmar, Robert T., Hoyt L. Sherman, and Ross Mooney, "*A Survey of Research in the Teaching of Sports*," *Research Quarterly*, October, 1949, 244.

Lawther, John Dobson, *Psychology of Coaching*. Englewood Cliffs, N. J.: Prentice-Hall Inc., 1951.

Leavitt, J. J., and H. Schlossberg, "The Retention of Motor Skills," *Journal of Experimental Psychology*, October, 1944, 404.

McCraw, L. W., "A Factor Analysis of Motor Learning," *Research Quarterly*, 20:316 (1949).

Mursell, James, *Psychology for Modern Education*. New York: W. W. Norton, 1952.

Oberteuffer, Delbert, *Physical Education, A Textbook of Principles for Professional Students*. New York: Harper & Brothers, 1956.

Ragsdale, Clarence E., "How Children Learn the Motor Types of Activities." *The Forty-Ninth Yearbook of the National Society for the Study of Education, Part I.*, N. Henry, ed. Chicago: University of Chicago Press, 1950, p. 89.

Seashore, Harold G., "Some Relationships of Fine and Gross Motor Abilities," *Research Quarterly*, 13:259 (1942).

Seashore, R. H., "Individual Differences in Motor Skills," *Journal of General Psychology*, 3:38 (1930).

Skinner, Charles E., ed., *Essentials of Educational Psychology*. Englewood Cliffs, N. J.: Prentice-Hall, Inc., 1958.

Solley, William H., "Effects of Verbal Instruction of Speed and Accuracy Upon the Learning of a Motor Skill," *Research Quarterly*, 23:231–40 (May, 1952).

Walters, C. Etta, "The Application of the Overload Principle to the Learning of Motor Skill," *American Journal of Occupational Therapy*. January–February, 1956, 1.

Welford, Alan Traviss, *Aging and Human Skill*. London: Oxford University Press, 1958.

6

Understanding individuals:
an essential

One must teach not only some thing, but he must teach someone.

PREVIOUS CHAPTERS HAVE DISCUSSED HOW INDIVIDUAL ADO-
lescents vary in capacity to learn the motor types of skills
and how individuals of the same age may differ in maturity and in
trait characteristics. Not only do individuals learn differently but
individual pupils also have varying needs. The effective teacher
recognizes that individual pupils must often be motivated differently, taught differently, and evaluated differently; and yet, he must
usually deal with these differing individuals in the same class. The
differing needs of individual pupils imply individualized instruction. Lack of such individualizing is a common professional weakness of physical educators and of physical education programs.

Growth is the essence of life, and the child is in the most rapid
period of growth. He represents, therefore, the organism at its live-
liest, most vivid, most active period. The extremely rapid growth
of childhood, the diversity of this growth, and the dependency of
this growth on specific environment for stimulus, all have implications in physical education.

How should the organism develop? Educators cannot specify
exactly the future needs of the child; hence education has stressed

versatility.   If the child is versatile, he is more likely to adjust to changing conditions.   The present generation has had to develop types of body control and skill not needed by preceding generations. With thousands of people per year being killed by automobiles, the need for exact movement control, emotional stability under duress, developed peripheral vision, health habits, and knowledge of first aid, not to mention pedestrian agility, becomes apparent.

Space flying has necessitated the development of new coordinations between hand and eye, new discriminations in body balance. Mechanized industry presents forces dangerous to the awkward employee.   Recreational sports as a leisure pursuit are on the increase. The complexities of modern civilization make precision of movement essential for efficiency, safety and recreation.

How can physical education develop versatility?   The skills of adult life are patterns woven from the part movements learned in childhood.   In the child, diffusion of energy from stimuli causes a tremendous variety of responses.   In the early developmental stages, almost any movement may be attached to a stimulus.   During this period the child learns the individual movements which are basic to skill acquirement.   Observation of the activity of infants and children would lead one to think that they make almost all possible movements.   But movements *as responses to the environment* are made more frequently and, therefore, become more subject to control.   The average person does not bring all possible movements under control.   By practice, comedians learn to make ear, face, and scalp movements which are not included in the learned movement repertoire of the average person.   Dancers, athletes, and highly skilled workers demonstrate movements not available in the learned responses of the average person.

The greater the variety of specific movements the child goes through in this early maturing and developing period, the more likely he is to possess the fundamental motor movement equipment to fit well the numerous demands of adult life.

The above statement implies a program of activities in the preschool, primary, and intermediate grades, characterized by an extensive variety of bodily movements.   Normal children might well have several hours of vigorous physical activity daily.

Variety problems at the high school level.   Motor abilities are, to a large degree, specific to the activity.   When physical education programs at the high school level are made up chiefly from a few of the traditional athletic games, they favor certain children over others.   Not only are the favored children more successful in the physical education program; their successes give them a social status denied those children less apt at the particular activities.

Perhaps physical education teachers should supplement the program with a greater variety of activities.   Then the majority could find activities at which they might excell.   Often teachers are reluctant to provide a broader and more varied program because pupils seem to prefer to engage in activities in which they are already familiar—involving those skills in which they have already enjoyed some success.   Many pupils lack the confidence to venture into new areas of experience.   They feel insecure in attempting the new. An example of such typical lack of assurance may be seen in the fearfulness with which many junior high school boys approach dance experiences.   Such difficulties are best overcome by effective leadership that instills confidence and helps the pupil to accept and adopt as his own the goal of becoming accomplished in those activities in which he is inexperienced.   (Program building is discussed in greater detail in Part Three.)

The three traditional major objectives of physical education— body-control skills, organic vigor, and social attitudes and conduct —imply vigorous participation in activity involving a great variety of bodily movements.   Group cooperative enterprise is implied also, but not the requirement of *a specific* game proficiency such as involved in football, basketball, or baseball.   None of these three games is a common recreational game of the majority of American adults; hence, the carry-over value is slight except for some spectator interest.

The three games mentioned are so much a part of the American culture that they are easy to make interesting.   Many children can learn them by imitation of better athletes.   All three games demand a vigorous type of activity, they are dependent for success upon group cooperation, and they seem to develop a great variety of body-control skills.   Yet, complete domination of the physical education program by a few major sports defeats the purpose of *greatest developmental value to the greatest number.*

Physical educators have difficulty finding the happy medium between activities at which the individual may experience success because of above-average achievement, and activities which are popular in the pupil's social environment and therefore possess social prestige. The pupils of high school age want to conform to the group. They are unwilling to strike out for themselves. They tend to be afraid of uniqueness and individuality lest such non-conformity adversely affect their social status.

Variety is essential. Teacher emphases are too often based on personal prejudice, college indoctrinated beliefs, or selfish personal desires, rather than on pupil needs. Emphasis only on certain specific types of activities may cause developmental malnutrition. The stereotyped patterns of child development such as prevailed in the seventeenth and eighteenth centuries did not fit the child for life. We know that such experiences did not foster a fullness of growth. A survival of the fittest sports program also is not adjusted to the individual pupil. Teaching sports fundamentals for pre-liminary varsity sport experience ignores the fact that most of the individuals will not participate in varsity sports and that other activities might be more valuable. To insist on either a "major" sports curriculum or the "natural activities" program, good as they both are, as the whole of physical education is educational myopia.

Extensive activity develops generalized habits. The preponderance of sense experience and the wide variety of interests of the entire pre-adolescent development make extensive rather than intensive motor training most adaptable to the pupil. He is not yet specialized in his interests. He will hang by his toes, juggle balls, walk rails, or perform balancing acts with equal fervor and intensity. Rhythms have appeal. So do hammer and nails, bicycles, hoops and kites, boats and rafts, swimming pools, bows and arrows. He should experience all these and much more. Muscles not used during the childhood stage appear in awkward and incompetent skill performance later.

Implications of variability. Variability pictured graphically by the normal curve has certain implications. It reveals that the 60 per cent of the adolescents in the vicinity of average can take on the basic movement skill, health habits, and social conduct patterns which are fundamental to successful later development. The 20 per cent above this group surpass them in learning. The 20 per cent below need more time, different methods, and perhaps corrective or adapted work.

The great middle group are not star athletes in high school. They need extensive intramurals. They need class guidance in skill acquisition for later expression on the playground. A regimen of health habits, social conformity in conduct codes, and emotional control should characterize their program. The basic body controls and balances make up their movement fundamentals. Similar recreations, similar social patterns, and similar vigorous activities produce group stability, solidarity, cohesion, and cooperation.

Ability levels. Techniques of instruction must be adapted to the ability of pupils. In physical education this ability depends on a great many factors. Previous training, health and vigor, habits of work, and level of maturity are all factors.

Those of greater ability seem to be better able to transfer skill or knowledge from one situation to another. They need less demonstration and detail drill. More avenues are open to them. Many people are willing to help a promising youngster. In the secondary school, the more mature, stronger, and more skilled individuals find varsity squads, trips, and games available to them, a field of experience denied those of lesser ability.

Those of lesser ability need more exact instructions, must be shown, and must be walked through new movement patterns. They have greater difficulty in identifying the movements needed in a skill. They need more repetitions and greater guidance when confronted with new situations. More care must be taken to provide effective motivation, to prevent discouragement and dislike for the activity. They cannot be left to their own resources with any certainty of further progress. Greater patience, more encouragement, greater kindliness must characterize the teacher's manner with the lower developmental levels.

Age and maturity. Age differences imply different maturity levels. An individual may have a mental age of 15 and a physiological age of 10. Actually, age in years (chronological) is a very crude measure of the physiological maturity of childhood and adolescence. The chronological age of attaining puberty varies about three years in the central 60 per cent. If we mean by age, the *level of maturity*, we should have a *physical education age* for classification purposes. Unfortunately we have no means of measuring or classifying pupils according to their average developmental level such as is found in mental measurements. Even if some type of data from height, weight, and anatomical age measures are combined with the rating of a group of experts on skill and bodily coordination level, only reasonably accurate developmental grouping may be made. The average teacher has not the time, equipment, or sufficient number of pupils to make such a classification.

Maturity classifications are advisable. Large junior high schools in which rugged and strenuous sports are included in the program are obligated to make some such classifications. The practice of actually eliminating the weaker ones by competition is too costly in overtaxed bodies, injured joints, and seriously retarded development. Crude classifications can be made by combining such factors as height, weight, strength, chronological age, and measures of physiological maturing. Physiological maturing is indicated in the boy by increased growth of hair on the face, lower voice pitch, and thinner, more rugged facial contour; developed breasts, increased width of hip, and menstrual periods are similar indices in the girl.

Degree of intensity, the problem of adolescent sport participation. The period of puberty and adolescence in the girl is not considered as trying and as dangerous as was once supposed. Girls, like boys, should have normal healthful exercise, be outdoors as much as possible, and have a balanced activity program that takes into account both the need of energy for growth and the inequality of the sexes in strength. High standards of strenuous physical skill acquisition should not be stressed for either boy or girl during puberty and during the *earlier* stages of adolescence. Herein lies the danger of interscholastic sports with the accompanying social pressure toward ever higher achievement.

Age of greater variability. The junior and senior high school years are periods of most common error in activity selection and method. During this period, greater variability appears in growth patterns and motor incoordinations. Greater attention to the individual is needed. Group generalizations are of little value to the teacher when the variability of this group is very great. Neither the boy who is growing six inches in a year nor the girl who is growing less than an inch in the same time conforms to group characteristics. The average height increment in the faster growing years is between two and two and one-half inches. The boy who is growing six inches may be atypical in his awkwardness and skill maladjustment. The girl who is growing less than an inch per year may be atypical in her lack of awkwardness, in her coordinated control.

Stages of development.   The continuity of the development pattern makes artificial any attempt to classify it into stages.   For the purposes of instructional emphases, however, certain divisions have been made.   These are based partly on developmental need and partly on interest.   The pre-school and primary grades have been characterized as the docile age.   In the nursery school and on into kindergarten, the child tends to respond to the strongest stimuli. Novelty, noise, movement, material for construction, for simple patterns, for locomotion have their appeal.   He is responsive to adult suggestions.   Variety of movement without complexity of requisite skill should characterize activity at this stage.

As he grows older, the child finds that suggestions of adults do not always conform to his chief interests.   The ninth to twelfth years have been characterized as the individualistic years.   He wants to decide for himself.   He is not as suggestible as to type of activity, nor is he inclined toward the cooperation of team activity.   He quits the side that is losing and allies himself with the winner.   He participates vigorously in natural activities but is not yet ready in strength or interest for complex team games.   If encouraged, he may develop considerable initiative and originality in activity invention at this stage.   He enjoys making up his own activities, making his own rules, and creating much of the meaningfulness of the activity out of his own imagination.   Under sufficient motivation he may, however, develop very high levels of movement skills.   This is evidenced in the accomplishment of some Little League baseball players and the expertness of some children who have experienced extensive training in dance.   Whether such early specialization is beneficial is still unclear.   It may be damaging to some youngsters and valuable for others.

Much has already been said about the social nature of the junior high and high school age.   Team games, social dancing, coeducational activity, and recreation belong here.   The team games should be adjusted to fit the child's strength and endurance.   Without sufficient conditioning, long distance running, football, and highly competitive basketball may overtax his strength, impede his organic development, or rob his system of energy needed for growth.   Careful health examination, individual clinical records for observation, avoidance of social pressure on competition, and homogeneous height, weight, and physiological maturity classification (for the purposes of competition) are some of the essential features of the sports program at this age level.   Because of individual variability, false generalizations may be drawn.   Some post-pubescents can be found in most large junior high schools and some physiologically immature individuals in most large senior high schools.   To judge the strength and endurance of the average by any atypical group and to set up an activity program based on the stage of development of the upper 10 to 20 per cent is extremely hazardous to the future health and development of students.

Some people conclude that the junior and senior high school age is an age of less vitality, energy, and endurance than the preceding years.   The contrary is true.   But because the student now appears to be more mature, and because he participates in many adult activities, we are startled when he shows evidence of being immature, weak, easily tired.   He is stronger than the pre-pubescent and may participate safely in a more vigorous program.   But he is large physically, has many of the social mannerisms of the adult, and we begin to expect much greater accomplishments from him.   We would never have expected as much from the childish appearing individual only two years younger chronologically.

The differences in rate of development of different body parts add to the confusion.   The difference in relative rank of various trait developments increases the difficulty of approximating his developmental level.   For example, the large boy (height and weight) may be completely mature physiologically, or may be a pre-pubescent. Yet because he is 5'10" and weighs 160 pounds, we expect him to be mature socially and emotionally.   Physical appearance furnishes insufficient data for classification as to maturity level or fitness for an activity.

Ability grouping.   The teacher may make adjustment within his classes by requiring a different quality of work from those of different abilities.   The more vigorous may participate longer or more intensively.   If the squad organization is used, the teacher may select squad leaders who excell; and he may have squads of any particular level of ability participate with others of similar ability.   Participation with those of better ability has certain advantages for those of a lower ability.   They can see more nearly correct performance and learn somewhat by imitation.   They have goals set for them which they can see and aspire to reach.   Sometimes they can get points of instruction from associates that they cannot get from their teachers. Requiring better performance of those of better ability is a common instructional device.

Homogeneous grouping is a much advocated method of adjusting to individual differences.   Let us remember the different relative ranks of individuals in different traits, their different rates of learning in each trait, and the difference in one individual's rate from that of other individuals.   Then let us ask ourselves whether we intend to group our students homogeneously for:

1. Height, weight, and age.
2. Organic vigor.
3. Strength.
4. Particular skills.
5. Health.
6. Anatomical age.
7. Motor educability.
8. Endurance.
9. Social conduct and attitude.
10. Interests.
11. Needs.
12. Improvement.

These are only a few of the possible classifications.   If we classify them homogeneously for one, they are very likely to be heterogeneous for most of the others.   A good procedure for regular classwork seems to be to classify according to the normal social group; then subdivide for various activities or various bases.   (Classification is discussed in further detail in Chapter 15.)

Individual instruction.   The good teacher will supplement his classwork with as much individual instruction, conference, guidance, tutoring, and demonstration as his limited time allows.   In the dressing room, on the playgrounds, after school, in club activities, he can give specific suggestions to individuals.   Rating sheets and tests offer opportunities for individual diagnosis and suggestion. The instructor may intersperse suggestions to individuals during the course of, and without interruption of, the activity.   Rest periods may also be utilized for suggestions.   By taking advantage of such opportunities for individual instruction, the teacher may partially adjust the activities to the individual—and thereby solve many of the problems underlying group instruction of what are of necessity heterogeneous groups.

SAMPLE TEST ITEMS

Yes-No

1. Does education stress specific training for specific future needs?

2. Has the need for precision of movement decreased as the world has become more highly mechanized?

3. Should the activity of the youngster in primary grades be limited to a practice of such skills as adults are now using?

4. Should coeducational activities replace present physical education activities in junior high school classes where the sexes are separated?

5. Should courses of study be essential in physical education?

6. Should class activity in physical education be of such a nature that the children will tend to continue similar activities after school hours?

7. Does the child need *vigorous* play?

8. Has the teaching of safety a place in the physical education curriculum of primary grade children?

9. Is there justification for devoting a large part of the physical education budget to the development of boys who show promise of unusual ability in motor skills?

10. Is physical education activity a contributor to mental health?

11. Does physical education offer great opportunity for teaching personality adjustments?

12. Should the same teaching techniques be used on the various ability levels in any one physical education class?

13. Can one learn all he needs to know in physical education by participation in sports?

14. Are height, weight, and chronological age adequate as measures of physiological maturity when classifying for participation in contact sports?

15. Is it advisable to set up high standards of strenuous physical skill acquisition for adolescents, with accompanying social pressure toward the attainment of these skills?

16. Are generalizations as to group needs of great value to the high school physical education teacher?

17. Does the intermediate grade youngster, on the average, take on more of the characteristics of the individualist than the primary school child?

18. Is an increase of the required time for the awkward youngster in physical education activities justified?

19. Can physical education students be grouped homogeneously as to their present level of attainment of the major objectives?

BIBLIOGRAPHY

Biddulph, Lowell G., "Athletic Achievement and Personal and Social Adjustment of High School Boys," Vol. 25, No. 1, *Research Quarterly*, pp. 1–7, March, 1954.

Brownell, Clifford Lee, and E. Patricia Hagman, *Physical Education— Foundations and Principles*. New York: The McGraw-Hill Book Company, Inc., 1951.

Jones, Harold E., *Motor Performance and Growth*. Berkeley: University of California Press, 1949.

Krogman, Wilton Marion, "Factors of Physical Growth of Children as They May Apply to Physical Education." *American Academy of Physical Education, Professional Contributions No. 3,* pp. 114–134, 1954.

Williams, Jesse Fering, *The Principles of Physical Education*. Philadelphia: W. B. Saunders Co., 1958.

Part Three

YOUR PURPOSES AND VALUES:
why teach physical education?

7

What are the purposes
of teaching?

"There is no road to success but through a clear strong purpose."
                                                            Munger.

SOME CRITICISMS OF THE PRESENT USE OF OBJECTIVES. ONE
of the keen criticisms leveled against lists of major teaching objectives, specific objectives, and more specific objectives is
that they are conceived, initiated, and followed up by adults.

Pupils' values important. The *first* criticism is that teachers do
not pay enough attention to their pupils' understanding of these
adult purposes of physical education; not enough consideration is
given to pupils' own purposes of physical education or their ideas of
what is valuable in physical education, in this lesson, in this activity.
Children learn more slowly (if at all) and forget more quickly those
activities in which they see little or no value. The point is not that
the activities and the objectives selected by the teacher are not
worthwhile. Rather, the point is that we have assumed that if
pupils do what we tell them to do they will attain the objectives we
have set up. Sometimes they do. However, too often learning is
greatly retarded by the teacher's failure to help the pupils understand the purposes and values of the activities.

The proposal that the teacher and pupils work cooperatively in selecting activities and deciding upon objectives does not imply that pupils are well prepared for these tasks. The cooperative plan provides excellent opportunities for the teacher to *guide* the children in understanding, in setting up new values, in broadening their judgments.

Progression not automatic. A *second* criticism of the usual concept of minor and major objectives is that if the smaller ones are attained the learner will have attained a larger objective. This "stair step" idea may happen to work, but almost without exception the major objective must be worked for as an entity—not as a culmination of many small objectives. Further, the stair step idea tends to provide no place for the new. The steps are set. Some new idea of what might be attained as a small objective spoils the neatly arranged sequence of steps.

Detailed specifics may obscure major objective. A *third* criticism of breaking down objectives into more detailed objectives has been recognized by teachers for years. Objectives can be analyzed in such detail that literally hundreds of small objectives result. The multiplicity of such a mass of details staggers the beginning teacher and confuses or discourages the more experienced teacher.

The beginning teacher is not to conclude from these three criticisms that analyzing or breaking down major objectives is useless. The moment we attempt to teach so that these more general purposes are accomplished, we are forced to analyze them in order to arrive at more concrete concepts of what the accomplishments are to be. However, these criticisms point out weaknesses and mistakes to avoid.

Newer purposes of education. Since 1918 the "seven cardinal principles of education"[1] have profoundly influenced and guided educational thought. They are:

1. Health.
2. Fundamental Processes.
3. Vocation.
4. Citizenship.
5. Worthy Home Membership.
6. Worthy Use of Leisure.
7. Ethical Character.

[1] U. S. Department of the Interior, Bureau of Education, *Cardinal Principles of Secondary Education,* Bulletin No. 35 (Washington, D. C.: Government Printing Office, 1918).

Leaders and teachers in physical education have made physical education contribute to these major objectives.

A newer list of purposes presented by the Educational Policies Commission represents a reinterpretation of the purposes of education in American democracy. These purposes with their analyses are presented here for two reasons. *First,* this presentation is a newer thought on how objectives might be constructed. For example, the four major objectives are broken down into descriptive statements. *Second,* this plan provides and encourages freedom, initiative, imagination, and ingenuity on the part of the teacher.

The four major objectives with their analyses follow.[2]

I. THE OBJECTIVES OF SELF-REALIZATION

The Inquiring Mind. The educated person has an appetite for learning.

Speech. The educated person can speak the mother tongue clearly.

Reading. The educated person reads the mother tongue efficiently.

Writing. The educated person writes the mother tongue effectively.

Number. The educated person solves his problems of counting and calculating.

Sight and Hearing. The educated person is skilled in listening and observing.

Health Knowledge. The educated person understands the basic facts concerning health and disease.

Health Habits. The educated person protects his own health and that of his dependents.

Public Health. The educated person works to improve the health of the community.

Recreation. The educated person is participant and spectator in many sports and other pastimes.

Intellectual Interests. The educated person has mental resources for the use of leisure.

Esthetic Interests. The educated person appreciates beauty.

Character. The educated person gives responsible direction to his own life.

II. THE OBJECTIVES OF HUMAN RELATIONSHIP

Respect for Humanity. The educated person puts human relationships first.

Friendships. The educated person enjoys a rich, sincere, and varied social life.

Cooperation. The educated person can work and play with others.

2 Educational Policies Commission, *The Purposes of Education in American Democracy* (Washington, D. C.: National Education Association, 1938).

Courtesy. The educated person observes the amenities of social behavior.

Appreciation of the Home. The educated person appreciates the family as a social institution.

Conservation of the Home. The educated person conserves family ideals.

Homemaking. The educated person is skilled in homemaking.

Democracy in the Home. The educated person maintains democratic family relationships.

III. THE OBJECTIVES OF ECONOMIC EFFICIENCY

Work. The educated producer knows the satisfaction of good workmanship.

Occupational Information. The educated producer understands the requirements and opportunities for various jobs.

Occupational Choice. The educated producer has selected his occupation.

Occupational Efficiency. The educated producer succeeds in his chosen vocation.

Occupational Adjustment. The educated producer maintains and improves his efficiency.

Occupational Appreciation. The educated producer appreciates the social value of his work.

Personal Economics. The educated consumer plans the economics of his own life.

Consumer Judgment. The educated consumer develops standards for guiding his expenditures.

Efficiency in Buying. The educated consumer is an informed and skillful buyer.

Consumer Protection. The educated consumer takes appropriate measures to safeguard his interests.

IV. THE OBJECTIVES OF CIVIC RESPONSIBILITY

Social Justice. The educated citizen is sensitive to the disparities of human circumstance.

Social Activity. The educated citizen acts to correct unsatisfactory conditions.

Social Understanding. The educated citizen seeks to understand social structures and social processes.

Critical Judgment. The educated citizen has defenses against propaganda.

Tolerance. The educated citizen respects honest differences of opinion.

Conservation. The educated citizen has a regard for the nation's resources.

Social Applications of Science. The educated citizen measures scientific advance by its contribution to the general welfare.

World Citizenship. The educated citizen is a cooperating member of the world community.

Law Observance. The educated citizen respects the law.

Economic Literacy. The educated citizen is economically literate.

Political Citizenship. The educated citizen accepts his civic duties.

Devotion to Democracy. The educated citizen acts upon an unswerving loyalty to democratic ideals.

Obviously physical education does not contribute to all of these major and minor objectives. The teacher will desire to teach so that physical education makes its rightful contribution to these educational purposes. The changing purposes of education suggest the necessity for a reinterpretation of the major objectives of physical education in terms of the ever-deepening and ever-widening of our understanding of American democracy.

"Ten Basic Needs of Youth." A still more recent set of guides, most of which have great meaning for teachers of physical education, are the Ten Basic Needs of Youth." [3] No phase of education can shrug off the responsibility of sincerely attempting to satisfy these needs:

1. All youth need to develop salable skills and those understandings and attitudes that make the worker an intelligent and productive participant in economic life. To this end, most youth need supervised work experiences as well as education in the skills and knowledge of their occupation.

2. All youth need to develop and maintain good health and physical fitness.

3. All youth need to understand the rights and duties of the citizen of a democratic society, and to be diligent and competent in the performance of their obligations as members of the community and citizens of the state and nation.

4. All youth need to understand the significance of the family for the individual and society and the conditions conducive to successful family life.

5. All youth need to know how to purchase and use goods and services intelligently, understanding both the values received by the customer and the economic consequences of their acts.

6. All youth need to understand the methods of science, the influence of science on human life, and the main scientific facts concerning the nature of the world and of man.

[3] Educational Policies Commission, *Education for All American Youth—A Further Look* (Washington, D. C.: National Educational Association, 1952).

7. All youth need opportunities to develop their capacities to appreciate beauty in literature, art, music, and nature.

8. All youth need to be able to use their leisure time well and to budget it wisely, balancing activities that yield satisfaction to the individual with those that are socially useful.

9. All youth need to develop respect for other persons, to grow in their insight into ethical values and principles, and to be able to live and work cooperatively with others.

10. All youth need to grow in their ability to think rationally, to express their thoughts clearly, and to read and listen with understanding.

CATEGORIES OF OBJECTIVES

Confusion exists in a discussion of objectives unless we specify whether we mean educational objectives, administrative objectives, teachers' objectives, pupils' objectives, class, grade, or lesson objectives, or the activity objectives. We have already discussed the newer educational objectives. Let us now consider some examples of administrative objectives.

Administrative objectives. Objectives set up for the administration of the department are the accomplishments which the department should strive to attain. Some of these administrative objectives are efforts made to achieve:

1. A progressive and modifiable course of study based on a sound, well-understood philosophy.

2. An interest in student progress toward major physical education objectives, and evaluation of this progress.

3. Adequate facilities and equipment conducive to greatest achievement in the program.

4. Efficient administrative routines with delegation of authority and democratic procedures.

5. Efficient teaching and high morale through in-service training, adequate salaries, and proper recognition of good work.

6. Adequate breadth of program so that all students may progress.

7. Community interest, support, and enthusiasm for the program.

Teachers' objectives. Many of the teacher's objectives are similar to those of the student. The distinction between the two is they are worded differently. For example, a teacher's objective might be "to demonstrate volleyball so that the student will learn it more easily." Or the teacher's objective might be "to teach badminton so that the student experiences a felt difficulty and is, therefore, anxious to learn." In the meantime, the student's objective might be merely "to learn hockey," or "to have a good time with this new equipment," or "to get a 'workout.' "

Many students' objectives have corresponding teachers' objectives —worded differently, of course. Some teachers' objectives do not find their counterparts in the students' objectives. Here are a few: to prepare the gymnasium so that it is in readiness for best teaching; to be prepared to demonstrate this new activity; to plan today's lesson so that it is related to former experiences and leads on to new or enriched experiences; to teach so that wanting to learn to swim becomes an objective of the student; or, to motivate the pupil to formulate his own objectives in his own way so that his efforts and attention are focused in the desired direction.

The students' objectives. The teacher doubtlessly tries to have the pupils set up objectives somewhat similar to those for which he wants the students to strive. In fact, if a teacher is unsuccessful in securing this type of cooperation and mutual understanding from the pupils, he is an ineffective teacher.

Sometimes the objective selected by the student is not at all the one which the teacher has in mind, or that which he thinks the student has in mind. For that matter, even if the teacher is wise enough to set up objectives with the active cooperation of the class, someone may not go along. Any individual can set up an undesirable objective instead of the agreed-upon desirable one.

For example, during a survey of a high school, the teacher and one squad in the class decided they would review for the survey experts several stunts on the mats. The teacher had in mind three objectives: (1) review; (2) showing the surveyors what the squad had learned; and (3) the development of organic vigor through the use of major muscles. The teacher told the squad that after the ten minute review they would play volleyball. The squad, with but one exception, performed rather well. One girl had difficulty performing the stunts. The teacher gave the girl several trials on each stunt and much encouragement. The girl, however, did not perform even one stunt successfully although she seemed to be trying very hard. The curiosity of one of the surveyors was aroused. At the noon recess period he sought out this particular pupil. After several minutes of tactful conversation, he discovered that the *objective was simply to waste as much time as she possibly could* so that there would be less time for volleyball, a game she labeled as "terribly sissy." She hoped to do the stunts until the class period was over.

Teachers sometimes fail to gain cooperation because they do not take the time and trouble to understand students. If the teacher in the above illustration had understood the attitude of the girl, he could have secured different conduct. The teacher must discover and sense attitudes and take steps to modify them if necessary. The following steps help to modify negative attitudes toward an activity: disseminating information about the activity secured from sport pages, books, magazine articles, photographs, or letters that college men, businessmen, or possibly a sport hero have written about the activity; enabling the student to see excellent players participate or movies of good teams in action.

Objectives of the activity. The activity objectives are also worded somewhat differently from those of the teacher but, of course, relate to the student. The student's objective might be worded "to get strong arms," while the objective of the activity would be worded by the teacher "to develop organic vigor through vigorous activities, some of which develop strength in the arms." The pupils objective is in terms of what he wants to learn. The objectives of the activity are in terms of what it *is to do for* or *with* the student. Throughout this chapter, we are most concerned with the objectives that arise through teacher-student cooperation. Adoption of desirable objectives by the pupils implies mature guidance and developmental teaching.

If someone presented an objective of physical education for your appraisal, you would first wish to know its classification. If the objective was well worded, could you tell whether it was an administrative, teacher, pupil, activity, class, or lesson objective? How?

Objectives of a class or lesson. The teacher with pupil-cooperation must set up objectives for a given class, grade, or lesson. He uses objectives that contribute toward the desirable accomplishments. He tries to help as many as possible of a given class or grade to reach these certain objectives. In the case of lesson objectives, the teacher tries to get the majority to accomplish the objectives set up for that single lesson.

In teaching tennis to a class of beginners, one specific objective will be the backhand drive. The teacher hopes to have the pupils doing backhand stroking by the time the course is over. But, the efficiency of this stroking will vary among the individual class members. The teacher knows that the more specific objectives include: (1) a suitable grip on the racket, (2) proper backswing, (3) proper position so that the back of the stroking shoulder is toward the net on backswing, (4) watching the ball until it makes contact with the racket, (5) adequate knee-bend to keep the head of the racket above wrist level, (6) shift of weight from back to forward foot on the stroke, (7) proper forward swing, (8) correct stroking of the ball, (9) correct follow through.

Even finer breaking down of objectives might include, for example, minor adjustments for stroking the low-bouncing ball. A slightly upward stroking and a turning of the racket on the stroke to give some top spin and a slight adjustment between the forehand and the backhand grip may be made.

These examples listed are entirely skill objectives. Courtesies of tennis might be a specific objective. The more specific objectives under *courtesies* might include accepting without adverse comment decisions as to "out" errors, commending one's opponent when he makes a nice stroke, giving him the benefit of the doubt when uncertain about the exact score, returning a loose ball on one's own side of the court when the opponent is serving so that he may catch it without expending extra energy, and the like.

The teacher's goal in these cases is to have the entire class accomplish *all* of the objectives selected for attainment. This goal may be unattainable, and yet it is the end toward which he continually strives.

SOURCES OF OBJECTIVES

Techniques for determining objectives. Because the objectives under chief consideration are those that relate to the students, we must find out what they are like. We have already learned that their needs, interests, abilities, and peculiarities tell us a great deal about them. But how are these facts discovered? *One* way is to observe children as they go about their daily lives, see their peculiarities, and note their abilities, interests, and needs. This method is more successful in elementary than junior and senior high school. A *second* way is to find out what experts in child psychology have discovered; this is most easily done by consulting the writings of such experts. A *third* way is to list all objectives mentioned by authors of texts on child psychology, and select those most frequently mentioned. *Fourth,* one may analyze the needs and interests of adults. (This method is limited because conditions will be different when the present generation of children reach adulthood.) *Fifth,* one may analyze the needs of society as set forth by frontier thinkers. *Sixth,* one may seek the information from conversations with children. *Seventh,* one may test children to ascertain their abilities. And *eighth,* one may compare a child or group of children with the average, to ascertain the peculiarities and needs of the former.

Individualizing objectives. These are methods of finding objectives for children by understanding children. Teaching based upon this information alone is too general to be helpful to a particular, individual child. The next step, therefore, is to study the individual carefully.

A physical education teacher cannot actually set up a separate set of detailed objectives for each child, especially if he is the only physical education teacher in a school of hundreds of children. In many localities, not only does he teach all the children in the school, but the classes are unusually large, the time short, and the class meetings held only once or twice a week.

The real problem, however, is reaching the individual student. All children are not identical. Assuming they are leads to poor teaching and disciplinary problems. The teacher is successful to the extent to which he reaches the individual, and many individuals are reached through the individualization of physical education. After the teacher has studied the individual and his background, he can individualize objectives.

Physical education as a source. We find physical education giving rise to different types of objectives, in terms of different kinds of changes experienced by the individual.

The objectives of physical education as a field fall into these seven divisions. These objectives are realized through participation according to the way the activities are taught. (See Figure 7-1.)

The teacher as a source. Not many desirable objectives could actually be secured without that all-important force, the teacher. The teacher analyzes the child, the group of children, and physical education. The teacher guides the selection of objectives. Regardless of the potentiality of an activity, worth-while objectives lie

OBJECTIVES INHERENT IN PHYSICAL EDUCATION

Objectives related to the skills of an activity, such as learning to serve in tennis.

Objectives related to knowledges, such as rules, strategy, and systems of play.

Objectives related to attitudes toward such things as activities, officials, spectators, and other participants.

Objectives related to appreciations exemplified in the recognition of good performance and of appreciation of the opportunity to serve as a leader.

Objectives related to feeling, such as enjoyment, pleasure, and exhilaration.

Objectives related to ideals, such as the "full life" and "a strong mind in a strong body."

Other objectives related to acquirements, such as organic vigor and bodily strength.

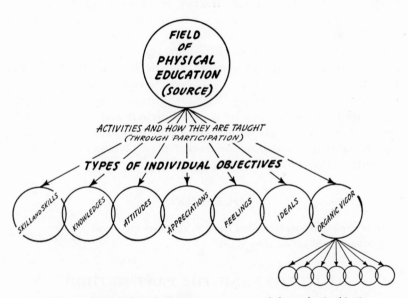

Fig. 7-1. Analysis of physical education as a source of the student's objectives. Each type of individual objective may be subdivided, as is organic vigor.

dormant unless seen, brought forth, and nurtured into development. The unavoidable and crucial responsibility placed upon the teacher cannot be overemphasized.

Some teachers teach several years and never fully realize the weight of this responsibility and the fine opportunity it presents. *What physical education does to and for a student is in the hands of the teacher.* He is more than an instructor of skills and a ball lender. He is the person who sees that objectives are attainable and attained, thus making it possible for the child to develop.

Textbooks and courses, as sources. Frequently objectives from textbooks and professional education courses are used. These short-cut methods, like most short cuts to education, are only partially satisfactory. True, many texts and professors present helpful lists of objectives. However, these can seldom, if ever, be satisfactory. Such objectives are not based upon intimate knowledges of particular students, a given environment, specific activities, and a certain teacher.

A curriculum-builder, author of a textbook, or professor may, of course, assume the average child, average environment, average program of activities, and average teacher, and thus arrive at objectives-to-be-used-on-the-average. This contribution is not to be disparaged or belittled. Such guides have directed and still help the teacher. But no author, professor, or curriculum-builder would claim for a moment that this type of general analysis is a substitute for the teacher's task of selecting objectives in cooperation with pupils. Teachers who expect to use, without critical analysis and careful application, the work done by textbook writers and teachers of professional courses are not unlike the pupil who expects to learn to play basketball by watching the teacher play. Neither develops successfully in the activity he has selected.

QUESTIONS

1. In terms of the student, what types of objectives are there?
2. Where do objectives come from?

OBJECTIVES AND THE PART METHOD

Questionable assumptions. Although objectives may have to be chopped into digestible pieces, the activity need not be presented to the learner as a series of segregated bits. Some teachers believe that the best way to teach any physical education activity is first to teach its various parts. These parts are sometimes called skill elements or activity elements.   Some teachers think these must be taught as isolated elements.

Experienced teachers are usually very quick to recognize that specific objectives facilitate effective teaching and learning.   Some of these teachers believe that the various activities, therefore, have to be broken up into parts and *learned separately* and that these parts have to be taught to the learner as *isolated* learnings.   The result of these beliefs is that the pupil is asked first to practice one skill, then another, and so on until all the parts of an activity are learned separately.

Activity elements and the whole pattern.   No case is being made for learning to play the game merely by playing the game and that *alone* (although conclusive experimentation may show this to be the best way to learn some activities).   On the other hand, no case is being made for trying to learn to play the game by practicing isolated parts of it.

Some evidence shows that the student should begin by learning the whole activity, followed by short periods of practice on parts of the whole activity that need special practice.   Following this short specialized practice, the participant immediately participates again in the whole activity so that the skill upon which he has been practicing becomes a part of the whole activity pattern.   Practice that is too long or too isolated upon a segregated element, such as the dribble, makes the participant dribble-conscious.   He learns the dribble outside of the whole pattern, basketball.   He still has to learn when, where, how fast, and what type of dribble to use as the game situations arise.   He must also learn to weave the skill element (dribble) into the whole pattern of the game.   The same principle applies to the other parts of the game.

Note that not knowing when to dribble, for example, is apt to be as disastrous in a game as not knowing how to dribble at all.   Those who overdo such fundamentals are criticized by the teacher and coach, but often this overemphasis by the player comes only because the skill was overemphasized by the teacher.

A part being practiced separately can be interrelated by tying it up with the game situation.   This act is done not merely by talking about it but by setting up a situation that resembles a game.

What has this to do with objectives?   Just this!   The teacher can set up a skill objective such as: correct technique in executing a particular type of bounce-pass with a guard directly between the passer and the receiver. The learner can understand and desire to attain this objective. However, the setting up, understanding, and desiring to accomplish this objective do not mean that the game of basketball must be broken up into and *taught* as isolated skill elements. Such skill objectives can be accomplished during the progress of the game. In this way, the objectives of skill acquirement are accomplished together with other objectives such as acceptable social behavior (teamplay, good sportsmanship), enjoyment, organic development, as well as specific skill objectives. In *some* activities teaching isolated skills first may be necessary for the sake of safety and protection.

As soon as the individual realizes that he needs special practice upon an activity element, or upon the desirability of playing fairly, or upon exercising self-control under fire, the teacher provides a special opportunity to correct his error or lack of ability. Sometimes this means going out of the game for short periods of practice on the side lines. At other times it means concentrating on a given skill during participation in the whole activity. At still other times it may mean being withdrawn from the game for unfair play or lack of self-control.

Evidence is not conclusive as to whether the whole, part, or the whole-part method is the best way to learn all physical activities. Perhaps no one of these three methods is applicable to all types of activities. But, we do know that merely because objectives are broken up into detailed accomplishments is no reason to break an activity up into skills-to-be-learned-in-isolation. Keep the importance and value of the whole activity to the student in mind.

If specific objectives are constructed for an activity, is it necessary that the activity be learned in specific parts? Why?

DIRECT AND INDIRECT OBJECTIVES

Emphasis determines direct objectives. The student and teacher cannot concentrate simultaneously upon all the objectives. Rather, one objective of a given type is singled out for special emphasis for a given period of time. Emphasis may shift to an entirely different type as the situation demands. The objective receiving emphasis for the moment is the direct objective for that moment; all others are incidental temporarily and, therefore, indirect.

The flow of emphasis from direct to indirect objectives, and vice versa may be constant—that is, the indirect objective becomes the direct objective when the teacher selects it for special attention or acquirement. This is *one of the tests* of successful teaching—to know when to concentrate upon a given objective. While the teacher is apparently deeply engrossed in seeing that a skill objective is attained, he does not miss an opportunity to change his emphasis and to focus attention upon the acquirement of another objective, such as good sportsmanship or self-control. The question of what objective to stress and when to select another one for emphasis is a matter of judgment—the teacher's judgment. In turn, this judgment is based upon what the teacher believes is most valuable for the pupil at the particular time and situation.

Indirect type of objectives. We tend to emphasize some types of objectives more than others. We tend to think of skill acquirement, for example, as a direct *type* of objective. We also tend to think of objectives that accompany participation in activities as indirect *types,* not because they are less important, but because they often occur concurrently with the type of activity that encourages their appearance. For example, organic vigor accompanies participation in vigorous activities. Organic vigor is a major objective of physical education; yet in the same sense that we do not directly call the student's attention to it, it is often an indirect *type* of objective. This fact raises the question: Do we too often leave the accomplishment of certain worth-while objectives to chance? That is, do we take for granted that they will be attained? The answer is unquestionably yes. Sportsmanship, fair play, courtesy toward officials and opponents during highly competitive games, organic vigor in less strenuous activities, safety skills, many desirable attitudes toward physical education, toward social conduct, and toward the teacher are examples.

Indirect *types* of objectives are of two kinds, associated and concomitant. They correspond to associated and concomitant learnings. Associated learnings are those rather closely related to the primary learnings. For instance, learning to dribble in basketball (primary learning), also involves learning the rules that limit the dribble. Learning these rules is one type of indirect objective (if the direct objective at the moment is to learn how to dribble). Some teachers emphasize the academic content of an activity at certain times with the result that to learn the rules becomes a direct objective.

Another type of indirect objective is related to concomitant learnings—those that accompany and are sometimes almost hidden from primary learnings. For instance, while the student learns to pivot according to the rules, he also learns to like or dislike pivoting, learns certain attitudes toward the teacher, learns that his shoes do not fit or tend to slip on the floor.

Not all associated and concomitant learnings are of the indirect *type* of objective. An illustration is found in this reference to shoes. Selecting and wearing properly fitted shoes may be made a direct objective early in the season. Ordinarily teachers think of the indirect *type* of objective as being related to associated and concomitant learnings of the pupil. However, at times the direct objective of the teacher is an associated or a concomitant learning of the student.

Teachers' and students' direct objectives may differ. Some teachers seldom, and sometimes never, give enough time and attention to the concomitant learnings because they are supposed to accompany the primary and associated learnings. It is as though some teachers assumed that nothing could be done to control this type of experience of the pupil. Often, the teacher's objectives might very well be to adjust the environment, to use teaching techniques, to present activities, and to guide the pupil so that the concomitant learnings are vital matters.

At certain times and places, the teacher's paramount and, therefore, direct objective might very well be to see that certain concomitant learnings receive a primary place in the student's learning. For instance, the teacher may make a concentrated effort to teach basketball so that it will be *liked,* which is the teacher's direct objective for the time being. Simultaneously, the student's direct objective might be to demonstrate successfully to the teacher that he can shoot fouls, shoot baskets, cut for the basket, or pass accurately. It follows that the teacher's direct objective is not always the student's direct objective. Furthermore, often unemphasized phases of physical education may assume the role of direct objectives for the teacher.

QUESTIONS

1. What determines whether an objective is direct or indirect?
2. Should the teacher's direct objective always be the student's direct objective?

Examining objectives. Accomplishing major objectives is no easy task. In fact, it is doubtful whether a person ever fully accomplishes them, but he begins to reach *toward* their accomplishment. Let us use an illustration to show this process. Assume that desirable social behavior is one of the major purposes. No teacher can begin teaching such a generality to a child. He must begin by teaching first one and then several *specifics* of social behavior which the child is guided to recognize as desirable and upon which he places value. From these acquirements he is led on to others. In this way he grows and develops. Eventually the child begins to recognize that acceptable social behavior is made up of many acts, knowledge, habits, and attitudes.

The teacher thus guides the many and varied experiences. The teacher *fuses* these experiences from time to time. Finally, the student, after a great variety of experiences, is better able to adapt himself satisfactorily to situations.

For example, one specific objective of desirable social behavior is self-control; and one aspect of self-control is control of temper. The boy who loses his temper in an activity and commits fouls finds that he is penalized for fouling; he incurs the displeasure of his teammates, other classmates, and the teacher; and he is less successful in skill-performances. Through teacher-guidance, gradually he learns to redirect the energy arising from this emotion (anger) into *socially approved behavior* in the activity. The boy also is led to learn to control his temper in many other and different situations. He also learns other types of self-control. And, as this process goes on, we can say that self-control is *growing* in this boy.

Through similar experiences in such characteristics as respect for the rights of others, friendliness, cooperation, fair play, and unselfishness, the boy gradually works toward the accomplishment of this major objective to a degree judged as satisfactory for persons of his age. His task, of course, is not completed. As he grows older, he is led to expect of himself a still greater development in desirable social behavior.

OBJECTIVES AND ACCOMPLISHMENTS

Difference between objectives and accomplishments. Accomplishments are the actual acquirement of objectives. An illustration will clarify this distinction. A student's objective might be to hit the bull's-eye in the archery target from a distance of 100 feet. It may take an hour, day, week, or month before this objective becomes an accomplishment. The objective may then become, to hit the bull's-eye more than 50 per cent of the time. This accomplishment may take weeks or months.

Immediate and remote objectives. Objectives and accomplishments related to skills are more immediate than the objectives and accomplishments of some of the qualities inherent in physical education that are more remote, such as control of temper. The remote objectives are more difficult to accomplish. It takes longer to accomplish them. Let us cite an illustration. A student has a bad temper owing to early home training and a failure to put forth effort to control himself. He is an excellent basketball player as long as he keeps a level head. The teacher assists him in setting up the objective: "to keep my temper during the game of basketball." He may learn to shoot goals, dribble, and pass in a relatively short time; he may take months and even years to accomplish the objective of keeping his temper in basketball games.

Why do we consider it easier for an immediate objective to be accomplished than a remote objective?

Immediate objectives and accomplishments often refer to concrete items that can be tested, measured, or directly observed as well as those that are accomplished more easily and readily.

Remote objectives do not lend themselves so easily to measurement, although they are none the less real. Enjoyment is a real phenomenon. We are at a loss, however, to know when a girl, for example, has accomplished such an objective as: to enjoy breaking up a dribble in a hockey game as much as most of the other girls seem to.   We cannot measure enjoyment.   The best that we can do is to judge by such outward behavior as smiles, yells, and actions indicating enjoyment.   Nevertheless, enjoyment is just as real as the dribble.

MEETING LARGE-SCALE NEEDS

The good life.   "It may all be very well to insist upon objectives to crystallize and give direction to teaching and learning, but is this the end?"   An experienced summer-session student posed this question.   He struck at the very heart of an important problem.   Teaching may be improved, the learning of certain skills, knowledges, and attitudes may be facilitated by the breakdown of objectives, but of what actual *value* are these objectives?

One test of these objectives lies in whether they fulfill the child's major needs.   Do they add needed body-control skills, needed social prestige, needed self-respect, needed energy supplies?   Do they add to his socio-motor tools and his social attitudes?   Do they furnish means of self-expression?   Do they develop greater confidence within the pupil in his own ability to meet life's problems?   Do they aid in resolving his frustrations?   Does the achievement of these objectives make him the type of citizen that contributes to the good of the state?   Is he becoming an asset to society?

Over-all needs.   Opinions have varied as to both the extent to which and the ways in which physical education may help meet over-all needs.   Minnie Lynn [4] has traced the development of man's concepts of physical education values from the thinking of early man to present concepts.   Ancient man's needs for fitting himself into a rugged natural existence motivated sturdy physical development.   At times in man's history, religious and political beliefs have reduced or opposed emphasis on physical development and adjustment.   Frequently, however, military demands have given strong impetus to the building of physical stamina and skills.   The gradual evolution of (1) concepts of individual worth, (2) the trend toward educational focus on whole personality, and (3) the realization by society of the need to conserve the physical resources of youth, all

[4] Minnie Lynn, "Major Emphases in Physical Education in the United States" (Unpublished Doctoral Dissertation, University of Pittsburgh, 1943).

have fostered physical education. Democratic society combined with outdoor pursuits to influence wide participation in sports and games. American individualism with its need and demand for more active leisure-time pursuits fostered sports and games. Repeatedly, wars focused attention on unfitness; and the pioneer concept of the need for a sturdy physique slowly changed to a concept of functional efficiency with its hygienic implications. The concept developed of recreation as leisure-time activity, as a means of social participation, and finally as therapy from the tensions and frustrations of increasingly complex civilization. With the changing concept of recreation came change in type of skills and conditioning and a growth of understanding of the social concomitants of cooperative-group physical activity. Later refinements of these concepts, particularly during wartime inventories of the physical status of manpower, brought out the need for *emergency* adjustive power. War analyses of physical inventories focused attention on the importance of healthy environment during the individual's developmental years, and on the repair and renewal processes commonly called rehabilitation.

Objectives and preparation for life. Objectives are valuable to the extent to which they modify the child's life in desirable, beneficial, and worth-while ways. How do objectives function in this manner?

Supervised physical activity helps provide the child with a *corpore sano;* it equips him with skills for safety and protection as well as for use in leisure-time activities; it assists in the development of a better personality; and it gives him experience in conducting himself acceptably, according to social and moral standards.

Objectives and present life. Physical education also contributes to making the child's education *real life* as contrasted to a hothouse type of life, or education in an academic vacuum. Observation of the average child's normal life forces the conclusion that a substantial portion of it is spent in physical activity.

Versatility of objectives. Many inexperienced teachers think of objectives as fixed, rigid, and prescribed. In actuality, the teacher has great freedom in manipulating and interpreting objectives. Major objectives need not be final. Just recently, we have added the acquirement of skills for safety as a major objective. General objectives are flexible and sensitive to changing ideas. The more specific objectives are surprisingly versatile in their applications.

VERSATILITY OF SPECIFIC OBJECTIVES

They may be constructed by any well-trained teacher.

The pupil may be trained to construct his own objectives, with the teacher's help.

They may apply to any phase of physical education.

They may apply to anyone.

They are applicable to the various kinds of school organization.

They are applicable to various activities.

They can be adapted to different levels of ability.

They are applicable to various communities.

They can be modified to conform to changes in the larger emphases in physical education.

Objectives are best conceived as versatile tools in the hands of the teacher. There is no one right way to construct them, select them, use them, or test them. This fact gives the teacher great latitude and freedom, but such prerogatives always bring unavoidable responsibility with them.

How would you help students better understand the importance that objectives play in their learning?

Being definite in selecting objectives. Better teaching is dependent in part upon the objectives that are specific enough so that both the teacher and the pupil know where they are going. To the degree that the teacher breaks down objectives that can be accomplished, are understood and appreciated, to that degree does his teaching take on effectiveness. *First,* the teacher has concrete ends toward which to drive; *second,* the pupil understands and can work toward real goals; and *third,* these goals make teaching easier, more appropriate, more applicable, and therefore more efficient. They *sharpen* teaching.

Let us illustrate this point. Suppose the teacher is teaching handball. One specific skill objective selected (for and by the pupil) is to learn to serve. As far as selecting actual ways and guides of how to teach the beginner to serve, the situation demands further analysis.

Without definiteness, teaching is merely muddling through, a hope-I-hit-upon-the-right-thing sort of procedure.

FACTORS IN SELECTING TEACHING TECHNIQUES

Age and grade of students

Previous background in similar activities

Physical condition

Quality of their coordinations

The purposes of teaching this activity

Type of handball used

Type of court available

The number of students being taught

Amount of time available

Any observer of teaching over a wide geographical area is impressed with the variety of objectives used by successful teachers. Even a given set of specific objectives does not inflexibly indicate a certain set way of teaching.

The experienced teacher is unable to tell the novice how to teach desirable social behavior, but he can tell the beginning teacher one, two, or three ways that have proved effective in helping the student learn control of temper when an opponent fouls him.

MEETING AND ASSISTING CHANGES

One's teaching program should be forward-looking and progressive. Suppose the major objectives are changed by the leaders. What then? Many teachers who read these pages have already experienced changes in the major objectives. Most of these teachers have changed their ideas of purposes because values changed. To the beginning teacher this seems sensible and proper, but *it is not* easy to do.

Many major students are taught during their college years that a certain set of objectives are *the* major objectives of physical education. They have been given the philosophical, scientific, psychological, and sociological reasons why these *are* the best major objectives. These prospective teachers will graduate and teach for several years, basing their teaching and program upon these major objectives. And then, a changed educational philosophy, a changed international outlook, or a changed role in education may force leaders to change these major objectives. Physical education must synchronize with national life as it exists, not as it was constructed in the academic atmosphere. And physical educators should take a hand in effective changes.

Teachers must change. Some teachers may find themselves quite out of step—old-fashioned conservatives—if sudden changes come. What will they do? Stubbornly fight for *the* major objectives they so religiously followed? If not, they must change their techniques, change their programs, change much that was truth to them; in fact, change themselves rather drastically! And if they do not change, the professional parade soon leaves them, branded has-beens. The question is, therefore, when such a time comes, what does one do?

Today, college youth know from experience that life is constant change. Events in the politico-socio-economic scene have changed and are changing with faster, more dramatic suddenness. For this reason, tomorrow's teachers probably will adjust a little more easily and quickly.

Teacher education changes. Another force is operating to make change easier for teachers. The trend in the professional education of teachers today is away from indoctrinated, panacean techniques and programs toward the development of such qualities as self-reliance, initiative, and careful evaluation. The new generation of teachers will thoroughly and enthusiastically follow the goals of physical education, but at the same time they will be alert to change and thus keep abreast of progress.

SAMPLE TEST ITEMS

True-False

1. If a teacher tells students they will get certain results from participation in an activity, they can be counted on to try to get these results.

2. Since students are not mature and experienced, they should have nothing to do with selecting objectives.

3. The specific objectives of an activity invariably lead to the major objectives of that activity.

4. The plan of presenting the objectives of education as proposed by the Educational Policies Commission is an example of the step-by-step process.

5. Physical education contributes to all the major and minor objectives of education as presented by the Educational Policies Commission.

6. Teachers' and students' objectives of physical education are identical.

7. The life of the student is one source of objectives of physical education.

8. Most of the objectives of physical education should relate to skills because of the nature of physical education activities.

9. The final selection of outcomes which the student strives to accomplish is one of the responsibilities of the teacher.

10. Physical education, regardless of the teacher, contributes to "the good life."

11. Because the major objectives of physical education are set up by leaders in the field, the teacher should accept these as invariable rules by which to guide his program.

12. The selection of teaching techniques is aided by selecting specific objectives which the student strives to attain.   The teacher's first task, therefore, is to break down the major objectives into hundreds of minor objectives.

13. The part method of learning is the best way for a child to learn physical education activities.

14. The whole method of learning is the best way for a child to learn physical education activities.

15. If the student is learning an activity by the whole method, the teacher does not call attention to correct or incorrect performances in parts of the activity.

16. Objectives invariably are either direct or indirect.

17. An objective may be of an indirect type but be a direct objective at a given time and place.

18. A teacher's direct objective is certain to be the student's direct objective, if the teaching is good.

19. Remote objectives are not so genuine and real as are immediate objectives.

20. Immediate objectives are apt to be more measurable than are remote objectives.

Multiple Choice

Below are objectives that might be set up for football.   They may be classified: (1) administrative objectives; (2) teachers' objectives; (3) students' objectives; (4) activity objectives; or (5) objectives of a specific lesson.   After each statement of objectives below, write the number of the type of objective that most nearly describes the viewpoint of the phrase.

1. Social prestige, emotional excitement and thrill, self-respect and self-realization.
(   )

2. A varsity sport to develop leaders in fitness.   A type of honors course for the top 10 per cent in physical achievement: i.e., for those of high rank in strengths, endurances, skills, etc.   (   )

3. Specific skills: kicking and catching, fast starting from line position.   (   )

4. Body control skills, energy, emotional control, willingness to labor, and sacrifice for a group-conceived goal.   (   )

5. Specific skills, certain physiological conditionings and fitnesses with social and emotional concomitants.   (   )

Matching

Directions: Put the number of the concept in the blank space before the definition which most nearly fits the concept.

CONCEPTS	NUMBER	DEFINITIONS
1. Objective		Emotionally colored idea of procedure or situation, desirable but scarcely attainable
2. Accomplishment		One's subjective judgment of what is of worth to oneself
3. Attitude		Tendency emotionally toned to act in a certain way toward a situation or group of similar situations
4. Appreciation		Anticipated and desired outcome
5. Skill		Achievement
6. Value		Ease and precision in performance of acts
7. Ideal		Sensitivity to the full worth of something.

Yes—No

1. Does the student know what he needs and how best to meet these needs?

2. Should the student help decide the objectives of the activity units?

3. Is there a fallacy in the step-by-step analogy of the minor objectives all building up to a major objective?

4. Do specific objectives tend to establish relationships (blend) before forming higher objectives?

5. Do specific objectives demand skill-element teaching?

6. Is progress in educational practice facilitated by regular steps—one objective to a prescribed next objective?

7. Does analysis of objectives into detailed specifics for daily achievement tend to clarify the major objectives?

8. Are the "Seven Cardinal Principles" and the purposes of education as presented by the Educational Policies Commission similar?

9. Can one be *completely* educated through physical education?

10. Should we expect our pupils to accomplish fully the major objectives of physical education?

11. May a generalized habit or attitude be developed from a variety of applicable but specific experiences?

12. Would it be advisable to have students propose the objectives of each activity period?

13. Do most suitable objectives vary with each student?

14. May the teacher bring out a variety of worth-while objectives from one activity such as volleyball, for example?

15. Should the teacher base his selection of lesson objectives on the needs of the average student?

16. Is a specific objective justifiable if it does not contribute to acquisition of one of the major objectives?

17. Are all other aspects of the school—administrative, supervisory, and so forth —justifiable only if they contribute directly or indirectly to the students' attainment of the major objectives of education?

18. Are the major objectives of physical education well established and are they universally agreed upon?

19. Should the teacher and the students attempt to agree upon the worth-while specific objectives of each activity?

20. Will ways of teaching vary with the type of specific objectives chosen for the activity period?

21. Can the teacher emphasize a specific objective (say a specific skill) to such a degree that there will be no associated or concomitant learnings?

22. Is it valuable to have some immediate objectives that offer the possibility of rapid accomplishment?

23. Can the remote objective be of much greater concern to the child than the immediate objective?

Matching

Below are two columns of words. Those in the left-hand column are numbered. Place a given word's number opposite the statement (in the right-hand column) that most closely corresponds to the meaning of that word.

WORD	NUMBER	STATEMENT
1. Principle		Minute and critical examination
2. Method		Proficiency in many things
3. Methods		Ability to guide pupil behavior effectively
4. Philosophy		Partially substantiated hypothesis
5. Scientific approach		A pellet-form of one's philosophy
6. Versatility		Study of man in his social relationships
7. Analysis		Factual study of the entire situation
8. Disciplinary ability		All factors included in the teaching process
9. Social distance		General but concrete ends set up for attainment
10. Theory		Results, accomplishments
11. Ingenuity		Detailed, concrete ends set up for accomplishment
12. Hypothesis		Value, consequences, purposes
13. Sociology		Conclusion based upon facts and near-facts
14. Aim		Degree of formality between persons
15. Major objectives		Assumption based upon reasoning
16. Specific objectives		Ways of facilitating learning
17. Outcomes		Cleverness in inventing and originating

Essay Type

1. In what ways is teaching in physical education (a) similar and (b) dissimilar to coaching athletic sports?

2. Defend either the negative or affirmative side of the following proposition: *Being an effective coach of athletic sports is more difficult than being an effective teacher of physical education.*

3. Do objectives demand or suggest or indicate ways of teaching?

4. What are the meanings of the philosophical, scientific, psychological, and sociological approaches to teaching? Why should a teacher understand and use these four approaches?

5. Construct an original aim of physical education.

6. Why is it more accurate to say that objectives lead *toward* the aim of physical education than to say that objectives lead *to* the aim of physical education?

7. In what ways do you distinguish between teaching and techniques of teaching?

8. Take the negative or affirmative side of the following proposition and defend it in approximately one hundred words: *Success in teaching is more dependent upon the use of specific techniques of teaching without a knowledge of the principles of teaching than upon the use of the principles of teaching without a knowledge of the specific techniques of teaching.*

9. Give two illustrations to show why the teacher's selection of techniques is considerably aided if he knows the specific purposes for teaching a particular skill or activity.

10. Briefly describe three ways you could teach volleyball to seventh graders to make it more valuable to these pupils than the ordinary way of teaching this activity makes it.

11. Give an illustration showing why teaching techniques and activity content are inseparable.

12. Give an example from your own experience showing the power of environmental factors upon human conduct or behavior.

13. If two teachers may use two different sets of teaching techniques with equal effectiveness in the same situation, why are some teachers ineffective teachers? If there are no best techniques of teaching, how can there be master teachers?

14. What are some of the difficulties encountered by the teacher who places objectives into such categories as (a) major, (b) specific, and (c) more specific?

15. The newer major purposes of education are related to: self-realization, human relationships, economic efficiency, and civic responsibility.   To which of these four areas does physical education contribute most richly?   In what ways?

16. If the teacher's and student's, activity, class, and lesson objectives are often dissimilar only in their wordings, why should objectives be divided into these categories?

17. What are the major sources of objectives?

18. Defend or attack the following proposition: *Since the student lacks the experience, judgment, and maturity of the teacher, the student should have no part in selecting the objectives of a given activity or lesson.*

19. Which of the major sources of objectives is apt to yield the most *valid* objectives?   Why is this source not used to a greater extent by teachers of physical education in the elementary, junior high, and senior high school?

20. What is the *ultimate* criterion of the value of any given set of major objectives?

21. If the establishment of specific purposes of teaching an activity aids the teacher in teaching, why should not teaching that activity in specific parts invariably aid the pupil in learning the activity?

22. (a) When may an objective be termed a direct objective?   (b) How do you distinguish between a direct objective and a direct type of objective?   (c) May an objective be a direct type of objective but be an indirect objective at a given time and place?   Give examples to illustrate your answers to (b) and (c).

23. If the statement, the teacher has not taught unless the student has learned, is true, how do you explain that the teacher and student may have different direct objectives?

24. Attack or defend this proposition: *The teacher is responsible for that which the student learns as well as that which he does not, but should, learn.*

25. Is the process of changing objectives into accomplishments the duty of the teacher alone? The student alone? Or the teacher and student? Why?

26. Explain these statements: "Activity is merely a means"; "Physical education is as much concerned with the child's present life as it is with 'Preparation for Adult Life.' "

BIBLIOGRAPHY

American Association For Health, Physical Education, and Recreation, *Developing Democratic Human Relations Through Health Education, Physical Education and Recreation.* Washington, D. C.: The Association, 1951.

Association for Supervision and Curriculum Development, *1956 Yearbook, What Shall the High Schools Teach?* Washington: National Education Association, 1956.

Broudy, Harry S., *Building a Philosophy of Education.* Englewood Cliffs, N. J.: Prentice-Hall, Inc., 1954.

Brubacher, John S., ed., *Eclectic Philosophy of Education.* Englewood Cliffs, N. J.: Prentice-Hall, Inc., 1951.

Educational Policies Commission, *Education for All American Youth—A Further Look.* Washington: National Education Association, 1952.

Educational Policies Commission, *The Purposes of Education in American Democracy.* Washington: National Education Association, 1953.

Hetherington, Clark W., *School Program in Physical Educatian,* Part II. New York: World Book Company, 1922.

Huizinga, Johan, *Homo Ludens: A Study of The Play-Element in Culture.* Boston: The Beacon Press, 1955.

McCloy, Charles H., *Philosophical Bases for Physical Education.* New York: F. S. Crofts & Company, 1940.

Mitchell, Elmer D., and Bernard S. Mason, *The Theory of Play,* Parts II–III. New York: A. S. Barnes & Company, 1948.

Oberteuffer, Delbert, "A Decalogue of Principles," *Journal of Health and Physical Education,* January, 1947, p. 16.

Oberteuffer, Delbert, *Physical Education: A Textbook of Principles for Professional Students.* New York: Harper & Brothers, 1956.

Wayman, Agnes, *A Modern Philosophy of Physical Education.* Philadelphia: W. B. Saunders Company, 1938.

Williams, Jesse Feiring, "The Inevitable Necessity," *Proceedings* of the 43rd Annual Meeting of the College Physical Education Association, 1939, 16.

Williams, Jesse Feiring, *The Principles of Physical Education.* Philadelphia: W. B. Saunders Co., 1958.

Wood, Thomas Denison, and Rosalind Frances Cassidy, *The New Physical Education.* New York: The Macmillan Company, 1931.

8

The student's values

. . . the secret of Education lies in respecting the pupil.

Emerson.

IF THE TEACHER SELECTS THE OBJECTIVES, HE IS THE ONE WHO hopes the outcomes or results of the learning experiences will achieve his idea of what is desirable; i.e., the objective. If the teacher is able to induce the pupils to accept the proposed objective, then teacher and pupils are in agreement as to hoped-for outcomes.

Meaning of value. The process of getting pupils to accept wholeheartedly teacher-proposed objectives implies the arousal of a want, a desire, a voluntary choice on the part of the pupils. Pupils must *value* the teacher's hoped-for outcome. Value is a matter of feeling. It exists only in the psychic nature of the one who feels the worth, makes the choice, desires the satisfaction. The given value may be a complexity of feelings common to mature, educated adults. This is the type of feeling we refer to when we speak of society's values. Any particular value may be felt by one individual, but not be felt by, and therefore not be a value to, another individual.

Value is one motive power behind action. We act as we feel. In discussing value we may forget the highly subjective and individual nature of feeling. Whenever the word value is used, we should examine the context to see to whom the feelings are attributed.

The feeling judgment may be the teacher's or the pupil's; or it may be an objective superimposed on the teacher and pupils by a value of the administrator or a community-group.

An abstract intellectual concept of a possible objective, without any accompanying individual feeling or desire, is *not a value!* Values are feeling attitudes toward facts, conditions, or behavior. They do not exist outside those possessing the feeling. The implication is not that value judgments are without evidence and reasoning. We hope they are based on factual evidence and reasoning. But the *judgment* must have feeling tone to be preferred and to get action.

Evaluation implies a weighing and a comparing of value concepts. The individual weighs, evaluates, makes relative worth classifications, and thereby builds his system of values. If he builds this feeling guide to his life pattern on mankind's experience, he is said to desire "the good life." "The good life" is a somewhat vague concept of a hypothetical hierarchy of values. It is imaginatively constructed out of ideals conceived by many individuals over centuries of time. It is probably never a real value concept; i.e., it is probably never desired in detail and in its entirety by any one individual. Clearer perhaps is that each individual has his own "good life" value concept.

The teacher automatically applies some criterion of values to the selection of activities. He may weigh the activities in terms of values set up by society, such as *unselfishness, respect for the rights of others, health,* and *fair play;* or he may make his preferences in terms of his own personal system of values, which doubtless includes some of society's values; or he may consider the system of values held by the pupil. The thoughtful teacher will have weighed the evidence and established in his thinking a ranking of values as to relative worth.

Some sources of values. Any teacher interested in helping even one pupil take unto himself one better or more mature value must know from where values come. Obviously, some values emerge from physical and physiological needs. Other obvious sources are: *second,* parents and adult relatives or adult neighbors or friends of the family; *third,* one's peers—other teenagers who are closely associated with the pupil. Less obvious are: *fourth,* one's own behaviors which elicit approval by or are associated with the affection of respected or liked teachers, parents, or others in position to judge; *fifth*, experiences—either accumulative or dramatic—whose consequences have had a chance to become apparent; and *sixth*, books and the mass communication media (press, movies, TV and radio). Knowing such sources is not enough.

How are values formed?   This question involves two phases. *One* is the forming of a value to substitute for another.   Often, this "just happens."   But, how does it happen?   By the individual's growing up, his maturing.   Or, perhaps, by a gradual amassing of the products from one or all of the value sources, so that the individual comes to realize (or perhaps vaguely becomes aware of) the need to modify or discard the old and possess the new value.

The *other* phase of forming values refers more directly to forming a new value.   This takes place usually in a gradual way by such means as: satisfaction of physiological and physical needs; satisfying emotional experiences; effects of life's punishments and rewards; inculcations by those in authority, who have prestige, who are respected and loved; personal reflective thinking and reasoning; imitation of someone else's values; and, identification of some *thing* (phenomenon, object, operation) as worthy and wanted.

The teacher can use these means without preaching.   He may be an example.   He may use other persons (who are accepted) as examples.   He may help the pupil anticipate consequences.   He may help the pupil *mentally* apply this-and-that value, or, actually apply values of different kinds.   He may help the pupil *see* (often for the first time) a given value and its place in a given, realistic setting.   This unusually important matter (even personal goals are dependent on one's constellation of values) is difficult in each case. Furthermore, the teacher usually must use a different set of methods and techniques in each succeeding case.

Some obstacles.   As one looks at this vital task, he might as well know of some of the reasons it is so difficult.   Here are a few: The community is neither sure nor clear about values which it emphasizes (and fails to emphasize the next day)!   The school is almost as vague about many important values.   The pupil notices that the school does not come out for or against a number of things which he has been taught are right, good, correct.   Values conflict with other values.   Everyday living makes the application of values quite difficult.   The individual, being only human in the face of such difficulties, becomes discouraged because he is not consistent in following his values. The impact of time, place, conditions, and circumstances upon values changes them—sometimes at the grave concern of the young person. Values vary in their duration from person to person. Adult failure at living values leads youth to practice duplicity in his values (giving partial truths, evasive answers, and the like). Pupils differ widely in their parental help, in their teachability, and so on.

Values change. *Circumstances and conditions* change man's personal values and society's values. The pupil, through the maturing process, also changes. Economic, educational, and political changes modify values for all of us. Not so long ago, leisure-time activities were considered by society as of value chiefly to the ne'er-do-well, the wealthy class, and children. After the onset of the depression of 1929, Great Britain and the United States began spending millions of dollars on recreation regardless of the individuals' socio-economic or educational levels.

Which values?   The young teacher finds that many of his former values have largely faded. He may remember when he placed little value upon caring for the health, welfare, and future of his players as compared with winning a championship. If *increased age* brings with it increased wisdom, the individual acquires new values, modified values, higher values. Furthermore, we teachers are faced with the question of the degree to which we should select activities that apparently are of value to most of the group, but of little or no value to a given few.

An activity may be of more value at one time, at one stage in the pupil's life, than at another time. At what level does the value of an activity cease or become negligible? We have to be alert to those activities that will be most worth-while to the pupil at each stage in his life. Then we must return to the former questions: Most worth-while individually, to the class, or to society? Now, or ten years from now?

Guidance in the selection of activities that are to be of most value is, therefore, an involved task; yet, the conscientious teacher will not allow these difficulties to prevent his practical consideration of the many facets of the problem.

INDIVIDUAL VALUES

Labeling a value as definitely individual or social is difficult. A social value such as *respect for the rights of others* may reflect upon the individual and affect him more than the group. An individual value such as *self-control* may reflect from the individual who uses it to the entire group. Most social and individual values are cyclic. They form beneficial circles. For the sake of discussion, the terms individual values and social values are used.

Pupil's system of values. The teacher faces the problem of offering the most valuable type of program. He goes as far as he can in offering a worthwhile program in spite of the limitations that exist. Activities are selected which are of most worth to the pupil as a member of the social group, in spite of the teacher's personal interests. Careful study is also given to the pupil's system of values. The child has his ideas of what is worth while, what is satisfying to him, although he may lack words to describe why he likes to run better than he does to read (if he does). At the less mature levels, the pupil does not judge his values. He is satisfied with the feeling of enjoyment in having the impulse of the moment satisfied.

The task of the teacher, therefore, is *first* to understand those activities or parts thereof upon which the pupil places some or much value—merely another step in understanding the pupil. This helps unlock the door to the formation of desirable attitudes. It is one basis of intelligent teaching. Is the pupil in a state of readiness if we try to teach him something upon which he places little or no value?

Values and consequences. Let there be no mistake here. The pupil has his own subjective feelings of worth. This statement means that rowdyism, bullying, beating the rules, and disobedience are values to pupils who feel like doing these things. The task of the teacher, after he understands the pupil's subjective feelings, is to guide the child into applying some judgment to and reflection on his values. He must be shown that certain of his values lead into blind alleys, cause the loss of his friends, lack permanence, or whatever may be the consequences.

Thinking of and *experiencing the consequences* of certain values and acting accordingly make the pupil examine his system of values.

Foreseeing or experiencing unwanted consequences helps force him to apply intelligence in weighing his values. This is one way of motivating him to raise his values, to acquire new and desirable ones. Almost invariably this process leads him gradually to accept and adopt many of the fundamental values approved by society. Such guidance accelerates the pupil's changing his values. It is excellent developmental experience for the pupil to examine his values critically, to see and foresee consequences, rather than to depend upon the teacher's thinking for him or waiting for him some day to see the error of his ways.

Anticipating values. Undoubtedly there are some adult-conceived values which the pupil at a given age cannot comprehend because of his immaturity, lack of experience, lack of judgment, lack of opportunity and training. The seven-year-old does not appreciate the *values* of teamplay. But the teacher anticipates and prepares him gradually for the time when he is ready for such an appreciation. Formerly, we teachers were taught that children were not ready for team games until they were in the sixth grade. Few efforts or plans were made to lead the pupil up to this level of maturity. Sixth graders were suddenly catapulted without preparation into a program of team activities. We assumed that when team games were started, the pupils would suddenly appreciate and recognize teamplay values such as *give and take, doing yeoman service so a teammate could score, accepting responsibility for team failure, the fun of playing appropriately in an integrated group unit,* and *the satisfaction of helping in team achievement.* But, children gain deeper feelings of value from an activity, sooner, if they have been *prepared* for it.

The value of emotional control needs introduction long before the age of fourteen. *Respect for the rights of others* is a value that should grow through the nursery and kindergarten ages. A tendency toward *sociability* has to be developed gradually in the introvert. The teacher *by example,* illustration, and demonstration gradually exposes and introduces the pupil to the worth-whileness of experiences beyond his present comprehension. We must remain critical of our present ideas of *when* to begin introducing these different values. Teachers are finding that children are ready far earlier for many experiences than thought possible a few years ago.

VALUE CONCEPTS IN TEACHING

Pupil opposition.   Introducing values is more difficult than has been described.   A teacher may gradually and circumspectly make a certain emphasis in an activity or guide the pupils into selecting a given activity for the chief purpose of exposing them to experiences that hold values *yet to be appreciated.*   The pupil does not know why, but he may not like and is not interested in this new emphasis, this new activity.   When such a reaction is *general* in the class, the teacher can be rather sure that the introduction was faulty.   But he does not give up trying to initiate the early beginnings of an appreciation of a certain value.   Pupils' specific likes and interests are *acquired!*   Taking on new likes and interests is part of their *education!*   The introduction of new values demands understanding of the pupil and ingenuity in making the new as acceptable as possible. Introducing to a high school pupil the idea of assuming considerably more self-direction is not easy.   Nevertheless, the skillful teacher can make just such an introduction.

A list of individual values.   Here are a few suggestions of the values, more individual than social, to consider in selecting activities for a physical education program:

1. Development and maintenance of organic power.
2. Utility skills such as walking, running, lifting.
3. Motor skills in individual and dual activities.
4. Self-control, emotional control.
5. Accurate, appropriate knowledges pertaining to physical education activities.
6. Proper attitudes toward play and recreation.
7. Self-expression.
8. Poise.
9. Perseverance.
10. Courage.
11. Self-discipline.
12. Pupil initiative in making selections.
13. Character development.
14. Carry-over skills.
15. Creativeness.
16. Confidence.

The young teacher is warned not to be too aggressive in modifying the values held by pupils or in introducing values which the pupil is not yet ready to comprehend and appreciate.

SOCIETY'S VALUES

Individual and social values.   Society's set of values is an expression of the experience of the race.   A democratic society considers as valuable that which is worth while to most persons, most of the time, under most circumstances.

In many instances the individual does not fall into the category of most persons.   Occasions permit or demand that the individual violate or ignore truth, health, courage, and other values set up by society.   However, man lives within society.   He may learn tragically or imperceptibly that some of his values get him into trouble, get him nowhere, or get him into jail.

The individual may adjust his values.   Experience teaches the majority of us that most of the time we adjust our system of values to those of society.   The individual may retain some of the values that conflict with those of society, but too many such conflicts and too great a degree of conflict are not tolerated by society.   The individual who retains too many values disapproved by society is ostracized or incarcerated.   The conflict between the individual values and those of society often arises because of the difficulties of sheer existence.   The pupil, like his parents, *wants to be recognized, wants to be successful, wants to be respected, wants to achieve self-hood.*   The values set up by society for the individual, such as *fair play, tolerance, courtesy,* and *loyalty,* largely overlook the personal desires, personal strivings, personal hopes of the individual.

On the other hand, the pupil must see and accept that most of society's values are worth while for the individual.   Society does not overlook the individual.   Society considers the fact that the individual is a member of a group.   Society's hierarchy of values for the individual are of the highest type, from the viewpoint of *group living.*   The pupil should be helped to understand that the satisfaction and expression of personal *desires* do not always represent personal *values* when all conditions and consequences are considered. The pupil experiencing difficulty in adjusting his system of values usually can be shown that he can secure the recognition and respect of his fellows, for example, by following a different route. The highway markers labeled *cooperation, self-control,* and *honesty* map the road recommended by society. *Selfishness, deceit, beating the rules* and *double-crossing* may get him along the road, but not far.

Social values. Both society's and the individual's systems of values include social values such as *friendliness, respect for the rights of others, consideration of the safety of others, adjusting to the interests of the group, alternating leadership and followership, give-and-take in competition, sense of responsibility to and for the group, law and order,* and *unselfishness.* These are examples of qualities and experiences of the individual that possess what we call social value. These values suggest the need for examining critically many a physical education program. Such values may indicate the elimination of some of the time-honored practices and the inclusion or invention of others. They may suggest new emphases to be made. The guess is hazarded that we have not even scratched the surface in enabling pupils to recognize and experience the many social values that are inherent in physical education activities.

Moral and spiritual values. Included among the *social* values of a good many persons are moral and spiritual values. The identification of these latter has served to highlight their importance. The ten moral and spiritual values effectively presented and discussed by the Educational Policies Commission [1] are: *human personality* (the basic value), *moral responsibility, institutions as the servants of man, common consent, devotion to truth, respect of excellence, moral equality, brotherhood,* the *pursuit of happiness,* and *spiritual enrichment.* Every teacher and teacher-to-be should carefully read this valuable booklet.

This chapter discusses some of these values of Western civilization. Some of the other parts of the world have also begun to accept these values because they are indices of man's slow climb toward *self-improvement* and toward man's *humanity*-toward-man.

In the face of such a development, though plainly gradual, it is difficult to understand the position of some educators who are saying in effect: "There's no use. Too many kids come to school and don't know or understand or appreciate *any* of these values. They are not taught in an increasing number of homes. Nothing but bedlam

[1] Educational Policies Commission, *Moral and Spiritual Values in Public Schools* (Washington, D. C.: National Education Association, 1951).

results when middle-class teachers try to get lower-class pupils to accept or respect middle-class values. Western values are through!"

Do we in education give up because something is difficult? Do we swerve hither and yon because a few intellectuals call down from their heights: "There's no use. We're at the end of the sway of Western values!" Have worthy values ever been anything but difficult to inculcate?

One of the unfortunate possibilities of *educators* preaching abdication in the face of difficulty is that prospective teachers may actually be led to *give up* the great values of Western civilization. And what values shall take the place of these jettisoned ones? Man cannot live, there cannot be any life of the mind, without values. Here we have no word from the group advocating the shelving of our present values. We point with pride to the writings of leading physical educators who place increasing emphasis on the importance of inculcating youth with these traditional Western values.

BIOLOGICAL VALUES AND PSYCHICAL CONCOMITANTS

A general type of value that is more directly related to the individual than to social situations is the biological. Biological values are particularly important because they emphasize the *basic,* age-long relationship between man and activity. Whether man's nature, his nurture, or both originally caused his hunger for activity is not important at this point. It is significant to note that activity enabled man to live. And it probably had a good deal to do with his evolution. Every normal person has drives for activity—even though many civilized adults repress these drives until such desires are beyond recognition and consciousness. Let us now consider seven examples of values of a biological nature.

Growth and development.   One kind of biological value is the stimulation which physical education activities give to *growth* and *development.* Activities affect the rate and kind of growth and development of the pupil. Some teachers have been shortsighted in offering programs only for the statistical, observed, or hypothetical *average* pupil in a given *average* grade or of a given *average* age. Most of their programs are based upon ideas and writings expressed prior to modern studies and concepts of education, learning, childhood, and adolescence.   One biological value of physical education is that no child enjoys normal development without beneficial kinds, amounts, and intensities of activity.   Man inherits a dependency upon activity.

Vigor.   Another biological value of physical education is *organic vigor*.   The individual inherits his basal organic vigor and the degree to which it can be developed.   Some other sources of organic vigor are physical activity, endocrine glands, and food.   Psychological sources of energy may augment biological sources.   Organic vigor is an expression of the strengths, resiliencies, responsiveness, and densities of the vital organs.   Individuals vary in their respective possessions of organic vigor.   In the past, physical education has adjusted itself too crudely to the individual's organic power—or failed to adjust at all.   Furthermore, we have failed to pay sufficient attention to beneficial kinds, amounts, and intensities of activity.   Too much and too intensive activity for growing youths may be disadvantageous.   One purpose of physical education is to maintain and develop organic vigor, not to devastate it.   Physical education for individuals must be adjusted to their respective capacities and needs for organic vigor.

Relaxation, rest, reduced activity.   The pupil also inherits needs for *relaxation, rest,* and periods of *reduced activity.*   Basal metabolism, the interphase of cell mitosis, the chemico-physiological results of fatigue, the rest periods of the heart, and sleep illustrate this fundamental law of nature.   Physical education must include activities and be organized to provide for these three complements of activity.   The length, amount, and spacing of rest, relaxation, and reduced activity depend upon the individual and the length and intensity of the activity program.   Some physical education programs are so poorly organized that normal pupils spend the majority of their time standing around.   McCloy [2] says, in commenting on this point: "We cannot obtain stimulation for growth and development in five minutes twice a week" doing vigorous muscular work.   We are certain that McCloy would not subscribe to the idea that we have orgies of vigorous physical activity in an effort to make up for lost time because we have the pupil only once, twice, or three times per week.   But, we do not think that McCloy believes in whole class periods

[2] C. H. McCloy, "Forgotten Objectives," *Journal of Health and Physical Education,* 8:512 (October, 1937).

without rest, relaxation, and reduced activities. The biological resultants of rest, relaxation, and reduced activity are as much the basis of life as activity and food.

Strength. Another value which has biological roots is *strength.* Some leaders seem to decry the direct seeking of strength. As Mc-Cloy [3] points out, although the pupil is a unity of mind and body, he is more body than mind; the physically undeveloped child develops feelings of inferiority; persons without adequate strength are easily fatigued and, therefore, susceptible to such minor ailments as colds, and work at a lower level of muscular efficiency; the strength of the organic system comes through vigorous activity.

One's philosophy of physical education would have to parallel McCloy's before he could agree with his statement: "I believe that a P.F.I. of 120 would, at the present stage of physical education and recreation in our country, be of more value to more people than would be the skill to shoot eighteen holes of golf in 72." [4] As far as teaching techniques, the program, and realized values are concerned, it makes quite a difference whether strength is directly sought or whether it is incidentally acquired as the pupil participates in activities. A great many acts and conditions in life are dependent upon strength, and it, in turn, arises from activity.

There are different kinds of strength, depending upon the kind of activity involved. For example, if the teacher is interested in the pupil's acquiring certain strengths that will enable him to do certain things or fill certain gaps, activities are selected accordingly. Strengthening certain muscles and muscle groups is beneficial to many pupils with structural and functional defects, in addition to those children who have no defects but simply lack the strength and muscle habits to avoid feelings of inferiority.

Skill levels. Another source of biological value is the *neuromuscular mechanisms.* Pupils differ in potentialities for neuromuscular mechanisms. Some pupils will probably be limited in the excellence of their performance in many physical education activities. Others seem to possess a tendency toward a high-order type of skill acquirement. If the individual's neuromuscular mecha-

---

[3] C. H. McCloy, "How About Some Muscle?" *Journal of Health and Physical Education,* 7:303 (May, 1936).

[4] C. H. McCloy, "Forgotten Objectives," *Journal of Health and Physical Education,* 8:512 (October, 1937).

nisms are to provide means for the realization of values, the degree of difficulty of the skills attempted and the rate of the pupil's progress from less to more difficult skills must be considered.   A teacher can eliminate unintentionally some values if the pupils become overly conscious of skill standards and norms.   No point is being made for the teacher's or pupil's being satisfied with poor performance, unless such performance represents the pupil's best.   Some ability is requisite to participating and, therefore, being in a position to enjoy any activity.   Yet at the present time some individuals go through twelve years of physical education classes and consider themselves worse than dubs.   They are dubs in the only physical education they had the opportunity of experiencing.   There has been too much glib use of that clever term, a physical education moron, as though the particular kind of physical education given to the individual were the only kind possible or worth-while!   Physical education activities should be selected in terms of the individual's neuromuscular uniqueness, if this biological equipment is to be a source of most value.

Physiological conditioning.   There are biological values in the activities that exercise *physio-chemical processes.*   The chemical expenditure and restoration during activity, and the conditioning of the circulatory, heart, and respiratory-regulating mechanisms are important values.   The time, intensity, and length of participation in activities are limited by these factors.   Exercise of these mechanisms keeps them flexible and adjusted.   The well-trained person normally enjoys a finely coordinated physio-chemical organization.   His heart and lungs are well synchronized.   Fatigue products are quickly eliminated.   Fatigue is postponed.   The teacher considers the physio-chemical relationships when he starts each class with a warming-up activity and closes with a cooling-down activity.   The teacher is alert to symptoms in the individual that may indicate an obvious upsetting of these physio-chemical relationships.   He avoids activities that tend suddenly, or over a protracted period, to throw into unbalance these relationships.

Satisfaction, joy, and release through activity.   The brain and the nervous systems are the means by which values are recognized and felt.   Through these mediums the individual experiences feelings of joy during and from activity, the satisfactions that arise from performance in activity, the divergence of worry that may result from long hours of sedentary tasks, and the releasing of tension and emotions. These psychical experiences are real even though they are difficult to explain. Man is individualistic in the extent to which he reacts to types of activity. The activity that brings satisfaction, joy, and release to this person brings just the opposite to another person. No one has a right to deny each individual his own particular taste for physical and psychical experience and expression. In fact, activities reach their highest physical value when the psychic experience is most pleasurable. The brain and nervous system are a source of value. They enable the pupil to make decisions, solve problems, use judgment, plan, create, and analyze.

More and more we use activities to make such developmental values available to the pupil. More and more we make these valuable experiences possible in connection with activities.

INHERENT, EXHERENT, AND FALSE VALUES

Meanings. Inherent values are those that are ingrained *within* the activity. Exherent values are those that are superficial, unconnected, supplementary. False values are those labeled false by someone who does not regard certain values as authentic. In the preceding paragraphs we were considering inherent values. Examples of exherent values are medals, cups, athletic scholarships, and grades.

Interpretations. Some teachers and coaches focus the pupil's attention upon the exherent values. This is unfortunate because so many inherent values can be recognized. Pupils under such tutelage not only miss many inherent values but are encouraged to look for exherent values in other life experiences. Pupils taught to expect exherent values are always asking: "What do I get out of it?" —meaning, of course, what *unrelated award* is forthcoming. There can be no question that exherent values are values. But, in terms of developing, educating, guiding the pupil to select *higher* values and *more permanent* values, the chief emphasis upon the pursuit of exherent values is shortsighted.

So-called false values do not exist. Some values held by one person may seem false to another person. In some cases an individual assigns value to an experience which seems or is proved to be invalid. One example is the value formerly assigned to breathing exercises— namely, the increased supply of oxygen carried by the blood to cells and tissues.   Research, observations, and the experience of the race sometimes show (to those who will believe) that the values they formerly attributed to certain objects and experiences are invalid.

A given activity or experience may not lose all of its value merely because certain supposed values related to it are disproved.   Some experiences have value but not in the way a person imagines.   Take the case of the individual who takes a leisurely stroll once a week. He may imagine he is receiving all the beneficial physiological results that accompany vigorous physical activity.   Of course, such slow walking produces very little organic stimulation.   Yet, the individual feels better.   Changes of environment, change of activity, the effects of the multifold stimuli of nature produce psycho-chemico-physiological results which make him feel better.   The psychical attitude has very definite effects on the physiological state.

Then, of course, there is the case of a person's believing that an experience has value when it may actually have disvalue.   Take, for example, the neurotic who says that bridge is relaxing to him, while the close observations of friends and his family testify that he is more "neurotic" after an evening of bridge.   The game is of some value to him, but it is a disvalue in the very area in which he imagines it is of value.

The teacher makes certain that the values used as a basis for activity selection are of the highest possible type, valid and authentic. This is particularly necessary if one considers the small amount of time available in a class period to permit the values to be appreciated and experienced.

POTENTIAL AND REALIZED VALUES

Activities vary in potential values.   Any desirable physical education activity has certain potential inherent values.   Some activities have richer potentialities than others.   For example, most teachers believe that swimming and basketball, given under proper conditions, are potentially more rich in values to most pupils than calisthenics given under favorable circumstances.   After considering the community, the school, the specific environment in which the activity is taught, the equipment, the pupil, and the teacher's ability, activities are selected that seem of greatest potential value to the individual and the group.

Bringing forth potential values.   Many inherent values of an activity remain within that activity, unrealized and undiscovered by the pupil.   Tennis, as taught by some instructors, can seem to be almost devoid of immediate value to the individual.   The game becomes little less than a set of boring drills.   But tennis, as taught by other instructors, seems rich in values immediately recognized and felt.

Why select an activity rich in potential values if the teacher fails to make them available to the student?   The first president of the University of Chicago reputedly taught Sanskrit as though it were an adventuresome sport.   Could it be that some teachers of adventuresome sports teach them as though they were Sanskrit?   One does not have to travel far to see physical education activities stifled with too much teacher domination, too meticulous attention to rule observance, too much stopping of the game for instruction, overemphasis on attainment of specified skills, too much emphasis upon one general type of activity throughout a month's program.

School administrators cannot be blamed for expecting more *realized* values from physical education.   They cannot be blamed for becoming impatient over the potentialities that go undiscovered.   If values of a given activity occur automatically, why must they be taught?   If these values we have claimed, and still claim, arise from activities without leadership and guidance, the term physical *education* activities is meaningless.   In fact, one wonders why more school administrators have not demanded that we show them values, not just claimed values.

One of the clearest examples of unrealized potential values occurs in the case of coeducational activities when the leadership is lacking. It is an open professional secret that these activities go only when the male physical educator fully cooperates in the leadership of this type of activity.

Teaching is a word of degree.   Teaching can be changed to *better* teaching.

CONDITIONS THAT LIMIT VALUES

Conditions related to the pupil.   The values within an activity vary according to certain conditions.   No activity has the same value for all pupils under all conditions.   One of these conditions has just been discussed—namely, the quality of the *leadership* of the teacher.   Reference has also been made to the pupil's *age* as a factor that determines the number, degree, and type of values realizable from a given activity.

The pupil's *sex* implies that some activities are of little or no value. Boxing, wrestling, and football have more disadvantages than values for girls.   The *ability* and *educable potential* of the pupil in physical education activities are other limiting factors.   Activities requiring a high order of coordination and neuromuscular mechanism have more values for pupils who have greater skill potentialities. What is the profit if a pupil spends hours attempting to master skills clearly beyond his capacity?   The pupil's *needs, attitudes,* and *interests* are well-known factors that limit the value of activities.

Physique, physical condition, and *structural* and *functional maturity* are four other factors that govern the values a pupil may experience from a given activity.   The more vigorous, competitive, intensive sports such as football, lacrosse, soccer, and wrestling have values for boys who are *fitted* to enjoy the values of such sports. Those who are not qualified for such activities may experience more disvalues than values.   The same principle holds for girls participating in hockey and basketball.

Conditions related to the situation.   *Facilities* and *equipment* and the *immediate environment* limit the values in activities.   Swimming, often rated as the most valuable physical education activity, has many disvalues if the water is unfiltered and unsterilized and the pool uninspected and improperly constructed.

Particular attention is paid to protective equipment in activities such as heavy apparatus work, hockey, and football.   Many constructive steps are yet to be made in modifying facilities and equipment so that activities become more worth-while to larger numbers of persons.   Some changes are being made; for example, the facilities and equipment of baseball have been modified and we have softball baseball.   In a few junior high schools the basketball goals are lowered two feet, a smaller ball is used, and the playing space is decreased in size.   The degree to which present activities may be changed if desirable is almost limitless.

Conditions related to the activity.   Most of these changes in facilities and equipment mean *revisions of the rules,* which, in turn, usually *change the content of the game.*   We are beginning to see a great need for many modifications in parent activities. Football has been modified so that it is of value to many thousands of boys who should not play it in its regular form. George T. Stafford, University of Illinois, has modified many sports so that they are suitable for students in the so-called corrective, restricted, or adapted groups. Much can still be done to change the rules and content of activities so that pupils lacking requisite degrees of motor ability for satisfactory participation may compete. Activities when suitably modified may be of more value to the majority of individuals.

Other conditions. Another condition that limits the value of an activity is the factor of *time.* This factor includes the length of the physical education period, the number of pupils per instructor, the time of day the physical education class is held, the number of times physical education is offered per week, the season of the year that a given activity is offered, and the length of time pupils participate in a given activity.

These and other conditions, such as the *local situation, teaching techniques,* and the *teacher's skill* are constantly operating to decrease or increase the number, degree, and type of values which a pupil or pupils recognize and experience from a physical education program or from one activity.

The well-trained teacher is most interested in the values that are actually *experienced by the pupil.* On the other hand, the stated values as outlined in books, pamphlets, and courses of study are of assistance to the experienced teacher. He, in turn, can contribute much to courses of study. The techniques of uncovering values in activities used by successful teachers may help those constructing courses of study. These various conditions that limit the value of activities are mentioned as areas in need of study and as facts to be faced by the teacher. They cannot be ignored by any teacher interested in better physical education teaching.

SAMPLE TEST ITEMS

Yes—No

1. Are one's values at twelve years of age the same as they will be at sixteen?

2. Do society's values change with time and experience?

3. Is the teacher likely to be able to arouse desired value concepts in all members of his class?

4. Are value concepts chiefly dependent on physiological maturation?

5. Should the teacher expect all members of a particular class to attain the same value concept?

6. Is the development of pupil value concepts an educative process?

7. Does the statement, "The teacher must educate the pupil to worthier values," assume that the value concept is a purely intellectual process?

8. Does the impulsive responding of the younger children to temporary and fluctuating drives imply the possession of value concepts?

9. Might the particular techniques chosen by the teacher induce contrary feelings instead of the hoped for value concept?

10. Does adjustment to society imply a change in value concepts?

11. Does the term social values imply that the pupils are in agreement as to worth-whileness of certain social behavior patterns?

12. Are the so-called biological values only values to those who recognize them as desirable?

13. Can the teacher see that pupil values are realized without developing pupil value concepts?

14. Is degree of realization of values highly dependent on the total learning environment?

True—False

1. The teacher of physical education always selects activities of most value for a given class.

2. The experienced teacher considers other systems of value besides his own in activity selection.

3. Activities that are of value to the group are of more worth than activities that are of value to a given individual.

4. The pupil is more apt to be interested in the immediate values of an activity than is the teacher.

5. Values change.

6. If an activity is of a given quality of value, it possesses this quality regardless of other factors.

7. If an activity is of little value to a few pupils in a given class, they should take it anyway because it is of value to the majority of the class.

8. Values can be placed into two distinct categories, individual and social.

9. The law of readiness is related to a pupil's system of values.

10. A pupil may be too immature to appreciate the value of activities which in a few years he will greatly desire.

Multiple Choice

1. To prepare the pupil for values not yet appreciated, the teacher should:
   a. Tell the pupil he will some day appreciate these things.
   b. Gradually lead the pupil through activities to experience to some degree the beginning of these values.
   c. Ignore the fact that the pupil does not like the new experiences.
   d. Refrain from offering any opportunities for participation in experiences that are not liked by the pupil.
2. Examples of individual values are:
   a. Courage.
   b. Initiative.
   c. Respect for the rights of others.
   d. Unselfishness.
3. Individual values and social values:
   a. Never conflict.
   b. Should conflict.
   c. Sometimes conflict.
   d. Should never conflict.
4. The development of strength is a biological value of physical education activities because:
   a. It is a guarantee that pupils will use strength for social purposes.
   b. It is necessary to carry on life's activities.
   c. It helps overcome feelings of inferiority in some pupils.
   d. It is synonymous with health.
5. Exherent values are:
   a. Often easier for the pupil to appreciate.
   b. More permanent than inherent values.
   c. Worth more to society.
   d. Worthless.
   e. More educational than inherent values.

BIBLIOGRAPHY

Crow, Lester D. and Alice Crow, *Human Development and Learning.* New York: American Book Company, 1956.

Drake, William E., *The American School in Transition.* Englewood Cliffs, N. J.: Prentice-Hall, Inc., 1955.

Educational Policies Commission, *School Athletics, Problems and Policies.* Washington, D. C.: National Education Association, 1954.

Estes, W. K., *et al., Modern Learning Theory.* New York: Appleton-Century-Crofts, Inc., 1954.

Fraser, Ellen D., Joan B. Bransford, and Mamie Hastings, *The Child and Physical Education.* Englewood Cliffs, N. J.: Prentice-Hall, 1956.

French, Will, and Associates, *Behavioral Goals of General Education in High School.* New York: Russell Sage Foundation, 1957.

Havighurst, Robert J., *Development and Education.* New York: Longmans, Green, and Company, 1953.

Lee, Mabel, *The Conduct of Physical Education.* New York: A. S. Barnes & Company, 1937.

MacLean, Malcolm S. and Edwin A. Lee, *Change and Progress in Education.* New York: The Dryden Press, Inc., 1956.

Nash, Jay B., *Philosophy of Recreation and Leisure.* St. Louis: The C. V. Mosby Company, 1953.

National Society for the Study of Education, *Forty-ninth Yearbook, Learning and Instruction.* Chicago: University of Chicago Press, 1950.

Oberteuffer, Delbert, *Physical Education: A Textbook of Principles for Professional Students.* New York: Harper & Brothers, 1956.

Scheffler, Israel, ed., *Philosophy and Education.* Boston: Allyn and Bacon, Inc., 1958.

Wheat, Harry Grove, *Foundations of School Learning.* New York: Alfred A. Knopf, Inc., 1955.

Williams, Jesse Feiring, "The Physical as Experience: For the Extension and Enrichment of Education," *Journal of Higher Education,* December, 1951, 464.

Williams, Jesse Feiring, *The Principles of Physical Education.* Philadelphia: W. B. Saunders Co., 1958.

Part Four

YOUR PROGRAM OF
STUDENT EXPERIENCES:
what should the student learn?

9

Program development in physical education

Sound plans lead to successful programs.

DOES THE TEACHER OF PHYSICAL EDUCATION EVER REACH perfection? What teacher can afford not to work constantly toward better teaching? The teacher interested in better teaching is bound to be interested in building a better program. While this text does not pretend to present a comprehensive treatment of the construction of courses of study in physical education, it is obviously necessary to discuss at least the fundamentals of program-building.

A supervisor of curriculum affirmed:

. . . staff personnel must come to understand—many yet fail to do so—that working on curriculum is *a way of life for the teacher*. Since change is inevitable and change is constant, the curriculum must be continuously revised. Tomorrow's problems and tomorrow's needs are sure to be different in some degree. Teachers can no more stop working on the improvement of instruction than doctors can quit working on the conquest of disease and the techniques of healing.[1]

1 Benjamin L. Simons, "Obstacles to Curriculum Development," *The Bulletin of the National Association of Secondary-School Principals,* 43:26–29 (February, 1959).

The teacher of physical education is inescapably involved in the advancement and betterment of school programs. Program improvement is a continual task. Changes in program plans are imminent as the purposes of education in American democracy are reinterpreted.

Existing programs of physical education are not spared criticism. The beginning teacher cannot be indifferent to the ineffective aspects of present programs. The following are some weaknesses of physical education programs in many schools:

1. Because teachers, departments, and schools have undeveloped philosophies concerning the purposes and content of physical education, many programs lack direction, consistency, and quality.

2. Often the physical education program is viewed as an end in itself rather than as a means of providing experiences for pupil growth.

3. The physical education program is often based on traditional practices rather than students' needs. Activities that are adapted to the developmental level of individual pupils are not available.

4. The physical education program usually does not provide for integration with other areas of the school program.

5. Students are not helped to develop sufficient skill in sports, games, and dance. Many physical education programs do not provide enough time for sustained concentrated effort so that pupils may develop satisfying levels of skill in any one activity.

6. Often concentration is on too few activities or too few objectives.

7. Programs are repetitious; each year's program shows a great similarity to that of the year before. Pupils are not grouped by grade or any other means in physical education programs, which causes too much duplication of material from year to year.

8. Pupils are seldom given adequate opportunity to help select the experiences that comprise the physical education program.

9. The physical education program seldom provides for a wide range of individual choices in different types of activity.

10. The values of coeducational activities are not realized.

11. Programs are largely recreational and not instructional in nature.

12. Not enough provision is made for *education* for leisure. Emphasis on individual and dual activities is lacking.

13. There is often a lack of a related, organized intramural program to serve as an experience laboratory for further development of the learnings acquired in physical education classes.

14. Written course guides or courses of study are either lacking or ignored in many schools. The selection of activities is haphazard.

15. Progression in achievement standards for various developmental levels is lacking.

16. The results of measurement in an attempt to further progress in the physical education program are not sufficiently utilized. There is a lack of evaluation of outcomes.

Thousands of school systems are engaged in curriculum revision to make education more meaningful and valuable to pupils and to society. Formerly curriculum construction and revision were tasks assigned only to outside experts. Today teachers and laymen are actively participating in this work. If the teacher is to improve instruction through what is taught, he must know something about program-building. If the school is to serve best and its purposes to be understood by the community, laymen should participate in the program-building process.

In small school systems, the teacher of physical education may believe he needs no outside help. Who else knows anything about or is interested in building a physical education program? One sure way to enlist a person's support of physical education is to invite him to perform some task which he can do well and which will bring credit to him. For example, serving on a course-of-study committee can awaken the interest of members. In the small school the music-art teacher might well serve on the course-of-study committee, not only because physical education and these two subjects are easily integrated but also because the physical education teacher and the music-art teacher can be mutually helpful throughout the year. The teachers who serve as deans of girls and boys, respectively, should also prove to be valuable members of the committee. Smaller schools are beginning to enlist at least the part-time services of a nurse or physician or both, and the teacher should ask a physician of the community to serve on the committee. Incidentally, this step often eliminates "doctor's excuses" which the teacher of physical education considers to be invalid. In addition, the community should also be represented through the P.T.A. and a businessmen's or service club.

The administrator is often the key to curriculum improvement. He should always be included as an advisory member of the committee, but he may seldom attend meetings unless the physical education teacher requests his presence for a specific purpose. He should be *kept informed,* however, of the committee's progress and can be helpful in suggesting ways of getting things done and in handling committeemen.

In some schools the initiative for revising the course of study in physical education will have to come from the physical education teacher. Assuming that he also desires to gain the support and cooperation of the school personnel and community and thus to educate them toward better programs of physical education, he may need some preliminary understandings.

To be developed effectively, the new program will need the attention of many people. These persons, faculty and lay people, must have good morale and must be able to see that their efforts will result in improvement of the program. Committee members must be carefully selected according to their teaching ability, experience, and other appropriate abilities.

A new program must spring from a conviction that the program needs revision. School staff and community groups must be convinced that there is need for a new program.

The teacher also must realize that for a group to work together effectively it must have skillful leadership. In order that a group work and plan together effectively in the development of a program, they must be able to work *as* a group. This involves all of the problems of human relations. The people must be able to give and take, to respect the viewpoints of others and to abide by the decisions of the group. Knowing this, the leader must improve relationships with others before he can improve the program. Teachers with many years of experience (and some with limited experience), having found that what they do *works,* may tend to be inflexible and resistant to change of any kind. They feel a lack of security in contemplating changes. A characteristic of both people and institutions is that they allow practices to prevail long after there is need for them.

The teacher must also realize that improvement involves more than an *easier* way to get the job done. In fact, an improved program may, and usually does, involve much more work and learning on the part of the teachers who are to conduct it.   Most new inventions, devices, and systems in business and industry are pointed toward *work simplification*.   In contrast to this, program-building may actually involve *work complication*.   Program improvement is not for the convenience of the faculty of the school!   It is for the improvement in learning experiences for the youth of the school.

Too often physical education programs are built around *facilities*. A few traditionally offered activities are fitted into the facilities at hand with various time apportionments allotted to various skills. Such an approach places the most emphasis on the subject matter or activities rather than on the desired types of pupil growth.   A more satisfactory approach to program development in physical education considers *primarily* the most significant *experiences* for pupil growth and development.   This latter approach requires that program-building begin with an examination of pupil needs, purposes, and objectives rather than with facilities, activities, and time allotments.

To focus the attention of the teacher on significant pupil experiences in program-building, the following twenty-five items are offered as an incomplete checklist of the teacher's responsibilities in program-building.   The sound program should be designed to develop pupils physically, mentally, and socially.   To accomplish this through *a program of learning experiences* the teacher should:

1. Foster pupil experiences which relate physical education to other areas of study in the total school program.

2. Select pupil experiences on the basis of the objectives which have been established.

3. Involve several representative and qualified persons in the planning of pupil experiences because an effective public relations program is a necessary source of support.

4. Select pupil experiences in a program on the basis of present knowledges about learning, pupils, education, and accepted principles of teaching rather than on the basis of past personal experience and traditional methods and practices.

5. Provide pupils who participate in experiences a share in the planning and control.

6. Plan pupil experiences on a developmental basis, based insofar as possible on the needs and the interests of individual pupils.

7. Include pupil experiences that call for independent judgment and promote competition to satisfy American needs.

8. Provide pupil experiences involving activities, behavior, and the development of attitudes that will be practiced outside of class.

9. Emphasize pupil experiences and skill in, and appreciation for, activities that will persist to the adult level.

10. Provide pupil experiences that will provide the pupil with the opportunity to develop leadership qualities.

11. Select pupil experiences on the basis of the sex, development, and skill of the pupils, on the basis of the equipment and facilities available, and on the basis of community attitudes and needs.

12. Widen the range of individually chosen types of activity.

13. Include passive as well as active recreational forms of activities.

14. Include combative and self-defense activities for boys.

15. Modify and emphasize certain objectives and pupil experiences for preparedness in an emergency or for special needs.

16. Provide experiences which place emphasis on the development of creative capacity.

17. Emphasize the development of self-reliance.

18. Provide experiences which *balance* capacities with respect to skills, knowledges, attitudes, and purposes and broaden personal development.

19. Foster self-initiated pupil experiences that are courageous, adventurous, and novel.

20. Provide broad learning experiences that develop the pupil as an integrated personality.

21. Provide unity from simple to complex pupil experiences; unify the concrete and abstract, unify doing and thinking.

22. Combine a continuity and relationship of pupil experiences from grade to grade with variety and flexibility.

23. Consider the relationship of pupil experiences between elementary school and junior high school, between junior high school and senior high school, and between high school and college.

24. Formulate a written guide outlining the sequence and relationship of planned pupil experiences.

25. Periodically evaluate the sequence and relationship of pupil experiences and revise the program on the basis of such evaluation.

QUESTIONS

1. What is an example of each of the above teacher responsibilities in program-building?

2. What other considerations should the teacher take into account in program-building?

3. Why does it make a difference if program-building begins with pupil experiences rather than with facilities and activities?

General steps in constructing a course of study.   A course of study in physical education should include criteria for selecting pupil experiences, the activities selected for attaining pupil objectives, materials helpful in such attainment, and evaluation of outcomes.   Consideration also is given to areas of integration with other related subjects or fields.

The trend is toward courses of study that are not too prescribed or limited.   The trend is away from a course of study restricted to physical education alone for a given school level toward an expansion in kinds of pupil participation.   The term pupil experiences includes helping select activities, setting up objectives, participating in such a way as to attain the objectives selected, and evaluating the results.

The concept of the course of study in physical education is also broader today because, *first,* it provides for integration with other areas of the school program, and, *second,* it is beginning to mean the entire program of physical education, from the kindergarten through the senior high school.   Unanimous agreement does not exist on all these points among writers of texts on the curriculum, but there is lack of agreement among these writers even as to the meaning of the curriculum and course of study.

The course of study is not a rule-of-thumb blueprint; it is becoming liberalized in scope, purpose, method, use, and application. With this partial escape from absolutism come less stereotyped steps to be taken in constructing a course of study.   The following six steps and questions are one way a course of study may be constructed:

1. *Backgrounds.*   What is the history of and attitude toward physical education in this community, this school?   In what tangible

forms are the attitudes manifested?   Why should a course of study be constructed or revised?   Who is interested at present in this task? Who would be helpful in assisting in such a task?   Does the financial condition of the school, the practical possibilities of increased facilities and equipment, the attitude of the school administrator and the community, and the possibility of more or a better trained staff justify the time, effort, and expense to be spent on the project?   Who should serve on the committee?   What philosophy or philosophies of education and physical education are to guide the committee?

2. *Purposes.*   What are the purposes of construction or revision in terms of the community, the school, the pupils, the teachers, and physical education?   What is the general purpose or aim of physical education conceived to be?   What are the purposes of the committee?   What are the major goals or objectives of physical education conceived to be?

3. *Analyses.*   What are the needs, interests, abilities, potentialities, appreciations, and peculiarities of the children according to grades?   Shall the answers to that question be the best guesses of the teachers responsible for these children, shall the answers be the expert judgments as found in the literature, or shall direct observation or scientific studies be used?   Which of these needs, interests, and so forth should be immediately satisfied in each grade?   Which can be deferred, and for how long?   What activities promise or have proved best to satisfy the needs, interests, and abilities of each grade? Which activities best match and challenge the ability of each grade?

4. *Syntheses.*   What are the pupil objectives for each activity? Each grade?   What areas should be covered in each grade?   Emphasized?   What philosophy or philosophies underlie the selection and synthesis of these experiences, activities, objectives, and materials?   How shall the content of physical education be selected for each grade (teacher-selected, pupil-selected, or cooperatively selected units)?   How shall the content of physical education be organized for each grade (topical units, theme units, significant-aspects-of-life units, pupil-need units, pupil-purpose units, pupil-interest units, or, by the subject-matter division and allocation method?   If the course of study is to be printed or mimeographed, what form should it take and what emphases should be made?

5. *Installation and evaluation.*   After construction, in what manner shall the program be introduced?   Installed?   What guides can

be set up to help the teacher in the use of the course of study?   In its criticism?   Is freedom granted the teacher in the rate of installation?   What checks are provided to insure best possible installation and experimentation?   What help is given teachers in using new materials, activities, and methods?   What criteria for evaluation are provided?   How long is the experimental period?

6. *Continuous revision.*   Who is responsible for initiating changes in the course of study commensurate with changing conditions and circumstances in the nation, state, community, and school?   From what other sources are suggestions for revisions sought?   What place does the teacher play in continuous revision?   Are objective data or untested experience the basis for revisions?

QUESTIONS

1. How would you go about building a program for physical education?

2. Do you favor the inclusion of laymen on a committee whose purpose is to construct or revise a course of study?

The following list includes a possible sequence of some of the steps that may be taken in program-building.   The order of these fourteen steps may be altered, some may be excluded, and other procedures may be indicated in particular situations.   However, the revision committee might consider the following approach as suggestive:

1. Determine the general philosophy of education and physical education.

2. Review the present program completely, examining carefully for strengths and weaknesses.

3. Determine the needs of pupils in the community.

4. Determine how physical education can help to satisfy these needs.

5. Establish objectives and attempt to agree upon which objectives are to be most strongly emphasized in relation to Number 1 and Number 3 above.

6. Clarify and define problems.   Examine those aspects of the program that need most improvement in contrast to the proposed objectives.

7. Visit other schools in similar settings to see how they have solved problems.

8. Study curriculum guides and courses of study from other schools and school districts.

9. Review recommendations in the literature and study the opinions of experts.

10. Conduct systematic, productive meetings. Possibly begin by working on only a part of the program—one general area of emphasis.

11. Keep the committee and the total faculty informed through distribution of duplicated copies of minutes and progress reports.

12. Plan a balanced, comprehensive program of pupil experiences and expectancies that will satisfy the objectives, taking into account the facilities, equipment, teacher load, and teacher abilities.

13. Compare this comprehensive program with criteria established by experts in the field and with the findings of research.

14. Consider the revised program as an experiment to be evaluated, revised, and reimplemented on the basis of the established objectives. To do this, a plan for the evaluation of the program should be formulated.

QUESTIONS

1. How might the sequence of steps suggested for program-building be altered, expanded, or amplified to better serve as a guide to a revision committee?

2. How would you go about determining the needs of the youth in the community?

Determining objectives. The beginning teacher may be somewhat confused about the role of objectives in the determination of program content. *First,* he may feel that statements of objectives are too theoretical and lack the concreteness necessary to be practical guides to program content. *Second,* he may find too many worthwhile objectives and not enough time to accomplish them. *Third,* he may be aware that in various situations agreed-upon objectives are similar, yet methods of reaching these objectives differ. He may fail to understand that these similar purposes may be accomplished through interestingly different methods.

From time to time in the history of physical education fitness has been the goal most worth striving for. During these times teachers have claimed to be giving additional emphasis to fitness in their programs.   Depending upon whether the particular emphasis was on social fitness, mental fitness, or physical fitness, the experiences through which pupils are guided might be quite different.   For example, emphasis on certain objectives may lead the teacher to include coeducational activities, international folk dance, passive recreational games, and many student-planning and socializing opportunities.   Emphasis on other objectives might lead the teacher to include prolonged periods of intense activity for the development of strength and endurance.   The identical objectives might be accepted by the teachers and groups in the two above examples but the *emphasis* on and perhaps the interpretation of the accepted objectives might differ, and hence the programs would be different.

Determination of objectives is one of the most important steps in program-building; and, therefore, it has been selected for special treatment.   Familiarity with the methods of determining objectives makes the teacher a more intelligent guide in helping pupils select and evaluate their objectives.   The teacher also should be well informed as to the individual and social acquirements which pupils need and in which they are interested, and the approximate age or maturity levels when such acquirements may be expected to be attained by pupils.

Objectives and pupil experience.   The objectives in a course of study should include *more* than the specific skills, knowledges, attitudes, and habits to be learned by the pupil by means of the activities.   This not uncommon conception of objectives has led some teachers to dodge the responsibility of setting up objectives.   Why? If the activities are well taught and the pupils participate, will not the pupils rather automatically accomplish most of these objectives even if they are not set up?   The course of study should intentionally provide, and the teacher make possible, certain experiences in addition to particular accomplishments ordinarily considered as objectives.   These experiences might be considered by some leaders as more important objectives than the conventional concept of objectives.   Reference is made here to experiences that provide opportunities for the pupil to *try out, receive guidance in,* and improve in such activities as *making decisions, planning, selecting, judging, evaluating, carrying responsibility, leading, following, choosing, succeeding, facing failure with intelligence, meeting and solving individual and group problems,* and the like.

The course of study should include as objectives such acquirements as have just been mentioned in order also that the pupil may experience *more* than selected bits of life as lived and conceived by adults. Is the world today, the people in it and what they do, to be considered as a constant? On the contrary, educators and intelligent laymen alike recognize that the school must better prepare children to meet the conditions of their present and *future* lives, whatever they may be. This attitude places the emphasis not so much upon specific skills, knowledges, and so on, as upon planning, evaluating, selecting, and the like.

The teachers of physical culture and physical training of another day were little concerned with the attitudes being formed by their pupils. Nor does it appear that they realized that the activities and objectives of that day might not fit into other conditions of American life. In fact, one force still operating against a modern program of physical education is the accumulated and combined attitudes of adults against their experiences in school or college physical education. Another negative force in some quarters is the inertia of a program of activities constructed for the ideas of a people in other times and places.

The pupil should be prepared not only for "the good life" but for its improvement. Does "the good life" exist today for most pupils? For most teachers? The difficulty with "the good life" commonly conceived in connection with objectives is that it is a certain kind of life made up of certain agreed-upon types of behavior. This concept of "the good life" is like asking the pupil to run a hurdle race in which the manner of running, the length of the race, the construction and spacing of the hurdles are adult-controlled. On the contrary, does not "the good life" change with each person if he creates a better life for himself and those about him? To use the analogy of the hurdle race, "the good life" is represented by the pupil who runs better, runs farther, runs with greater satisfaction over hurdles made and spaced by himself. Preparation for and improvement of this type of "good life" must take place under the guidance of the teacher who considers the pupil's efforts within the frame of reference, the experience of the race. Again this new emphasis gives the pupil opportunities to try out, evaluate, create, and select, under the guidance, direction, and interpretation of a good teacher. Gradually the pupil is led to expand and deepen his methods and criteria of evaluation. That is, the teacher not only helps the pupil interpret his efforts in terms of something better but aids him in gradually acquiring a basis for making his own judgments of what is better.

Objectives and interrelationships. Good drivers of automobiles possess what the layman calls "split vision." That is, they have the ability to be watching the road and at the same time see what is going on on both sides of the road. Coaches of sports have learned to recognize this peripheral vision as a desirable characteristic in their athletes. The program-builder must possess a type of split vision. He sees the objectives of physical education, but he also sees the objectives of other school subjects which are near the periphery of physical education. He is interested in this latter group of objectives not only as they represent possible areas of integration but also because they serve as a means of better orienting physical education in the whole school program.

Many schools are attempting ways of insuring better integration, whether it be through the curriculum, teaching techniques, or administrative maneuvering. Subject matter lines are disappearing, at least in part.

Tomorrow's teachers of physical education, including those of us who are teaching now and will be teaching tomorrow, will need a considerably broader viewpoint, founded upon wider fields of interests. This is the only way we can keep alive to interrelationships with other fields and *contribute as much as possible to the development of the individual.* At the same time we cannot afford to lose our professional skill in the precise field of physical education. That is, because a teacher is broader in his interests and therefore better able to integrate his special field is no reason he should be less expert in his specialty; in fact, quite the contrary is indicated.

Restatement of objectives. The major objectives of physical education need reinterpretation.

The major objectives presented by any recognized authority may satisfactorily present *his* concept and reflect some of the ideas of his time. Yet, the constantly changing conditions and circumstances of modern living bring ever-changing ideas, emphases, and demands. The major objectives of physical education, as they are related to the program of physical education need restating because of such changes.

We suggest, *first,* that this restatement recognize the larger purposes of education to which physical education makes contributions. Present statements of major objectives of physical education may be interpreted in terms of the larger purposes of education. However, the present *wording* of many major objectives directs attention too exclusively toward stated goals without showing the close relationship between them and the new, larger purposes of education. We need an ever-broadening view of the purposes of physical education.

This question brings us to the *second* suggestion—namely, that the restatement of the major objectives of physical education should recognize need for integration. Too many administrators and too many academic colleagues still consider physical education one of the special subjects. Perhaps, too many teachers of physical education teach it as though it were a special, if not an isolated, subject. Many of those responsible for recent revisions of school curricula verbally testify that teachers of physical education have difficulty thinking of physical education as contributing to the common units of a core curriculum. If the major objectives of physical education are worded so that integration is recognized or perhaps emphasized, physical education teachers would be more apt to realize that integration is part of their responsibility. It is *essential* that teachers of physical education work toward contributing to the individual's emotional adjustment and social maturity as much as toward his organic vigor and acquirement of skills. If the wording of these latter objectives remains as it is at present, we will work toward the accomplishment of these objectives as ends rather than using them as *means* that lead on.

Third, we suggest that this reinterpretation of major physical education objectives recognize the need for the individual development of more self-direction and creativeness so he can improve himself and the social order in which he finds himself. As with a course of study, objectives should take into account the importance of the self-development that comes from *creating, exercising self-discipline, achieving desirable kinds of recognition, judging, planning, leading, following, initiating, socializing, carrying out orders, overcoming difficulties, respecting the rights of others, carrying responsibility, helping those less adept,* and other such types of experience. These activities are as worthy of accomplishment as the acquirement of recreational skill.

Finally, this suggested reinterpretation of major objectives should also include the objectives now connected with physical education. These objectives are, for example: organic vigor, natural urges and drives satisfied in socially desirable ways, normal functioning of the metabolic and nutritive process, neuromuscular control, skills for recreation.   Without a doubt these are vital, essential, fundamental. But, the point of our three suggestions is that these commonly understood major objectives are of most value *only as they contribute toward such a purpose as self-realization.*   It is not obvious that the major objectives of physical education, as they are stated and interpreted at the present time, are to be projected and applied to the larger purposes of life.   Judging from our physical education teaching methods, the majority of printed courses of study in physical education, and the views of hundreds of experienced teachers, the present wording of the major objectives of physical education actually fails to express the wider, deeper, further implications.

Surprisingly, the American Association for Health, Physical Education, and Recreation has not attempted to revise the major objectives of physical education even though the revised major purposes of education continue to be changed.

The core curriculum and the integration of physical education. During the past fifty years the high school curriculum has undergone many changes.   It is now broader, more flexible.   In the past every pupil took every subject or dropped out.   At present, high school pupils, generally, can elect more courses than at any previous time.[2] Teachers are not as confined by rigid requirements.   They may plan experiences with a great deal of leeway.   The trend seems to be toward giving young people the opportunity and encouragement to help in the planning of learning experiences.

The traditional curriculum centered around subject matter has been severely criticized by many educators and vigorously defended by others.   Critics of the traditional subject-centered offerings of American secondary schools maintain that measures must be taken to give more meaning to and make more functional the learnings acquired in the school.   They say that traditional subject matter emphasis is not in accord with what is now understood about the

2 Association for Supervision and Curriculum Development, *What Shall the High School Teach? 1956 Yearbook of the Association for Supervision and Curriculum Development* (Washington, D. C.: National Education Association, 1956), p. 72.

nature and conditions of learning.   They claim that the total program is unnecessarily fragmented when it is compartmentalized into
various subjects, and that in many subjects, periods of time for learning experiences are too short for real interests to be satisfactorily
satisfied.   Pupils, they feel, have inadequate experiences in planning
for the satisfaction for their own needs because activities are planned
and dominated by teachers in rigid curricular frameworks.   Critics
further declare that traditional curriculum plans lack the proper
setting for effective guidance.

Partly as a result of such reactions against the traditional subject
curriculum, the core curriculum approach has emerged.   This approach to curriculum planning has had such growing emphasis in
recent years that we must stop here to examine the relationship of
physical education to the core.   What is core?   Let us review the
statements of some leaders in this educational movement.   Anderson [3] describes the core curriculum:

A type of curriculum organization at the secondary school level that uses
the problem-solving approach is the core curriculum.   The core curriculum
is a way of organizing some of the important common learnings in the high
school curriculum, using a problem-solving approach as its procedure,
having social and personal problems significant to youth as its content,
and the development of the behaviors needed in a democratic society as its
purpose.   This represents a fundamental reorganization of the curriculum
of the secondary school, rather than just a combination of the traditional
subject matter.   According to this definition, the core goes beyond the
unification of two subjects into a unified studies plan.

Another explanation of the core curriculum is offered by Faunce
and Bossing:

In modern education the term core has come to be applied to that part
of the experience curriculum which is concerned with those types of experiences thought necessary for all learners in order to develop certain behavior
competencies considered necessary for effective living in our democratic
society. . . .   The core program, then, refers to the total organizational
activities of that part of the school curriculum devoted to the determination
of the personal and social competencies needed by all, and the procedures,
materials, and facilities by which the school assures the adequacy of the
learning experiences essential to the development of these competencies.[4]

3 Vernon E. Anderson, *Principles and Procedure of Curriculum Improvement*
(New York: The Ronald Press Company, 1956), pp. 316–317.

4 Roland C. Faunce and Nelson L. Bossing, *Developing the Core Curriculum*
(Englewood Cliffs, N. J.: Prentice-Hall, Inc., 1958), pp. 54, 57.

Caswell [5] defines core as: "A continuous, carefully planned series of experiences which are based on significant personal and social problems and which involve learnings of common concern to all youth."

What implications does this curriculum design have for physical education? Some physical educators, anxious to more completely relate physical education to this modern core approach, have sought ways of including physical education in the core. In fact, some believe that physical education belongs *in* the core since it is part of the general education of all students.[6] Some teachers have experimented with such plans with apparent success. These persons feel that physical education should not be departmentalized. They believe that the experiences in physical education should show close relationships to the other broad fields of experience of students in the secondary school, much as they do in the self-contained classrooms in the elementary school. These persons, anxious to keep in step with the newest current practices, have advocated that the core program holds promise for the improvement of physical education.

The beginning teacher should be aware of the possibility that inclusion of too many objectives or of objectives not traditionally those of value in physical education *may weaken rather than strengthen* the physical education program. The authors of this book feel that caution is needed in attempting the almost total integration of physical education into a core curriculum. The following are some reasons for this point of view:

At present few physical education programs have adequate time to accomplish the purposes of physical education. Pupils need time for intensive activity to accomplish the important objectives of physical education, and projects, pageants, and group and committee work necessarily limit the accomplishment of other objectives. Time-consuming student planning to show relationships in physical education, especially for boys, is not needed as much as in some other areas of general education or core programs.

The worth and application of a well-planned physical education program is often readily understood by pupils. Because they are

5 Hollis L. Caswell, *et al., The American High School: Eighth Yearbook of the John Dewey Society* (New York: Harper & Brothers, 1946), p. 143.

6 Jack R. Frymier, "Physical Education in the Core Program," *National Association of Secondary School Principals Bulletin,* v. 39, No. 211, May, 1955, pp. 116–120.

meaningful, the activities of physical education may very well stand by themselves. Relationships with the broad fields of learning are in some instances necessary and important, but in many other instances are, of necessity, highly artificial, trumped up, and unmeaningful. Actual relationships should exist for integration; relationships should not be *created* or manufactured.

Pupils in physical education are usually dressed and ready for activity of quite a different nature than they experience in the core program. Physical activity is different and the setting is different. Such change does not compartmentalize or fragment the experiences of youth unnecessarily. The uniqueness of class organization is orderly, logical, necessary, and valuable, and the learnings remain meaningful. Learning sports and games that better fit pupils for leisure and develop fitnesses are not provided for in other settings in the school. Other learnings concerning group planning, human relationships, democratic living and problem solving can be provided in other areas of the school. With the time squeeze that exists in physical education, primary efforts must be exerted in providing the unique experiences that are available to pupils through physical education. Physical education *is not* primarily the "whole child" in planning, decision making, discussion, and intellectual problem solving. It *is* primarily the "whole child" in learning, doing, and performing invaluable specific types of activity. For some types of learning, the core is important in providing relationships between various fields of *knowledge*. These relationships are not often as vital in physical education. The core approach is undoubtedly valuable and needed for some kinds of learnings; it provides interest and relationships particularly in the area of social and personal problems. But in physical education, development may take place better outside the core. The unique contributions to the growth and development of pupils through physical education experiences should remain undiluted, and, in fact should be strengthened.

A graphic representation, Figure 9-1, may serve to clarify the relationship. This figure shows that as the physical education circle moves into or under or is further eclipsed by the larger circle, less and less time and emphasis are apt to be possible for developing organic power and vitality and the important neuromuscular skills in games, sports, and dance. Smith, Stanley and Shores have pointed out some of the limitations of the core curriculum that support the

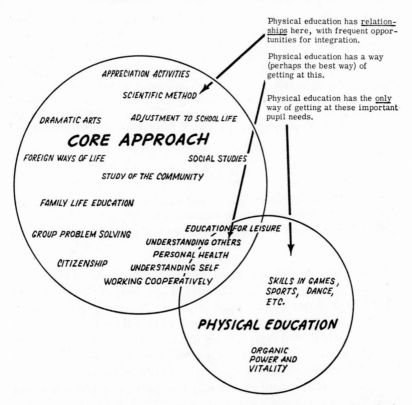

Fig. 9-1. *The objectives of the core programs do not completely eclipse physical education. Physical education uniquely emphasizes the development of the individual's strength, endurance, flexibility, and skill in bodily movements for work and leisure; it stresses uniquely the development of skills, understandings, and appreciations in sports, games, and dance.*

caution of the authors: [7]

The core of the curriculum, although of first importance, is not the whole of it. A well-rounded education should result in several types of learning products: skill in the manipulation of things; skill in the manipulation of ideas, in the sense of logical analysis; skill in the processes of group discussion and cooperation and in personal relations with others; the understanding of ideas, both in the sense of their consequences in action and of their place in a conceptual system; appreciations, in the sense of

[7] B. Othanel Smith, William O. Standley, and J. Harlan Shores, *Fundamentals of Curriculum Development*, rev. ed. (Yonkers-on-Hudson, New York: World Book Company, 1957), p. 647.

adequate standards of the good and the beautiful and of sound personal tastes and enjoyments. Undoubtedly, much can be done in the core program to develop these capacities and skills. Some of them, however, require specific attention outside the core. The development of sound personal tastes and enjoyments is one such case. Skill in the intellectual, as well as the physical sense, requires practice and drill that cannot be obtained incidentally in the core program. The principle that skills should be learned in connection with use in sound doctrine, but that principle does not preclude special periods devoted to practice of needed skills and abilities.

QUESTIONS

How would you reinterpret, reword, and reorganize one given set of major objectives so that they conform to the suggestions made?

What do you believe is the proper relationship of physical education to core programs?

Health and the objectives of physical education. Let us consider the question regarding the uses of the word health in a statement of the major objectives of physical education. Some courses of study and texts mention the word while others do not. Many school principals and superintendents are confused if not incredulous when they are told: "Health is not an objective of physical education." More controversial is whether health is a factor to be considered in a restatement of the major objectives of physical education.

Defending the thesis that the program of physical education should be constructed and conducted in such ways as to ignore the health of the individual is difficult; but, physical education is not limited to health outcomes alone. If one assumes that health is "a state of complete physical, mental and social well-being and not merely the absence of disease or infirmity," [8] then physical education is partially interested in health. If we accept this comprehensive view, health becomes *one* of the outcomes of physical education. The program of physical education and the way it is conducted should consider, among other things, the health of the individual. Under such a program health includes the various pseudo-categories, mental and social, as well as physical.

[8] Constitution of the World Health Organization, p. 3, from *Chronicle of the World Health Organization*, 1:29–43 (1947).

The reasons for this discussion are threefold. *First,* many experienced teachers have maintained that the program of physical education and the way it is taught should *ignore* health considerations, implications, and outcomes. *Second,* some school administrators are confused by the point of view just mentioned and as a result assume still further biases against physical education. *Third,* since health is a larger goal than organic vigor and is more easily comprehended and related to such larger purposes of life as self-realization, desirable human relationships, and civic responsibility, then the reinterpretation of the objectives of physical education can include the relationship between physical education and the individual's health. The conscientious effort, the literary gymnastics, and almost fearful avoidance that some speakers and writers demonstrate as they try to discuss the major objectives of physical education without mentioning the word *health* is astonishing and regrettable.

Appropriate programs show variation. As was noted earlier, the same objectives can be achieved through the pursuit of differing programs. There is no one best program of physical education, but many *programs.* A comprehensive, graded program that would best fit conditions and circumstances throughout the country cannot be recommended. Local conditions would prevent the universal adoption of any proposed program. The next chapter will discuss some of the forces that tend to make programs different in various schools and communities. Several texts give a more detailed treatment of the physical education curriculum. These books consider specific activities and their suitability and recommended time allotments for various developmental levels. These books may be regarded as basic guides in program-building.

SAMPLE TEST ITEMS

True-False

1. The appointment of a course of study committee is not needed if no persons in the schools thoroughly understand physical education.

2. The teacher of physical education can count on the principal's recognizing the need for a revised course of study, if one is needed.

3. The trend is toward liberalizing the content of a course of study in physical education.

4. The course of study does not need to be revised more frequently than every five years, on the average.

5. Too frequently the course of study is merely an adult-conceived program of activities designed for living in the present adult's world as he knows it.

6. Our idea of "the good life" today is identical with that of a generation ago.

7. A teacher of physical education is less expert in that position if he has to spend some of his time in integration.

8. New conditions in this country suggest the need for a reinterpretation of the major objectives of physical education.

9. Agreement is unanimous that health is an objective of physical education.

10. A course of study should be so organized and presented that it recognizes the soundest principles of the psychology of learning.

11. A course of study in physical education should provide for some activities that stimulate courage and seem adventuresome to the pupil.

12. A course of study in physical education should emphasize a balance of the capacities of the pupil rather than narrow specialization in one type of capacity.

13. A sound philosophy of physical education must underlie the building of a course of study in physical education.

14. Physical education programs should be based, for the most part, on traditional practices.

15. Physical education programs should not provide a wide range of individual choices in different types of activity because teachers know better than pupils which experiences are of most value.

16. Written course guides should be very detailed and describe precise plans for daily lessons.

17. Teachers of physical education should plan programs without consulting the administrator because including him in planning may indicate weakness on the part of the teachers.

18. Program planning should always result in the teacher's work being simplified.

19. If two schools adopt the same objectives, their programs should be identical.

20. A revised program should be considered as an experiment to be evaluated, revised and reimplemented.

21. The core approach represents a fundamental reorganization of the secondary school curriculum.

22. Some attempts at integration may be artificial and unmeaningful.

23. Health should not be included among the objectives of physical education.

24. The desire to appear to be consistent prevents some person from keeping abreast of the times.

25. Changed conditions and circumstances mean changed programs.

BIBLIOGRAPHY

Alberty, Harold, *Reorganizing the High School Curriculum,* Rev. Ed. New York: The Macmillan Company, 1953.

American Association for Health, Physical Education, and Recreation, *Physical Education for High School Students.* Washington, D. C.: National Education Association, 1955.

American Association of School Administrators, *American School Curriculum, Thirty-first Yearbook.* Washington, D. C.: The National Education Association, 1953.

Anderson, Vernon E., *Principles and Procedures of Curriculum Improvement.* New York: The Ronald Press Company, 1956.

Association for Supervision and Curriculum Development, *A Look at Continuity in the School Program, 1958 Yearbook.* Washington, D. C.: The National Education Association, 1958.

Association for Supervision and Curriculum Development, *Research for Curriculum Improvement, 1957 Yearbook.* Washington, D. C.: National Education Association, 1957.

Benne, Kenneth D., and Bozidar Muntyan, *Human Relations in Curriculum Change: Selected Readings with Especial Emphasis on Group Development.* New York: The Dryden Press, Inc., 1951.

Cassidy, Rosalind, *Curriculum Development in Physical Education.* New York: Harper & Brothers, 1954.

Cowell, Charles Clarence, and Helen W. Hazelton, *Curriculum Designs in Physical Education.* Englewood Cliffs, N. J.: Prentice-Hall, Inc., 1955.

Douglass, Harl R., *The High School Curriculum.* New York: The Ronald Press Company, 1956.

Faunce, Roland C., and Nelson L. Bossing, *Developing the Core Curriculum,* 2nd ed. Englewood Cliffs, N. J.: Prentice-Hall, Inc., 1958.

Frymier, Jack R., "Physical Education in the Core Program," *National Association Secondary School Principals Bulletin,* 39:116–20 (May 1955).

Hughes, William Leonard, and Esther French, *The Administration of Physical Education for Schools and Colleges.* New York: A. S. Barnes, 1954.

Krebs, R. E., "Using Special Subject Teachers as Resource People in a Core Program," *National Association Secondary School Principals Bulletin,* 40:146–8 (May 1956).

Krug, Edward A., *Curriculum Planning.* New York: Harper & Brothers, 1957.

National Society for the Study of Education, *Adapting the Secondary School Program to the Needs of Youth, Fifty-second Yearbook,* Part I.   Chicago: University of Chicago Press, 1953.

Romine, Stephen A., *Building the High School Curriculum.*   New York: The Ronald Press Company, 1954.

Saylor, J. Galen, and William M. Alexander, *Curriculum Planning for Better Teaching and Learning.*   New York: Rinehart and Company, Inc., 1956.

Simons, B. L., "Obstacles to Curriculum Development," *National Association Secondary School Principals Bulletin,* 43:26–9 (February 1959).

Smith, B. Othanel, William O. Standley and J. Harlan Shores, *Fundamentals of Curriculum Development.*   New York: World Book Company, 1957.

Voltmer, Edward Frank, and Arthur A. Esslinger, *The Organization and Administration of Physical Education,* 3rd Edition.   New York: Appleton-Century-Crofts, Inc., 1958.

Williams, Jesse Feiring, *The Principles of Physical Education.*   Philadelphia: W. B. Saunders Co., 1958.

Williams, Jesse Feiring, C. L. Brownell, and E. L. Vernier, *The Administration of Health Education and Physical Education.*   Philadelphia: W. B. Saunders Co., 1958.

10

Selecting student
experiences

*When an idea is hammered into an inflexible doctrine,
still another prejudice is born.*

EVERY TEACHER TRIES TO AVOID ERRORS OF JUDGMENT IN program-building and pupil guidance because mistakes may be harmful to students. Despite the best critical judgment of the teacher, an occasional error is only human. However, the more the teacher is aware of possible sources of error, the better he can guard against them.

At times the teacher has difficulty recalling that he takes *himself* to the task of building the program. What the teacher thinks, feels, and does largely determine the activities selected unless the committees assisting him in program-building overrule his judgment. What are some of the factors that cause the teacher to make errors in judgment?

Traits of heredity. Although the determined individual may accomplish wonders in overcoming his biological heritage, it does set limitations and serves as a basis for tendencies. If a person has given little thought to possible sources of errors in his judgment, little can be gained if he blames his heredity for his poor judgment! Such conditions as the teacher's health, certain types of physical defects, vitality, certain types of emotional stability, and intelligence may be partially related to biological inheritance. These qualities do not *directly* modify the teacher's part in building a program so much as they may by *indirect* influence.

The teacher in excellent health with great vitality may *inadvertently* select a program of activities that assumes the possession of these qualities to a similar degree, by the pupils who participate in the program. The teacher who has an inherited defect might inadvertently build a program that too obviously recognizes those pupils with physical defects. Such examples illustrate the need for recognizing heredity as a possible source of error in judgment, as a program is being constructed.

Personal experience. Teachers rely to a considerable degree upon their experience as one basis of program-building. This use of experience is justifiable if it is the kind of experience that has *educated* the teacher. Past experience is helpful if present conditions and circumstances also are fully considered. But if a teacher's experience is based solely upon his subjective judgments and his incidental observations, his experience is a curious mixture of truth and fancy. The plea here, then, is not for abandoning personal experience, but for extreme care in its use. It should be looked upon as only one preliminary source of ideas and not the final yardstick.

In any case, *tested* experience is a much more reliable guide than untested experience. Regrettably, some experienced teachers resort to untested experience as the sole justification for program-building. If this were in fact the only guide or the best guide in the construction of a program, we would still be teaching such activities as the exercises of Delsarte. The point is re-emphasized that changed times and changed conditions mean changed programs. The adults of tomorrow will find themselves in a world that differs from the world of today.

A different kind of experience that applies to both the mature and the novice teacher relates to life-experiences, apart from teaching. These, like other experiences, form many of the bases or sources of attitudes. Lack of a desire to understand and to be sympathetic, indifference, refusal to consider all possible factors basic to a decision, a desire for personal renown instead of consideration for the welfare of others are a few examples of attitudes that teachers may have acquired from life-experiences.

One traumatic experience, or an accumulation of experiences over a period of years, is often forceful enough to influence the teacher's selection of activities unless they are recognized and discounted. Teacher *A* tells of a serious injury incurred as a high school pupil while attempting to perform on parallel bars against his wishes. Later on when he became a teacher, he refused to include this type of activity in his physical education program at any grade level, regardless of other factors. He was asked in January to resign from his first position because he refused to cooperate with the administrator who advised and finally demanded that some apparatus work be offered. Teacher *B* relates that, beginning with junior high school and continuing through college, the physical education program to which he was exposed was the "here is the ball" type. These years of observing and experiencing an irresponsible program prejudiced him against the *game* type of program. He admits that during his first three years as a teacher, his programs of physical education were restricted to formal activities only. When we take the trouble to examine some of our experiences in the school, home, and street, we can better understand some of our attitudes and thus take the first step in guarding against errors in judgment arising from them.

The teacher's cultural background, his former associations, his pre-college education, his educations gleaned from the playgrounds, movies, alleys, market place, and church, all combine to help make him what he is. The prospective teacher does not automatically drop the influence of these kaleidoscopic experiences when he begins his undergraduate professional preparation. Four or five years of teacher education under the most favorable conditions result in effecting only some changes in attitudes. When the student becomes a teacher, the basis for his choices of activities often antedates the years in college. Unfortunate experiences in these previous years imperceptibly and negatively influence his judgment as a teacher, especially if he fails to recognize experiences as a possible source of poor judgment.

Professional education. The beginning teacher is also influenced in his program construction by his professional preparation. If he has attended a given institution, he may select a program of physical education that includes posture exercises, marching, calisthenics, and heavy apparatus because of the program and recommendations of the major professors in that institution. If he has attended another institution, the program he selects as a teacher is apt to consist of games and sports. If he has attended a third institution, his school program may be weighted with rhythmical pageants and recreational activities. The type of program with which a teacher is indoctrinated as a student-in-training may overbalance other factors. Sometimes the novice teacher's program is not a fair interpretation of his professional education. Not infrequently, the novice forgets the *modifying* and *limiting* remarks that accompanied a professor's proposed programs of physical education. On the other hand, a few students-in-training are indoctrinated beyond reason. Occasionally they are not warned that programs of physical education must be constructed with many factors in mind; at least, some young teachers forget that they were so warned.

The successful beginning teacher carefully evaluates his professional education as a vital influence in determining the program he constructs, and guards against using it indiscriminately. The chief responsibility of the young teacher is to interpret his professional education properly in terms of the pupils, school, and the community in which he is teaching. He should not feel disloyal if he adopts a type of program for a given situation that was not followed at his alma mater or recommended by his professors.

The beginning teacher has his own career to make. For this reason, there is a decided trend in teacher education to emphasize self-reliance, ingenuity, and initiative on the part of students-in-training.

Attitudes. In addition to attitudes that arise from traumatic experience or the accumulation of many experiences, a myriad of other attitudes arise from such sources as the teacher's education, his imitation of others, suggestions arising from such a medium as moving pictures, and from individual applications of and personal differentiations of the general, nonspecific attitudes of approach and avoidance. We are just beginning to recognize fully the major role that attitudes play in pupils' behavior and conduct and the absolute necessity therefore of helping them attain desirable attitudes. In most instances, the first step is for the teacher to ferret out and analyze his own attitudes. After isolating and identifying them, he may wish to modify them if he desires to decrease or eliminate prejudices, intolerances, and biases.

The teacher's attitudes toward teaching as a profession, children, the community, his own responsibilities and duties, and the purposes of education and physical education affect the kind of program he constructs. Once pauperized, unplanned programs of physical education were in existence because teachers lacked proper training. But today there is no reason for such an excuse. Inappropriate programs exist today partially because those who construct and conduct them do not care enough to be satisfied with only the best and to consider such qualifiers as *this* community, *this* school, *this* class, and *this* pupil.

What are the requisite attitudes of the teacher as a program-builder? Their number and variety are legion. Here are a few examples: a desire to know, appreciate, and understand the needs, potentialities, interests, peculiarities, and abilities of each pupil; a desire to serve the community by providing the best possible program for its children; unselfishness, sympathy, tolerance, and patience toward the pupils; alertness and progressiveness in following trends in physical education; a desire to adapt one's ideas and plans to those of the administration; and enthusiasm, courage, and firmness in working for the best interests of the child.

Too often a list of attitudes such as this is read without interpreting them in terms of action. Some teachers who lack the requisite attitudes reason something like this: "You can easily talk about being cooperative, enthusiastic, and interested in the pupils' welfare, but you don't know my job. You have no idea what I have to put up with." A few unanalytical teachers eagerly admit they have all the requisite attitudes, without bothering to find out if they actually possess these qualities. And, a few teachers regard teaching as a sort of trade. They regard any discussion of the necessity for self-analysis as so much theory. This general attitude is summed up in this oft-repeated dodge, "I'm just that way," the inference being that no change is possible, so why find out if change is needed.

Increasing attention is being given to the actual activities of teachers. The trend today is to find improved tools that measure these activities. The results of such research raise a still further question. Why does the teacher perform the activities he does and in the way he does?

The common answer to this question is that the teacher lacks a proper professional education. This statement is difficult to believe because one of the chief purposes of professional education today is to reform the attitudes of prospective teachers. The knowledges and skills acquired by the teacher-to-be miss their mark if he does not form appropriate attitudes. Of course, students-in-training can major for four or five years in physical education and still harbor attitudes after graduation that prevent the proper selection of activities. Inexperienced and experienced teachers alike must face this question if they are to work toward improved teaching: "Do I possess the requisite attitudes to take the responsibility of program-building?" This question digs into the problem of curriculum construction far deeper than a mere consideration of knowledge and skill in program-building. This question calls for some thorough-going self-analysis.

Too much has been written about the dangers of self-analysis. If the teacher refuses to face the facts and try to ferret out mistakes, how is he to improve? No attempt is made here to overlook pathological types and degrees of introspection. There is a definite attempt here to emphasize that much improvement in teaching is self-improvement, and that this is based in part upon self-analysis. Too often a maternalistic attitude is expressed by writers or speakers toward the young teacher's ability to engage in any fruitful self-analysis. Their idea seems to be that the inexperienced teacher cannot discover a substantial number or the types of his attitudes which serve as obstacles to improvement. Our experience shows, to the contrary, that even as early as the first semester of the junior year in college, students-in-training show considerable ability in isolating attitudes that may possibly warp their judgments in program-building.

For example, one young woman's ideas were strongly influenced by those of her high school physical education teacher. In spite of what her college professors said and what she read in textbooks, she found herself rejecting their ideas in favor of the ones formed by her high school teacher. Self-analysis helped her recognize this attitude as a possible source of error in judgment, and she can begin the process of reforming her attitude. This self-analysis helped her see that she *took herself* to the task and responsibility of program-building.

Beliefs. The sum-total of the teacher's experience, including reactions to environment, professional education, attitudes, and whatever influence his hereditary traits may have upon these factors, all influence his beliefs.   The young teacher may not have developed a seasoned philosophy of physical education; yet he has one, and it profoundly influences him as a program-builder.   How carefully he attacks the problem of program-building, how conscientious he is in continually evaluating the program, and how carefully he considers all the other forces and influences that are considered in program-building is affected by his purposes and values.

Some experienced teachers have never taken the time and trouble to prepare a written statement of their philosophy of physical education.   Unrecognized influences cause the teacher to construct a program based in part at least upon unvalidated assumptions and permit that unscientific process of taking-for-granted.   The teacher himself is unaware of the origin and basis of the feelings which cause his preferences.   Experienced teachers are invariably astounded at the puzzling results when they prepare detailed analyses of their respective philosophies of physical education.   Here are a few of the items in an analysis of one experienced teacher:

1. I do not believe in classification of pupils.
2. I believe in taking into account individual differences in pupils.
3. I consider vigorous athletic games much superior to physical education activities.
4. I consider the chief values of physical education to be exercise, strength, speed, endurance, and coordination.
5. The so-called social and character-building values of physical education are overrated.   They are best developed at home and out of school.
6. I believe in such disciplinary measures as giving the class calisthenics when they "get smart" in physical education class.
7. I believe in drills on fundamentals as the best way to learn.
8. I do not believe in testing.
9. The success of my program is judged in terms of how well the boys can play the games.
10. There is little you can do to improve a boy who "hasn't got it."
11. My obligations to the community are satisfied when I teach its pupils and turn out good athletic teams.
12. Our present generation is too soft on the boys.   I do not believe in making the junior high school boys' program any easier than the senior high school boys' program.
13. Boys do not know what they're interested in; they're not old enough.
14. My grades are based upon the boys' attitudes and how well they can play games.
15. I select a program that I know is good for all the boys in the class.

16. High school athletes should be excused for the semester in which they are participating.

17. I do not believe boys and girls should ever play together in the junior and senior high school.

18. I believe a boy should show considerable improvement in a game before letting him take up another game.

19. The physical education period should be spent in work, not recreation.

This teacher not only found contradictions in his convictions, but by detailed analysis prepared himself to check the justification and soundness of his beliefs. It is not difficult to visualize the type of program this teacher had been using. A teacher's conception of the kind and degree of results he expects from physical education, and the type and scope of the values he places upon various areas in physical education, furnish a fairly good index of the type of program he would construct.

SAMPLE TEST ITEMS

True-False

1. A teacher's biological heritage has considerable influence on his selection of activities.

2. Experience automatically renders the teacher capable of wisely selecting activities for a physical education program.

3. Experiences in life automatically render the physical education teacher capable of making satisfactory selections of activities in program-building.

4. Recognition of possible sources of attitudes that may affect judgment is a first step in guarding against such influences.

5. A teacher's professional education may be of such a nature that he selects inappropriate activities for his program.

6. Some prospective teachers ignore the limitations of programs of physical education mentioned in texts and by their professors.

7. The act of selecting activities is governed not by the teacher's knowledge but by his attitudes.

8. The teacher should not engage in self-analysis because it is dangerous.

9. Students-in-training are too immature to recognize personal attitudes that may interfere with the satisfactory construction of a course of study in physical education.

10. Young teachers do not possess a philosophy of physical education.

11. Experience is bound to be a wise teacher in guiding one through the process of selecting activities for his physical education program.

12. Your professional education can give you biases and prejudices toward certain types of activities.

13. One can get all the data he needs for building his program by consulting his professors and reading the standard texts in the field.

14. One's knowledge governs his selection of activities.

15. Recognizing the source of one's own attitudes by self-analysis is a valuable type of training.

BIBLIOGRAPHY

Anderson, G. Lester, and Arthur I. Gates, "The General Nature of Learning," *National Society for the Study of Education, Forty-ninth Yearbook,* Part I. Chicago: University of Chicago Press, 1950.

Andrews, Emily Russell, *et al., Physical Educations for Girls and Women.* Englewood Cliffs, N. J.: Prentice-Hall, Inc., 1955.

Bookwalter, Karl W., and Carolyn W. Bookwalter, *Fitness for Secondary School Youth.* Washington, D. C.: American Association for Health Physical Education and Recreation, 1956.

Brownell, Clifford Lee, and E. Patricia Hagman, *Physical Education— Foundations and Principles.* New York: The McGraw-Hill Book Company, Inc., 1951.

Cowell, Charles Clarence, *Scientific Foundations of Physical Education.* New York: Harper & Brothers, 1953.

Cowell, Charles C., and Helen W. Hazelton, *Curriculum Designs in Physical Education.* Englewood Cliffs, N. J.: Prentice-Hall, Inc., 1955.

Daniels, Arthur Simpson, *Adapted Physical Education: Principles and Practices of Physical Education for Exceptional Students.* New York: Harper & Brothers, 1955.

DeWitt, Raymond Talmadge, *Teaching Individual and Team Sports.* Englewood Cliffs, N. J.: Prentice-Hall, Inc., 1953.

Dexter, Genevie, *Teacher's Guide to Physical Education for Girls in High School.* Sacramento: Bureau of Textbooks and Publications, California State Department of Education, 1957.

Halsey, Elizabeth, *Physical Education for Children, A Developmental Program.* New York: Dryden Press (Holt), 1958.

Knapp, Clyde G., and E. Patricia Hagman, *Teaching Methods for Physical Education. A Textbook for Secondary School Teachers.* New York: The McGraw-Hill Book Company, Inc., 1953.

LaPorte, William Ralph, *The Physical Education Curriculum, A National Program.* Los Angeles: University of Southern California Press, 1957.

Loewendahl, Evelyn, *How to Develop Physical Functions in the Growing Individual.* New York: F. S. Croft & Company, 1954.

Meyers, Carlton R., "Suggested Criteria for the Selection of Program Content," *The Physical Educator,* 9:103–105 (December, 1952).

Nash, Jay B., "Physical Education and Recreation for Life Adjustment," *Education for Life Adjustment: Its Meaning and Implementation,* Harl R. Douglas, Editor. New York: The Ronald Press Company, 1950, 267–289.

Part Five

YOUR WAYS OF TEACHING:
how is physical education taught?

11

Principles, methods, and techniques

*Ignoring chart and compass, some teachers are adrift
in physical education.*

WHEN W. G. ANDERSON WROTE HIS BEST METHODS OF TEACH-
ing Gymnastics [1] in 1896, he advocated the formulation
and use of "principles in Physical Education." He spoke of the
need of "principles of teaching" in this field. This marked the
beginning of the recognition that no physical educator should start
out on the teaching voyage without chart or compass. Much time
and persuasive effort, however, were needed before these suggestions
were widely accepted.

Previous to 1896, each person in the field was a law unto himself.
What he *believed* about teaching, about program, and about administration was the way it was done in *his* school! Then, men like
W. G. Anderson saw that such practice was chaotic and would lead
to disintegration of the budding profession. Surely, some *guides-to-
action* might be worked out over the years.

[1] W. G. Anderson, *Best Methods of Teaching Gymnastics* (New York: Hinds,
Noble & Eldredge, 1896), pp. 7–29.

PRINCIPLES AND INDIVIDUAL BELIEFS

For a beginning teacher in physical education, today, to follow only that which he believed would be as senseless and disastrous as for some novice spaceman to start for the moon with nothing but his vehicle and his belief that he could reach it. For, many thousands of teachers in physical education since 1896 have taught a good many years, in a good many differing situations, with a good many different youngsters and arrived at similar conclusions. The similarity of these conclusions built *principles* of teaching, or guides-to-action.

Sources of principles. The principles of teaching in the following chapters came from five general sources. *First,* 2,476 secondary school teachers replied to three questions: What do you do that represents competency? What do you do that goes beyond the call of duty? What do you do that aspires toward reaching the highest level of being an effective teacher? Thousands of detailed items were sent in. These were placed in categories that served as the basis of generalizations in the form of guides-to-action. *Second,* textbooks, articles, and researches on teaching, some of them dating back to the turn of the century, were searched for guides-to-action. The most consistent and best supported were incorporated in the list of principles. *Third,* college department heads in nineteen fields of human activity and knowledge recommended authoritative sources of facts or near-facts pertaining to physical education and teaching. A total of 6,459 (most of them near-facts) items were garnered, classified, generalized into guides-to-action. *Fourth,* beginning with 1940 and continuing up to the present moment, several graduate classes of experienced teachers in a course devoted to the critical analysis of principles examined the professional literature for principles. These were subjected to criteria of acceptability, and subsequent revisions were made. To these were added acceptable principles which were formulated to fill existing gaps in aspects of the field for which no principles existed. *Fifth,* teachers and teacher educators who have used this textbook since 1941 have sent in proposals regarding other possible principles, and those meeting the criteria have been incorporated.

These sources should assure the reader that the guides-to-action are not the just result of armchair thinking, as fruitful as that may be in forming generalizations. At the same time, we have roughly indicated some things about a principle which suggest that we have come to closer grips with its meaning.

Definition and purpose of principles. Pull out of the dictionary the nineteen definitions descriptive of principle. Here are some: rule of action, generalization indicating action, basic proposition denoting action, conclusion exercising an influence to act or on action, a rule consistently directing action. These descriptive phrases imply that the rule or generalization is based on truth or the nearest we have to available and acceptable truth.

The meaning of principle is: *A statement of belief used as a guide to action,* based on generalizations accruing from (1) *appropriate facts resulting from scientific methods,* (2) *outcomes of the philosophic process,* (3) *certain consistent experiences of the race or profession,* and (4) *man's relevant insight and intuitions.*

The *purpose* of a physical education principle is twofold: to better insure *consistency* (a) in acquiring goals and (b) in the practice of physical education.

Principles, not how to's. Principles do not purport to tell the teacher *how* to teach. Four decades ago, prospective teachers were taught literally thousands of *techniques* of teaching. Later, *methods* of teaching were of great concern. Yet, the emphasis was still on how to. Today, the emphasis is on principles or guides-to-action. Principles constitute one of the foundations of methods. They are one of the foundations of purposes. They form the pathway that leads toward ends or goals. Every principle of teaching *leads toward an objective* or goal of physical education. When the application of a principle is the concern of a teacher, the principle becomes a temporary goal, but most of the time principles are *means to* ends.

Principles are formulated by people. Once they are applied, they in turn react on people, not only on the student but also on the teacher and what he does, as well as on some of the people in the community (at least indirectly). That is, principles have a *relationship function between people and things.* And, in the case of principles limited to people, they have a relationship function *between* and *among* people.

One concept which beginning teachers should learn before they teach is that principles are not permanent or static. As soon as the *underlying* facts and near-facts change, the principle changes. The major student will do well to think of these guides-to-action as the best we have, but because we have them, they are the *beginning* of their own revision or elimination.

The worth or value of a principle depends on its purpose and its application. Obviously, one could not say that a principle was valueless merely because it did not result in solving some problem in one situation.

A principle is important or significant more because of what it *implies* as it is applied than because of the facts supporting it. It is not of importance because it is a principle but because of what it *makes possible*. Think of the improved teaching which principles can help persons attain who lack the *knack* of teaching, if they only follow these guides!

Although the best supported principles usually are based on scientifically-determined facts, no principle is scientific. The formulation of a principle, as one generalizes upon the supporting facts and near-facts, is a *philosophic* process. Which principle to select for use in a given situation is a *subjective* decision. When and how to apply it also is a *subjective* process. Principles operate toward obtaining some good, another philosophical concern. Principles cannot take on the indifference of science. The point is not that principles comfortably bask in the sunlight of being unscientific. Rather, it is that principles are only the best we have as guides and, they are only the beginning.

The mature teacher must know the facts that underlie a principle. The curious beginning teacher also might want to know what lies beneath a principle. The thinking that led to the amassing of facts and near-facts remain connected with the principle. This thinking is actually part of the principle.

Principles are not levelers-of-thinking. Two persons could look at the same principle and not only think differently about it but apply it in quite different ways. In spite of the fact that principles emerge from *discontent* over failure, confusion, and waste, professional persons of equal caliber may disagree as to the value of a given principle. A good deal of this disagreement stems from the heavy influence of local situations. A principle can be stable in one situation and explosive in another!

Wisdom is needed in the application of principles.   The consequences of this application may be professionally fatal to he who
applies it in a given situation.   Local conditions and circumstances
must be considered.   Principles do not command.   They may be
suitable in this place, at this time, with these persons but not suitable in a neighboring situation.

A principle brings together what should be with what is.   This
is always a difficult, risky responsibility.   The practical person knows
what is and usually does not want it changed.   The thinker tends
to know what should be and usually would like to see it applied.
The physical educator must combine these two views, as he applies
principles.   The difficulties and the risks are worth the effort.   For,
the selection and application of principles form one of the most
powerful forces in determining professional destiny.

Principles guide the profession in what it does.   They are based
on the closest approximation to truth that we have and know.
They emerge as a result of the best kind of thinking we know how
to do.

One reason principles were slow in winning acceptance on the job
is that they involve *interpretation*.   This process is used when a
principle is formulated.   It also is employed when a prospective
user considers needed action.   Interpretation is a mental process
increasingly needed, yet almost neglected in the education of most
of us.   In fact, almost no one in schools and universities excepting
doctoral candidates (and their professors, it is hoped) even begin to
be aware of the need of interpretative skills and the almost total
lack of instruction pertaining thereto.

Avoiding confusion about the place of personal beliefs.   The
word belief has confused some persons in its connection with principle.   In their confusion they say in effect, "A belief is a belief, and
one is as good as another.   When it comes to teaching, you follow
your beliefs and I'll follow mine."   The purpose of formulating
principles in medicine, mathematics, and the various other fields
of human endeavor is to avoid the confusion and conflict of having
professional persons follow their own respective personal beliefs.
This latter idea would send any profession back to the days when
each professional man was a law unto himself.   Imagine no doctor
following the principles of medical practice!

A belief may be judged by three criteria: (1) the pragmatic one, namely, *what are the consequences* (large and small, to me and to others, now and later); (2) the realistic one, namely, *what is the amount and quality of the evidence* which supports the belief; (3) the idealistic one, namely, *what is the purpose* (and attached values) of this belief. And, sometimes another criterion is also used for idealism, namely, *what are the relationships of this belief;* that is, how does this belief relate to and interact with other facts, ideas, and beliefs?

A prospective teacher who says, "I'm going to follow my own beliefs about teaching and bypass any principles of teaching which are given in class, by excellent teachers, and in books; these guides to action may be all right for some people, but I'm going to use my own head," should ask himself: Would I go to a *novice* physician, *beginning* surgeon, *inexperienced* engineer, for professional help who took this same point of view?

Again, let us emphasize that principles are *guides,* not demands, *to action.* Even the secondary principles of teaching (a few of which are given in the ensuing chapters) are meant simply as *guides.* By way of explanation, secondary principles are smaller in scope than are principles. Because statements of secondary principles cover less scope, they are more concrete. Thus, they may be mistaken by the beginning teacher for how-to's. At the other end of the scale, the larger in scope a statement of a principle becomes, the more general, vague, and indefinite it becomes. Principles vary in scope and can be made so small that they become teacher *activities,* but they still avoid telling the teacher *how to* perform the teacher activities.

The attempt has been made in the following chapter to make the scope of a principle proportionate to the *quality and quantity of the evidence* which supports that principle. The scope of a principle also has been adjusted to the estimated degree of certainty we have that the principle may be acceptably applied in most situations. The larger and looser a principle, the wider the space between the guide-lines and thus the greater freedom of action. This wider scope permits opportunity for more varied interpretations of what to do in a given situation. Thus, large principles have strong, wide support in facts or near-facts.

APPLICATION OF PRINCIPLES

In spite of other views to the contrary, the present authors do not believe that principles should be applied no matter how much they may be needed if the local situation will spell disaster or defeat for physical education or for those who teach it in that situation.

Principles are the guides that indicate action that *should* take place. Yet, some physical educators who pride themselves on being practical persons even fail to make use of principles of body movement! Ignoring principles permits faulty principles to go unexamined. Defensible principles go unused.

Some obstacles to application. Here are some of the reasons principles are not applied:

1. *Lack of knowledge.* Some professional workers do not know about principles. Regardless of blame or reasons, they are uninformed.

2. *Negative attitudes.* Some physical educators who are fully informed, *fail to use principles.*

3. *Nervous system resistance.* Some practitioners who are informed and have no particular negative attitudes, are unable to overcome the resistance of the nervous system to change to the new. They find reasons for continuing the old system without the use of principles.

4. *Immaturity.* Some professional persons do not mature emotionally and socially as they grow up in other ways. They seem *unable to accept responsibility* in proportion to their abilities; they are self-centered, consider themselves exceptions—resenting regulations, and show other signs of professional immaturity. Such persons have motor skills but not the kind of mental-social skills needed to select and apply principles.

5. *"Anti-Tradition" complex.* Some teachers object strongly to the established order when it interferes with their desire to be different and to reject anything that has been handed down in the past. They eagerly accept advice to follow their own beliefs.

6. *Local conditions.* Sometimes local conditions contradict the application of certain principles. This is used as an outright alibi to avoid using all principles. (Local conditions include finance, persons, and facilities.)

7. *Timing.* The use of a given principle may be ill-advised "at this time."

8. *Personality conflicts.* Sometimes the only obstacle to the application of principles is the familiar fact that two fine persons (e.g., a physical educator and a principal) permit their apparent mutual irritation to prevent the improvement of physical education.

9. *Philosophy.* The professional person's philosophy may be an obstacle. Philosophy is an even greater obstacle if it is not formulated and examined.

Aids to application. Application (use) of a principle in physical education is *an operation of establishing and maintaining relationships between the principle and the local situation* (which includes persons and things). Broadly conceived, this application also includes *noting results in a reflective way and perhaps, in turn, adjusting the principle itself.* Thus, application of a principle resembles the kind of operation of relationships experienced in some other activities in life. *It demands abilities similar to those required in operations of relationships in these other activities,* e.g., getting along with persons.

Certainly, application of principles includes the opposite of the obstacles listed above: *knowledge, affirmative attitudes; overcoming the resistance of* one's nervous system, *maturity* (including cooperativeness); *recognizing that tradition has passed on some desirable things; accepting negative local conditions with poise, with ingenuity and determination to improve* when the time is right, and *using affirmative local conditions; keeping professional improvement above small bickerings* by recognizing that perhaps one's own *personality may need rounding;* and, *examining critically one's own philosophy* of physical education.

In addition, the implementation of principles demands *intelligence and effort.* Intelligence and effort are both needed to *select* and *use* the right principle—and to evaluate—and to re-examine the principle.

The practical use of principles requires *skill and judgment.* As in different parts of "the good life," principles may compete for primacy. Which one to select *requires judgment.* Applying a principle *requires skill in selling, persuasion, diplomacy;* for example, persuasive skill is needed if a principle of physical education conflicts with a principle of school administration.

Criteria for applying principles. Here are a few criteria which the teacher might use to prepare himself to apply principles.

1. Can the principle be accomplished?
2. Is it feasible?
3. Do I have the ability to put it over?
4. Is this principle *the* one to do this particular job?
5. Should I consult with someone? If so, whom?
6. What does the selected principle demand of me and the situation?
7. How shall I start to apply it?
8. Judging from the underlying facts, what is the real purpose of this principle?
9. Precisely what outcomes may I expect? What unwanted consequences may happen?
10. What support do I have?

METHODS AND TECHNIQUES OF TEACHING

How shall one teach? Some intending teachers now may have the thought, "At last! Now we're going to discuss what I want to know. How do I teach? What methods shall I use?" Some decades ago, most books devoted to teaching in physical education emphasized how-to. But when the college students then preparing to be teachers began to gain teaching experience, they realized that the authors of such books and the instructors who followed them, were mistaken. Granting them the best intentions, these persons simply had no way of knowing the *students* a given teacher had in the various classes. These authorities had no way of knowing the *school* in which a given teacher taught, not to mention the administration and its *policies.* The textbook writers and the professors had no way of knowing the *community* in which a given teacher taught. Nor could they know the type of *program* that fitted the local situation.

Thus, these young teachers, as they matured, vowed that this well-intentioned false emphasis should not be continued in the teacher-training departments. As the protest grew and as some of these critical young persons became teacher educators, the domination of how-to gradually disintegrated. Today it is virtually extinct.

Methods of teaching. Let us move closer to teaching methods. *First,* a method of teaching is a *general way of guiding and control-*

ling learning experiences. Like principles, methods vary in scope. Some are large-scale, such as the traditional lecture method. Some are refinements of a larger method; for example, the demonstration is a refinement of the method usually called the use of sensory (audio-visual) aids. As methods are broken down into small ways of teaching, they are called *techniques* (another kind of technique of teaching will be discussed later).

There is not and should not be anything sacrosanct about any method of teaching. As such devices as TV, tape recording machines, and other attention-getting devices are invented, teaching methods will and should incorporate those that aid teaching. As researchers and educators produce new ideas about how to make teaching more effective, one's repertoire of methods can be expanded. Young teachers never visualize themselves as old-fashioned, behind-the-times, or archaic. But look around you!

Kinds of methods. The teacher is helped in his effort to help the student learn by having quite a variety of methods from which to choose. While some methods lend themselves better to certain subjects than others, an imaginative teacher can use most of the methods. Those listed below have been used successfully by many teachers. These methods have been used by fitting the method to the students, to the purposes one is teaching, to what one is teaching, to where one is teaching (some communities have preferences), and to one's own capabilities and talents. After the novice begins to feel some confidence, he should begin gradually to try out, modify, and adapt different methods to the task at hand. Such gross experimentation and professional development, at first, should be done with help and advice from an effective and experienced teacher.

What, then, are some of the methods from which to select a method? Some of these are so well known they will be only mentioned: (1) *telling;* (2) *explaining;* (3) *questioning* (sometimes called the Socratic Method); (4) *answering student's questions;* (5) *demonstration* (some regard this as part of the next); (6) *use of sensory aids* (note the inference that in physical education other senses are used besides hearing and seeing); (7) *mechanical assistance* (here the teacher grasps the racquet, bat, or club and moves it; or, he grasps the student's arm and moves it); (8) *unit* (in this method the teacher organizes the semester's or year's program into logical or psychological blocks or units of work, placing similar experiences together; sometimes these units roughly parallel or are connected with units of work in academic subjects); (9) *project* (similar to the unit method except that the purposes of a project are more directly connected with students' objectives and interests; not infrequently the students suggest projects); (10) *laboratory* (geared to the point of view which the teacher tries to have accepted by the students that the physical education facilities, equipment and supplies constitute a laboratory; that it provides a chance to experiment with how one may learn most quickly, most surely, most easily; emphasis is placed on the student becoming aware of his needing help so he may accept teaching more easily); (11) *problem and problem-solving* (a method differing chiefly from the laboratory method in that the students become aware that they have problems related to performance; this is followed by engendering the attitude, "Now, how shall *we* go about solving this problem which I have?"); (12) *group* (techniques revolving around the group); (13) *formal and informal* (the short verbal commands given to a class with their immediate response in some prescribed manner and the informality of instruction given during the teaching of a game or sport; these two methods frequently refer to the ever-changing amount of social distance used by the teacher as the teaching situation changes); (14) *direct and indirect* (combination of methods used by the teacher in directing learning; as a rule most teachers teach skills in a direct, straight-forward manner but teach attitudes, for example, indirectly in a tactful and suggestive manner); (15) *stop-the-game* (to have the activity cease before the teacher demonstrates, explains, or calls attention to something; usually not used unless several participants have common difficulties or unless a high level of performance is expected as in practice sessions connected with a varsity sport); (16) *keep-the-game-going* (not stopping the activity to correct; sometimes even the individual who needs help does not stop, as the teacher moves close enough to him to quietly give a suggestion).

What method to use. Such an array of methods to choose from may serve to confuse rather than to clarify. Some young teachers are discouraged from trying methods by seeing them performed inexpertly. A quicker way to become prejudiced against a given method is to try it out without knowing enough about it. Such a teacher hoodwinks himself as he says, "Don't tell me about that method. I tried it out. I know from experience!"

On the other hand, in a given situation, the chief method used might vary considerably among several teachers of equal effectiveness. And, each of them may be as successful as the other. How can this be? The following factors help a teacher determine which method he should use:

1. The teacher's skill in using a particular method.
2. The nature of the activity.
3. The backgrounds of the students.
4. The students' growth, development, and maturity levels.
5. The objectives set up for accomplishment.
6. The nature of the local school.
7. The make-up and type of community.
8. Possible departmental policies.
9. The theory or theories of learning used by the teacher.
10. Previous experience with these students.
11. The type of evaluation to be used.
12. The teacher's personality.
13. The availability of human and other aids.
14. The welfare of the students.
15. The teacher's philosophy of education and physical education.
16. The types of techniques in which the teacher is most expert.

Techniques of teaching. The *first* type of teaching technique has already been referred to, namely, a small part of a method. Having a student *demonstrate* a golf swing or a lay-up shot, is an example. A *second* type is the special *way* that the teacher uses a method and the *ways* he performs the thousand-and-one activities during the day.

Techniques of this *second* type are more difficult for beginning teachers to be natural about. The tendency is to commit the unforgivable sin of teaching, namely, straight imitation of one's former instructors or of a colleague. Techniques of this *second* type go to make up the teacher-personality which a teacher is always building. Most of these techniques are bits of behavior which he has acquired without knowing it through the years. As long as they do not detract from his teaching effectiveness, they help make him different from the other teachers.

The *second* type of technique also is typified by voice inflection, some distinctive movement of the hand, a particular kind of gesture, a certain look that comes when the teacher is displeased, or pleased, and so on.   After a teacher has had five years of experience, he has accumulated a good many of these techniques.

The student while he is still in college should make it a point to notice the techniques used by all instructors (and coaches).   He will see that the techniques which help the teacher are those which seem to be a part of him.   They fit his personality.   This is one reason why one does not imitate others in detailed manner any more than one would try to imitate the personalities of other persons.

In addition, the prospective teacher should observe high school teachers at work.   Of course, formal observation is required of the major student, but reference here is made to doing some observation on one's own, if this is permitted.   The major student also can ask for help from some of his instructors about being an effective teacher, one who can make his teaching come alive!

What is the best way of teaching?   This question has been bandied about until some of the answers dodge the sincerity of the major student's understandable concern about what *is* best.   Again, as in all issues, the matter is philosophical.   The pragmatist claims that he can give the immediate answer, "The best method or technique is the one that works best."   But, as a number of authorities in philosophy have pointed out, the pragmatic view leaves out an important consideration, namely, the *means* to accomplish the results.

Quite a different answer comes from he who says, "The best way of teaching is the one that serves the most worthy purpose."   This view is being considered more and more, even though higher purposes often mean less flashy consequences and the returns on "How did it work?" are less optimistic.

Still another answer comes from he who says, "That method or technique is best which enables the pupil, the teacher, and the profession to improve most."

Another answer says, "That way of teaching is best which scientific evidence shows to get the results most quickly and with least effort (expenditure of energy) by the teacher."

The major student may find that his instructor says that this is a somewhat fruitless question if the student is looking for a *universal* answer.   His instructor may make the point that *that* way of teaching is best which best *fits the situation,* gets the most worthy results, and is most challenging to the pupil. Understandably, it takes quite a period of time for the teacher to gather all this evidence. This may be desirable for, in the meantime, the young teacher finds that there are a good many best ways of teaching.

FORCES INFLUENCING WAYS OF TEACHING

Objectives influence methods and techniques. A discussion of teaching automatically assumes that worthwhile objectives have been agreed upon. An aim partially determines the quality of teaching, and objectives partially determine the types and directions of teaching techniques and methods.

Many years ago, the objectives of physical education were conceived to be the accomplishment of such attributes as military discipline and large muscles. Today, the objectives have changed to other acquirements. Teaching methods become quite different when the objectives set up for the pupils are changed to such a degree. The teacher, therefore, continually asks himself: "What is it I am trying to do for and with these students and why?" The objectives of physical education are the highway signs for ways of teaching.

Selecting an aim of physical education and formulating objectives are empty gestures if the teacher does not find *ways* of accomplishing or striving *toward* these worthy ends.

As mentioned in Chapter 2, purposes or objectives are powerful influences in determining the methods and techniques selected, how they are used, and the emphasis given to them. After an activity is selected, these questions arise: Why am I teaching this activity? Why am I teaching it now? Why did I select it for this class? Answers indicate ways of teaching.

Environment, an ever-present force. The child, as we find him in the schools, is the result of his environment, his inherited characteristics, plus what he does with these two factors. Environmental influences actually change the child's physical make-up—even affect his intelligence. The school should form one of the strongest of these environmental forces playing upon the child. And, the school environment could well be made a much more vital and permanent influence upon the pupil.

The student as a force in determining ways of teaching. The student must be viewed as an absorbing organism as well as a reacting one. Within the limits of basic inherited equipment, he reacts in terms of how he has been taught to react to the stimuli received from his environment. This absorbing of thousands of stimuli of many different kinds sets the stage for what the pupil is, does, and thinks (again disregarding his inheritance). Looking at this process from a different viewpoint, we see the environment throwing out *cues,* absorbed by one or more of the receiving mechanisms (senses). These in turn help suggest attitudes and behavior and sometimes profoundly stimulate the emotions.

The teacher's chief concern actually centers upon such questions as: Is the student getting it? Is he understanding it? Is he assimilating it? Is he developing? In the teacher's enthusiastic concentration upon answering these questions in the affirmative, he may find himself using techniques of instruction he never heard of, and using them effectively. Regardless of the name of a specific way of teaching, it is valueless if it does not produce desirable changes in the learner. Dewey said that no teaching has taken place unless the pupil has learned. Learning means that changes have taken place. Learning means changes in such phenomena as the pupil's nervous system, body build, his appreciations, emotional control, attitudes, and outlook. Granted, all changes occurring within the child are not due to school education or physical education. In fact, many *desirable* changes are correctly attributed to other agencies, forces, and conditions. But this does not free the school from its massive responsibility.

Teaching sometimes includes not only what the teacher does but what he fails to do. If there are certain desirable skills or other worthy outcomes of a given activity which are essential but which are not learned because the teacher has failed to teach them effectively, we are forced to place responsibility where it belongs. Teaching includes seeing and grasping the opportunity to teach all that should be taught.

Teaching begins with the student: what he knows, what he is, what he can do, what his interests are; and good teaching helps him learn and grow.

The teacher, a factor. Methods and techniques of instruction are adaptable also to the points of *emphasis* selected by the teacher. Teacher X may emphatically stress the accomplishment of the major objectives of physical education while the activities are actually regarded as incidental. Teacher Y selects skill execution as his point of emphasis while the activities themselves and their corresponding objectives receive little attention. Teacher Z emphasizes enjoyment and pleasure—the recreational aspects of activities. To him all else is incidental. Most teachers use all of these and other points of emphasis shifting from one to the other as the occasion and their best judgment indicate. In each case, however, teaching methods and techniques, are adapted to the emphases which the teacher believes should be made.

Ways of teaching also are adaptable to the *uses* which the teacher wishes to make of them. One teacher may use demonstration in an entirely different way and at different stages of the pupil's learning than another teacher. Teacher A may demonstrate several skills very slowly before the class has participated in the activity including these skills. Teacher B may have the squad leaders demonstrate the skills at normal speed only after the class shows or feels a need for them. Teacher C may show a moving picture of some outstanding performer executing these skills. All of these are teacher's adaptations of *demonstration*.

Teaching methods and techniques also are adaptable to the different *ideas* of the ways students learn. Some teachers believe that the best way to develop students is to let them participate (learn by doing) and teach each part of the activity in logical order. Other teachers will maintain that the activity elements be learned in order of increasing difficulty. Still other teachers hold that the activity be taught as a whole (let them learn to play the game by playing the game) and thus keep interest at a high level. Regardless of the various claims for the superiority of different ideas, teaching should be adapted to fit our best knowledge of the ways children learn best.

The teacher must create a type of environment in which the cues, atmosphere, and stimuli are favorable to learning. In fact, the pupil and teacher both help make and are parts of the environment. But the teacher has a far greater opportunity and responsibility for controlling it. Therefore, the task of the teacher is not only to manipulate the environment to facilitate learning but also to guide the student so that he in turn assists in creating an environment favorable to his own learning and the learnings of others.

Cues operate as suggesters to the individual because he has been *conditioned* to react in a given way. Some gymnasiums, physical education classes, and the teachers responsible for them suggest little else but disorganization and confusion.   Disorder, dirt, and lack of repair in the gymnasium; lack of preparation for and organization of the classes; a slovenly manner of speech, disorderly dress, and a lack of poise on the part of the teacher are a few negative cues. What a responsibility this places on the teacher!

Positive cues to *physical education* are found in: an open space; areas marked out for games; equipment in sight; cool air; light; the teacher dressed for activity; and the teacher who is visibly prepared and eager to get started.   The students have been conditioned by the teacher to this atmosphere of readiness and preparedness to respond to these cues that mean physical activity.

Observe how sensitive children are.   Bring in a substitute teacher unknown to them, and their resulting reactions are unpredictable! The students do not act like themselves.   Their attitudes and behavior are different.   Or, even making so slight a change as the regular teacher appearing before the class in street clothes results in observable reactions in students.

Principles influence ways of teaching.   More basic than these other forces that influence the ways one may teach are principles of teaching.   For principles can call attention to the importance of these other forces and suggest that they be made operative.

Although principles are the beginning of their own modification or elimination and should not be used if the time, place and conditions are not right, nevertheless, they are the best guides, based as they are on the best evidence available and on the tested and considered experience of many thousands of teachers.

Furthermore, principles give direction to teaching because they point toward goals or objectives.   Certainly, if a given objective becomes the center of attention (at least for the time being), the way in which the teacher teaches is apt to be quite dissimilar to that appropriate for attaining some other objective.

Without principles of teaching, the teacher must rely on his own untested personal beliefs as he considers ways of teaching, or, he must turn to some other teacher for his belief.   Sometimes it is easier to see the impact of this state of affairs if one considers some other profession such as medicine, as was done earlier in the chapter.

Let us now turn to a discussion of principles of teaching so that the prospective teacher may directly see how helpful they may be as guides to action.

12

Anticipating, planning, preparing

Unsound planning—erratic results

THREE IMMEDIATE TASKS FACE THE TEACHER WHO IS GETTING ready to face a class or to come to a new teaching situation. These three duties are: *anticipate, plan,* and *prepare.* These duties indicate work to be done well before school begins, or before the class begins. These duties assume that the teacher already knows (1) the *nature* of children of the age-range to be taught, as well as (2) the *natures* of these *individuals.* The teacher must also know (3) himself, (4) the thing he will be teaching, (5) the policies and regulations of the school, and (6) the expectations of the community. Some people would insist that two other things be included. The teacher must know (7) the physical education program, and (8) the profession with its standards and beliefs regarding best practices and conduct.

These eight enumerated items stand for not only that which the teacher should know but also for the corresponding abilities. Most of the preparation which these eight items require has been taken care of during the years spent in college, or as a part of one's professional experience and growth. They are more general than the three duties mentioned at the outset.

Let us consider some principles that guide the teacher as he *anticipates, plans,* and *prepares.*

PRINCIPLES OF ANTICIPATION

Before the prospective teacher has his first day of directed (practice) teaching, he can get a head start if he will learn that the main difference between the novice and the expert teacher is the ability to anticipate. No one was born with the ability to anticipate. It comes with trying, noting results, and improving in this ability.

The prospective teacher will be surprised at the speed with which he will learn to anticipate questions from the pupils, learning difficulties common to many in a class, possible disciplinary problems, possible accidents, and the like:

Let us formulate a few principles that will be helpful guides.[1]

▶ QUESTIONS. **The teacher should anticipate questions.** The novice teacher often is unprepared for appropriate pupil questions. Not to be able to give clear concise answers to sincere pertinent questions is embarrassing to any good teacher. Involved answers not only take time away from participation but confuse about as often as they clarify.

▶ LEARNING. **The teacher should anticipate learning difficulties.** The teacher discovers that certain activities and parts thereof are learned more slowly than others. He studies and experiments with ways of making such learnings easier to grasp. He apportions the time for various learnings and anticipates that some learnings are not retained as long as others. Talks with experienced teachers let the young teacher know whether the learning difficulties he observes are common or whether there may be some weaknesses in his teaching.

▶ DISCIPLINE. **The teacher should anticipate the possible need of discipline.** Few novices are apt to neglect this principle. In fact, the danger is to be *overly* conscious of it, with the resulting defensive, looking-for-trouble attitude. This principle includes such matters as anticipating the environmental set-up that may encourage misconduct. Anticipating possible causes of the need for discipline

---

[1] Sentences in boldface type in this and the following chapters are principles of teaching.

and then avoiding those causes is one reason expert teachers have so few disciplinary cases.

▶ ACCIDENTS. **The teacher should anticipate accidents which might occur in the shower-locker-dressing rooms, field, pool, and floor, and should provide safety measures to prevent them.** This principle like many principles may draw the remarks, "That's just good common sense. Anybody knows that." Judging from the number of accidents, this principle of teaching is either not known or not applied. Anticipating accidents refers not only to controlling the environment but also to controlling participation. The adventure inherent in many activities stems partially from the danger elements. To eliminate all of these elements from activities would be a mistake. Unpreventable accidents are bound to occur in physical education unless it is made a passive, insipid program. However, to fail to anticipate all *preventable* accidents and take precautionary measures is crass neglect.

▶ MOTIVATION. **The teacher should anticipate the need for motivation.** This principle of teaching applies not only to introducing a new activity and to participation, but also to parts of the activity and to knowledges and attitudes as well as to skills. At least one pupil in a class has to be motivated almost each time something is being taught. Sometimes all pupils may have to be motivated.

▶ FUTURE ACTIVITIES. **The teacher should anticipate the physical education program that will be used in the future.** The application of this principle helps give continuity, relatedness, and cohesion to the program. The principle is based on the psychological theorem that in teaching we *begin with* where the students are, what they can do, what they know. It includes the early dissemination of information and early use of bulletin board materials about the new activity before it actually is introduced. Also included is the use of lead-up activities, planning the month's, semester's, and year's programs, and providing for relationships between the school program of physical education and the community recreation program.

▶ FACILITIES, EQUIPMENT AND SUPPLIES. **The teacher should anticipate the facilities, supplies and equipment that will be needed.** This principle applies to the next class as well as to next year. It includes repair and replacement. The need to anticipate having facilities ready for use is also included. Not only do pupils form unwanted attitudes toward the hindsighted teacher but his failures too often require him to make unreasonable, last minute requests of the business office, the custodian, colleagues, and others.

▶ BACKGROUNDS OF THE PUPILS. **The teacher should find out in advance the general background of abilities of class members.** This principle aids in avoiding disciplinary problems, wasted time, negative attitudes. The principle helps indicate the amount of time and attention to be given to, and the type of introductory steps to be taken in presenting activities.

▶ THE PREVIOUS PROGRAM. **In many situations the new teacher should anticipate having to use, at the start, the program, class organization, and routines established by his predecessor or those now in operation in a school.** If a new teacher is to work in a department under the direction of another person, he will not expect to effect changes for some time. Should the teacher replace another in a school where only one teacher is hired to teach physical education, he should not anticipate the immediate inauguration of his own program. The teacher plans, of course, for the time when he can start his own program and set up better routines, class organization and management, keeping in mind the local school and community situations and realizing that any program must be flexible.

PRINCIPLES OF PLANNING

Before considering a few principles of planning by the teacher, the intending teacher should be warned about some mistakes that a good many novice teachers make with reference to planning. *First,* even though planning may be the next step after anticipating, the beginning teacher should avoid overplanning. Granted, some professional persons do not plan carefully enough, and better professional work should result from better planning. Nevertheless, a conscientious individual, with a flair for the planning *kind* of mental activity, can make too many plans, make too detailed plans and spend too much time in planning. For him, planning becomes *the* thing, his *major* concern and object of too much attention.

A *second* mistake that some prospective teachers may make is to carry out plans, regardless of a change in the situation. After all the time, effort, thinking, and work spent on planning, putting the plans into operation is the logical or sensible thing. Nevertheless, sometimes the intelligent thing is *not* to carry out some carefully made plans if the situation changes.

Third, related to the second is the mistake of insisting on initiating a planned action when evidence indicates it will not be accepted. After the lesson has been started and one sees that the plans are not going well, changes are indicated. Better give up a plan which encounters serious obstacles (which were not anticipated!) and which jeopardizes worth-while parts of the program or other plans that are working well, than to try to jam things through.

The reader will recognize that in all three of these mistakes, the crux of the matter is the *soundness* of one's judgment. Sometimes one would plan almost to the nth degree. Sometimes one would carry out a plan, regardless of a changed situation.

Let us consider a few principles of teaching related to planning.

▶ **The teacher should make his plans so that they fit into the local situation.** Following this guide may be difficult. Sometimes the new teacher may not be accustomed to the conditions which prevail. Sometimes he may be quite positive that others in the school are mistaken, or are following old-fashioned or low standards. Sometimes he feels frustrated in being unable to try some of his excellent ideas. One of the fastest ways for a beginner to become unwanted is to make plans that are counter to the *established* situation. The kind of plans he *can* make are those that demand some patience, plans that will lead to the possible eventual adoption of his good ideas. Put the plan away on the shelf and make plans for how it can be used later on. The principle here rests on a rather sound foundation: Keep Perspective! A young teacher *learns* that there are other good ideas, that sometimes it would be professionally disastrous to carry out some of his good ideas at this time.

▶ **The teacher should make plans geared to the present but also with an eye to the future.** This kind of planning better insures smoothness. For example, lead-up activities can be planned so that the transition to the main sport is one smooth operation. Or, they can also be planned so that each lead-up activity is an entity, a thing unto itself, and the student is not led psychologically toward the main sport.

▶ **The teacher should make plans that consider the status and welfare of every possible person who is or may become involved.** This is one of those principles that is so comprehensive and fine-sounding that everyone nods his head in agreement.   The word possible is the escape-door which enables one to accept this principle.   For, no teacher can actually plan anything so that *all* of these individuals are taken care of.   But, the status and welfare of as many people *as possible* can and should be considered in his plans.

▶ **The teacher should make plans in terms of practical conditions but these plans should be directed to the highest, finest accomplishment possible.**   This principle guides the teacher toward being realistic in facing obstacles and difficulties, yet at the same time it guides him toward gaining the best possible results from the situation.

▶ **The teacher should make plans so that when the class begins, efficiency and effectiveness of teaching will be better assured.**   This is another over-all type of principle that cuts across many of the principles which are presented in the following pages and chapters. Efficiency must be the mark that is characteristic of all the procedures that surround the actual instruction itself.   The teacher, of course, has to perform such procedures as starting class, calling the roll, organizing the class for the activity or activities being taught that day, and other noninstructional duties.   If the supplies, equipment, and fields or floor are not ready for immediate use, time is wasted.   Inefficient ways of calling roll waste further time.   Further moments slip away if the most efficient ways of getting the class members participating as soon as possible after the beginning of the class are not followed.   When one looks at the small number of minutes of active participation available, one sees that efficiency in noninstructional duties is a must.

▶ **The teacher should adjust all plans possible to the objectives for this day's lesson.**   Again the escape-door is the word possible. The point here is so obvious that its importance may be overlooked when getting ready for the actual class.   Usually other plans can be subordinated to those related to the realization of the day's class goals.   Or, better yet, these other plans can be made to augment those concerned with objectives.

▶ **The teacher should plan in terms of the students.**   Although previous principles alluded to the status and welfare of the student, he is so important in any planning that he is singled out in this important principle for special emphasis.   This guide to action reminds the teacher to *know* each of these particular pupils—their strengths and weaknesses in knowledges, skills, appreciations, and attitudes pertaining to the day's lesson as well as pertaining to the entire program of physical education. The principle reminds the teacher to consider the slow and fast learners, those with low or with high quality neuromuscular potential, those who are troubled and those who apparently are strong, well-adjusted personalities. That which the teacher does, thinks, says, and *is* should be *in terms of the learners!*

PRINCIPLES OF PREPARATION

The third obligation before learnings occur or before the class begins is preparation. After anticipating and planning, the teacher *prepares.* This means that the plans resulting from his anticipating certain conditions and circumstances are made into preparations. There are two distinct types of preparation, namely, personal preparations and technical preparations. We shall now consider some *sample* principles—guides to action for the teacher—regarding these two phases of the preparatory function of the teacher.

Principles of Personal Preparation

Although no line of distinction holds between personal and technical preparations (since the teacher does both of them), it is helpful to label acts of preparation that refer directly to the teacher as personal and those that refer more to physical education as technical.

▶ APPEARANCE. **The teacher should be prepared for each class from head to foot.** This statement includes clean, neat, appropriate costumes, hair, complexion. Mentioning such matters as clean teeth and fingernails hardly seems necessary, but appearance is too frequently neglected by teachers of physical education. Some of us apparently overlook or forget the fact that pupils are more strongly influenced by example than they are by precept.

Any experienced teacher who has, of absolute necessity, taken charge of a class in street clothes knows the effect this slight change has upon pupils' behavior. The teacher's costume is part of the environment that yields cues to pupil behavior.

The teacher should be dressed in a costume appropriate to the activity. He should also have changes in costumes so that they can be cleaned frequently.   Women teachers of physical education so far have paid more attention to such matters than have the men. The latter, however, are gradually turning to a variety of costumes made of materials that look neat and are easily and inexpensively cleaned, pressed, and mended.

Children, their parents, and other teachers also expect the teacher in physical education to have an easy, erect, poised bearing and carriage.   They expect him to have a fairly well-developed physique.

▶ **The modern physical educator should be careful of his appearance on occasions other than in physical education classes.** His clothes should be in appropriate style and fit, his shoes in good repair, cleaned and brushed (even at the heel!), shirts and blouses freshly laundered, and headgear becoming and appropriate.   These aspects of appearance are usually corrected, if they need to be, during the years as a college student.   Sometimes a beginning teacher forgets these basic essentials when the unfamiliar responsibilities of teaching are heaped upon his shoulders.

Fewer physical educators, who were college athletes, now wear their letter-sweaters in public except upon such informal occasions as picnics, hikes, and winter-sport parties.   On the street and in the classroom, the teacher does not call special attention to himself by such inappropriate dress.

As the novice prepares to be seen for the first time in the town or city in which he is to teach, as he prepares to meet his first class, he makes certain that his appearance is above reproach.   Thereafter, he makes it a *habit,* if it has not been made so previously.   The point is, not only does his grooming set an example and earn him respect, but it also insures his being accepted, it removes the possibility of immediate criticism or fun-poking, and it gives him a feeling of confidence and poise.

A group of superintendents of schools, called together to make suggestions for the improvement of tomorrow's physical educators, pointed out that they were often embarrassed by physical education men who appeared in the principal's office in sweat-suits.   Nothing short of a real emergency should prevent one's having appropriate dress.

▶ ATTITUDES.   **The teacher should meet his class with eagerness and affability.**   He should:

- demonstrate the possession of appropriate energy and forcefulness.
- maintain a friendly feeling toward pupils regardless of past experiences.
- be approachable, helpful, and sympathetic.
- be so prepared that he has a feeling of confidence as he gets ready to teach.
- show an interest in all of his students and demonstrate that he understands them.
- be courteous, kindly, and polite to pupils regardless of their attitudes toward him.
- be so well prepared that he permeates belief in the worth and value of his field, regardless of the attitudes of others toward this field.
- maintain a consistent attitude of fair dealing.
- be ever ready to show that he can be human yet objective in his dealings with students.

These ten examples of attitudes which the teacher has prepared himself to have and to hold, are sufficient to show that one must be *mature* if he is to be a teacher. And, when he fails to hold such attitudes, his immaturity betrays him.

▶ HEALTH. **The teacher should develop and maintain good health.** This broad principle might be divided into some subsidiary principles because, for the sake of discussion and writing, health often is divided into emotional, physical, and other aspects. But, within the individual there are no such categories. Many students, colleagues, and many persons in the general public expect the physical education teacher to have abundant health. Such an expectation arises from their observation. Most of them have never known anyone in the school or community who has such vigorous health as the physical educators seem to have. Such an observation is matched by the experience of most physical educators.

▶ PERSONALITY. **The teacher should develop and maintain a stable, likeable personality.** Personality and health are closely related. In fact, most authors of textbooks dealing with healthful living, list health as one of the essentials of good personality. And, certainly no one would deny that when health is considered as a unity, personality permeates the quality of that health.

Because of the particular duties which a teacher performs and because of the differences in ages of student and teacher, as well as the age-range of public school children, the belief that a good teacher has a good personality is not surprising. Further, the most consistently found factor in teaching success in the various researches is the teacher's personality. It seems to be *the* ingredient that counts most in making or breaking the teacher's efforts to help someone learn.

Principles of Technical Preparation

Like the lawyer, physician, or surgeon, the teacher must be prepared in more than personal ways. He must have the technical knowledges and skills which enable him to render *quality* of professional service.

Some of the principles that guide the physical educator in this phase of being prepared to meet the class refer to the child, some to the school, the department, the teaching-learning process, the program of physical education, and the provisions for the program such as facilities. And finally, some of these principles refer to the relationships with certified and noncertified associates in the school, the profession and in the community.

▶ INFORMATION ABOUT THE LEARNER. **The teacher should know the nature of those within the general age-range of his students, as well as specific and appropriate information about the individuals in his classes.** Part of this principle guides the teacher to recall pertinent facts from the fields of physiology and psychology. Part of it guides him to review the backgrounds, personalities, potential, and status of those he is about to teach.

This principle also is made intentionally broad enough to include technical preparations performed before the teacher begins to teach in a *new* situation. Obviously, that part of the principle referring to those whom he is to teach, guides the new teacher to find out general information about these learners beforehand from the principal or supervisor (or superintendent of schools in smaller communities). Such general information is replaced by specific facts about these young people and their backgrounds, as fast as good judgment permits. The good judgment of an inexperienced or a new teacher can be supplemented by that of the principal, supervisor, department head or some experienced teacher. Experienced teachers new to a situation are eager to get the most reliable information of this kind possible.

▶ INFORMATION ABOUT THE SCHOOL. **The teacher should know essential information about the school and its operation.** This principle also includes several parts. Some information about the school covers the organizational structure, the system of ordering materials, the general budget pattern, registration and scheduling, and the like. Such basic information is secured by each incoming new teacher. This kind of information tends to have few changes from year to year under a given administrator.

Another part of this principle refers to the rules and regulations of the school system, as well as the particular school. The following are examples: attendance matters; pupil traffic plans between classes; fire drills; teacher assignments during noon recess; teacher arrival time in the morning; first-aid and emergency care plans; disposition of those who appear to be ill; accident reporting and responsibility; handling of lost and found articles; school announcements; school assemblies; use of student helpers; readmission of pupils to classes after illness; annual reports; relationship with and reponsibilities for phases of the school health program.

Before meeting the class, the teacher should recall some pertinent rules and regulations. "Expect what *might* happen and know *beforehand* what to do," is a bit of wisdom that any experienced physical educator could give his novice colleague. This not only enables him to act sensibly, instantly and correctly but it also enables him to attend to the major task of teaching with much greater confidence. He *knows* what to do in all situations involving the rules, regulations, and policies of the school.

▶ INFORMATION ABOUT THE DEPARTMENT. **The teacher should know all appropriate information about the department.** As in the previous principle, this too refers to the advisability of the new teacher's knowing essential matters about the department before the first day of school. For example, the department relationship in the school's chain-of-command, the jurisdiction and responsibility of the department head and the staff members, and similar kinds of general information are all important.

Other necessary information applies more immediately to the teacher preparing to meet the next class. Here are some examples: the teacher's locker room duties; keeping of absence records, test scores, performance scores and estimates, and the like; time allowed for pupils preparing for class, showing, and preparing for the next class; responsibility for facilities, equipment, and supplies; disposition of those not dressed for activity; possible departmental regulations about types, colors, and styles of costumes; disposition of those assigned to the adaptive physical education program; common signs, symbols, and commands indicating routine pupil-response (such as fall in!); locker assignment, towel collection, and similar routines; the collection of fees and their disposition; the use of test results, and the like.

▶ THE TEACHER-LEARNING PROCESS. **The teacher should recall pertinent principles of teaching and of learning.** Here, again, we have a principle of teaching that embraces several parts. *First,* the teacher should recall those principles of teaching which are particularly pertinent in terms of his strengths and weakness. Also, he will recall those principles of learning which underlie learning and motor learning in particular. *Second,* he will consider those particular principles of teaching and learning, which apply to the class he will next meet. As every experienced teacher knows, classes have personalities. Some classes can be approached and taught by using principles which do not work with other classes. Thus, the teacher recalls the sorts of techniques, methods, and principles which usually work with particular classes. Classes in physical education also vary in their level of performance. Some aspects of learning will have to be emphasized with one group and other aspects with another class.

Third, the teacher should have in mind how the class will be called together, the ways activities will be presented the first day, ways of getting the group into activity, methods of explanation, demonstration and motivation, length of time spent in each activity or part thereof, how the groups or squads in the class will be changed from one activity to another, and how the class will be handled in the locker room before and after the activity period.

Mentioning these items at this time helps to emphasize the inseparable relationship between teaching and class management. Teachers, as they face their first day, wish they had begun some of the preparations during their college years!

The new teacher cannot select beforehand the teaching techniques that definitely fit the classes he meets for the first time. Even though he is fortified with previous information about these pupils and with knowledge of the community and school, still he does not *know* the pupils. On the other hand, this necessarily incomplete background does not mean that the teacher should face his classes with no particular teaching techniques in mind. Individuals differ, but they are also similar in many respects.

The new teacher with experience uses those techniques that

proved successful in previous situations, with changes to fit the local situation as far as he knows and senses it. He cautiously and alertly feels his way along.

▶ THE PROGRAM. **The teacher should know the elements and criteria of a good physical education program and know the details of that program which will meet the needs of the individuals in the class he will next teach.** Again we encounter a principle of teaching that is broad enough to embrace the teacher's professional preparation as well as his estimate of the kinds and intensities of the needs of the individuals in this class. The principle also is broad enough to include the best current views of professional leaders of what constitutes a good program. Furthermore, this principle includes the program of activities that will be taught to the class on a particular day.

▶ OBJECTIVES. **The teacher should recall the general objectives of physical education, the objectives of the department and the objectives for the semester and then consider the objectives for the activities to be learned as well as the objectives for the grade** (e.g., seniors), **class, and lesson.** And, with this background, **the teacher should consider the objectives which the class and individuals in it may have.**

This principle is rather self-evident without further elaboration, but a word is needed about cooperative planning in setting up objectives with the pupils.

A few educators believe that the novice and new teacher are taking chances in permitting students some experience in self-direction and self-expression. These educators believe that the best thing for the new teacher to do is to adopt measures that will keep the students well under control until the teacher has established himself. On the other hand, the first class meeting or two is not too early for the teacher to begin to establish a cooperative, friendly atmosphere. If classroom teachers can set up controlled situations that permit expression and planning during the first days of school, why cannot the physical education teacher do likewise? No final answer to this question is justifiable or sensible at this time. Too much depends upon the ability of the teacher and the type and background of the students. The teacher's job will be made both easier and more effective if both he and the students are working for the same goals in the day's lesson at least part of the period! Such matters also should enter into the teacher's thinking as he gets ready for the class.

▶ RELATED ESSENTIALS. **The teacher should check on the readiness, adequacy, and availability of all facilities, equipment, and supplies that will or might be used, and he should check on the time alloted.** The experienced teacher comes to learn that he is *responsible* for such preparations. Are the fields properly lined? Is the tape recorder, piano, TV, victrola, movie machine, or projector in good repair and ready to go? Are all facilities, equipment, and supplies free of hazards, serviceable, in good condition, and safe? Are balls inflated properly, goals and targets properly set, nets ready for play, the shower-dressing rooms clean and orderly? The time element mentioned in the principle is a reminder to check on the possible change in schedule. Special assemblies and other meetings are not uncommonly called at the last moment by the principal. The teacher must bother to find out for sure that his class at the 10:00 a.m. period is to be of usual length.

This principle also includes such simple but essential bits of preparation as to where the class will sit or stand, checking out and recording of equipment and supplies, foot traffic in the shower-dressing rooms, and the like.

Preparatory steps at the beginning of school also are included. For example, before the first class starts, a complete and detailed inventory is made of all office, gymnasium, pool, and field equipment and supplies, together with a report of the condition of each item. The teacher also obtains all necessary blanks, forms, roll books and the like before the first class starts. He ascertains the exact amount of money in the physical education budget and any restrictions that may apply to it if such information is available to him.

▶ PERSONAL RELATIONSHIPS. **The new teacher should exhibit tact, reserve, and good judgment.** He should avoid negative comparisons of this locality, this climate, this town, this school, with others. He also should avoid superlative statements of a complimentary nature. He knows he should avoid subjects of conversation that are directed at persons, personal affairs, financial affairs, religious matters, political parties, or one's alma mater. The new teacher is a master listener.

In the midst of all these preparations a teacher sometimes forgets one essential: namely, to begin the year right with his associates.

Although the adage, "First impressions are strongest," is not always true, beginning the year by creating poor impressions has no advantage. The novice may overlook the fact that he is judged severely by his colleagues as to appearance, behavior, and casual conversation. Many a young teacher starts the year with two strikes against him because of some innocent, thoughtless remark.

▶ **The new teacher should aim to establish and maintain cordial relations with the administration, his colleagues, the students, the janitor, and other employees.** The new teacher does not pattern his degree of cordiality after those who have served in this school before. He is pleasant but is also modest and reserved. He is as sincerely cordial to the janitor as he is to the principal—that is, his degree of cordiality does not vary with school station and rank. **He should avoid confidences.** He refrains from giving the appearance of trying to "get in" with the group of teachers who are returning to school. He shuns participating in whispered conversations. He avoids positive commitments and statements of his policies. No reasonable person expects a newcomer to know what his policies will be until he has had an opportunity to become familiar with the situation. This last sentence provides a sensible, justifiable answer to those old-timers who wish to pump or test the new teacher.

During the days or hours before school begins, the new teacher is sometimes told of the errors and mistakes of his predecessor. **Neither by word nor gesture does he indicate agreement in condemning his predecessor.** In fact, he should be prepared to keep the conversation on impersonal subjects. As a rule the persons who condemn the predecessor also will condemn the new teacher.

The new teacher should secure so many vital types of information that there remains no time for these taboo conversational subjects. Teachers familiar with the local schools are usually ready to give professional advice to the new teacher. It goes without saying that the new teacher does not follow all the advice given him, although he does not say so! He may tactfully gather several viewpoints. As a rule, this process can be done casually and, therefore, is carried on beyond the first days, weeks, and months of school.

▶ THE PROFESSION. **The teacher should recall and keep in mind the best for which his profession stands.** This step in his preparation for the next class refers to such matters as articles in professional periodicals appropriate to the coming lesson, ideas proposed by professional writers in books, discussions and talks heard at professional meetings, and the like. He should recall that the test of a professional person is the *quality* of his service, that personal information about pupils should be kept confidential (note the practice here by doctors, lawyers, and theologians), and that the welfare of the child is the eternal criterion of the worthiness of that which the teacher does. No existing professional code for physical educators, as of this date, covers the kind of ideals for which the teacher, in his teaching, should strive. Unfortunately, we also have not yet matured enough as a profession to have established standards of professional conduct and practice to consider as a preparatory step.

▶ PARENTS AND OTHER NONSCHOOL PERSONS. **The teacher should know and give consideration to the interests, wishes, beliefs, and attitudes of community members who are interested in the welfare of their children.** "Parents" and "nonschool persons" refer to those persons to whom we usually give the label the community. Certainly as the teacher prepares to start the new school year or prepares to meet the next class, he considers pertinent beliefs and attitudes of those who live in the community, particularly the parents.

This kind of principle is applied automatically by the teacher who has been in a community for a few years. The teacher who is new in a community but who is experienced is very careful to find out beforehand how the community feels about physical education in general, and particularly those phases of it he has learned are apt to be criticized. The prospective teacher might very well learn from the experiences of these two classes of teachers.

The novice should not feel that he must be subservient to community members. Nevertheless, he should see clearly that he teaches in the community. He should know the kind of things the community likes and dislikes. The novice never starts something new without discussing it with the principal or department head.

SAMPLE DISCUSSION QUESTIONS

1. Can a beginning teacher omit any one of the eight kinds of information listed in the first paragraph of this chapter and still be prepared to meet his first class? Why?

2. Is learning to anticipate an ability that is attained by trial and error, like many other learnings?

3. How can a beginning teacher in physical education anticipate learning difficulties in students that he does not know very well?

4. How can a teacher find out before classes begin about the general background of the ability of each student?

5. When a school employs a teacher, does it not hire him for his ideas as well as his ability to teach?   Why, then, is the novice teacher admonished not to expect to have his ideas adopted?

6. How does one make plans for the future and at the same time make them with an eye to the future?

7. "If the student is the one I am supposed to be teaching, why am I expected to consider the status and welfare of every possible person involved in education of the young?"   Discuss.

8. How can a teacher plan in terms of practical things like budget and facilities and at the same time plan in terms of highest outcomes?

9. Why should we be concerned about appearance?   Can't one be a top-notch teacher and not pay much attention to these superficial things?

10. Students learn physical activities by participating in them.   How much planning is needed to get a class to participate?   I can see the need for planning in academic subjects but not physical education.   Discuss.

11. Is the principle referring to abundant health too severe?   Are there not good teachers in the field who have even a low quality of health?

12. Why is the general information picked up in psychology classes not enough to supply adequate information about the learners for the teacher?

13. "I don't see why I have to bother finding out, beforehand, a lot of things about the school.   I'll be hired to *teach the kids,* not to pass a test about the workings of the school system.   Am I right?"   Discuss.

14. "Let's be practical for a moment.   I can understand how principles can help the *experienced* teacher, but how can they be helpful to the novice who already has so many details to think about?   Trying to remember principles *complicates* instead of simplifying teaching.   Also, there are so many principles I can't see how anyone can figure out which one or which few are the really important ones."   Defend or attack these opinions.

15. Which set of objectives is most important, those set up by the textbook writers for physical education in general, the department's, those for the semester, for a given activity, the grade's, the class's, or those for the lesson?

16. Is it all right to turn over to a student helper the details of getting the facilities, equipment, and supplies ready for the class?

17. Suppose you realize after your first months of teaching that you are not as well prepared technically as others in the department although you are better prepared in the area of general education.   Should you try to fill the gap in technical preparation?   Why?   If your answer is yes, how can it be done?

18. What standards of professional conduct would you propose if you were named as a student member of a national committee to produce a set of such standards?

19. How could you give consideration to the wishes of the community and still not be subservient to them?

Note: These sample questions emphasize the why of the principles and their application. We suggest that an essay test be used for the chapter, and that the questions follow this pattern of having the student *reason* and *apply*.

BIBLIOGRAPHY

Brownell, Clifford Lee, and E. Patricia Hagman, *Physical Education— Foundations and Principles.* New York: The McGraw-Hill Book Company, Inc., 1951.

Bucher, Charles A., ed., *Methods and Materials of Physical Education and Recreation.* St. Louis: The C. V. Mosby Company, 1954.

Burton, William H., *The Guidance of Learning Activities,* Rev. Ed. New York: Appleton-Century-Crofts, Inc., 1952.

Butler, Frank A., *Improvement of Teaching in Secondary Schools.* Chicago: The University of Chicago Press, 1946.

Cantor, N., *The Teaching-Learning Process.* New York: The Dryden Press, 1953.

Cowell, Charles Clarence, *Modern Principles and Methods in High School Physical Education.* New York: Allyn and Bacon, Inc., 1958.

Grambs, Jean Diana, and William J. Iverson, *Modern Methods in Secondary Education.* New York: William Sloane Association, 1952.

Knapp, Clyde G., and E. Patricia Hagman, *Teaching Methods for Physical Education, A Textbook for Secondary School Teachers.* New York: The McGraw-Hill, Book Company, Inc., 1953.

Kozman, Hilda Clute, Rosalind Cassidy, and Chester O. Jackson, *Methods in Physical Education.* Philadelphia: W. B. Saunders Company, 1958.

Oberteuffer, Delbert, *Physical Education: A Textbook of Principles for Professional Students.* New York: Harper & Brothers, 1956.

Spears, Harold, *Principles of Teaching.* Englewood Cliffs, N. J.: Prentice-Hall, Inc., 1951.

Vannier, Maryhelen, and Hollis F. Fait, *Teaching Physical Education.* Philadelphia: W. B. Saunders Company, 1957.

Watkins, Ralph K., *Techniques of Secondary School Teaching.* New York: The Ronald Press Company, 1958.

13

Initiating and advancing
learning—I

Not only is there an art in knowing a thing,
but also a certain art in teaching it.

Cicero.

THE LAST CHAPTER PRESENTED THREE TEACHING OPERATIONS to be taken *in sequence,* preparatory to actual instruction. Once teaching and learning begins, such a neat prediction of sequence is not possible except as outlined in Chapter 14. What the teacher does next, after he helps to trigger learning, depends on the moment-by-moment situation. Most of that situation involves the learner—what he does, what he says, how he handles the ball or racquet, how he reacts to the bounce of the ball, and scores of other possible responses.

Teaching-learning situation not simple. The teaching-learning situation also includes other factors. Let us look at two of them. *First* is the teacher—what he does or says, his attitude, his acuity of observation, his excellence of analysis, judgment, and understanding. *Second* is the immediate environment—the sureness of footing, temperature of the water, direction and speed of the wind, and the like. Amount of noise is another environmental item that often influences both teaching and learning.

With so many items that may be of influence and the unpredictability of how pupils may respond individually and as a class, clearly what the teacher does next cannot be planned in an orderly 1-2-3 sequence.

Teaching involves selecting alternatives.   The student majoring in physical education should not be disturbed by this complexity and unpredictability.   It resembles the game situation which faces him in the team sports.   After play starts, what he does moment-by-moment, calling sometimes for split-second decisions and action, depends on what is happening.   This "what is happening" is the situation.   Sometimes the alternatives in sports are encountered so quickly there is not time to think things over.   Sometimes the outcome of a game depends on one man selecting the right hair-trigger response.   No one would want to remove these situations from the sport.   They are the very essence of the game.   They are the challenge, excitement, and adventure of many sports.   They constitute the anything-may-happen-next, the tantalizing unknown.   These, too, make teaching challenging, exciting, and adventuresome.

No assurance can be given that what the teacher does, once learning begins, is a logical operation.   But, it *is* a *psychological* operation.   The teacher selects what seems crucial or best in light of the teaching-learning situation.   After learning begins, the teacher selects one of a number of operations to fit the changing situation.

Teaching operations.   In this chapter, eight teaching operations are discussed, together with their respective principles, which guide the teacher.   These teaching operations are followed in the next chapter by seven others.   Then, in the subsequent two chapters, only one operation is discussed in each, namely, evaluation and guidance.

Counting the three operations discussed in the last chapter (anticipation, planning, and preparation), at least twenty operations are available to the teacher.   The prospective teacher should think of the operations as in a reservoir, *ever before him available for use* rather than thinking of them as they appear in a textbook, one after the other in several different chapters.   The eight submitted in this chapter are not separate from those in the next chapter.   Nor should the operations presented in the present chapter be thought of as belonging together.   The operations in the next chapter are separated into a different chapter chiefly for convenience in using this textbook in a course for major students. The remaining two operations, evaluation and guidance, are assigned separate chapters for the same reason. The prospective teacher might well think of the twenty operations as used in each situation change of teaching.

In the present chapter, the operations discussed are: (1) presentation, (2) explanation, (3) class organization, (4) routines, (5) use of sensory aids, including the well known demonstration, (6) providing for pupil participation, (7) individualization, and (8) socialization. Looking ahead briefly, the seven operations in Chapter 14 are: (1) observation, (2) analysis, (3) diagnosis, (4) generalization, (5) direction, (6) motivation, and (7) discipline.

The pupil initiates his own learning. The teacher can only help him. The first teaching operation in some situations might very well be motivation, not presentation. Or, in another situation, the first operation might very well be to provide for participation. In still another situation, the first operation might be launching one of the established routines, or it could be explanation, and so on.

PRESENTATION

In order to help kindle learning, the teacher *presents* that which he hopes will be learned. Sometimes, a general overview of an entire unit is briefly presented. On most occasions, a *review* of the last lesson may be briefly presented, perhaps followed by a presentation of the next thing to be learned. Often, a review of the last lesson is indicated as a desirable start. On still other occasions, a brief overview of a new activity is presented. Or, the presentation might be that of a brief report of a summary evaluation of the class's performance in a test of their performance in a game.

Presentation described. To *present* a lesson, an activity, and the like, the teacher offers an idea, a challenge, an invitation to the class members. Something to be learned or recalled is held before their mind's eye for *consideration* and *action*. The presentation is made as interesting as possible. The test of any given presentation is the degree to which the class wants to *do* something and then *does* something about it.

Each presentation for each day is planned in terms of each particular class, the experience of the teacher, and in terms of the wisdom gleaned from the experiences of hundreds of thousands of teachers, namely, principles of teaching.

Beginner's beliefs not enough.   Telling the prospective teacher that *whatever he believes* is the way to present a lesson, a unit, or an activity is the best way to flatter him, but it would be intellectually dishonest.   The accumulated wisdom of the race, of a profession, or of a family can help prevent our going through the errors of the past.   If we are intelligent, we learn through the doing of *others!*   Much of this accumulated wisdom contradicts what the less skilled person *believes.*   Certainly, one reason intelligent younger persons go to college is to crystalize their beliefs and values!   The major student who does not modify any of his beliefs about how to teach is either a genius-in-teaching-promise or he is headed for years of trouble.   The idea that each beginning teacher starts out with nothing but his beliefs and values as guides to action is an idea that may make him feel like a valiant Viking but gives him little credit for *wanting* to modify his beliefs!   It also gives little credit to the profession, for surely the professional heritage of guides to action has value.

Principles of presentation.   In actual teaching, a number of other operations may be used simultaneously with presentation. For example, as one introduces or reviews an idea he might demonstrate a movement or ask the students to try out (participation) the movement.   Or he could briefly describe or explain some part of it. The following principles are guides to better presentation.

▶ Permit class to become familiar with the **equipment and facilities.**

▶ Discuss, very briefly, the **main purposes of the activity.**

▶ **Arouse curiosity;** establish felt difficulties.

▶ **Provide participation** in the whole activity.

▶ **Analyze pupils' respective performances** in various aspects of activity as they participate in whole activity.

▶ **Demonstrate difficult parts of activity.**

▶ **Demonstrate for a few pupils** that part of activity with which they are having difficulty without interfering with the remainder of the class's participation.

▶ **Keep demonstration of, and participation in, a part of the activity closely related to the whole activity.**

▶ **Give explanations** that do not interfere with participation.

▶ **Provide for questions** after reasonable degree of participation.

▶ **Reach temporary conclusions regarding abilities.**

▶ **Maintain group attention,** when it is desired, by having pupils placed advantageously; by aiming what is said and done at their level; by being master of what is taught; by sheer exertion of personality; by wording and planning what is to be said and done so that it is concise, clear, and colorful; by planning the lesson so that attention is usually sought at appropriate times and places.

▶ **Help pupils set up their own objectives and values.**

▶ **Evaluate results** of presentations; follow with plans for the next lesson in light of this evaluation.

▶ **Observe the routines and procedures of class management and organization.**

▶ **Establish and maintain a positive attitude and atmosphere;** make the pupil feel that he can learn the activity; the learning should be meaningful to him.

▶ **Recognize that pupils vary** in their assimilability and personality as well as in their comprehension and physical education backgrounds.

▶ **Keep alert to students' reactions** to explanations and demonstrations.

▶ **Use more reward techniques than punishment techniques** when class is learning an activity.

▶ **Maintain an informal type of poise;** avoid showing irritation and discouragement; avoid nervous mannerisms.

▶ **Keep alert to a waning interest** or appearance of discouragement; be prepared to make the learning easier or seem easier; or in rare cases subtly change to another similar activity.

▶ **Locate or distribute pupils** so that their chances of success are enhanced.

▶ **Keep the learning moving** at a rate that is challenging but not overwhelming.

▶ **Aid pupils in summarizing the chief learnings of the lesson.**

The above principles emphasize individual differences, pupil responsibility, pupils' values, the objectives set for accomplishment both by the teacher and the pupils, progress from the easy toward the difficult, and appraisal of the presentation operation.

EXPLANATION

Principles of explanation.   Trying to help pupils learn a skill may retard their learning.   Any good explanation, clear, concise, and to the point, can prevent this.   If the teacher does not over-explain and an ververbalize, explanation can speed learning.   Most teachers tend to feel that *verbal* communication is the main way to teach.   This idea probably arises from school and college experiences.   Over-explaining often is an error made by ineffective teachers, no matter how much experience they may have had.

Explanations are *word-pictures of human motor action.*   To find out if the learner has the correct picture, ask him "What were you thinking about?" after he has attempted performance of a skill.   Another question might be, "What is it you were doing just now?" or "As you were performing that skill, what was it you were trying to do?"   Replies to questions such as these reveal quite accurately whether or not the teacher's explanations have been caught.

Another key to explanation is to explain *briefly* the action which the bat, racquet, ball or other instrument should go through *rather than* to direct the learner's attention to what *he* does with *his* hands or wrists or arms.   The idea here is to inject as few things as possible for the learner to think about.

As one studies the following principles of explanation, he again becomes aware of the fact that, as in presentation, this teaching operation is not an isolated act.   To avoid the excesses of explanation and to keep activity interest focused, the teacher almost always combines demonstration with explanation.

Careful regard of explanation principles will do the most to make explanation a helpful rather than retarding learning experience. Here are some principles of explanation.

▶ **Develop a vocabulary that is meaningful** in terms of the activity, keeping in mind the mental level of the group.
▶ **Shorten and simplify words and phrases,** but keep them complete enough to be understood.
▶ **Make explanations serve their purposes.**
▶ **Begin explanations with what the learner knows.**
▶ **Make sure that the class interprets sentences correctly.**

▶ **Practice giving the major purposes of an activity** in a short time with the help of illustrative devices.

▶ **Learn the origin and development of the activity.**

▶ **Keep the explanation moving forward** at a reasonable yet challenging rate.

▶ **Avoid beginning any explanation if the situation is unfavorable.**

▶ **Show enthusiasm** if it is expected from the pupils.

▶ **Avoid repetition of words and phrases.** Repetition of ideas that clinch points is necessary.

▶ **Adopt mannerisms** that add to, and eliminate those that detract from, the explanation.

▶ **Be as clear and brief as possible.**

▶ **Make use of the relaxation or rest period,** sometimes, for explanations.

▶ **Control your speech**—rate (about 150 words per minute), low pitch, varying inflection, rich texture, clear enunciation, proper pronunciation.

▶ **Display a sense of humor** at appropriate moments.

▶ **Make explanations simple, logical, and coherent.**

▶ **Use visual aids** when appropriate.

▶ **Use the corner of a gymnasium** when the acoustics make lengthy explanations to them in class front difficult. Under such circumstances, decrease rate of speech and lower pitch of voice.

▶ **Stick to the point** of the explanation and complete it quickly.

▶ **Allow pupils to settle comfortably** before you begin talking.

▶ **Maintain an easy, alert carriage while talking.**

▶ **Postpone even a moderately long explanation** if the class is to travel quite a distance before beginning the activity.

▶ **Avoid preaching and haranguing;** pupils like activity.

▶ **Establish and maintain a courteous, positive approach.**

▶ **Use the blackboard.**

▶ **Let pupils try explaining** if experience shows that certain of them can perform this function creditably.

Although whole-class explanation is usually necessary when introducing a new activity, the teacher also must give individual explanations. Some professional player-teachers, such as one finds in tennis and golf, are masters in this ability to paint word-pictures that the *individual* catches, that give him that flash of insight which enables him to really see, instead of partially getting the idea. One of these professional player-teachers told one of the authors that there were about *one hundred ways of explaining* every single skill involved in his sport. Surely the professionally-minded teacher should be willing to work out a dozen ways of explaining what is to be learned.

CLASS ORGANIZATION AND MANAGEMENT

If a chronological sequence in the teaching operations were possible, class organization would be among the first. Another, closely related operation, is establishing routines, or routinization, which is discussed later in this chapter.

Class vs. group.   In this discussion about the class, nothing is held to be sacrosanct about the group or about group process. Even to call a class a group, *tends to remove it* from the psycho-socio-politico-educational matrix of which it is an inescapable part. Further, it is quite inaccurate to describe a class as a miniature of society. The expectations of the community, the responsibilities thrust upon school personnel, the requirements by law, and the great differences in age-education-experience ranges culminate to make the school a benevolent despotism. The obligations of the teacher to teach the ideals of the West, to set an example for the young, to police their conduct, to teach the rudiments of educational tools and media, constitute part of one side of the educational coin. On the other side, and be it remembered an inseparable part, is the student fighting to free himself from adult domination, his voluntary and close attachment to his peers, his running to these peers for sympathy, solace, sign, and assurance, his off-and-on readiness to accept responsibility, and so on. The necessitated amalgamation of these two disparate populations and viewpoints within a school is hardly a replica of society! Rather, it is part of a picture of the school as it actually is.

As much as the authors would like to present the class as an optimistic picture of the group, they cannot in honesty do so. The law of the state requires that the young go to school until they are of a given age, barring expulsion, suspension, or dismissal. The law of the state requires that certain subjects be taught. The law requires that the teacher must have taken certain professional courses. Some of these courses are designed to motivate the teacher to help the pupil learn, or at least help him want to learn.   Local school regulations result in certain pupils attending each scheduled class in physical education.

In most schools, no attention is paid to the *appropriateness* of the clientele in a given physical education class, as far as abilities or interests are concerned.   In small high schools, all seniors are in one class.   In large schools, this class includes part of the seniors.   In a very small school, junior and senior classes are combined.   No matter how much, how often, and how long physical educators have expressed the wish (and given good reasons for it) for homogeneous grouping, few principals gear their high school schedules to this convenience of the physical education department.   Nor has the proportion of schools that do so increased in the past twenty-five years.

What we are saying to the prospective teacher is that the chances are good that his classes will be homogeneous in but this respect, the pupils will be from *about* the same age and grade.   This means that there will be real divergencies in height, weight, speed, strength, endurance, skill, background, and interests.   And, in many a school intelligence, as measured by any of the nationally-standardized intelligence tests, will vary considerably.

This condition is not cause for alarm.   Tens of thousands of physical education teachers have faced these same conditions ever since physical education became a subject.   This does not mean that we ought to stop trying.   We continue to assume that teaching could be more effective if the students were somewhat similar in the abilities needed in physical education.   But, this plan of classification is not geared to the interests of other subjects and teachers.

Principles of class organization and management.   Before considering some of the principles of teaching which guide one in organizing and managing a class, bear in mind that this operation is usually the one with which beginning teachers have the most difficulty.   Most experienced, ineffective teachers also are weak in this crucial part of their task.   Here, then, are some related principles.

▶ Try to have physical education classes **scheduled at times which are most beneficial** to the pupils.

▶ Try to have **facilities, equipment, and supplies** of satisfactory quality provided in adequate amounts.

▶ Act on the knowledge that the teacher's **appearance, manner, and attitude** become cues for pupil behavior.

▶ Make certain that all needed **facilities are ready** before the period begins.

▶ Act on the knowledge that **proper markings on field and floor** facilitate the control and conduct of classes.

▶ See that necessary **regulations governing pupil behavior** are known and understood, and that they are carried out. (The individual may possess self-control or he may acquire it. But, without regulations, a class rather easily slips into the role of a crowd without self-control.)

▶ **Provide areas according to types of activity and according to types of participants.** (Persons in a class vary in a number of ways as mentioned above. Some of them are slow enough, weak enough, clumsy enough to warrant areas that are safe and protected.)

▶ **See that facilities are laid out with reference to the sun** (tennis and baseball) and other factors such as prevailing winds.

▶ Make sure that students know and understand the time limits **for use of the locker-shower-dressing rooms,** and that these limits are followed.

▶ **Arrange all equipment** such as lockers in orderly fashion. Use of them, such as foot traffic, should follow a regulated pattern. (This arrangement and pattern should be made in terms of the source of natural light, location of toilets, dressing space, and entrance-exit.)

▶ **Call the class together** by means of an understood, uniform sign or signal, given at the same time with reference to the beginning of the class period, and the same agreed-upon spot each time.

▶ **Arrange a plan of taking attendance** which is accurate, time-saving, easy to record, provides a chance for the teacher to see each student, and (perhaps) provides a chance for the student to respond. (The latter provision stems from the belief of some teachers that the roll call should be personalized. Some teachers also believe students should be helped to understand the necessity for attendance being taken.)

▶ Consider formulating some scheme for injecting an **inner type of organization** within the class. (Some teachers do this by having regular teams formed within the class. Other teachers use the familiar squad system, with the squad leaders often serving as class helper.)

▶ **Modify activities** and/or their respective rules in order to fit the activities to the situation.   (In spite of the list of activities one finds in textbooks, the number of activities which have caught on in high school is not great.   The teacher should feel obligated to help the situation by becoming inventive and creative.)

▶ Act on the knowledge that **most accidents connected with physical education are preventable.**   (Any one or all of these factors may demand action: (1) providing proper playground surfacing; (2) selecting and fitting activities for and to the class; (3) being alert to and controlling pupils during participation; (4) making pupils aware of their need to prevent needless accidents and securing their cooperation in this prevention; (5) giving instruction that prevents or lessens the number and severity of accidents; (6) removing hazards such as posts or buffering them or planning activities and pupil-traffic to avoid unremovable hazards; (7) placing equipment so that it is least hazardous; (8) being alert to near-accidents; (9) continually studying ways of reducing chances of accidents; (10) purchasing equipment and supplies and providing facilities that have a low potential for accidents; (11) inspecting the environment frequently with special attention to equipment with movable parts such as swings and materials that wear out such as ropes; (12) replacing and repairing with dispatch unsafe equipment or supplies; (13) making reports at once to superior officers of the existence of needed action in cases of unsafe conditions or materials if such action transcends one's jurisdiction; (14) removing from use any unsafe equipment or supplies until proper action is taken; (15) giving proper safety precautions and emphasizing responsibility for knowing and responding to safety precautions; (16) being able to render expert emergency care if necessary; and (17) disposing of equipment and supplies that will not be used again in the class.)

▶ Take necessary measures, before the class leaves its assembly-spot, quickly and clearly to **let each student know the necessary details** of what is about to happen.   (This usually includes: (1) the activity; (2) exactly where to go; (3) the route and manner of getting there; (4) dividing the class into sides, teams, squads, and the like; (5) which team or squad will be up first or will be on which side of the net or will defend which goal; (6) any changes in the usual rules; (7) those who are captains or leaders; (8) who will officiate; (9) who are the scorers; (10) the length of time to be spent at this activity; (11) what is to be done then; (12) any special relationship to marks or grades; (13) this participation as possibly being related to other matters such as a part of a tournament; (14) any newsworthy note such as a tie-in over-all points for the year between Squads I and II; and (15) a possible word about reassembling at the usual spot. These fifteen teacher activities serve several quite important purposes. They avoid the common causes of wasted time, confusion, and argument. They allow participation to begin almost immediately. They contribute to a positive attitude on the part of class members toward the teacher, the activity, the program, the department, and physical education, and toward the idea that leisure-time pursuits need not be haphazardly planned. They eliminate causes of misbehavior and the need for disciplinary action. Some teachers *unintentionally plan* that pupils misbehave. Most misconduct in classes can be avoided by building *channels* of conduct. One set of these channels are comprised of details such as those pre-participation activities listed above.)

▶ **Formulate a program** that promotes good class organization. (Considering the nature of the adolescent as well as his welfare, (1) the program should include activities related to the out-of-door hours, days and months; (2) each lesson should include at least one new and challenging situation, stunt or activity; (3) the program should balance the factors of instruction, drill, recreation, practice, and review; (4) it should reflect not only a recognition of the psychology of learning but also the interests and welfare of the class; (5) most lessons should balance active participation and rest and relaxation; (6) each daily lesson should reflect the learners' past experiences as well as those that are anticipated; (7) the program should be planned in terms of progressive demands for increased skill, the other objectives set up, social and cultural backgrounds, the expectations of the community, and the aspirations and motives of the learners; (8) the program should be a part of a general plan for the entire school system and the students should be made aware of the need for this kind of planning; (9) the program should include not only teaching about the activity, teaching the activity, teaching the learner by means of that activity, but also teaching the *principles* of movement involved and the *significances* of the activity.)

▶ Recognize that **the teacher is an active force in class organization.** (Even the beginning major student in physical education realizes that the way a teacher *communicates* with his class affects its conduct. Pronunciation, rate of speech, pitch of voice and its volume, enunciation, and inflection all affect class response. A shrill, high voice accompanied by rapidly uttered words fail to indicate poise and stability to a class and, in turn, fail to engender stability and poise within members of that class. Many young teachers do not make themselves heard by all members of a class. This is one common cause of irritation and resulting misconduct. The teacher's *manner* is another active force in class conduct. An overly sarcastic, domineering, or meek manner on the part of the teacher, for example, weakens teacher control of class conduct. Other factors related to this principle are the teacher's appearance, forcefulness, self-control, promptness and decisiveness, dependability, fairness, and the like. The teacher must not only know what is going on, he also must look as though he knew. This helps keep a class on its toes, it sets the atmosphere and tempo of the class and brings the class to the viewpoint that "this teacher is all right.")

▶ **Eliminate from class** anyone who is unable to respond normally and take judicious action with reference to his case. (The ill student is sent to the school nurse, the slightly indisposed one may sit along the sidelines or participate in some mild activity, the unruly one dealt with according to the conditions and the nature of his misconduct, and so on. The basic plan of class organization for girls should be more flexible than for boys.)

▶ **Exercise care in following the regulations of the school regarding the readmission after absence** and keep an accurate record of excuses. (Establishment of rapport with local physicians usually results in bona fide excuses.)

▶ **Formulate a policy regarding the attendance of athletes** in physical education classes and carry out the agreed-upon policy.

▶ **Make assignments to the adaptive program in accordance with instructions from the school medical advisor** or some physician who serves in that capacity.

▶ **Formulate a policy regarding the organization of those in the adaptive program,** and follow it without exception. (The beginning teacher may find himself in a department which organizes these classes very differently than was done in college, in his high school, or than was recommended by his major department. At some *appropriate* time and place he *might* suggest a reconsideration of the policy.)

▶ **Follow the department's policy regarding making up absences.**
▶ **Continually study the status of class organization and management** and assess the degree of cooperative working relations with the class members.   (The authors feel compelled to warn beginning teachers that all is not sweetness and light in the help teenagers give when formulating regulations and the like.   At the same time, some very fine teachers believe that perhaps something here is more important than the students' help.   Physical education classes offer the chance for young people to sample some duties which they are expected to be able to do as young adults, but which they have little chance to learn to do in school.   Furthermore, the experienced teacher comes to recognize that if he expects the students to obey the rules, carry out regulations, pursue objectives, and so on, these expectancies are far more apt to be realized if students discuss them beforehand.)

(With the cautionary word about starting slowly and alertly, realizing that mistakes are bound to happen and that the whole process of *establishing* such things as objectives and regulations will be slow, here are some kinds of experiences that physical education teachers might provide for their pupils: (1) to recognize, accept, take, carry through and anticipate responsibility, (2) to make decisions that affect self and others, (3) to manage, (4) to lead, (5) to participate in imaginative or creative activities, (6) to follow, (7) to carry out a project to its conclusion, (8) to obey, (9) to conform, (10) to help set up guides of conduct as well as know the reasons for such guides.)

▶ **Adjust the length of time spent on a given activity to the conditions at hand.**   (Some of these conditions are: (1) age of the pupil, (2) school level, (3) number of times per week the class meets, (4) length of class period, (5) purposes of the program, (6) number of pupils in the squad or the class, (7) number of activities taught during the semester besides the one under consideration, (8) degree to which facilities are available and equipment is adequate, (9) the weather and climate, (10) the backgrounds of the pupils, and (11) their abilities.)

▶ **Keep supplies in good repair.**   Store them properly and in orderly fashion when not in use, have a record of each item and its condition, and maintain an efficient, accurate system of checking all supplies in and out.

▶ **Keep a running account of equipment and supplies needed for next year** and issue requisitions for them at appropriate times. (This principle includes the task of knowing the date of purchase, the date of arrival, the date the item was first put into use, and the date it was discarded with an indication of severity of use.)

▶ **Make certain that equipment and supplies used during the class are adequate in number and satisfactory in quality.**

▶ **Establish instructions about the program** so that the new students at the beginning of the year and those who arrive during the year are quickly oriented.

▶ **Follow the grading plan set up by the department.** (Not infrequently this plan is flexible enough to permit a teacher to consider as many items as he wishes, as long as they are related to the purposes or goals of the department's program. Some of the items or factors which are being used by various departments are as follows: (1) level of performance at the outset, (2) improvement in skill as well as other appropriate criteria, (3) knowledges, including rules, strategy, and the like, (4) attitudes toward the activity and the program, (5) cleanliness, including costumes, (6) citizenship, (7) sportsmanship, fairplay, and the like, (8) scores made on performance tests, (9) posture, figure or body-build, carriage, (10) degree of physical condition as determined by tests, (11) leadership-followership, (12) versatility and skill in self-testing activities, and (13) personal responsibility such as being on time, carrying out regulations, rules, routines, and the like. See also Chapter 15 where evaluation is discussed in detail.)

▶ **Provide a plan of placing students in certain categories** in order to enable the teacher to be more intelligent, understanding, and effective. (Many teachers use these categories as the basis of class organization. Many plans are available. For example, the class can be organized on the basis of age-weight-height. The class can be divided solely on the basis of proficiency in the next activity to be taught. Some departments use the results of the health examination. One obvious division is on the basis of sex, although coeducational activities ignore the validity of such a category for most activities because the underlying purpose changes. Some departments classify on the basis of some general motor ability test, assuming that such an ability exists. Sometimes an activity almost forces a department to categorize members of a class if strength and speed and similar specifics count a great deal in performance.   Some take the view that the superior ones in any type of classification should learn to adjust to the dubs, and vice versa.   While some persons assume that homogeneous grouping increases teaching effectiveness and a number of other claimed advantages, supporting facts are lacking at this time.   On the other hand, teaching is *easier* if a class is divided into squads formed according to abilities in the activity being taught.)

▶ **Carry out the department's and school's policy regarding type of dress for physical education classes.**   (The women have come a long way in costuming girls for participation in physical education types of activities—swimming, dance, various games, and sports.   The day of *one* style, *one* color, *one* material costume is passing.   This does not mean, however, that common sense is jettisoned.   If the department insists on providing costumes [usually for a fee], it must weigh the cost and effects of laundering against the advantage of mass buying [one color, one style, one material].   With the cost of education continually being appraised, some expenditures, currently connected in people's minds with education, may be eliminated.)

(Related to this principle regarding costuming is the long-term practice of some boys to ignore their appearance in physical education classes.   Some evidence shows that the traditional soiled, untidy dress associated with the boys' program is being changed.   Any alert, experienced teacher knows that his appearance and that of the student is a factor in class management.)

▶ **Consider that class management begins as soon as the students are under the jurisdiction of the physical education department and continues until they are no longer under the department's control.**

▶ **Establish and use some students as helpers** if this plan fits into the school's and department's policies.   (The most common provision for this plan is that of having squad leaders.   This part of class organization is now so well known that it need not be described.)

ROUTINIZATION

Formulating, establishing, and carrying out routines is the backbone of class organization and management because routines can be applied almost automatically. That is, routines *are* followed. If a routine ceases to engender that much confidence in its being followed, a new routine or a modified one is indicated. Routines streamline the day's tasks both at home, in the work-a-day world, and at school. Stopping for a red traffic light is inescapable even to the "let's have more freedom in the classroom" advocates.

Advantages of routines. Routines require a very minimum of supervision once they are established. They should be worked out (most of them) with student cooperation and thus with effectiveness. Routines eliminate the repetition of directions or things to do, and thus they are timesaving also. They help teach respect for rules, regulations, and laws. And, because students know what the others are doing, routines facilitate cooperation and teamwork within the school and within the class.

Changing procedures to routines. Making a routine become a concrete, understood, followed rule-of-action requires planning, work, cooperation, and patience. The need for the routine must first be sensed. Some necessary routines may not be sensed by primary school children. Much of their school work is concentrated on *doing*. Thus, drilling on these necessary routines becomes the point of emphasis. But, in the secondary school understanding the need for routines is seldom a problem. Occasionally, discussing the need of some routine that may appear to curtail past freedom may be necessary. Discussion and explanation are often required to describe how the routine works and the part each class member is to play. Once the mental part is taken care of temporarily, the class goes through the routine in slow motion, analytically. This enables the class members and the teacher to identify possible problems or errors. The class tries the routine again, avoiding the errors noted previously. This process continues until, upon the given sign or signal, the class responds.

Let us look at some routines that apply to various aspects of the teacher's task.

A. *Healthful school living.*

1. Knowing the location of, steps to follow in the use of, and types of injuries that should be treated through the use of the first-aid equipment. Knowing how and where to find the school physician or a physician.

2. Taking safety precautions in the use of such apparatus as parallel bars and high bar.

3. Refraining from participating in pranks that may lead to injuries and accidents; for example, running on the platform of the swimming pool and scuffling in the locker and shower rooms.

4. Inspecting equipment and having a definite place for it.

5. Checking the temperature of the gymnasium (58–60°).

6. Keeping clean and in repair the locker room, shower room, towel room, lavatories, gymnasium, and field.

7. Eliminating materials that are fire hazards.

8. Keeping the gymnasium costumes clean and sanitary.

9. Keeping the drinking fountains clean and sanitary.

10. Keeping the shower room floor free of soap; keeping the liquid soap system in operation.

11. Being alert for signs of illness, overfatigue, and undernourishment in pupils and sending all questionable cases to the nurse.

12. Planning beforehand what to do in such cases of emergency as fainting, broken bones, nosebleed.

13. Checking on the artificial light and lighting systems in the gymnasium.

14. Selecting activities that are not too hazardous considering the facilities available.

15. Checking on the sanitation, filtration, and sterilization of the swimming pool.

16. Eliminating the sources of disagreeable odors, if possible; if not possible, using a deodorant.

17. Providing a reasonable length of time for shower baths.

18. Keeping halls and exits clear of obstacles.

19. Keeping gymnasium and field free of accident hazards.

20. Providing a suitable program for the physically handicapped.

21. Providing some system for a clean towel after a shower bath and after washing.

22. Providing warm water for washing and showers.

23. Eliminating the habit of expectorating on the floor of the gymnasium and locker room.

24. Determining whether the weather indicates an indoor or outdoor program.

B. *Record keeping.*

1. Taking attendance; recording excuses.

2. Itemizing equipment and supplies on hand, and their condition.

3. Recording equipment and supplies ordered.

4. Keeping results of tests, scales, ratings, classifications.

5. Noting reports of progress; grades.

6. Recording available and pertinent data from the health examination records.

7. Recording teaching schedules; sports schedules.

8. Keeping an account of appointments for conferences.

9. Recording injuries and accidents; dispositions made of each case.

10. Keeping a record of participation of squad members in activities, data, amount of time, location, name of sport.

11. Selecting, following up, and recording borrowed supplies.

12. Establishing a system of records and reports.

13. Writing, recording, and filing plans.

14. Recording estimates of the degree to which students demonstrate positive and negative physical, social, and mental traits.

15. Writing and recording the aim and objectives of physical education for each grade, for each activity.

16. Preparing a course of study.

17. Writing and recording a statement of one's philosophy of physical education.

18. Writing and recording an outline of each public address delivered, including the date and occasion.

19. Recording all lesson plans, even though they are discarded, with written revisions appended.

20. Making a note of occasion when techniques of instruction fail to bring results and occasions when they seem to work unusually well.

21. Keeping a carbon copy of all correspondence; promptly answering correspondence.

22. Keeping a permanent record of the results of all test data.

23. Reporting absences, tardiness, marks, promotions, and other similar information required by other offices, promptly.

24. Keeping a register if so required.

25. Making a written annual report of accomplishments and problems.

26. Recording the program of activities in which each grade participates.

27. Keeping records up to date.

28. Constructing and submitting budgets.

29. Recording and reporting accidents, illnesses occurring in class, and cases dismissed from class and sent to the school nurse.

C. *Routines regarding facilities, equipment, and supplies.* The following routines, as in the lists above, are not complete but they are indicative of procedures to be taken care of almost automatically:

1. Repairing or discarding equipment that is broken or worn out.

2. Inflating balls.

3. Deflating balls not in active use.

4. Cleaning, laundering, labeling, and storing equipment and supplies not in active use.

5. Having towels and physical education costumes laundered frequently if this is the school's responsibility; seeing that students supply themselves with clean towels and costumes if possible; if not, taking steps to secure these materials.

6. Providing the best quality of equipment and supplies possible under budgetary limitations.

7. Keeping fresh supplies in first-aid kits.

8. Providing facilities and equipment for drying wet supplies.

9. Providing satisfactory types of storage space for different kinds of supplies and equipment.

10. Protecting equipment rooms against fire and theft.

11. Providing safe places to store personal belongings and valuables.

12. Keeping shelves, cupboards, and storage areas clean.

13. Providing physical education costumes for the indigent.

14. Keeping all parts of the gymnasium and the fields in good repair throughout the year.

15. Being sure that the plumbing is in good order.

16. Keeping the swimming pool clean and sanitary throughout the school year.

17. Making available physical education facilities and supplies for community use, if this is in conformity with the administrative policies of the school.

18. Helping and cooperating with the janitor so that no unnecessary dirt and refuse are deposited in auxiliary rooms.

19. Checking on the proper use of toilets, showers, and liquid soap system.

20. Anticipating needs as regards facilities, equipment, and supplies, and presenting this information to the proper authorities so that they fully realize the importance of these needs.

21. Dividing the fields into areas for various groups for use during recess periods, before and after school, and out-of-school hours.

22. Taking all precautions possible in connection with facilities and equipment to insure the safety of pupils.

D. *Routines and guides to the conduct of classes, and instruction.* The following list of eighty-four items consists of procedures, many of which are routines in the sense that the experienced teacher performs them at the right time, place, and occasion without thinking much about it. On the other hand, some of them are *secondary* principles of teaching in that they are guides to action. These small-scale principles do not tell the teacher the *way* to do something; that is, they do not give the how of conducting classes or the how of instruction. Thus, they are not methods or techniques. They are large-scale principles broken down into specific, small principles. They guide more definitely what the action should be. Sometimes this breaking down of a principle makes it seem less vague and less ideal. In conducting classes and in instruction, such activities as the following routines and secondary guides are indicated:

1. Maintaining order as class moves to gymnasium or locker room.

2. Conforming to agreed-upon traffic plan in locker room.

3. Dressing in physical education costumes as quickly as possible; locking lockers and otherwise making street clothes and valuables safe.

4. Avoiding the practice of loitering in a locker room.

5. Responding immediately and correctly to the signal to assemble.

6. Responding to roll call.

7. Responding immediately to routinized commands or signs.

8. Preparing and distributing supplies according to plan.

9. Following policies regarding absences.

10. Passing with dispatch and order from one activity center on the floor or field to the next.

11. Greeting visitors.

12. Following out lesson plans (with judicious flexibility).

13. Providing an adequate period of activity for warming up.

14. Providing an appropriate period of vigorous activity.

15. Providing an appropriate period for cooling down.

16. Selecting techniques of instruction that are in conformity with the principles of mental health and psychology.

17. Making use of the bulletin board.

18. Appraising the effectiveness of the bulletin board.

19. Conducting the class on scheduled time.

20. Establishing and following a given approved plan of marking.

21. Collecting and storing supplies; replacing equipment.

22. Dismissing class properly and on time.

23. Passing to the locker room in orderly fashion.

24. Following pre-arranged plan for taking a shower bath, securing towel, taking care of physical education uniform, preparing to leave locker room, moving to next class.

25. Conforming to the rules of activities.

26. Conforming to school regulations and customs.

27. Caring for personal property.

28. Caring for school property.

29. Memorizing the names of class members the first day.

30. Being punctual.

31. Using the same terminology for desired routine responses.

32. Requiring obedience when necessary in a congenial manner whenever possible.

33. Securing a mastery of the lesson to be taught.

34. Securing attention and order before speaking or teaching.

35. Selecting leaders as early in the year as possible.

36. Making use of student leaders.

37. Providing opportunity for developing leadership in others not selected as leaders.

38. Giving ready and sincere acknowledgment of excellence, merit, and ability.

39. Enlisting student aid whenever appropriate in such matters as making decisions and formulating rules.

40. Informing leaders of daily plan of lessons sufficiently in advance.

41. Providing a program of activity for those who arrive before the class assembles.

42. Providing programs of activity for those who remain after classes.

43. Developing the spirit and practice of self-discipline and class responsibility.

44. Placing emphasis upon positive rather than negative conduct.

45. Supervising all activities during the class period.

46. Cultivating a good speaking voice.

47. Beginning the class period with the group together and dismissing with the group together, whenever appropriate.

48. Avoiding special attention to students of the opposite sex; avoiding "crushes."

49. Adopting a sympathetic attitude toward students, and avoiding remarks that appear to ridicule, nag, or slight students.

50. Avoiding the habit of blowing the whistle too frequently.

51. Trusting rather than watching.

52. Permitting no one to get away with conduct that may lead to habits that will have to be broken later.

53. Remembering requirements, agreements, assigned responsibilities.

54. Avoiding participation in an argument at any time.

55. Encouraging enthusiastic responses.

56. Refraining from giving a series of progressive commands or orders until each prerequisite command is understood and learned.

57. Encouraging and permitting courteous attitudes.

58. Keeping the right degree of social distance according to the situation.

59. Avoiding the malpractice of holding grudges, or the after-effects of difficulties in or outside of class.

60. Striving to be a good teacher even at the temporary sacrifice of being thought of as a "good guy."

61. Keeping control continually of the teaching situation without being dictatorial.

62. Keeping control of one's temper and maintaining poise at all times.

63. Conducting the program so that students enjoy it but also in such a way that they respect it.

64. Displaying a sense of humor at all appropriate times.

65. Using proper disciplinary measures appropriate to the kind and degree of misconduct.

66. Giving minor problems and major problems proportionate time, energy, and thought.

67. Keeping the classwork moving toward objectives that have been selected.

68. Finding and considering interests, peculiarities, abilities, and needs of students.

69. Determining the relative value of activities before they are selected and after elements in the teaching situation are considered.

70. Helping students set up their own objectives before or during each lesson.

71. Providing an expanding program of physical education experiences.

72. Stimulating students to develop new interests in other areas of school life.

73. Taking time to explain school regulations, if necessary.

74. Stimulating students to respect the rights and privileges of others.

75. Adopting and applying health procedures.

76. Stimulating the superior student to be helpful to others.

77. Administering, constructing, or selecting tests.

78. Integrating physical education with other school subjects wherever and whenever this is possible and advisable.

79. Adapting the program to the facilities and equipment available.

80. Arranging contests within class periods and between classes.

81. Avoiding teacher domination during participation.

82. Providing a variety of activities for each grade without sacrificing an opportunity to learn each activity reasonably well.

83. Using the physical education period as an opportunity or for guidance and personality adjustment.

84. Recognizing commendable fellowship.

USE OF SENSORY AIDS, INCLUDING DEMONSTRATION

Human learners do not like to have the instructor talk very much when they are supposed to be doing something that requires coordination and control unless they feel they need help. Although what learners like is often an unreliable guide, in this case their feelings point in the right direction.

Talking by the teacher demands but one of the senses of the learner—hearing. Sensory aids make use of any and all of the other senses: kinesthetic, tactile, taste, sight, and smell. The so-called practical arts kind of courses—music, art, home economics, industrial arts, and physical education—use all of these senses. The longer-established courses formerly made use of but one or two, hearing and sight. Thus listening and reading, with the use of the blackboard and charts, is the traditional way that the teacher expected the learner to learn. Many courses and subjects are taught traditionally even today. We tend to teach as we were taught, not as we were taught to teach. Some physical education teachers *think* they are really teaching when talking!

One of the first mistakes made by persons in professions involving the practical arts is to think in terms of audio-visual aids, instead of sensory aids. For, to restrict one's thinking to aiding the learner by means of what he hears and sees overlooks the importance of the other senses. This may account, in part, for the failure on the part of some teachers to have members of the class get acquainted with a new piece of equipment by feeling it, manipulating it, touching it, testing its weight, and if it is a ball bouncing it, throwing and catching it. The audio-visual limited view of sensory aids would have the home economics teacher ignore the senses of taste and smell! And, some physical educators fail to see that demonstration is one of the sensory aids.

Excessive talking not only robs learners of the time and opportunity for trying out, getting the feel, and such concrete experiences, but it also slows learning by complicating the learning process. It gives the learner more things to think about as he tries to learn. Furthermore, some of these verbalizations get in the way of other things he may be considering such as feel, space sensing, angle sensing, hunches, observations, and the like.

Principles of using sensory aids, including demonstration. The following principles of teaching apply the use of sensory aids and demonstration to physical education:

▶ **Make certain that the sensory aid selected is appropriate** to the skill, unit, or activity being taught.

▶ **Consider sensory aids as supplements to teaching,** not as substitutes for teaching.

▶ **Avoid permitting enthuiasm for sensory aids to disrupt judgment** as to the amount of time devoted to this part of teaching.

▶ **Use sensory aids for appropriate purposes.** For example, use photographs and drawings for illustrations that will be needed several times, the blackboard for temporary illustrations, and the bulletin board for materials that are more permanent than either of the other two. Movies help in the analysis of skills as well as in the presentation of excellent performances of whole activities. Photographs are useful in illustrating such fundamentals as grip and stance.

▶ **Place sensory aids in appropriate places.** For example, the movie film loses some of its teaching force when used in a room that is not dark and on a projection background that is unsuitable. The bulletin board should be placed in a spot where it is most apt to be noticed by pupils who have time to give attention to displayed materials.

▶ **Keep sensory-aid devices in good condition.** (Before any lesson in which a sensory aid is to be used, the teacher should test the equipment.)

▶ **Select sensory aids that are related to former experiences.**

▶ **Make certain that the sensory aids selected clarify** rather than complicate, facilitate rather than make more difficult.

▶ **Encourage the use of sensory aids** to consolidate learnings and to express ideas.

▶ **Select the most fundamental, most easily understood method first,** when and if selecting between sensory aids and verbalization as the initial step in teaching.

▶ **Check on the major learnings** subsequent to the use of a sensory aid, not only to evaluate the scope, kind, and degree of learning, but to evaluate the sensory aid itself.

▶ **Use the more permanent types of sensory aids** such as moving pictures and photographs as ways of recording important activities of the year such as playdays, demonstrations, or exhibitions.

▶ **Integrate physical education with other activities,** such as photography, drawing, making lantern slides, and lettering.

▶ Avoid assuming that the use of sensory aids decreases the need for the **effective application of the principles of presentation, explanation, and demonstration.**

▶ **Use a few excellent sensory aids** in preference to many of fair quality.

▶ **Make full use of sensory aids for their various purposes.** Sensory aids are used: (1) to present model performances, (2) to present a whole activity to beginners, (3) to present performances of unusual persons or teams from distant cities, (4) to provide concrete experiences, (5) to make learning more interesting through a variety of teaching techniques, (6) to provide additional experiences to the pupil so as to enable him to draw conclusions better, (7) to save time, and (8) to gain and maintain attention.

▶ **Determine the specific purpose of the demonstration** before presenting it. For example: (1) a demonstration of the whole activity when introducing an activity so that subsequent practice and instruction has direction and meaning, (2) a demonstration of a detailed skill to a pupil who is having difficulty with the execution of it, (3) a demonstration of a skill in varying situations to show him it is used differently in different parts of the game or as the game changes, and (4) the demonstration as a motivation procedure.

▶ **Make certain that the demonstration creates the kind of model desired.** We strongly advise that the teacher practice any planned demonstration beforehand.

▶ **Select a few skilled students to try an activity after a demonstration,** to show the class that it can be done.

▶ **Use student demonstration sometimes** when it is more effective than demonstration by the teacher.

▶ **Keep the demonstration at the students' general level of ability.**

▶ **Provide opportunities for participation** as soon as possible after the demonstration.

▶ **Make the demonstration long enough to accomplish its purpose** but short enough to avoid interfering unduly with participation.

▶ **Demonstrate any major error in performance,** as well as the correct performance.

▶ **Conduct a demonstration ordinarily at the tempo used in actual game situation,** except when movements are too fast or complicated to be adequately observed and assimilated.

▶ **Give at least one good reason for performing a skill a certain way** during a demonstration. (This statement does not apply to introductory demonstrations.)

▶ **Direct observation and attention during a demonstration by word and gesture** instead of relying on students' memories.

▶ **Prepare the class for precisely what is to be demonstrated.**

▶ **Adapt complexity and detail of demonstration to level of maturity and ability of class.**

▶ **Place the class and the demonstrator(s) in relatively advantageous positions.**

▶ **Make sure that an introductory demonstration reinforces socially approved conduct as well as skills.**

▶ **Permit class to imitate the demonstrator** as he presents a certain skill, thus using the kinesthetic sense as well as visual and auditory.

▶ **Make use of the largest assimilable whole,** ordinarily, in demonstrations. Even in demonstrating parts, they should be tied in with each other and related parts or, better yet, the whole activity.

▶ **Make it understood that pertinent questions should be asked** after the introductory demonstration, prior to participation.

▶ **Secure a skillful person as a demonstrator** if you are unable to appear to advantage in that role.

▶ **Provide the demonstrator(s) with equipment similar to that which the class is to use.**

▶ **Develop interest and group responsibility** by permitting the class to prepare an introductory demonstration.

▶ **Evaluate results of demonstration,** partially in terms of students' evaluation of it.

Modern mass media and other aids.   The press, TV, and radio are particularly suited to aid teachers in physical education. Not only do the first two provide many excellent pictures, but in most communities the physical education teachers are well enough known to be of influence in some of the pictures shown on TV. At the present writing, the chief value of these media is that of most sensory aids, namely, motivation. But, the authors believe that TV may prove to be a real boon to increasing the effectiveness of teaching physical education and athletic activities. Devices such as the tape recorder, video tape, and the teaching machines hold real promise as *supplementary* aids to the teacher, particularly as they are combined with other media. For example, the use of 35 mm. transparencies taken of the class as they perform, together with the use of a tape recorder, is probably a far more effective supplementary teaching aid than a purchased moving picture film that costs five times as much.

As physical educators take some of the responsibility for keeping expenditures down, as taxpayers become increasingly concerned about the cost of education, the department may have to use the combined imaginations of its staff members to figure out economical ways of providing valid sensory aids. And, even in localities where budgets are open-ended, every supplementary aid to teaching should be tested for the validity of its purpose.

PROVIDING FOR PUPIL PARTICIPATION

Physical educators, doctors of medicine, most educators, parents, and others interested in the welfare of human beings believe that physical education is a valuable field. They believe this because of the outcomes to themselves and to others. In spite of the finger-pointing at "spectatoritis," there certainly are some values in watching others participate. But, greater value and more different values accrue when the individual participates in the variety and the types of activities which are good for him. Thus, providing for participation is one of the key teaching operations.

Principles of providing pupil participation. Because of the importance of this task, it seems advisable to submit *secondary* and *tertiary* principles, those that are more concrete, specific, and detailed. The teacher should:

1. Utilize the greatest possible amount of class time for participation.

2. Arrange the activity so that there is maximum participation and minimum teacher participation.

3. Use some participation time for other than skill learnings and

development of organic vigor—for example, desirable social and human traits.

4. Devote most of the class period to those learnings that will be most valuable.

5. Divide class period into review, drill, practice, play, and instruction, according to the needs and interests of the group, the nature of the activity, and the purposes agreed upon.

6. Provide for some participation in appropriate and supervised activities with students of opposite sex.

7. Provide, if possible, for participation in activities with other schools occasionally.

8. Incorporate a modified intramural program in the physical education program at appropriate school levels if this is the only way to provide this type of experience.

9. Guide students in helping them select activities in which they are to participate so that the activities seem more meaningful and valuable.

10. Work toward 100 per cent spontaneous participation throughout each period.

11. Eliminate some participation problems by permitting different groups in the class to participate under student leaders in some activities.

12. Stimulate reviews, drills, and practices so that students try to perform them correctly.

13. Distribute skilled and unskilled participants in contests in such a way that the activity is most challenging, enjoyable, and safe to the greatest number.

14. Provide a warm-up at the beginning and a cool-down at the close of the class period.

15. Provide for alternate leadership and followership in such a way that neither the individual nor the class unduly suffers and both benefit.

16. Provide, regardless of heterogeneous or homogeneous grouping, some opportunities for skilled participants to perform together, and for unskilled to perform with the skilled participants.

17. Keep in mind throughout the period and the year that activity is the medium of physical education for educating the child.

18. Make practice and drill periods long enough for profitable learning but short enough for maintaining interest and enthusiasm.

19. Make certain that the student understands the value of drills.

20. Lead the student to experience a felt need keenly enough so that the result is self-directed practice, even outside of school hours.

21. Guide and lead the student to set up his objectives of the activity and understand teaching objectives, if possible.

22. Keep in mind that most persons learn motor activities more by imitation than by verbal direction.

23. Avoid practicing too long on a small isolated skill.

24. Give brief instructions at beginning of each class period.

25. Allow for individual differences in performance as students try to imitate the demonstration model and follow explanations.

26. Work for ease and relaxation of performance as students learn a new activity.

27. Avoid expecting speed, coordination, strength, and endurance all at the same time; or avoid expecting speed and coordination at the same time in a new activity.

28. Plan and conduct some *vigorous* activities.

29. Avoid participation that leads to apparent excessive fatigue.

30. Keep in mind and be alert to variance among students in the rapidity with which fatigue sets in.

31. Eliminate activities that are unjustifiably expensive in terms of space if the class is large or the available space small.

32. Utilize available extra spaces on the field or floor. Invent or modify activities that fit into such spaces.

33. Provide activities that lead up to the new activities.

34. Modify rules or content of an activity in order to make it better fit the group, the facilities, or the purposes of the activity.

35. Explain rules without unduly interfering with participation.

36. Work toward the goal of enabling each student to be successful in achieving something worth-while to him in each physical education period.

37. Help students check on the attainment of their self-selected objectives.

38. Make sure that first attempts in learning an activity will be reasonably promising of success.

39. Construct tests to evaluate results of participation.

40. Enable each student to know his standing in any evaluated trait or ability at any appropriate time.

41. Diagnose errors in skill, knowledges, and conduct that are evidenced.

42. Devote some time to remedial teaching, based upon diagnosis.

43. Help students discover gradually the ever-increasing number and degree of values to be gained from the activities.

INDIVIDUALIZATION

No one ever taught a class, or two people—even most Siamese twins have two brains! One teaches the *individual*. Not only the novice is apt to forget this. Some ineffective teachers who have taught for a good many years fail to *individualize* their teaching. They toss something to be learned to students as if they had identical thresholds of receptiveness, identical abilities, potentials, intelligence, and identical motivations. As pointed out in the last chapter, some of the golf and tennis pros do better than this! The individual learner *must* be reached, he must be hooked in the language of the fisherman and William James.

Principles of individualization. The following principles guide the teacher toward this gaining of the attention, the interest, and the notice of the individual learner.

▶ Let the student observe that you **notice him** sometimes.

▶ **Vary speech, demonstrations, explanations, and visual aids** so that each student's background, physique, ability, physical competence, and intelligence are recognized.

▶ Make sure to **adjust teaching to varying maturities.**

▶ Permit a reasonable amount of **individual variation** in performing skills.

▶ During explanations, **use examples that come from the hobbies and interests of various members of the class.**

▶ **Avoid overdoing individualization** to the point of spending too much time and attention on one student at the expense of others.

▶ Consider the student's **degree of sensitivity.**

▶ **Recognize individual talents,** good performances and improvement, and earnest effort.

▶ **Concentrate when possible on the individual's improving his own level of performance,** attitudes, sociability, and so on.

▶ Be alert to evidence of extreme frustrations and conflicts.

▶ Strive to make it possible for each student in each class to experience success at something considered by him, the class, or the teacher as worthy.

▶ Provide some opportunity for individual creative work or individual self-expression.

▶ Provide opportunities for carrying responsibility by the individual.

▶ Recognize that the rate of learning, development, and improvement varies from student to student.

▶ Provide some opportunities for decisions to be made by each student.

▶ Provide opportunities for the student to lead and to follow.

▶ Permit program flexibility, to meet individual needs.

▶ Practice social equality in dealing with students.

The prospective teacher may already be aware of the growing concern of many modern men of wisdom who write articles and books about where Americans are heading as *individuals*. The concern about the gradual taking-over of the life of the individual is widespread. More and more of the individual's former privileges, rights, initiatives, responsibilities, and chances to simply *be himself* are disappearing. They are being taken over by various governmental agencies at different levels, by social and welfare agencies, by organizations and other structured groups. The step from group dominance and control to the group as *the one* greatest good and goal is slippery. The step is not as long as it may seem to groupism.

This same alert prospective teacher may feel this concern about the individual is not related to his teaching in physical education. Yet, it is the work of such persons as *individual* teachers and *individual* parents that preserves the dignity of the human personality and the rights of the individual. No point is being made for the teacher to use silly techniques for the purpose of providing orgies of self-expression. Nor is it being emphasized that we should be soft with these growing, learning youngsters! Nor is it being said that these young people—intelligent as they are—know more than the teachers! Nor is there a concern that discipline and restraint may twist the personality beyond recovery! Rather, we stress that the concerned teacher should do all that he feels is wise to help the individual sense, believe, and feel that *he counts,* even in a large impersonal high school.

SOCIALIZATION

In the same breath that we discuss principles of individualization, we should discuss principles of socialization. Overemphasis on either one as a general practice fails in the proper development of the student. A nation, an organization, a team is strong only insofar as its *individual* members are strong—and as they are strong as an operating unit. Part of the necessary education of the individual is to be appreciative of his dependence upon others and to learn that through cooperative effort many worth-while accomplishments are gained. He also should come to see that worthless or harmful outcomes may emerge from cooperative effort. Nor are the *ends* the only test. No outcome can be truly good if the *means* are dishonest, unethical, unjust, and the like. In fact, a third test of group effort must be applied, namely, *what is the purpose of that effort?*

We are suggesting that socialization is not automatically a good thing. It is good if it meets the three tests. Fortunately, most physical education classes, most of the time, receive unquestioned benefits because most teachers take this socialization teaching step *intelligently.*

Principles of socialization. The following guides indicate not only that the chance should be given to work with others, within the conditions of the three tests, but also that the student must work within the conditions set down. It is not difficult to talk of cooperation and forget that the team and the activity each has set down stipulations, laws, and conditions to be followed. Here, then, are some of the principles of socialization.

▶ **Provide many opportunities for the individual to participate as a member of a team.**
▶ **Promote conformance to regulations, rules, and codes.**
▶ **Provide for changing leaders.**
▶ **Stress the importance of, and necessity for, the specific work performed by each member of a team,** for the dependence of one skill or set of skills upon another skill or other skills.
▶ **Engender the "our team" idea,** even though the players vary.

▶ **Recognize the worthiness of self-subordination for the good of the team,** as well as stellar performance for the good of the team.

▶ **Show the gearing of individual objectives with team objectives.**

▶ **Emphasize team solidarity** as distinct from dissension.

▶ **Promote transfer of training** from team sport experiences to life.

▶ **Recognize improvement in socialization of class members.**

▶ **Promote sociability** as well as the accomplishment of successful team performance.

▶ **Promote the ability to give and take,** and the necessary personal yielding to the will of the majority.

▶ **Encourage and adhere to the other standards of social behavior:** fair play, sportsmanship, and so forth.

▶ **Allow expressions and feelings of pride and satisfaction in team accomplishment,** with the admonition that the sportsman wins with modesty and that few victories are the result of one man's play.

▶ **Encourage the feeling of responsibility for team failure,** with the admonitions that the sportsman loses with dignity and that few defeats are the fault of one man.

DISCUSSION QUESTIONS

The reader is reminded that in the foregoing pages the chapter has presented primary, secondary, and tertiary principles of teaching together with teacher-student routines that serve as guides in teaching. Recall too that this and the following chapter should be thought of *as a whole.* In fact, Chapters 14, 15, and 16 also deal with teaching operations and their accompanying teaching guides. Nevertheless, there is merit in discussing some questions related to the contents of each chapter before going on to the next. The following discussion questions are samples of some matters that may need elaboration. Some refer to the next chapter.

1. In your experience in student assistant teaching, trial teaching, directed or practice teaching, or any unofficial teaching, is there any teaching operation discussed in the foregoing pages which you would omit?

2. Should the prospective teacher and the beginning teacher hold to that which he believes, as he considers how he should teach, or should he make use of the ideas and related experiences and suggestions of those who have served ably in the profession for a number of years? Why?

3. Of the principles of presentation listed, can you pick out one or more that seems meaningless to you? Are they meaningless to others?

4. Of the principles of explanation, which one or two do you think are *most* important if you want to explain something effectively?

5. If the professionals in golf and tennis find it advantageous to devise about one hundred ways of explaining how each skill is performed in their sports, do you believe that you should try to match them?

6. Do you think that a school actually is a replica of a democratic society? Why?

7. What is the main point being stressed in the principles of class organization and management?

8. Why should great care be taken in class organization and management before the class leaves the assembly spot?

9. Would you add some factors to those submitted for consideration in grading?

10. Do you favor classes made up of individuals of similar levels of ability in physical education? Why?

11. A good many procedures are listed under routinization. Would you ignore some of these? If so, which ones? Are unwanted consequences probable?

12. In the question above, if you believe that all of these routines and procedures are essential, about how long will it take to establish them?

13. What is your present belief about sensory aids to teaching—are they devices for the lazy teacher? Can better teachers use them to advantage? Defend your position.

14. Some physical educators consider demonstration as a teaching operation rather than one phase of the use of sensory aids. Where would you classify it? Why?

15. Do you think that individualization is as important as indicated in this chapter? Why?

16. If you were to list the teaching operations presented in this chapter in order of their importance (or value), where would you put providing for pupil participation? Why?

17. If large-scale or primary principles were used in the section on participation, there probably would be two, three or four. They would be formulated, for example, something like this: The teacher should provide a chance to participate in activities that are beneficial. Would a few general guides like this better serve the beginning teacher than specific, concrete, detailed principles? Why?

18. Do you think that the experienced, effective teacher could use the general, large-scale type of principles of teaching better than the beginning teacher? Why?

19. Unquestionably, a few experienced teachers are ineffective. If they should begin to use teaching principles, would it be easier or more difficult for them than for beginning teachers to begin to use teaching principles? Why?

20. Someone has likened the use of principles by the teacher to the use of chart and compass by the navigator. At first it is easier to steer without such guides because they get in the way in the early stages. Do you believe that teaching can become more and more automatic, less and less dependent on the teacher's judgment? Why?

SAMPLE TEST ITEMS FOR THE CHAPTER

True-False

1. Teaching consists of orderly steps taken in predetermined sequence.

2. The modern teacher knows how a student will respond to any teaching.

3. Teaching is somewhat like a sport in that you cannot predict accurately what will happen next.

4. There are only seven teaching operations that initiate and promote learning.

5. Presentation of a lesson should be geared to at least one of the major interests of the class.

6. The only way to learn something is by doing it.

7. In presenting a new learning to a class, a teacher should begin with something difficult.

8. Leave it up to the students to set up their own objectives, as the teacher sets up his objectives for a given lesson.

9. A teacher's explanation of how a new skill should be performed should describe in accurate detail exactly how it is performed by the best performers.

10. Explanation and demonstration are two separate teaching steps and should be used separately by the teacher.

11. If a teacher expects the student to become enthusiastic about an activity, he should visibly show enthusiasm for it.

12. While the class is in session, the teacher should maintain a businesslike atmosphere, reserving a show of a sense of humor for out-of-class occasions.

13. While a class is resting after a strenuous period of activity, the teacher should not attempt to explain anything because fatigue minimizes understanding.

14. The beginning teacher can count on his classes in almost all schools being arranged on the basis of homogeneous grouping.

15. The teacher's appearance and manner are cues to student behavior.

16. One good way of adding variety to the program is to have a different way of signaling the class to assemble each time they meet.

17. The rules of an activity should never be modified by the teacher until they are changed officially.

18. Before a class leaves the assembly spot, the members should know about how long they will have for the activity in which they are about to participate.

19. Regardless of the teacher's possible disagreement, the physical education program should fit into the school's program.

20. The quickest way of taking attendance is always the best way.

21. All children of the same age should be given the same amount of time for participation in each activity.

22. Class management begins when the class begins.

23. Teaching would be a wasteful bedlam if there were no routines.

24. Regardless of other considerations, high school students are too immature and disinterested to be helpful to the teacher in establishing routines.

25. The term audio-visual aids is too limited an idea for the teacher in physical education.

26. Use of a wide variety of sensory aids of fair quality is better than a few of high quality.

27. The teacher should use demonstration for showing the right way to perform a skill and should not demonstrate some error in performance being made by members of the class.

28. The time to use demonstration is at the end of the class period when the class can more accurately remember it for the next lesson.

29. The progressive teacher will use every new mechanical aid to teaching which the school can afford.

30. Seldom permit a student to see you observing his worst efforts.

31. One should teach all students similarly if he is to be fair.

32. Leaders are born, so select them as squad leaders.

33. The effective teacher constantly works to have students participate spontaneously, but if they do not, he should make them want to.

34. A class period should begin gradually and reach the height of intensity just as the class period ends.

35. If the class is not obviously fatigued at the end of the class, the teacher cannot be said to have taught effectively.

BIBLIOGRAPHY

Brace, David Kingsley, *Health and Physical Education for Junior and Senior High Scshools*. New York: A. S. Barnes & Co., 1948.

Brownell, Clifford Lee, and E. Patricia Hagman, *Physical Education—Foundations and Principles*. New York: The McGraw-Hill Book Company, Inc., 1951.

Bucher, Charles A., ed., *Methods and Materials of Physical Education and Recreation*. St. Louis: The C. V. Mosby Company, 1954.

Cowell, Charles C., and Hilda M. Schwehn, *Modern Principles and Methods in High School Physical Education*. Boston: Allyn and Bacon, Inc., 1958.

Knapp, Clyde G., and E. Patricia Hagman, *Teaching Methods for Physical Education, A Textbook for Secondary School Teachers.* New York: The McGraw-Hill Book Company, Inc., 1953.

Kozman, Hilda Clute, Rosalind Cassidy, and Chester O. Jackson, *Methods in Physical Education.* Philadelphia: W. B. Saunders Company, 1958.

Oberteuffer, Delbert, *Physical Education, A Textbook of Principles for Professional Students.* New York: Harper & Brothers, 1956.

Vannier, Maryhelen, and Hollis F. Fait, *Teaching Physical Education in Secondary Schools.* Philadelphia: W. B. Saunders Company, 1957.

Williams, Jesse Feiring, *The Principles of Physical Education.* Philadelphia: W. B. Saunders Company, 1958.

14

Initiating and advancing
learning—II

". . . progress, man's distinctive mark alone. . . ."
—Browning.

WE HAVE SEEN THAT THE TEACHER PREPARES FOR HIS WORK through three sequential operations. Once the students come under his jurisdiction, he chooses from further operations, depending on the teaching-learning situation. Eight of these were submitted for consideration in the last chapter with their accompanying guides-to-action.

In the present chapter, the following seven operations are discussed and described in similar fashion: (1) observation, (2) analysis, (3) diagnosis, (4) generalization, (5) direction, (6) motivation, and (7) discipline.

The prospective teacher should remind himself that the principles of teaching are guides. They are neither formulas nor how-to's. He will do well to remind himself that guides-to-action are found in all of the other professions. Such principles are based on the best that the profession knows. When new facts and information make elimination or revision of a given principle advisable or essential, the change is made. Such a process is not new in any profession. Even scientific theories and laws are being changed!

Let us now look at the first of the teaching operations to be considered in this chapter, that of observation.

OBSERVATION

Observation is a teaching operation that *may* serve as the first in a series of five related operations. When the teacher observes the student in order to analyze his performance or conduct and in turn directing his learning, we have an instance when this series occurs.

The prospective teacher is warned that in the following discussion of these five operations a good deal of time and space are used to describe an overall process that actually may take but a few seconds to perform! The experienced teacher may very quickly observe, analyze, diagnose, generalize, and say a word or two to direct the student's learning.

The teacher's observation of the individual as he practices or performs does not refer to the kind of observation usually connected with directed teaching. Neither is reference made to the kind of observation employed in guidance.

If teaching hints, suggestions, and directions are to be effective, they must be based on more than a casual looking at the performer. The teacher *must actually see* the significant movements performed, their timing, the place they were performed, their relationship to other movements made by the performer and by other possible performers. Effective teaching is based in part upon accurate analysis, followed by accurate diagnosis, followed by valid generalizations or conclusions, and finally the direction of learning. This entire chain of mental operations is based on the assumption that the analysis, in the first place, was based on accurate observation.

Principles of observation. Here are some principles that guide the teacher in this teaching operation.

▶ **The teacher should know the activity being performed, the performer, he should know *about* the activity and know *about* the performer.** The teacher must be familiar with such factors as: (1) the skills involved, (2) skills similar to those of other activities, (3) the basic mechanics of movements like the skills being performed, (4) the different ways that effective participants (including the champions) have performed these skills, as well as, (5) definite information about the present performer and his abilities and his potentials.

The accumulated background enables the teacher to see with the eyes of experience and knowledge. There are reference-points with which comparisons can be made. The reference-points aid in looking for commonly accepted movements and distinctive and crucial actions. Thus, observation includes not only seeing what is actually going on but also seeing or sensing *relationships* between the action-at-hand and previously observed actions.

For example, as a teacher observes the pupil practicing or participating in basketball, he observes this individual as he performs the fifteen to twenty fundamentals with the eyes of one who knows. Thus, for each move that he sees, he has reference-points to tie to, to compare with, to establish relationship with. This refers not only to such a fundamental as passing or pivoting but the more complicated team movements such as screening. Effective teachers and effective coaches bring their experiences and ability to see relationships to bear upon what is happening before their eyes.

▶ **The teacher should be able to isolate and identify the significant movements of the learner or the performer.** This principle is related to the first one. The teacher does not pay equal attention to all movements. He checks on the basic movements and body positions. Should they be reasonably sound in the beginning stages, the teacher shifts his attention to the more commonly made mistakes. Perhaps he is alert enough, expert enough, or fortunate enough to have some part of the movements catch his eye. The eye is caught because the timing is off, or the angle of body part or angle or release of the ball is wrong, or the application of leg power is at odds with the application of power of the torso, and so on.

▶ **The teacher should develop his observational ability to the point of effectiveness.** This principle is another of the obvious statements which are apt to be overlooked because of their basic common sense. Experimentation has shown that the most accurate and most telling observation comes from constant changing of attention and eye-shifting from one point to another, not in any particular order. The eyes dart quickly here and there from one body part to another, as the performer is observed, or from one player to another. In some activities where very swift, sweeping movements are made with an extremity, the eye of the teacher shifts from one point to the other, closer to the body than the end of the fast-swinging leg or arm.

▶ **The teacher should observe comprehensively.** This means that before the teacher can analyze he must see the movement as a part of a unity. Actually, this point of being comprehensive in one's observations also means that what goes on *before and after* the skill being observed is important. The timing and direction of the pivot in basketball, for example, are judged correct or acceptable depending on what happened just before the pivot and what is to follow after it is made. The teacher *must* be able to isolate and identify any given movement which warrants his attention as a part of the entire situation. A player might make a well executed pass time after time, but the situation instead might call for a shot at the basket in each of the occasions.

This principle also includes the point that the teacher adds *connectivity* to that which he sees, in order to really observe. That is, he does not view the movements of the performer, either during the same skill or successive skills, as a series of only isolated movements. Rather, he sees them as connected, as making up a whole overall movement. The catch-stop-pivot-pass-or-shoot is seen as a unity. A player might be able to perform any one of these acceptably as an isolated skill but fail to perform it properly as a part of a progressive movement. This criterion of comprehensiveness also includes performing under fire. The psychological aspect is a part of comprehensiveness in observation.

▶ **The teacher should make sure of the accuracy of the senses used in observation.** This principle means simply that he has visual acuity, hearing accuracy, and the like. The information brought in by the senses must avoid being distortions of reality. Nor does this principle forbid the use of instruments that favorably supplement man's senses, such as a telefoto lens.

▶ **The teacher should adopt and maintain a favorable mental attitude.** This principle is one of the most important, yet commonly overlooked aspects of observation. It refers to the desire and will to observe accurately and reliably, and to the fact that the teacher should have no prejudices, no prejudgments.

▶ **The teacher should make as certain as possible that a given observation is made from the best possible spot in order to see accurately and dependably.**

▶ The teacher should be or become skillful in estimating measures related to observation of motor performance such as angle, distance, width, height, time, and size.

▶ The teacher should know and keep in mind precisely why a given observation is being made.

▶ The teacher should guard against seeing into a situation that which he hopes he finds.

▶ The teacher should recognize that experience in performance in physical activities or in teaching in physical education is not a guarantee of expertness in observation.

▶ The teacher should guard against using one observation as the basis of analysis and diagnosis, unless this is unavoidable.

ANALYSIS

This teaching step refers to the *teacher's* analysis of the student(s). Normally, we think of analysis as being confined to the teacher's examination of the pupil and his performance, or of a team's performance in terms of players' movements on field or floor. But, analysis also may refer to the teacher's examination of the activity, the environment, the purposes, his own teaching, and the performance of others for the sake of comparison.

Analysis by the pupil of himself, as mentioned in the discussion on motor learning, is a task that must be handled *very carefully* by the teacher and coach. It is not included in the following discussion although some of the points may apply.

The teacher's analysis consists of breaking up into elements whatever it is he examines. The teacher first must really *see* what there is to be *sensed* (weighed, seen, touched, heard, felt). Secondly, as a skill is observed, analysis calls for the teacher's recognizing the significant *parts* of the skill and perhaps identifying them.

Almost without knowing it, the teacher then takes the third step and classifies these skill-parts, even if it is no more than registering them mentally as correct or erroneous. In a complex skill, this classification would include more than two categories. For example, in the common catch-throw or catch-pass kind of skill combination, the categories might be before catching, catching, before throwing, throwing, and after throwing. And, under each of these categories might be sub-categories for skill-parts performed by feet, legs, torso, head, neck, arms, and hands. All or most of this part of analysis may be done instantly by the teacher without his being aware of the mental processes of *classification*. This classifying task includes the *ideas* the teacher associates with the skill parts. This classifying action is inseparably geared to observation. The two go on in such close connection that they form almost a single quick operation.

The fourth stage of analysis is verification. Sometimes classification has to be a temporary process. The teacher, if he is unfamiliar with the pupil, the activity, or some other factor, may not know for sure how to classify what he sees so that it *makes sense* in terms of the diagnosis which will follow analysis. Consequently, he checks his first judgment of classifying the skill-parts. He makes more sure which skill-parts were accidental, and which were intended. This means that he needs to see the pupil perform a skill more than once. Even this brief discussion explains why it usually takes longer for the teacher to help a new student.

Also included in this *verification* stage of analysis is making certain that the sequence of performing the skill-parts *as observed* was actually the sequence performed. This verification stage also may find the teacher breaking a skill-part into still smaller parts.

Fifth, this grouping or classifying of skill-parts is *related to* the knowledge and experience of the teacher. The teacher thinks, "In the light of what I know about this skill, this learner, the purposes and goals set up, and the like, and in the light of what my senses tell me about what has gone on before my eyes, what is my analysis?" At this pre-diagnostic moment he wonders if he can effectively help the learner.

This next phase of analysis is often unnecessary. However, if the teacher knows that he lacks the knowledge and ability to deal with the problem, he should, lastly, postpone action until he is competently ready.

Let no teacher-to-be think that these six stages are good theory but unnecessary. One of the authors will never forget the experience as a novice coach of watching one of the country's top university coaches spend two weeks in the midst of a "hot" season going through these stages of analysis (plus diagnosis and generalization). Only then did he step up casually to the player who had been off, and tell him in fifteen seconds what to try. At no time during those two weeks did the player even know that he was the object of extremely intense, comprehensive observation and analysis. Every teacher in physical education will not follow this pattern of carefulness, patience and close study.   But, this failure to follow cannot be because such quality of analysis is impractical!

The example used above was that of analyzing a skill.   The same six stages also apply to analyzing an activity, the environment, attitudes, purposes, or whatever needs to be analyzed, in order for the teacher to make an intelligent diagnosis.

Principles of analysis.   The following guides help the teacher perform analysis.

▶ **Identify exactly what it is that is to be analyzed.**   This prevents the teacher from rushing into doing something because the learner badly needs help.   Many teachers admit they rush in.   They view the situation as, in the words of William James, ". . . one great blooming, buzzing, confusion. . . ."   In contrast, this principle guides their collective finger on *exactly* what part of the teaching-learning situation needs to be analyzed.

▶ **Determine whether he** (the teacher) **possesses the background and skill to perform the indicated analysis.**

▶ **Specify the purpose(s) of the analysis.**   This gives direction to the teacher's effort, thought and energy.   "Precisely why am I doing [or going to do] this particular analysis?" is a question that helps bring sense and clarity.

▶ **Identify the size of the thing to be analyzed.**

▶ **Determine whether the thing to be analyzed is a common experience of the average physical educator.**

▶ **Determine the significance of the thing to be analyzed.**   This principle is another common sense statement.   Yet, this guide is not followed frequently.   Some well meaning teachers take the time, trouble, and energy to analyze something that is not significant in terms of the purpose(s) set up.   And again, there are the unfortunate consequences of a young teacher's following his beliefs when a five-second conversation with someone who *knows* may save the novice five days or six weeks of worry, or even his job!

▶ **Identify the main values involved with the thing to be analyzed.**   The activity, the skill, or whatever it is that the teacher is analyzing may have few if any values connected with it.   Or, it may be very crucial because of the large number and size of the values involved.

▶ **Determine whether the thing to be analyzed is a carryover from traditional practice** (but actually no longer valid).

▶ **Determine whether the thing to be analyzed is something that can be rectified, after diagnosis, generalization, and direction.** Many a teacher would be saved heartaches, wasted time, and hours of work if he simply found out whether the situation could be improved by him.

▶ **Consider the consequences of the analysis.**

▶ **Determine the relationships between this analysis with other analyses.**

▶ **Consider the possible future of any analysis made.** One also should think of to what a given analysis-diagnosis may lead. Analysis, like a good many things that teachers do, has a future.

DIAGNOSIS

The very use of the term diagnosis reminds us of the key stage in the physician's relationship with his patient. Like the physical educator, he observes with all senses (as recommended by Hippocrates about 2300 years ago), then analyzes, and only then makes his diagnosis. If his observation is inadequate, incorrect, or if his analysis is inaccurate, what chance does he have of making a correct diagnosis?

The physical education teacher, like the physician, observes and analyzes, and then says to himself, "What is wrong here? What is or is not normal?" Questions like these assume that the questioner has a background of technical knowledge. He has the ability also to compare what he sees with that which he knows or has seen or experienced first-hand. The physical educator, because his purpose usually is different from that of the physician, does not ask himself only the what's wrong here question.

Part of diagnosis might include asking questions of the learner. Recall from the last chapter that some teachers ask such questions as, "What are you trying to do?" "What do you think of when you perform this skill?" "Are you trying to . . .?" Another aspect of diagnosis usually includes comparing this pupil's movements with those of other pupil's movements who have similar appropriate characteristics such as age, height, weight, body-build and the like.

Or, the comparison might be made with best form, typified by some of the top performers.

The teacher mentally tries out each of the possible causes of erroneous performance. He keeps asking himself, "What do the pupil's movements in this skill *indicate?*" Is it a matter of muscular weakness? Lack of endurance? Low quality neuromuscular coordination? The usual tension of the beginner? Disinterest? *What?*

Sometimes the teacher, intent on a correct diagnosis, will ask another and perhaps still another teacher, whose judgment he respects, to help in the diagnosis. Another outside aid is the use of a testing device. This might be a standardized test of the skill. It might be a mechanical device. It might even be a pencil-paper test such as a temperament inventory.

The work of the teacher-diagnostician resembles the searching efforts of the detective. And, like the detective presented with a good many clues at first, the teacher attempts to identify the clue within some *large* area of possibility.

As the possibilities are considered, they are tested. Some of this testing might consist of mental experimentation. Some of it might be actually *trying out* temporarily selected solutions. For example, if the teacher decides to see if the reason is a lack of hand strength more than it is a lack of eye-hand coordination, he can quickly test these two abilities.

In the meantime, the teacher with a fine technical background, who has kept up-to-date, and who sharpens his skills of diagnosis, continues to attempt to *connect* the student's performance with that of comparable performances. He may review mentally kinesiological principles that are appropriate. He might turn to a study of his anatomy textbook. These sorts of knowledge, study, and experience help the more expert teacher make correct diagnoses more rapidly, and accurately.

Another thing that recognition of the fine diagnostic ability of the experienced, effective teacher might suggest to the novice is that, on the job, such valuable help can be had for the asking. No matter *what* the novice might *believe,* and no matter how sincere he may be in that belief, the chances are great that the teacher who has proved his ability as a diagnostician will have quite a different belief!

Principles of diagnosis. To guide the teacher as he diagnoses the performance of a pupil, he should:

▶ **Look for connections between the situation being diagnosed and other similar situations** with known diagnoses that proved to be correct.

▶ **Consider and submit to trial** (at least mentally) **the various possible reasons for the problem** or difficulty in the situation.

▶ **Make sure that his diagnosis is based on errors that continue to occur with some consistency** and pattern in the situation.

▶ **Attempt to connect, as an early step, the cause of difficulty with the pupil's violation of some fundamental law or principle.**

▶ **Assess one's capability to make an accurate diagnosis** of this particular situation.

▶ **Obtain at the earliest possible moment a general notion of what the most likely causes may be,** and at the same time keep the mind open for unusual and unexpected causes.

▶ **Rule out obvious biases** and search for and eliminate hidden ones.

▶ **Continually seek the implications** of that which has been observed and analyzed.

▶ **Make use of all possible sources of help** such as experts and evaluative tools.

▶ **Try out the correct diagnosis** (until it is unquestionably the right one), **before generalizing,** and then recommend what the pupil should do.

GENERALIZATION

In this operation the teacher pulls together a number of ideas and suggestions. He has made his diagnosis, based on observation and analysis, and now he is prepared to pull together *all* factors and forces which will enable him to draw a justifiable conclusion. He pulls together selected bits not considered up to this moment, for example, pertinent facts about the nature of adolescense, about the laws of learning, about this environment, about this school, about the level of maturity of the pupil being studied as well as his present levels of ability and estimated potentials.

To be able to generalize accurately, not only must the teacher have bits of evidence from appropriate areas, but he must have the ability to select those that are pertinent. To see *relationships* between data from observations, the results of the analysis, and the diagnosis, and, on the other hand, the data from all of the pertinent remainder of the environment is the key to making a justifiable generalization.

Generalization is one place the experienced teacher has an advantage over the beginning teacher. If he has been a successful teacher, he has built many reference points back through each of the years he has taught.

Another reason for care in making generalizations is that sometimes a little point may have a great effect. No teacher knows what may happen to an idea once it is tossed out upon the air waves, or into the mind of a student.

The teacher also should connect his conclusion to the end in view. Unless his purpose is to say something meaningless, he would not make the generalization that what this performer needs is to be told to keep on trying. This points up one of the differences between the effective and ineffective teacher. The latter is apt to say a good many things that do not *pinpoint* exactly what it is the pupil should try next. Often, he says things that he hopes will make the pupil feel good. Conclusions must be accurate if they are to enable the teacher to direct learning effectively.

DIRECTION

We are now ready to consider what the teacher does after he observes, analyzes, diagnoses, and generalizes. After generalization, he directs learning. That is, he gives *direction* to learning.

Perhaps a few prospective teachers might think, "Well! All there is to it is to see that the kid made a mistake and then just tell him what to do. It's all just plain common sense if you've ever played the game." The effective teacher knows that teaching is not that simple (would that it were!). Effective teachers possess abilities in all five of these teaching operations.

The word direction is a word avoided in the vocabularies of some physical educators. *It is used quite deliberately here.* If the teacher is able to go through the other steps skillfully, he is ready to give authoritative instruction! Another intended meaning of direction is prescription. Still other synonyms are cut out work for, show the way, lead the way, conduct, or guide.

Not only are some physical educators afraid of the word direction but they continuously use the "soft" approach instead of *directing* learning, regardless of the situation. Here we are speaking of method. Of course, authoritative instruction need not be given in an authoritative way. Yet, the teacher should be an authority in what he is about to tell the student. If he is not, he must begin again with observation. Or, perhaps he needs to know more about the activity. Nor should he forget that once he knows what to tell the learner, there should be a score or more (at least) of ways of saying it.

Aspects of direction. *First,* one of the main keys to effectiveness as a teacher is to do or say that which will help the learner *catch the essence* of what he is to do. *Second,* in directing the learner after he has made a mistake worthy of attention, teacher's words should be doubly graphic, acutely descriptive. Bear in mind that the teacher already has given some word pictures before the first attempts. Further, the learner must show progress. This verbal phase of the direction of learning finds many physical educators at a loss to *etch* sharply what the pupil should do, without making his thoughts turn inward so long, so often, or so violently that he gets tied into knots.

Third, a sequence of movements quickly begins forming a motor pattern (undoubtedly with one or two errors mixed into the pattern). Once it has become a pattern, the learner does not feel like another change (unless results are unsatisfactory). He resists taking on a new movement. He does not like the discomfiture which comes with trying to forget the old as he tries the new. He says, "It doesn't feel natural this new way."

Fourth, sometimes, time is not of the essence but in a physical education class it is. There are so few minutes per period for the teaching-learning process! So many learners need help!

Fifth, psychologists tell us that the *fastest* way to bring about the kind of a change in which we are interested is to make errors unpleasant and right movements pleasant. This making errors unpleasant does not mean that the teacher needs to be unpleasant in his attitude, manner, or speech! But it does mean that the learner should not be permitted to get away with (unintentionally) major errors without at least having them called to his attention.   And, if the movement is performed correctly, there should be a rewarding sign.

Sixth, most teaching in this field is of the *type* we have been describing.   As soon as the pupil begins to try to do what he has seen demonstrated or heard verbally described, from that point on the teacher's *main* task for a while is to help eliminate errors.   This means that most of the instruction at this stage is what we are calling direction, directing the learner's attention to a major mistake and directing his attention to the right movement.   This accounts in part for the fine reputation many physical educators and coaches have for being effective teachers.   It demands a great deal of patience.

Seventh, the point that people do not forget physical education skills as easily as they forget some academic acquirements because the former have to be overlearned, is further evidence that the teacher in this field has to be persistent.   The term, overlearned, hides the long hours of *helping* the learner perform with acceptable consistency.   In a good many school subjects, which students take concurrently with physical education, to *know* is enough.   But in the latter field, one can know what to do with acceptable consistency and be able to *perform* only once in ten tries, even after a good many class periods.

Eight, think of the patience the student has to have!   He is the one who is making the mistakes, whose errors are being pointed out by the teacher, who feels clumsy, who knows, but cannot *do.*   Is it any wonder that a good many of them become discouraged, impatient, and some come to have negative attitudes toward physical education—and its teachers!

Ninth, the direction of learning (authoritative instruction) calls for patience by the teacher about himself.   The beginning teacher is overly apt to blame himself for the inability of the learner.   This impatience with self should not upset the novice.   Think of just one of the paradoxes of teaching.   The performer must learn a number of things the teacher cannot teach him!   The kinesthetic feel must be learned by the performer in a number of activities.   But, so far we know of no way to directly *teach* feel.   Yet fine former college performers admit they never learned feel until college days were over.   The best we can do is to give suggestions, ask questions, and direct attention, but we cannot *teach* the very thing we want the player to acquire!

Tenth, sometimes the teacher should be impatient with himself and is not.   The well intentioned novice is apt to direct the learner's attention to how his body parts move as he performs, to the end-result of some body-part(s), to the errors being made, or to some level of skill or intricate nicety which is considerably beyond present attainment.   Such efforts are made with the best of intentions.   Yet, good intentions may direct the learner down the wrong road. Again, we see the limitations of following what one *believes* instead of following the route of tested, examined experience, as is the practice in other professions.

Sure!   Consider trying something new.   But, before actually experimenting with it on an unsuspecting class, in an unsuspecting school, in an unwarned community, the better part of wisdom is to check first with the department head and/or the principal.   No novice should ever get the idea that there is a conspiracy against newcomers with new ideas.   But let it be said in passing, that the old, catchy saying that even though I do not agree with you, I will defend with my life your right to believe what you like, went out the window after Belsen, Bataan, and Buchenwald.   Individual beliefs that lead to great harm to others cannot be ignored or countenanced.   The three ancient and honored professions (medicine, theology, and law) long ago recognized that in their services, members had to be responsible for the professional practice, behavior, and standards of their fellow members.   If teaching ever becomes such a profession it will have this kind of responsibility to shoulder.

MOTIVATION

The fallacy of the automatic working of interests as the key to motivation still exists in some schools.   "All you have to do is to interest them."   That is a different idea from this one, "The student's interest is. . . ."   Both of these ideas are different from, "She is interested in . . . because. . . ."   This kind of indefinite talk has centered in this word, which Dewey is credited with throwing on the education band wagon many years ago.

Dewey's use of interest has also been misinterpreted.   Nothing he ever wrote (and no record of anything he ever said) could be construed to mean that teachers should make it a principle to connect their teaching to the *minor, transient interests* of youngsters. And, *most* of their interests are of this small-scale, ephemeral variety. Hundreds of thousands of teachers have spent millions of hours trying to find out such minutiae. Today it may be a certain song or comic strip. Tomorrow, a special way of wearing one's clothing or doing one's hair. And, the next day it may be a certain Hollywood star or a special connotation given to a word, in or out of the dictionary.

The futility of tying one's teaching to such here-today-gone-tomorrow interests rests in this fact. When they are gone, the student jettisons everything connected with them. What splendid disdain the teenager shows for *anything* connected to yesterday's discarded interest! And therein lies the reason for many failures to stimulate youngsters to want to learn. The teacher finally discovers the loss of *that* student interest and starts the scramble to find another— not only to discover another or a new minute interest but also to try to twist the subject or warp the interest so that some tempting connection exists between the thing to be learned and the trivial, temporary interest.

In contrast, *motives* are the steam that is used to help push and prod and coax the human machine to move. This analogy is descriptive even though it, like most analogies, is not accurate in all respects. Saying it more formally, motivation occurs by means of using man's *motives*. Now, *if* by interests someone actually *means* motives (and sometimes this is the case), then he would be correct in his *meaning to say* that motivation occurs by means of using man's basic and more permanent interests.

But let us examine the place of motivation in the teaching-learning process. Even an elementary course in psychology clarifies that man is goal-seeking. We will do a great deal and go through almost anything to attain our goals. If there is no easier, faster, better way to reach a goal, we even will *learn* in order to attain it! In order to learn, if a more desirable alternative is lacking, we even will practice, drill, go through the embarrassment of having someone tell us of our errors, and push ourselves past the point of fatigue!

A number of the things that you want are also wanted by almost every other normal human being. These wants or cravings seem to be common to man. Some of them are necessary to his physical survival. For example, breathing, eating, drinking, and maintaining proper chemical balances. Thus, we might call them basic or universal *needs*. And, as the course in general psychology points out, there also are cravings which involve other people, and, still other needs that involve personal cravings such as a desire for self-esteem or wanting power or a desire for success.

These three categories of motives might be expanded into eight in order to make them seem more tangible: (1) activity motives—processes of the energy of life and natural response to stimuli; (2) subsistence motives including man's economic activities—organic needs such as hunger, thirst, and temperature balance; (3) social recognition and approval—organic needs such as early dependence on the care of others, and orientation with others; (4) mastery motives—to succeed, dominate, excel—reaction to resistance; (5) conformity motives—obedience to lawful authority, submission—fear and pain; (6) sex motives—relations of *all* kinds to the opposite sex, conditioned symbols, sublimination; (7) security motives—concern for security of self, for one's offspring; and (8) acquirement motives—drives to have, to collect, to acquire.

More definiteness and concreteness about motives may come to the prospective teacher if we expand the eight into twenty-five motives:

1. Reaching for or toward material gain.
2. Competing for results, scores, rewards, honors, recognition, a position.
3. Desire to be approved as "one of the gang," as courageous, as worthy.
4. Wanting to advance, get ahead, be on the first team.
5. Being ambitious for attaining things for self, for our team, our school.
6. Desire to play, relax, recreate (recreation).
7. Desire to create, to start something new, to be original, to have a new self.
8. Desire to express self in some way or ways—verbally, artistically, *et cetera*.
9. Making things, constructing, putting things together, building.
10. Entertaining others, "listen to me, see me, see my ability."
11. Meeting other persons, socializing, sharing.
12. Collecting, saving.
13. Mastering, conquering, exerting power, dominating others.
14. Bettering, improving self, conditions, chances for success.
15. Expressing curiosity.

16. Manipulating—purposeful and concentrated, even when idle.

17. Seeking adventure, the unusual, the unexpected, taking chances for a goal.

18. Seeking security, certainty, the dependable.

19. Love, affection.

20. Protection of others, sympathy, kindness, altruism.

21. Tackling certain fears and avoiding other fears.

22. Battling the elements of nature.

23. Struggling, meeting challenges, striving, making the effort.

24. Being a good citizen, a good team man, a dependable person.

25. Seeking biological and physiological satisfactions and balances.

A number of years ago, the list of man's motives numbered over 6,000 if one tallied the various lists of different items proposed by the various psychologists.

Now, if man's basic needs are not satisfied, tensions disequilibria result. The person may not be aware of these tensions. He, therefore, may not identify them. Nevertheless, they are there. Something basic within him *must* be satisfied. They knock for recognition. "I am hungry." "I am thirsty." "I can't hold my breath any longer."

These disequilibria tensions release energy. Man goes into action when tensions are not satisfied. He *seeks* food. He does something about being hungry. Some psychologists call these drives.

As all of us have observed, these drives in the baby are random and they are uncontrolled. But when the developing human learns some *patterns of behavior* to satisfy these drives, he then has motives! Thus, motives are a combination of man's inner drives together with learned patterns of behavior to satisfy the needs. Motives are connected with a large part of life and living. They are relatively permanent. These motives are neither isolated forces nor necessarily the one and only catalyst. For, many of them may unite to drive a man to act and to continue to act. A person might start to do something because he wants to dominate others but end up doing this same thing because of his love and affection for his offspring.

When a motive is recognized by the individual who is experiencing a given drive so that the end-result wanted by him is seen by him, it becomes a *purpose*. How he may gain the end-result is not important to him at this point. Thus motives enjoy not only relative permanence and are geared to living, but they are psychologically cemented to man's purposes.

Some of the things man seeks are things that society has determined are worthy. We call them *values*. The *symbols* of these values also are largely determined by the society in which we live. But, the symbols vary from person to person. Take for example the motive of the need for security. One phase of this motive is that we feel we must obtain and retain status. For some people the value symbol for status is the acquirement of material riches. For a teenager this might take the form of a certain make and style of vehicle.

Part of the task of helping students mature is suggesting (at least indirectly) that they adopt more permanent and more other-centered value symbols of status than a car or plane. For example, somewhat more maturity is gained if they come to see that status can be had by turning out for a team, joining a choral group, turning out for dramatics, and the like. Still further steps toward maturity may be taken if the teenager comes to find status in joining and working for a great cause, joining and working for a worthy organization.

Again we see that motives are more fundamental and reliable as bases of motivation than are interests. They are geared to man's more dominant values, his value system.

Still another reason that the use of motives is the springboard to motivation is that they are part of the force and substance which form *attitudes*. Dominant values, major purposes, and motives unite to help the individual determine what his attitudes shall be and to what degree of intensity they are held by him.

Most powerful motivation results when several motives are united and brought into play. One of the reasons American young men and women go through a good deal in order to gain a college education is that several motives are at work. And, these motives are so apparent that seldom does an adult have to motivate the young person to go to college. But, after he is in college and faces the tasks to be done and the standards to be met, he may need to be reminded of the motives involved such as social approval, success, security, and acquiring a college degree.

Incentives are stimuli acting from outside the individual. They may come from persons, objects, or situations. They are environmental conditions so arranged that they stimulate desired student responses. The teacher is a vital part of this stimulating environment. He must not become so dominant a part of the environment that he carries on most of the activity. Instead, he must remain the instigator of *student* activity. *He attempts to focus the energy drives of the students on the learning experiences by use of incentives which promise satisfactions and pleasurable activities.* When he can achieve such focus of student energy, he finds the need for imposed control reduced to a minimum.

Utilizing natural activity. Activity is a characteristic of normal individuals. In fact, normal children find it annoying to sit still and keep quiet for even relatively short periods of time. Learning, itself, implies activity on the part of the learner. But undirected and random expenditure of energy may be very uneconomical as a learning procedure. When the natural activity of the healthy student is guided by the mature and understanding adult, learning is accelerated. The teacher understands the student's wants. Women teachers use personal appearance as a basic incentive in physical education classes in junior and senior high school. The teacher attempts to direct the learner's activities by environmental and personal suggestions, and by helpful constraint.

Types of incentives. In all teacher attempts to guide and control student behavior, the question arises as to what kind of incentives the teacher should use. Any incentive is better than none, in so far as the rapidity of learning of those activities to which it applies is concerned. No incentives really act by themselves. The dread of failure and the hope for success are dual stresses in motivated activity. *Avoidance incentives add to the dread of failure, and rewards add to the hope for success.* Which phase of this motivating dichotomy exerts the most drive depends on a great many factors. Previous success and failure experiences of the individual vary his amount of tension to each; for example, an athletic coach may feel that he is not so much concerned about winning but that he hates to lose. Success occasions little congratulation. On the other hand, loss of a game seems to produce much emphatic, noncomplimentary comment.

In general, experimentation in the field of incentives has indicated that praise, satisfaction, and reward are better techniques for fostering learning than reproof, rebuke, criticism for error or failure, and the like. Individuals vary tremendously in how various incentives affect them. Reward incentives such as praise seem to be much more effective as an aid to learning when applied to the less skillful or less able students than when applied to the superior. Criticism for error, of teacher-expressed dissatisfaction at level of achievement, and the like appear more effective incentives with superior students. The combination of both types of incentive is better than either alone. Perhaps the superior performers need more criticism to keep them challenged and to keep them from being satisfied with anything but their best efforts; and the less successful students need more praise to keep them from becoming too discouraged to put forth their best efforts.

The teacher should bring into play as many incentives as he can focus on the learning activities. Incentives to other types of activity and incentives that conflict should be removed in so far as is possible. If social approval is the most effective, stress that particularly; but if mastery motives seem to be the most powerful, give the individual rewards such as responsibilities for direction and leadership, demonstration, and the like. *Stress the incentives which focus on the learning activities the strongest driving force available.*

We assume that the teacher will keep in mind the total learning situation. The recommended use of strong motives does not imply the development of antisocial or personally harmful phases of motivation. Appeals to selfishness, cultivation of dislike for a rival, and encouragement of notoriety-seeking are examples of malpractices in the use of incentives.

An abbreviated list of incentives and devices used by some teachers include:

1. Stressing freedom and independence of the student; having them choose objectives and select leaders, captains, chairmen, and student assistants to the teacher.

2. Teacher comment or reaction to student achievement; use of compliment, praise, or temporary but complete refusal to notice.

3. Emotional appeals through pep talks, inspiring stories, alumni speeches.

4. Animated and enthusiastic demonstrations by the teacher; followed by impelling and exacting demands on student effort, with personal interest in and individual guidance for each student.

5. Individual progress records, graphs, statistics: self-rating scales,

scoring records, batting averages, time records in events, strength indices, and the like.

6. Good equipment—gives opportunity to take pride in appearance.

7. Public recognition by newspapers, radio, assembly programs, movies of activities, bulletin-board publicity, banquets, and the like.

8. Competition, cooperation, and corecreation in games, tournaments, playdays, intramurals, exhibitions, pageants, and so on.

9. The awarding of prizes, ribbons, pennants, letters, medals, and the like, for successful achievements.

Two types of motivation. One type of motivation is characterized by persisting, annoying, uncomfortable tension. Pain and discomfort, mental or physical, are present. The individual must escape the stimuli to ease his tensions. He acts to remove the cause of the unbalance and to avoid the producing situation. Failure, social disapproval, insult, and tissue injury are examples of stimuli producing avoidance behavior. The visceral tensions from such stimuli may be tremendous.

Another type of motivation is characterized by pleasantness and pleasurable emotion. The individual acts to prolong and perhaps increase the intensity or amount of the experience. Success, physical comfort, social approval, praise, petting, and dancing are examples of stimuli which motivate the individual to seek further, or more intense stimuli.

This latter type is characterized by tensions and drives, just as the avoidance type is. If the individual were complacent and satisfied, he would not be stirred to seek activity by the stimuli. Sometimes the drive to this seeking type of motivation becomes very intense. Sex is the common example, but there are many others. Power, success, admiration, social approval, and beauty of art, music, and literature may become increasingly sought after by the individual experiencing these as personal satisfactions.

Analysis of motivation reveals childhood beginnings. The type in which furtherance or increase of stimulus is sought begins with the cuddling, rocking, petting, and praising of the youngster. He learns to seek praise, social approval, and the like. But the origins of extreme desires for power, fame, and social approval seem to relate to both escaping and seeking motives. Early need for social recognition, for example, can be thwarted until it turns into an abnormal craving. Napoleon is a classic example of abnormal craving for recognition and power. He is supposed to have been an object of derision to his schoolmates. Restraint and disapproval fostered in him the development of voracious hungers for mastery and recognition.

Strong stimuli, strong satisfactions.   Too much failure distorts one's motivation. Unfortunately, many teachers fail to realize the effect of the avoidance motivation present in competition, rivalry, and even in awards for success. Someone loses when someone else wins. Rivalry implies that some students *fail* to equal or surpass their rivals. Situations in which students try arduously, and yet almost continuously fail to win or to earn coveted awards, often cause maladjustments in personality. Such situations are inimical to education. An increasing number of teachers are giving awards and recognition for *personal* improvement rather than for total accomplishment only.

Failure.   Too many disappointments teach students to give up too easily, or not to try at all. Students blame the teacher or the examination for their failure, in order to escape the greater annoyance of admittting their own weakness. They may claim that they were not well, worked too hard, learning was of no value, they are in no hurry to learn, an additional year in school is what they really want.

Students denied praise and recognition for success may seek attention and notoriety by misbehavior. The male group attitude that the good student is a "sissy" is a reaction to escape the feeling of inferiority, a feeling engendered by failure to attain desired levels of success. The so-called "sissy" defends himself by speaking of dumb athletes. Has competition taught these boys to enjoy the failure of others? The competitive system of relative grading may be a major cause of such attitudes.

How can one develop aversions to subjecting his own behavior to reason and analysis? Narrow, illiberal, bigoted thinking and behavior have more than ignorance as a causal factor. Underlying fear that one may be wrong and a felt need to avoid any such humiliation also are factors. Persisting unrest due to a conflict in motives may cause this adjustment by stressing the stimuli to one motive and suppressing the stimuli to the other.

Too many disappointments and failures tend to make one over-sensitive to criticism and failure.   Failure in little things takes on undue significance.   *The teacher must make available to the student, activity which has as its outcome results interpreted as personal successes by the student.*

The teachers of tomorrow can go a long way toward erasing a concept which permeates education and even physical education.   This is the unfortunate, unfair, and sometimes tragic viewpoint that success and failure are inflexible labels.   The point is not to have the pupil avoid facing failure.   No mature person ever grew up who avoided that.   Nor is the point here to lower standards.   Nor is this the place to discuss the bases for awarding most grades in physical education.   Rather, the point is that we recognize and let the pupil recognize that success and failure are elastic words.   No person is so highly successful in all phases and activities of life that we can say of him, "He is a success."   Or, of another, "He is a failure."

Analysis of drive.   The curious upper division major student might be interested in an analysis of how a *drive* functions.   Because of its basic connection with motivation and discipline (which follows) a brief account is presented here.   The original source of human energy is food.   Food is transformed by the body's metabolism into various elements and into energy.   The neural, circulatory, and endocrine systems of the body distribute the energy throughout the body and function in maintaining a state of relative equilibrium or chemical balance.   Need for food will upset this balance, create tensions, and activity.   Hunger leads to activity in general, produces visceral tensions.   When aroused, this hunger drive energy seems to flow over and produce faster learning even in nonrelated experiences.

Thirst, fatigue, extremes in temperature, tissue injury, and the like produce other tensions or drives.   The hormones secreted from the glands of the body cause chemical changes, unbalance, drives. The hormones from the sex glands, for example, raise the general activity level.   Excessive thyroid secretion produces hyperactivity, irritability, and nervousness.   Deficient thyroid secretion reduces the individual's activity.   The hypothyroid is characterized as sluggish and lacking in alertness.   Anemia and feeble-mindedness are other conditions which often reduce the activity of the individual so afflicted.   Ill-health is frequently the cause of behavior classed as lethargic and indolent. Even long thwarting of an individual's desires may condition him into a pseudo-laziness, an unwillingness to try.

The life processes are continually producing energy which flows out into activity. Activity fosters greater energy production. The healthy individual is active, curious, exploratory, and manipulative in behavior. Until he learns specific patterns toward which his drives are oriented, he tends to approach, examine, and manipulate any stimulus which is strong enough to catch his attention.

Overstimulation usually causes avoidance reactions, whether the stimulus be extreme cold, heat, pain, light, or the like.

Overstimulation produces diffuse and deep visceral changes, a state of tension which is akin to emotion. Perhaps emotion is originally just some form of diffuse tension owing to very strong stimuli. Later, conditioning may attach this stirred-up state to milder stimuli. When these milder conditioned stimuli release emotional energy, the overt responses may be facilitated or they may be inhibited. Inhibition may be caused by motivation of an avoidance nature; or it may be caused by an overcharge of energy which diffuses throughout the individual, overexcites him, produces such a variety of random activity that focus of energy on specific response patterns is prevented. The system is flooded; hence, direction of current is impossible.

Motives, not push buttons. Regardless of the fact that the basis of motivation is motives, regardless of their strong connections within man's nature and behavior, they are not automatic. The intelligence and judgment demanded of the teacher who uses them explain why even experienced, effective teachers spend *a great deal of time* planning on how to get Bill or Mary to *want* to learn or to improve. Possibly researchers will find that still more judgment will be needed. For, should they establish that gross temperament accounts for some persons responding to the incentives and methods used by some teachers and not responding to the incentives and methods of other teachers (of equivalent quality as a teacher), our judgments will be further tried and tested. Let us now look at a few summary statements that re-emphasize that motives are not automatic.

1. Which motive is strongest in a given situation with a given person has to be discovered.

2. Motives that coax rather than club are usually superior even among animals.

3. Specificity in symbols gains quicker responses. "We serve good meals" on a roadside sign attracts fewer drive-in customers than "delicious strawberries."

4. Symbols that are closer to *sensory* mechanisms are stronger than others.

5. In numbers 3 and 4 above, the point may not be that quicker responses and stronger incentives are *wisest* to use, even though they are more sure-fire.

6. Nevertheless, examples of numbers 3 and 4 illustrate the power of motives. We seldom grow enthusiastic over service. Mentioning boys and girls that need our help comes closer. Meeting a youngster face-to-face who obviously needs our help is closer yet. The son or daughter of a close friend who needs us badly and who comes to us personally is almost certain to motivate action.

7. Human behavior—response to incentives—depends on such forces as the following: inherited mechanisms (such as the quality of the nervous system and of the sense organs), acquired experience (sum of habit patterns), present psycho-physiological state of the person, the incentives, and who (if anyone) is associated with them.

8. One cannot elicit behavior that is not built into the person's neural patterns. One cannot get appreciation of an oral reading of Shakespeare's Hamlet from some Ubangi savages. Polysyllable words will not motivate monosyllable persons.

9. Conflicts among and between motives are one source of life's trouble—which car, which girl, which college, how spend this $10 bill? The necessary choice between two good motives is especially frustrating to the young. If both are approximately worthy in one's philosophy of life, of about equal force in attaining toward one's master purpose, the experience of having to choose is frustrating to the most civilized adult.

10. Our feeling tone for words carries over to other situations. For example, an especially bad set of experiences with a man named Smith results in a feeling tone for Smith that carries over. Thus, some motives that should work, do not.

11. When trying to stimulate, negative symbols are not advisable. Keep attention on the positive.

12. Sincerity pays. Truth is stronger than fiction. To over-

describe in an effort to sketch the wanted end-result sometimes back-fires.

13. Usually, enthusiasm accompanying an incentive helps.

14. The strength of motives is not some academic matter. A person who really has some basic need that *must* be satisfied will sacrifice even life itself in order to gain it.

15. The overconcern of today's youth in the welfare of self and family can be diluted and should be replaced by greater and wider concerns. Not only has American youth been socially and idealistically minded in the past, but if tomorrow's citizens are not concerned with causes worth fighting for, what of the future of democracy?

16. The young teacher should *expect* that motives *may* lead on to other and often deeper motives.

17. Our difficulty in motivation has been that, as teachers in physical education, our vision has been small and short. We have been attempting to stimulate students in some matters that are actually trivial instead of stimulating them to learn and be guided by underlying principles.

18. We must keep in mind that motives are tools, devices in our hands. What works for one with rapidity and effectiveness may not work at all with another student (even though some day that motive may be the touchstone for this other student).

19. You cannot get a youngster to put his talents to work unless you can reach him and get him to give of himself.

20. Teachers ought to develop the ability to become masters at sensing when they have activated a given student's motives.

21. As in all human motivation, the teacher must plan his work so that the learner's wants or needs (at least one of them) are *not* met. If needs are met, there are no motives.

22. The teacher who permits mild demands for learning and insipid appeals to improve can expect dull responses.

23. When the biological cravings (water, food, and the like) are satisfied, higher motives come to the fore and become the springboards to motivation.

24. The teacher should realize that by the use of motives to attain motivation of the learner he is providing a wonderful chance for the learner to reach and move toward his potential.

Some principles of motivation.   As has been indicated, motivation tends to be quite individualistic in terms of both the teacher and the student.   Nevertheless, guides-to-action for motivation have been worked out.   Let us look at a few.

▶ **Find out as early as possible the one or two motives which are most active with each student.**
▶ **Set up an environment which is most conducive to wanting to learn.**
▶ **Connect in as many ways as are available the thing to be learned with the most active motives.**
▶ **Use incentives that are strong and sure-fire.**
▶ **Develop skill in motivation** by taking the time to organize learning.
▶ **Plan pupil experiences that will reach the main motive(s).**
▶ **Present the lesson and explain in such ways that the learner sees connections** between parts of skills and between skills is challenged to connect them in actual activity.
▶ **Try to teach what is needed when the student feels that need.**
▶ **Keep appeals and incentives within the maturation level** of the pupil.
▶ **Be quick to cover several different incentives and make use of several different motives so that almost at once many pupils are challenged.**

DISCIPLINE

Maintaining discipline, so that learning may take place effectively, is one of the crucial and persistent problems of teachers.   Teachers-in-training, beginning teachers, and experienced teachers-in-service are all concerned about properly handling troublesome students. More teachers, and parents for that matter, are distressed by the misbehavior of adolescents than by almost any other problem. Even pupils in classes report that they are disappointed by the behavior of some of their peers.   The public and parents want more strictness in school and expect schools to raise the behavior standards of children.   Actually, too, the majority of high school students want teachers to be tougher on those pupils who misbehave and disrupt the activities of the school. Almost everyone agrees that discipline is needed.

Discipline, a recognized problem.   One study of several hundred high school students who were about to enter college, indicated that these youngsters considered the necessity of dealing with the uncooperative a major disadvantage of teaching. Another investigation involving over two thousand teachers-in-training showed discipline to be their most important concern. A survey of the reasons why teachers drop out of the profession after one or more years of service indicated that the problem of working with unruly pupils was a most important factor.

One beginning teacher said, "Books by authorities avoid and gloss over the answers concerning discipline. What they say is great in theory but superficial. Let's be realistic. Troublesome students are my greatest problem." Another beginning teacher said, "If I could just teach without the annoying problems caused by difficult students! Teaching would be pleasant if it weren't for the small percentage of students who are unruly." Still another first year teacher said, "Understanding that Phillip comes from a broken home, that he is a nonachiever in all of the classes in which he must read, and realizing that he is not accepted to the degree he should be by his peers—still does not make more tolerable the discord he causes in my physical education class. I am at a loss as to what to do." The teacher-in-training must be prepared to deal with these perplexing problems.

How might the teachers who made the above statements be answered? First, we might suggest that all of the principles of effective teaching enumerated in this and other chapters be employed. That is, if we individualize and motivate and effectively teach, then we will have no discipline problem. But this answer is too pat and too simple.

Some teachers have few discipline problems. This is caused by their personal qualities, their organization and planning, and their ability, through one technique or another, to cause students to want to do what is desired. But again, a statement about personality plus organization and good planning is an oversimplification of the solution of discipline problems.

Discipline merely means the guidance and control of behavior. Ideally, all discipline is directed toward the student's achievement of self-discipline, the result of positive motivation. The teacher who is able to guide student activity by stimulating and focusing student motives in the right direction has reduced the need for control by force and authority to a minimum. In addition, he is teaching, as concomitants, habits and attitudes toward work, toward the specific learning experiences, and toward life.

Few teachers are so expert in teaching and organizing the learning situation that they do not have some problems with student behavior. Pupil behavior is, in part, dependent upon the mental and emotional health *of teachers*. Some poorly adjusted teachers take out their own problems on pupils: they thwart and dominate pupils and are constantly under stress because their classes are out of hand. They become upset and distressed over pupil misbehavior to a disproportionate degree. Actually some people may be constitutionally unsuited for teaching and working with energetic young people.

Forces of discipline. Society is characterized by standards, customs, rules, laws, and manners. The schools are expected to teach these, but in some situations today this is a difficult task. Some people say that parents are soft, that education is soft, and that this approach does not promote vigorous intense effort or sustained application toward worthy accomplishment. Many worthy accomplishments are not interesting at the outset. This is even true of the acquisition of motor skills in games that ultimately result in great satisfaction. At the outset intensive application is necessary to get past the annoying phase of learning.

Society demands certain conformity to its regulations. This kind of discipline is a continuing and important feature of life. In addition, society prizes highly the learning of tact and consideration of others. Dependability in doing one's job, conformity to group regulations, promptness, assumption of responsibility for getting work done, honesty, and tolerance are examples of highly desirable products of learning. They are some of the disciplines of civilization. One learns such behavior just as one learns the easier lessons of the class, though more slowly. These more mature aspects of learning are harder to teach, and children need much guidance and help in the process of attaining them.

Natural and social laws may often be broken without immediate reprisal. Acceptance of, approval of, and obedience to law require long education. Socially approved traits such as industry, thrift, caution, neatness, punctuality, exactness, concentrated and sustained application to uninteresting tasks for the accomplishment of a distant goal, enforced logical attack on a problem, all contribute to self-discipline. Their acquisition requires intense, but often uninteresting practice. One may *know* of the usefulness of such traits long before practice of them has made them a voluntary part of his behavior. No method of education could furnish such training without the use of techniques of some restraint, compulsion, and exacting requirement.

The teacher should not think that the easier the learning task the greater the interest. The learning problem must be a real challenge to the learner. *Need for vigorous and intense effort is more likely to add to than to detract from interest in learning.* In worthwhile pupil attacks on learning, the teacher must require the pupil's best efforts.

Justifiable disciplinary action. Only two reasons justify the use of disciplinary techniques: one is the necessity of such technique, at times, to protect the individual or group; the other is that learning may thereby be facilitated. The first reason applies particularly to young children. At times also the older student or student group needs protection from some incorrigible student, or from some milder student maladjustment. The second reason, that learning may thereby be facilitated, is deceptive in its apparent simplicity.

We must have order for learning to occur. The purpose of this order is to help the child learn, not to please the teacher with the control he can establish. Students must be reasonably orderly and quiet so that they may hear instruction or see a demonstration. Some order is needed so that the roll may be accurately taken. Pupils must be punctual so that the group may get under way and not lose valuable time. To remain on the bench or in the dugout during a softball game is a safety precaution to keep students from being struck by a bat, and such a rule must be observed. Kicking a leather basketball on a wet field will damage equipment, and such behavior must be corrected. Running with muddy street shoes on a well kept gymnasium floor does not show proper regard for property. Putting a shot in an unsafe area is extremely dangerous—perhaps fatally dangerous, and such behavior cannot be permitted.

Some discipline problems are unique to physical education because of the setting and the nature of the activity. Students come to physical education classes ready for activity, eager to move about and release energy. Still, at times they must be quiet and orderly so that class routines may be attended to and so that instruction may be given. In addition, physical education teachers normally are dealing with larger groups than other teachers. Sometimes, acoustics out-of-doors or in large rooms are a problem. When weather is uncomfortably hot or cold, or when there is too much wind, pupils may be upset in a physical education setting but perhaps not in a classroom setting. There is also an element of danger in physical education. The speed of movement, possible collisions, potential danger in the handling and use of objects and apparatus add to the necessity of sensible controlled behavior.

As we have seen, *learning wrong responses should be made annoying to students, just as correct responses should be made satisfying.* The difficulty lies in the adjustment of the degree of annoyance so that the individual will be dissatisfied, and yet not so upset that he is unable to learn the approved behavior. The student may become confused and cease to learn when he is overstimulated.

Disciplining the child may require considerable firmness to protect him from serious injury, to protect others, or even to protect property. Facilitating his learning may require some punishment, but punishment should be given with guidance toward correct behavior. *The teacher must display objectivity about the wrong behavior,* and a very evident feeling of kindness and concern for the child and his welfare.

Discipline problems of a serious nature necessitate diagnosis of underlying causes. The behavior itself may arise from emotional upsets or conflicts that are not immediately apparent. These may originate in the home, in the social life of the child, or elsewhere outside of school. The physical inactivity of the schoolroom may be a real cause. Repressions of tendencies to talk, to help a friend, to have moments of fun and relaxation may be causes. Uninteresting assignments and too difficult or too easy assignments may be causal factors.

Students will do *something!* If the teacher does not find them something to do, they will supply the need themselves. Mischievousness is usually just excess and misdirected energy.

The teacher does not treat the immediately manifest symptoms but the underlying causes. Just as the doctor diagnoses the patient and prescribes for his specific disorder, so must the teacher diagnose the pupil and treat him for his specific disorder. Just as weakness, fever, and loss of appetite may have many and diverse causes, so may nonobservation of rules, impertinence, and emotional outbursts have many causes.

This approach is a little difficult for the beginning teacher to acquire. He is likely to be more concerned about changing the symptoms than the underlying causes. Disorder in the school concerns the beginning teacher, not disorder in the pupil. If the pupil can be repressed, he causes no confusion. True, he may lose his initiative, become more of an outcast, lose whatever slight confidence he had in himself, or lose his interest in learning and self-betterment; but he satisfies the teacher if he becomes outwardly docile and conforms to the routines of the mass education process. Perhaps he waits until after school to turn loose the pent up energy from his frustrations and rebellions in anti-social behavior. He may even become a nonquestioning, overly obedient, submissive type of individual. In this case the teacher should be greatly concerned. A democratic state cannot afford to pay out money for the production of such citizens.

The teacher may select any *methods* he may wish to control pupil behavior. The method he employs, however, should educate as well as control. Many physical education teachers are very effective disciplinarians. They are able to be more firm with pupils than many other teachers in the school. But in many respects these physical education teachers, unfortunately, exhibit a decidedly undemocratic philosophy. Realizing that they cannot teach without control, they strongly impose their will on their classes and demand good behavior. In some instances this is a harsh top sergeant insistance that provides a superficial control and keeps the group in line. Authoritative control has been typically and traditionally the role of the physical education teacher. Many physical education teachers and athletic coaches have developed strong authoritarian characteristics and are able to boss and control others, get the job done, and still maintain the respect of most people. Traditionally athletic coaches have not been concerned with freedom of choice or decision making for team members. Such an approach may work fairly well with a highly motivated group, but when the same procedures are applied to groups that are less highly motivated, negative reactions sometimes develop.

Let us assume that the better teacher is guiding the child. Such a teacher is not lacking in firmness where firmness is needed. He is kind but objective. He treats the behavior problem without fuss and ado, usually privately. His techniques involve informal conferences, private suggestions, mild punishment for wrong behavior with direction toward the correct behavior, and sympathetic helpfulness. *His punishment is as mild as it can be, and still be effective.* The student's idea of the meaning of the punishment is important. This teacher uses punishment to clear up the trouble and sometimes even to ease the feeling of guilt. This excellent teacher may literally be *helping* the student protect himself from his own rash impulses.

Often students appreciate such constraint. They respect and admire the teacher who exacts a high grade of performance and spurs them on to better performance.

Principles of discipline. The following are some of the primary and secondary principles, which may guide the teacher as he attempts to help pupils develop acceptable social behavior.

▶ **Develop discipline on the basis of understanding the purposes of desired behavior.** Give reasons for requirements.

▶ **Work for good group morale.** The spirit and enthusiasm of the group as a whole may help to minimize some individual behavior problems.

▶ **Avoid discipline based on coercion or force.** Stress the development of attitudes and enthusiasm and not just surface behavior.

▶ **Remember that the individual is important** and that control based on recognition of the dignity and right of the individual is better than discipline based on submission and humiliation.

▶ **Continually seek discipline which is based on fair play** for everyone.

▶ **Direct discipline toward developing self-reliance, self-control, self-direction.**

▶ **Avoid sarcasm.** Do not shame or belittle pupils before a class.

▶ **Make corrections of behavior privately,** whenever possible, not in public.

▶ **Avoid insignificant punishment.** If punishment is necessary and there is no formula for punishment, punish decisively and promptly after fair warning has been given and has been understood by the pupil. Punishment changes its very nature in the presence of others.

▶ **Avoid trying to bluff.** If the teacher does not have the answer he should admit ignorance.

▶ **Practice patience,** realizing that behavior characteristics are slowly learned and that pupils must be continually corrected.

▶ **Establish a climate of firmness and consistency** without harshness or a punitive atmosphere.

▶ **Maintain self-control at all times.** Teacher anger or irritation is perfectly appropriate and normal. Such normal behavior on the part of the teacher is good for both the pupil and the teacher, but such teacher behavior should not involve loss of control or extreme emotional outbreaks.

▶ **Attempt to rule out bias felt toward some students.**

▶ **Make a diagnosis of causes of behavior problems** within limits. But the teacher should remember that he is no psychotherapist and should limit his treatment.

▶ **Recognize that misbehavior is normal** and to be expected. The teacher should be more concerned over the student who is retiring, withdrawn, and who never misbehaves than over the normal active youngster who creates the occasional disturbance.

▶ **Avoid delays in routines** since these periods of inactivity provide the opportunity for misbehavior to occur. Keep things moving rapidly—don't delay—be organized.

▶ **Realize that class organization and control is for the purpose of helping students** and not for the convenience of the teacher.

▶ **Expect students to do what they are told to do when they are told to do it.** But, the teacher should not tell them to do too many things or be constantly fussing.

▶ **Do not demand apologies from students,** especially before groups.

▶ **Provide for recognition** of difficult students in approved, acceptable ways.

▶ **Employ a sense of humor,** yet avoid having pupils be the object of humor or jokes.

▶ **Practice a remedial approach** to discipline problems, avoiding retribution, revenge and vindictiveness. Be a sympathetic guide to improved behavior, not an avenger of evil doing.

▶ **Gear the technique used for correcting undesirable behavior to the individual and the situation.** This might vary from a glance or a soft correction to a sharp reprimand, depriving of a privilege, physically restraining or excluding from the group, or even referral for administrative assistance.

▶ **Recognize that the main job in control of behavior is to stimulate and focus motives in the right direction.** Attempt to be objective.

▶ **Avoid sacrificing the good of the majority for one or two problem cases.** The whole group should not be deprived of privileges because of the conduct of a few individuals.

▶ **Separate disturbers quietly and individually.** Use physical force, if legally permitted, as a last resort, for this is an admission that the teacher cannot handle the situation in any other way.

▶ **Keep ahead of the group.** Anticipate problems before they arise. Anticipate solutions before incidents occur.

▶ **Set up, practice, and follow routines** so that students know what is expected.

▶ **Expect less than perfection.** Point toward it and aspire to it as a worthy accomplishment but realize that it is seldom achieved.

▶ **Never use school work as punishment** or an excuse from classwork as a reward.

▶ **Handle all cases possible** but promptly refer those cases which seriously interfere with the progress of the group.

▶ **Provide the opportunity to think and plan, to assume some responsibility for establishing and accepting standards, and to determine some courses of action.**

▶ **Realize that there are many upsetting factors in the lives of youngsters** and that adolescent behavior is variable, therefore minor incidents might be best minimized or ignored.

▶ **Set standards of conduct rather high at first,** for it is easier to relax high standards than it is to be lax and then attempt to impose more stringent expectancies.

▶ **Realize that discipline is more than punitive action** and that self-discipline and self-control are difficult to establish with an authoritarian manner.

▶ **Understand, when using group control, that turning the group against a pupil may be more damaging than firm authoritarian correction by the teacher.**

▶ **Use a positive, not a negative approach.**

▶ **Have an emergency plan ready in case of interruption.**

▶ **Be meticulously careful about your own appearance.** Watch that your voice does not betray a feeling of irritation, fatigue, or lack of enthusiasm.

▶ **Do everything possible to make the environment conducive to learning.**

▶ **Organize, when helpful, student groups and leaders;** use student proctors and managers and other democratic procedures to the extent that seems feasible.

▶ **Set up necessary routines at once,** but have no rules or routines unless they help the learning situation. Avoid a treadmill atmosphere.

▶ **Take good care of your health** so that you have energy. You will need to be alert every minute. Plan your work so that you can keep your eye on the whole group—to be out of sight of the teacher may be a temptation.

▶ **Avoid being puritanical.**

▶ **When direct action is necessary, act promptly.**

▶ **When correcting, stress the procedures for improvement** more than the errors already committed.

Extreme conditions. In a few situations, school discipline has deteriorated to such an extent that the students test the new teacher's *ability* to enforce school regulations and procedures. Extreme measures may be necessary to handle this abnormal situation. The teacher should anticipate the situation, decide upon suitable techniques, and make sure they are both legal and permitted by the administrator.

When pupils behave loudly and disturbingly and the class is disrupted, every teacher desires to have an effective operational system of discipline. About the only easily understood system of discipline involves methods which depend upon compulsion, coercion, force, and fear to control behavior, but this is not recommended. Modern methods apply techniques of developing self-discipline, self-control, and self-reliance.

Schools in recent years have assumed a more nondirective approach and have operated in an atmosphere of more permissiveness. This is in marked contrast to the authoritarian approach of fifty years ago when corporal punishment was an accepted and respected method of guaranteeing control.

Common conditions.   Some teachers-in-training in physical edu-
tion assume that because they have an attractive subject and will
have a close relationship with students, they will have but minor
problems with discipline.   This is in part true, but behavior problems exist in good programs and in well-run schools, and are occasional problems for even highly skilled teachers.   Moreover, if behavior is traditionally poor in a particular school or community, a
new teacher, or a teacher new to the school, will have difficulty
making rapid or appreciable change.   In fact, decisive efforts to
raise behavior standards may do more to develop the hostility of
pupils than to improve their behavior.

The behavior and viewpoint of adolescents is developed in many
ways; through parents, peers, and community attitudes, and only
partially by teachers.   It is unlikely then, that one teacher in one
class can so completely alter the social and emotional climate and
the general attitude toward teachers and school, that great changes
can be quickly made.   Yet, this does not imply that the effort should
not be made.   The teaching of desirable behavior is as important
an objective as any the teacher might include, but the teacher should
not be discouraged if his efforts are only partially successful.

Sometimes, uncomfortable physical conditions in the learning environment irritate the students and make them harder to control.
Ill health is a contributing factor to behavior maladjustment.
Harsh discipline techniques, for which the individual does not understand the reasons, cause negativism and rebellion.   Moreover,
students will imitate each other in misbehavior as well as in correct
behavior.

Poor selection of the activities in the curriculum may bring about
student unrest.   If activities are unchallenging, too hard, too easy,
remote from interest, if expectancies are too high or too low, pupil
unrest may develop.

The teacher should appreciate the general loosening of social institutions and of family control in today's world.   The adolescent
feels a need for independence.   The adolescent does not want to be
organized and dominated, and he is not as readily organized by
adults as younger children are.   Typically the adolescent does not
want supervision and direction.   He does not openly desire adult
regulation.   He is more apt to seek advice from friends than from
teachers or parents.   He *does* want to conduct himself as an adult.

Capitalize then on this desire on the part of the adolescent for self-direction. Give guidance that will enable the adolescent to choose proper courses of behavior for himself. Most adolescents realize that the wise guy, though he may amuse the group, also disrupts the group.

If all standards are established by the teacher, and enforced by the authority of the teacher, through constraint and forced obedience, characteristically the adolescent reacts against such control. If, on the other hand, the teacher allows the group to set standards to determine what appropriate behavior is, then the social pressure of the group to which the adolescent belongs determines the properness of behavior. This approach is superior to adult supervision and regulation.

Such approach takes a bit of doing. Implementing this kind of plan uses some valuable class time, it takes some discussing, and some effective leadership. But, a few hours spent in developing standards, in developing social skills, and in developing discussion skills may be just as important as learning motor skills, and, in fact, if the discussion is effective and fruitful, and if standards are set and observed as a result of such planning, progress might be made in the subsequent development.

Physical force. Constraint and forced obedience may be necessary at times for the protections of the individual student, or for the protection of the group. Punishment, in the sense of pain, suffering, loss, dissatisfaction, failure—any stimuli which will cause avoidance reactions in the individual—may be needed as a deterrent of behavior. Discipline, in this sense, should never be used unless an alternative, teacher-approved course of action, is known to the student. Punishment of a student, when he does not have sufficient guiding cues to proper adjustment, may stir up strong, disorganized emotional responses.

Once the proper learning atmosphere is established, the teacher may undertake the re-education of the problem cases. Harsh punishment may create conditions which prevent future success with special problem cases. This is one reason that physical force is outlawed in many public schools or is used only as a last resort in others, and perhaps should never be used. However, possibly in some cases, severe treatment will make expulsion unnecessary. The teacher should remember that the misbehaving student is a result of partial failure of education up to the present.   He is in even greater need than the average of kindly guidance, firm as it may need to be.

Since *the beginning teacher* is inclined to be lacking in confidence, he is often overly severe.   He, of course, must be more cautious about proper social distance than the experienced teacher.   His very youth makes him more likely to be taken for one of the gang. He does not yet know an adequate variety of techniques, he has more trouble keeping his emotions out of the picture, and he has not yet the prestige and dignity of the experienced and well-known teacher.

When measures of physical force are employed, they are usually used on hostile young people.   Hostility cannot be eliminated with hostility.   All we get is more hostility; we cannot get anything else. Corporal punishment, if it is to be used effectively, must be administered by persons whom children love and respect.   Such practices may be all right for parents, but the relationship of teachers to pupils is not close enough to justify the use of corporal punishment as an effective means of correcting behavior.   Institutions attempting to rehabilitate delinquent youngsters, under the most expert modern psychiatric advice, have discovered that corporal punishment is ineffective and have abandoned its use.

School administrators usually think well of teachers who are capable of handling their own discipline problems.   Obviously a great many referrals to the office by one teacher is a sign of the weakness of that teacher.   Actually, some teachers retain their positions more because of their ability to control student behavior than for their ability to direct learning.   Everyone expects the teacher to handle his own discipline problems if he can.   Even the appeal to the parents for help must not be too frequent.   The intelligent parents are likely to know their youngster and his weaknesses.   They handle him at home and they expect the teacher to do even better at school.

DISCUSSION QUESTIONS

Note: Some questions refer to Chapter 13.

1. How can the teacher individualize his teaching for a class of fifty members?

2. Is it sensible to try to play up the importance and place of the individual in a world that is increasingly by-passing him?

3. Is the group or the individual really most important?

4. Is it tougher for an individual to lose a match in tennis singles which he wanted very much to win, or for a team to lose the championship in, say, basketball? Why?

5. Do the ends justify the means of accomplishing a desired something, or, do means also carry the responsibility of being just, ethical, and honest?

6. How far should the individual adjust to the group?

7. If the lone voice in a group can be right or wisest, why the emphasis upon majority votes?

8. Granting that the teacher must be or become a keen analyst, is he apt to make the student overly introspective and too self-analytical?

9. How could a teacher be a good observer of athletic performance and a poor analyst?

10. What are some of the things that could go wrong when the teacher has expertly observed and analyzed a given motor performance, some part(s) of which was erroneous?

11. How can a major student improve his ability to diagnose before he begins to teach?

12. What is the difference between diagnosis and generalization?

13. How could two teachers watching a performer agree on what they saw, make identical analyses and diagnoses, and then reach quite different generalizations?

14. What sorts of traits would a teacher have who would be expert in observation, analysis, diagnosis, and generalization but be very poor at directing or guiding the learner?

15. In most instances do you believe you would reward (praise) correct performances and make unpleasant (psychologically) errors of performance? Why?

16. Motivation occupies the top spot of importance in assessing a teacher's effectiveness. "If you can't motivate, you can't teach!" But, could not a teacher be an effective stimulator of having learners learn the wrong things? Then, would you rather be (if you had to choose) a top-notch motivator who did not know the details of human movement, or, an expert in skill performance and a poor motivator?

17. What extremely keen interests did you have in high school that you jettisoned while still in high school?

18. What would you do if a student struck you with his hand or pushed you because you insisted against his will that he take a shower at the close of the physical education class?

19. What proportion of disciplinary situations that you have seen could have been prevented? How could they have been prevented?

20. In the disciplinary situations you have seen or personally experienced, what proportion were caused by poor organization of the class or class activities?

21. What steps would you employ if you were interested in having your physical education classes establish their own standards of conduct?

22. How are you going to handle the confirmed bully on the school playground? The pupils who imitate him? The parents whose children have been bullied?

23. Suppose the ring leaders of a given class use their influence to disorganize the class, how are you going to handle the situation?

24. What will you do if the pupils whisper and chat as you explain a new game in physical education class?

25. A child in your physical education class is very clumsy and awkward. He becomes very discouraged, gives up, and starts disorder in your class. How are you going to prevent further occurrences?

26. What kinds of disciplinary problems do you expect will give you the most trouble?

SAMPLE TEST ITEMS

Essay-type Questions

Note: Some questions refer to Chapter 13.

1. Can you overdo individualization?   If yes, in what ways?

2. How can you under-do individualization?

3. Why is providing a chance for self-expression so important?

4. Can a group often arrive at wise decisions if its members are quite unintelligent?   Why?   How might it be able to once?

5. If the rights of the individual are so important, why should he have to conform to rules and regulations?

6. How could a teacher or coach promote transfer of training of some trait like good sportsmanship from the field of play to ordinary living around the neighborhood?

7. The detailed description of analysis took a good deal of time to read. Could it actually be done in seconds by a good teacher?   How?

8. How could a major student learn to analyze the motor movements of others while still in college?

9. Select one skill such as the one-hand shot in basketball, and trace through what you as a teacher would do: observation, analysis, diagnosis, generalization, direction.

10. Why should the teacher consider the values connected with whatever it is he is analyzing?

11. Why should a teacher take the time and trouble to compare the analysis being done at the moment with some previous ones of this same kind (if possible)?

12. How could asking the performer a question like, "What are you trying to do?" help in the teacher's diagnosis?

13. Since diagnosis by the teacher is not a life-and-death matter as it may be with the physician, why should accurate diagnosis be stressed so much?

14. Why is not diagnosis enough before the direction of learning? That is, why is generalization necessary?

15. Considering how important word-pictures are of the movement to be performed or the pattern which the club or bat is to follow, describe in word-pictures *only* how to set in a volleyball.

16. The importance of having a repertoire of word-pictures for any given skill has been emphasized. Why?

17. Why cannot the teacher teach kinesthetic feel?

18. Will top-sergeant domination eliminate breaches of discipline? Why?

19. The child of ignorant parents is overdisciplined at home. At school, this child runs wild both because the discipline is less strict and because it rebounds from the extremely strict routine at home. The child is in your physical education class and begins the year by causing you much trouble. How might you handle this case?

Yes-No Questions

1. Do motives have to be learned?

2. Are incentives internal stimuli?

3. Is the urge to vigorous activity a result of learning?

4. Are organic drives focused toward specific patterns of behavior even before learning takes place?

5. Does the psychological rather than the logical method imply that appeal to motives may be more important than a logical sequence in order of presenting learning experiences?

6. Does the term *purpose* imply that the drive is entirely intellectual?

7. Does the teacher *motivate* the student?

8. Is the hungry person necessarily less efficient in learning activities during the period of his hunger?

9. May overstimulation of drives to learning inhibit that learning?

10. May pleasures experienced increase the drive toward those pleasures?

11. Would a toothache be classed as a motive?

12. Does failure increase the desire for success?

13. Is there a danger that intense degrees of competition and rivalry may maladjust personality?

14. Has the student who enjoys the lack of success of others learned this type of enjoyment?

15. Are organic needs causal factors in the learning of desire for social approval?

16. May sex hormones add to energy available for sport participation?

17. Is there any place in modern education for restraint and forced obedience?

18. Is the learning of self-discipline facilitated by an environment devoid of external restraints and controls?

19. Should the student be punished by being made to expend extra time and effort at some type of learning experiences?

20. Should excellent work be rewarded by excusing students from learning activities?

21. Should the amount of criticism and reproof of a student be proportional to his degree of failure to achieve approved standards?

22. Does the use of antisocial incentives occur in many school situations?

23. Are we born with a conscience which directs us and makes character education unnecessary?

24. Should a large number of activities be included chiefly because of their disciplinary value?

25. Do activities in which students must work strenuously but in which they are not interested have more disciplinary value to the student than the more interesting activities?

26. Is the teacher chiefly responsible for securing the correct mental set for the activity of the day?

27. Is the use of negative incentives occasionally justifiable?

28. Is easiness an important factor in the arousal of interest in the activity?

29. Should the erring student be induced to cooperate in the selection of his punishment?

30. Should students discuss and agree on conduct codes?

31. In order to stop the immorality and degeneracy of the adolescent period, should the discipline be severely firm and objectively just, without any leniency for mistakes?

32. Do individual differences make it impossible to secure perfect moral responses?

33. Is cheating best prevented by assigned reading on the nature of morality?

34. Do educators agree that strict discipline is a prerequisite for greatest achievement of ultimate values in class work?

35. Are fear and force ever justifiable as means for maintaining discipline in high school?

36. If a student openly defies the teacher, should the teacher ignore it?

37. Should *incorrigible* students be handed over to the higher authorities?

38. Is it good pedagogy to make many rules even though some of them are not obeyed?

39. Are the rude knocks from companions at school good for all children in that they take away self-centered notions?

40. Does strict repression encourage lying and deceit?

41. Is self-assertiveness usually a compensation for feelings of inferiority?

42. Is the child's attitude toward conformity to approved social standards primarily the result of his innate brightness?

Note: *If some of the above questions cannot be answered by yes or no, why?*

BIBLIOGRAPHY

Bennett, Elizabeth, "An Ounce of Prevention," *Journal of the National Education Association,* 45:346 (1956).

Bringhurst, Jack R., "Practices and Principles of Classroom Discipline" (Unpublished Master's project, University of Southern California, 1957).

Brown, Judson S., *et al., Current Theory and Research in Motivation—A Symposium.* Lincoln, Nebraska: University of Nebraska Press, 1953.

Brownell, Clifford Lee, and E. Patricia Hagman, *Physical Education—Foundations and Principles.* New York: The McGraw-Hill, Book Company, Inc., 1951.

Hymes, James L., *Behavior and Misbehavior.* Englewood Cliffs, N. J.: Prentice-Hall, Inc., 1955.

———, "Something Is Wrong Someplace," *Journal of the National Education Association,* 45:343 (1956).

Knapp, Clyde G., and E. Patricia Hagman, *Teaching Methods for Physical Education, A Textbook for Secondary School Teachers.* New York: The McGraw-Hill Book Company, Inc., 1953.

Kozman, Hilda Clute, Rosalind Cassidy, and Chester O. Jackson, *Methods in Physical Education.* Philadelphia: W. B. Saunders Company, 1958.

Lambert, Sam M., "Pupil Behavior," *Journal of the National Education Association,* 45:339 (1956).

Oliva, P. F., "High School Discipline in American Society: A Primer on Democratic Discipline in its Social Context," *National Association of Secondary School Principals Bulletin,* 40:1–103 (January 1956).

Ryans, David G., "Motivation in Learning," *The Psychology of Learning, Forty-first Yearbook of the National Society for the Study of Education,* Part II. Bloomington, Illinois: Public School Publishing Company, 1942, 289–331.

Sheviakov, George V., and Fritz Redl, *Discipline for Today's Children and Youth,* revision by Sybil K. Richardson. Washington, D. C.: Association and Curriculum Development, National Education Association, 1956.

Van Til, William, "Better Curriculum—Better Discipline," *Journal of the National Education Association,* 45:345 (1956).

Wilson, Guy M., "Psychological Basis for Motivation," *Educational Administration and Supervision,* 38:350–58 (October 1952).

15

Evaluating, measuring, grading

"For he that reads but Mathematicke rules
Shall find conclusions that avail to work
Wonders that passe the common sense of men."
Robert Green, 1594.

Most undergraduate students preparing to be teachers of physical education are required to take a course in tests and measurements. *This chapter is in no way a substitute for that course.* Rather, we are about to take merely a critical approach to measurement and evaluation.

Before beginning this critical discussion, the importance of measurement and evaluation in physical education should be made clear. If the teacher fails to perform these functions, he does not know to what degree, when, and whether objectives are accomplished by the individual pupil, the class, or the entire student population. Without the facts and information that come from testing and appraising, the teacher does not know what emphases or changes to make in program and in teaching. Of all the reasons for testing and evaluating in physical education, the ones just mentioned are the most fundamental.

A few decades ago teachers could be excused for using the hunch-guess method to determine what physical education did *for* the pupil, *with* the pupil, and *to* the pupil.   Today, *no valid excuse remains* for hoping, wishing, or taking for granted without *making as sure as possible* of the facts.

This point is emphasized at the outset of this chapter for two reasons.   *First,* a few persons who read the following critical approach might gain the impression that this is a *skeptical* approach toward testing and evaluation.   *Second,* too many educational administrators comment to the effect that physical education could be doing an excellent job if it only accomplished that which it enthusiastically *claims.*   There is but one way to answer that criticism satisfactorily.

A CRITICAL APPROACH

Tests and measurements as a process in education and particularly in physical education are frankly criticized in the first part of this chapter.   Attention is then directed to evaluation as distinct from measurement.   Measurement in physical education is then considered, followed by a discussion of marking or grading.

As we discuss this first part, let us keep in mind that it is not only a *critical* approach but a critical *approach.*   Every teacher interested in the better teaching of physical education desires to face the claimed weaknesses, disadvantages, abuses, and misuses of measurement, as well as the claimed values, advantages, and uses.

Physical educators—leaders in modern educational philosophies. Teachers of physical education have been practicing for years what many others are just beginning to talk about—namely, such procedures, programs, and concepts as the play way, the activity curriculum, the whole child, and learning by doing and through experience.   Generally speaking, school education is still educating minds instead of educating persons.   School education in most areas still attempts to duplicate life (education is life) by means of *passive* techniques such as reading and listening.   The purpose of this discussion is not the criticism of educators whose educational philosophies rest upon the concepts of the Schoolmen of the Middle Ages, erudition instead of functional wisdom.   Rather, it is to point out definitely that physical educators have been and are leaders and pioneers in certain educational movements.

Physical educators—laggards in tests and measurements? Physical educators are leaders in many aspects of education, but the field of tests and measurements is not one of them. In spite of the very early tests of strength and physical dimensions and the irregular appearance of testing devices for physical education since the middle of the nineteenth century, we have not kept abreast of the testing movement in education. At the present time, some of us are so busy following the laggards in the educational test parade that we appear to be unaware of the fact that the parade leaders made an abrupt turn two or more decades ago.

Unscientific influences. Attempts to belittle, thwart, and stifle such qualities as *wholesome skepticism, avid curiosity, determined truth-seeking,* and *courageous experimentation* defeat the very essence of the scientific spirit and attitude. As Huxley states the proposition: "Science commits suicide when it adopts a creed." When the movement of tests and measurements in physical education fails to foster the scientific attitude *toward itself,* such a movement destroys the very force that created it.

This discussion is no attack on imaginary malpractices. Let us listen to those test enthusiasts who argue that test-making should be left to the experts, in the same manner that we entrust our automobile, our radio, or TV set to expert handling. One statement runs: "No, I would not advise any of you to experiment with tests. It is difficult enough for men trained in the science (*sic*) of test-making to construct standardized tests, much less you who are so untrained. It is better to do no testing at all than to use subjective (*sic*) tests such as any but the experts would make. . . ."

A scientific influence. In contrast to the above type of professional guidance is a suggestion from a well-known maker of tests of physical education:

. . . Second, he [the teacher] should study his own local situation and ask himself what information he wants or can well utilize in order that he *may do better teaching.* Third, experiment; and in the experimentation, be sure that the results are utilized—not just filed. A few years of such experimentation will enable one to determine what tests will contribute to the efficiency of teaching, and which ones may be left entirely to the research worker. [And which ones should be discarded.] [1]

[1] C. H. McCloy, "The Future of Tests and Measurements in Physical Education, *The Journal of Health and Physical Education,* 11:56 (January, 1940).

Objectivity vs. subjectivity.   Some pseudo-experts in the field of testing, who have reached the ears of teachers of physical education, have attempted to give the word objectivity in connection with tests and data a sort of approved status.   At the same time they use the word subjectivity with derision.   Have we reached the point where it is possible to silence a teacher merely by labeling his proposal for a marking plan, for example, as subjective?   The fact of the matter is that tests and measurements are quite subjective.   The content of all tests is subjectively determined.   The selection of a given test to use for marking, classification, or other purposes is a subjective process.   The administration of a test is a subjective procedure. The taking of a test by the pupil is subjective.   The recording of the test data may be open to human frailties.   The interpretation of data and drawing of conclusions are subjective.   Someone has to decide the action that is to be taken after conclusions are drawn, and this obviously is a subjective process.

Therefore, speaking of *degrees of subjectivity* with reference to tests and test data is more accurate than to pretend that some tests are the essence of objectivity.   Objectivity in tests usually refers to scoring only.   No one would question the desirability of each teacher's attempting to decrease subjectivity as much as possible with regard to tests and measurements, but the accusation of subjectivity need not muddle one's clarity of thinking or observation. If one is too concerned over the matter of objectivity of testing, he may not be alert to the limitations of the resulting data, sensitive to possible misapplications of statistical techniques, and awake to exaggerated claims for testing in general or some tests in particular.

A given test of physical education may have its claims for being objective, but the alert teacher desires to know: What is the purpose of this test?   Of what value is it?   Of what value to the pupil, now and later, are the test items?   Are these questions too severe a subjective test of objective tests?   Perhaps!   But answers to these questions will go far toward preventing teachers from attempting to build whole programs of physical education based upon test items, from directing our teaching toward the accomplishment of only the trivia and minutiae resulting from one, two, or three objective tests in physical education.

Validity—actual or implied?   The test maker, after selecting a supposedly existent trait to measure, sometimes assumes (1) that he is in possession of an adequate knowledge of the simplicity or complexity of the trait, (2) that responsible persons agree with his understanding and diagnosis of the nature and content of the trait, (3) that a testing device will measure this trait, (4) that the items of the test represent measurable uniform units or increments, (5) that limited experimentation will or will not *prove* that this device actually measures the trait, and (6) that the remaining statistical treatment used in standardizing a test is sufficient to launch a test upon the market.   The mere listing of some of these tasks and danger signals cannot help but stimulate respect for the test maker who devises an acceptable standardized test.   But most such tests are useful to teachers because of their aid in avoiding objectionable degrees of subjectivity and in their reliability.   This leaves the question of the *validity of a test unanswered.*

No one knows better than the genuine test expert that no amount of statistical juggling increases the actual validity of a test.   The attempt to show statistical validity by means of computing a correlation between the scores of the new test and those of an established test is unacceptable because the established test is also subject to the question, precisely what trait or traits does this test *actually* measure?   That is, eventually and invariably we end by having to admit that the original test consists of *someone's ideas* of the factors of a trait or ability and how it can be measured.

Let us illustrate the care with which one must consider the question of a test's validity.   Assume that a teacher who will use the test desires a test that actually measures what it purports to measure. Suppose that we wish to devise a test for measuring physical condition.   First of all, we will have to assume that physical condition can be isolated for measurement.   We will probably agree that we must have several items in the test or have a battery of tests, since physical condition is a multifold trait.   In fact, thirty-five nationally known physiologists (also leaders in physical education who are doctors of medicine) reported the following factors as the *essential constituents* of physical condition: age; heredity; native capacity; family history; case history; somatic health; nutrition—accessory food factors, biochemistry; emotional factors; reaction time; speed; strength; muscle tone; endurance; susceptibility to fatigue; respiratory efficiency; perspiratory efficiency; weight—in relation to height, width, stability, build; distribution of weight; work output per pound; cardiac condition—pulse ratio, cardio-vascular adaptation, size of heart, pulse variation, pulse change, return to normal, critical pulse, rise in systolic B.P., minute volume of heart, amount of hemoglobin, blood pressure, amount of buffers, pulse rate, chemical condition of blood, hemopeitic mechanism, alkaline reserve of blood; indices that the whole organism is geared together for best functioning; freedom from structural and functional disorders—compensation, adaptability, resistance to disease; good functioning of the endocrine glands; good functioning of the sympathetic nervous system; normal basic metabolism; skin; eyes; hair; teeth and gums; arches of feet; lack of obesity; proper functioning of sense organs; neuro-muscular control; subjective sense of well-being; attention and alertness; morale and zest; good functioning of the digestive processes; posture.

Thus, physical condition has a good many component factors, and some of them appear capable of being isolated for measurement. If some factors are isolable, we may be able to apply quantitative measurement to them and get some valid results. The trouble is that the factors are *interrelated*. Consequently, we have a large number of factors, some isolable and some not, and all of them interrelated. Does it not become increasingly difficult to devise a valid test of any one factor? In fact, is it possible?

One reason so many factors were listed by the physiologists and physicians may be because the term physical condition does not have similar meanings to these men. McCammon and Sexton [2] after studying various programs conclude that: "Various measurements of fitness and response to conditioning, when applied to the same individual, give different answers, suggesting that current testing methods omit consideration of the question, 'fitness for what?' "

This fact poses rather interesting questions: What degree of agreement can we expect to get from a representative sampling of physical educators as to the precise nature of *any* of the traits or factors we test and measure in physical education? What degree of agreement would we expect to get as to how *any one* of these traits or factors could best be measured? How many of these physical educators

2 Robert W. McCammon and Alan W. Sexton, "Implications of Longitudinal Research in Fitness Programs." *Journal of the American Medical Association*, 168:1440–1445 (November 15, 1958).

would agree as to need or value of testing any one trait, or set of traits?

We speak rather glibly of such a factor as strength and are rather confident of our devices for measuring it.   Increased knowledge of strength yields complexity rather than simplicity to our understanding of it.

Agreement among one's colleagues as to the *precise* meanings of many of the traits or factors which we optimistically attempt to measure is difficult to find.   If experts do not agree as to precisely what a given factor such as strength is, how do we know what to attempt to measure, or when it has been measured?   Coupled with such questions is another, suggested by the paragraph above: Will more careful analyses of a trait, which we assume exists and can be measured, become increasingly complex and begin to involve other traits, most of which are not now measurable?   If this is true of a factor such as strength, how much more is it true of a still more complex something called physical condition?   The present devices for measuring strength obviously are based upon *someone's ideas* of strength, *someone's ideas* of how it is expressed, and *someone's ideas* of how this expression can be harnessed and measured.   Does not the same hold true for physical condition and the other traits which we assume can be isolated?

We may secure records of some of the reactions to stimuli of the human organism, but whether these activity phenomena are expressions of an isolated human trait or factor is seriously questioned. Merely to *measure* some reaction of the human being to a stimulus does not mean that man *is made up* of isolable, measurable variables.

Any discussion of the validity of tests would be incomplete without calling to mind the ever-changing nature of the human organism.   One of the difficulties of attempting to apply the type of techniques used in the physical sciences to education is that the basic elements in education change.   Another difficulty of this attempt is that predictions of a human being's precise reactions to a given stimulus are highly fallible.

Another reason a test may lack the validity claimed for it is that the test deviser, recognizing his inability to measure some human condition, trait, or ability, substitutes some measurable factor which he *believes* is a component part of the original trait.   Thus a test maker desiring to construct a device for measuring *physical condition* might select *strength* as the substitute variable.   That is, he purports to measure physical condition and, assuming a close relationship between it and strength, substitutes the latter for the former.   If this substitute factor is to be judged as a *valid* substitute, the ratio between the substitute and the original factors must be constant.   Yet if strength is a valid substitute for physical condition, the ratio between the two shall be constant regardless of such factors as age, body build, motivation, and the like.   In the case of strength, a delirious person may manifest extraordinary strength.   So may a person highly motivated by fear.

Misconceptions in using tests.   The misconceptions of standardized or any other tests, *result from the fallibility of human beings*—those who assume the existence of distinct, separable human traits, those who make the tests, those who administer the tests, pupils who take the tests, and those who interpret the test results and recommend and take some action.   Note that many of these sources of fallibility lie within the teacher.   Thus, a brief discussion of some ways that tests may be fallible and made more fallible seems pertinent.

Most of us strive toward the finding of certainty.   One symbol of certainty to a teacher of physical education is a key, formula, process, or device that solves one's problems.   Thus, a teacher of physical education, who, after lifting the eyebrow of cynicism toward testing and tests for too many years, may come to place faith in a particular test.   The teacher's hope is that, although the test is not panaceanic, it will help eliminate some teaching problems, solve other problems, and facilitate the desired results of teaching.   Most experienced teachers of physical education have gone through the period of doubt as to the value and practicability of standardized tests.   We then learned a little more about tests and testing.

Standard tests: their selection, use, and interpretation.   Caution should be used in the selection, use, and interpretation of standardized tests.   The following nine reasons explain why.

First, before selecting a standardized test, the teacher ought to know what it is that he hopes to measure, rather than just testing to be testing.

Second, related to the above is the decision of the purpose for testing; i.e., is the purpose of the test compatible with the purpose for testing? For example, one would not select a diagnostic test to use for classification purposes.

Third, if these two purposes coincide, is the test appropriate for the type of program of physical education to be used; i.e., will it diagnose weaknesses for *your* type of program, classify for *your* type of program, measure achievement in *your* type of program, or motivate students in *your* program?

Fourth, the test should be appropriate to the local situation. This criterion is often overlooked. A standardized test may not fit local conditions, circumstances, and persons.

Fifth, a standardized test does not automatically yield data that conform to scientific criteria. The administration of the test may be faulty.

Sixth, securing agreement is difficult, among those interested in the physical welfare of children and youth, on what things are of sufficient worth to justify the establishment of national norms. Changed objectives mean changed program emphases and, in turn, changed types of tests. Even if all those now interested in the nation's physical welfare reached an agreement as to the items to be included in, and the standards for an achievement test, another generation would find the experts disagreeing. We teachers should be wholesomely skeptical, yet open-minded, of national norms or standards as goals for which *our* students should strive. Needs are personal and specific.

Seventh, one criterion of the use of a standardized test is its value in pupil guidance. After spending time, thought, energy, and perhaps money, one should secure useful results. The results of a pertinent standardized test may indicate a change in the entire physical education program, a change in emphasis, a change in the participation of some students, and so on. The test should indicate areas, kinds, and degrees of experiences needed.

Eighth, we must avoid doing foolish things on the basis of the results of a standardized test. One test maker advocates excusing from physical education all students who score in the upper quartile of *his* norms! The astonishing thing is that some teachers who use his test have followed his advice! Each child deserves to be given opportunity to develop his own potentialities. Such aspects as growth, fitness maintenance, and self-expression are only fostered by participation.

Ninth, standardized tests should result in better teaching. Do the tests supplement and improve the teaching? Or does the teacher neglect many of the other values to be gained from physical education in order to have his students rank high—in the test items —in the city, county, state, or nation?

Misconceptions of the functions of measurement. The foregoing discussion of test selection is related to the larger problem, misconceptions of the functions of measurement. If measurement is the essence of science, any criticism of measurement borders almost on the sacrilegious, in the minds of some persons. Yet, the greater the scientist, the more ready is he to admit such weaknesses of scientific measurement as are listed below. The purpose of presenting these facts is to explore further the reasons for a critical approach to tests and measurements in physical education. The following points refer to scientific measurement in physical education and its limitations:

1. Measurement is not concerned with the purpose, value, or consequences of physical education.

2. Measurement is based upon both the assumptions of measurement and the assumptions of physical education.

3. Measurement lacks the tools and techniques for evaluating itself.

4. Experts in measurement often fail to try to prevent unthinking acceptance of that which goes under the name of scientific measurement in physical education.

5. Measurement fails to include the not-yet-measurable yet valuable phases of physical education. As far as measurement is concerned, these latter do not exist.

6. Measurement is always fallible. Tools of measurement constantly are improved, and new ways of manipulating data are invented. Yet, before these improvements are made, some of us act as though the present tools and statistical methods were infallible.

7. Measurement is limited largely by the needs and interests of physical educators and test experts. Do they correctly interpret the needs and interests of children?

8. Measurement yields data. These data may answer the ques-

tion how much? but how much of *what,* and *why,* remain unanswered as far as measurement is concerned.

9. The statistical aspects of measurement, such as the mean, tend to direct attention away from the individual pupil.

10. Measurement assumes the existence of isolable human traits.

11. Measurement in physical education at best is trial and error. We can only try to get results in the best way we know at a given time.

12. We do not know the motives behind the expert in measurement. Work can be done in this field for selfish reasons.

13. Measurement is circumscribed by its tools.

14. Measurement yields data from which we generalize. This generalizing is merely stating what seems most probable to us about some aspects of pupils' behavior as we now understand it.

15. The value of measurement is not scientifically but philosophically determined.

This incomplete list of limitations presents for our consideration the proposition that measurement is circumscribed in scope, purpose, and place in physical education. Someone may reply: "Of course scientific measurement in physical education is limited. Who claims otherwise?" We are not so much interested here in who *claims* otherwise as we are concerned about the teachers who, after taking a course or two in tests and measurements, lose their perspective and judgment relative to the appropriate uses and justifiable interpretations of tests and measurements in their teaching program.

Experts in educational measurements are becoming more critical. Let us now consider some reactions of leaders in the field of tests and measurements in education to their own work. We shall observe not only a definite tendency toward frank criticism but the emergence of a recognition of the value and essential nature of *subjective* data as revealed through evaluation, not measurement. The following viewpoints are not so much the opinions of individual experts in educational measurement as they are composite opinions of these experts.

1. The mysticism, novelty, and superficial lure of standardized tests have passed. We now want a nonscientific answer to a nonscientific question—namely, What are the basic values of testing?

2. Tests must be related to the program being followed.

3. Judging a teacher's ability by comparing the scores made by his pupils with norms is unfair, vicious, and disastrous in terms of the teacher, the program, and the pupil.

4. Tests may deter the progress of education just as easily as they may aid it.

5. Testing procedures that lack the fundamental purpose of pupil guidance are defenseless.

6. Intelligent pupil guidance is based not only upon the results of objective data but upon all evidence, including the intangibles acquired about the pupil.

7. Obviously, testing has been based upon the assumption that education is not a complex process. Testing will be a highly questionable process as long as this assumption is taken.

8. Tests should yield satisfactory data regarding *all* the desirable, measurable outcomes of a given field because tests aim to point out to the teacher those variables which the test purports to measure. This pointing-out to the teacher influences what he teaches and how.

9. Pupil guidance depends not only upon discovery and diagnosis of difficulties but upon the selection and application of techniques of prevention and remedy. Obviously no series of objective tests supplies all this information.

10. The pupil's scores should be in terms of his own previous and concurrent records, not in terms of group norms.

11. Rates and levels of learning, various reactions to experiences, individualization of the program, and integration demand a disregard of intercomparisons between individuals, similar grades, and schools.

12. A teacher who doubts the value of tests is not to be blamed. There is frequently too great a discrepancy between that which is tested and that which is deemed worthy of teaching.

13. Test results not supplemented by and interpreted in terms of the teacher's judgment (that is, in turn, based upon sufficiently careful observations) are unjustifiable factors in pupil guidance.

14. Education is interested in something that does not exist in exact amounts—namely, the *potential* growth and development of the child.

15. A test may be objective in terms of scoring the test, and yet leave unmeasured personal factors vital in the complete evaluation of pupil achievement.

16. Self-analysis, self-appraisal, and a statement of personal evaluation of a pupil regarding a given learning-experience may be far more vital as a basis for guidance than a score in a test covering this area of learning.

17. Types of tests and their emphases have mirrored the development of the program, its major objectives, and its needs. Now that we have moved forward to new practices, new programs, and new objectives, we need new tests—new types and new content. Unfortunately, the prestige and inertia of the older tests tend to perpetuate the traditional objectives, practices, and programs.

18. Evaluation techniques stimulate teachers to analyze the purposes of teaching a given field, to think of pupils instead of curricula, and to discard former, taken-for-granted conceptions of the nature, needs, and interests of pupils.

19. Most recently constructed courses of study list as objectives such intangibles as the acquirement of proper attitudes.

EVALUATION

In this chapter, for the sake of emphasis, let us regard measurement and evaluation as distinct processes. Actually these two processes overlap in that area where measurement is judged to become less accurate, reliable, and objective, and evaluation is judged to become less subjective and more reliable and accurate. In fact, in some quarters the tendency is to use the term evaluation as embracing not only its distinct functions but measurement's functions as well. Viewed in this manner, evaluation may be represented as a scale at one end of which are very precise types of measurement and at the other end of which are types of personal judgment. On the other hand, occasionally a writer considers measurement as the broad and inclusive term and evaluation as only a phase of measurement. This lack of consistency in interpretation of terminology in psychology, education, and physical education is known to most teachers. This condition denotes a lack of precise, clear, well organized thinking on the part of the leaders. In an effort to avoid confusion, let us attempt to distinguish between measurement and evaluation for the purpose of better understanding this chapter.

Terms explained. Measurement in education may be regarded as quantitatively determining the answers to the extent to which, the degree of, the amount of, how much, how many, and similar

questions regarding certain educational phenomena. Evaluation
may be regarded as a way of trying to find out answers to such questions as: Of what value is this experience to the child? What does
he think of this experience? How does he feel about it? Does he
understand its place (if any) in the social order? Of what value is
it in terms of society's welfare? What is the pupil's or the teacher's
judgment regarding the importance of this learning? How well
does the child analyze his difficulties in learning this act? How
well does this learning function in the child's life?

Measurement assumes standard units of educational data—that
is, that they are equal and interchangeable. Measurement is assumed to devise and construct standard units for educational data
through assigning numerical terms to educational data. Evaluation, to personify, desires to know the value of that which is assumed
to have been measured. It regards as valuable many experiences
and learnings not describable in numerical terms, not capable of
being dogmatically put into standard units. Evaluation questions
whether all that exists can be expressed in numerical terms.

Evaluation is interested in securing the most accurate answers to
questions, but these answers are not necessarily in numerical form
or in some *measurable amount*. Evaluation does not decry measurement because of the latter's use of numerical terms, standard
units, its theses, and the like. Rather, evaluation proposes that *in
spite of the fact* that many worth-while experiences in education are
not measurable at present, they are so essential to an understanding
of teaching and learning that we must consider them and find out
all about them.

Evaluation would also question the value of all that is measurable, and question the value of measuring some phenomena that are
now measured. Nevertheless, evaluation assigns a value to the
units that measurement counts. For example, a boy may get a score
of 84 on some strength test, but evaluation must decide what each
of those 84 points is worth to the boy in comparison to each of the
96 points that he might have scored.

To summarize, evaluation emphasizes the value of a given experience or learning to the child (now and later on to the child as
an individual and to the child as an integrating personality in the
social order), and it emphasizes the use that is made of all that is
learned. (How? In what respects? To what extent are the learn-

ings made a part of life?   How functional are they?)   Measurement emphasizes different kinds of numerical accountings of educational phenomena which are purported to exist in some measurable amount.

Evaluation in physical education.   The ascendancy of the child over the subject as the pinnacle of attention in education is not new. (This statement is not to claim the substitution has actually taken place in many schools!)   The child-centered curriculum, the child-centered school, education for life adjustment, and all the other satellites of the movement of the child as the center of education are older concepts in the history of man than subject-centered education.   Education continues to pass through periods in which the *real* center of attention in school subjects is all but forgotten.   Yet even during such periods, one of the marks of the good teacher is his understanding of and his efforts to understand those whom he teaches.

As might be expected, accompanying the change of emphasis from subject to child is the change to a recognition of the place of evaluation.   This transition is not difficult to understand.   The more thoroughly we understand the child and the more he is studied, the more we recognize that we must surely go *beyond* the present tools of quantitative measurement to find out what his education is doing to, for, and with him.

Also interesting is that the final test of physical education is in the hands of society, not the educators or the physical educators.   This test is not made up of measurable bits.   It consists of estimates and appraisals of physical education as reflected in the lives of persons. How valuable has physical education been to you, Mr. and Mrs. Adult?   The emphasis upon evaluation seems to promise foci of attention in teaching physical education that we have largely underestimated in the past.

Measurement may tell us how strong the pupil is in terms of the available tools and certain assumptions.   Measurement may tell us how much he improves in his strength scores (whether this improvement is caused by growth, development and maturation, or special exercises, is often not revealed).   Measurement also may tell us some things about the pupil's status and improvement in certain skills, speeds, reaction times, and the like.   But what of the pupil's attitude toward this program?   How important is the attainment of these skills and strengths in the pupil's system of values?   What of his understandings regarding the implications and projected applications of such acquirements?

If a teacher cares not a whit for the pupil's desires, values, attitudes, personality, and character, perhaps a glance through another pair of glasses might be of interest.   Assuming that the teacher is interested in his profession, and assuming that physical education really has worth-while contributions to make to the individual pupil, the indifference and even antagonism of many adults and post-school youths toward physical education must be of concern to the teacher.

Regardless of how practical and conservative a teacher may wish to be about the outcomes of physical education, he cannot dodge the fact that most of today's pupils in physical education are tomorrow's voters for or against physical education.   The weight of adult public opinion, based upon its former school experiences, already has broken down the door to the academic stronghold of several subjects and put them to flight.   The importance of considering the pupil's attitudes, interests, and values goes beyond the one consideration, his present education.   The importance of these matters affects his reactions, opinions, and votes as an adult citizen.

Evaluation, purposes, and outcomes.   The major planned purposes as well as the actual outcomes of physical education should be related to the real life and thinking of the pupil and society. The leaders in physical education may need to change not only the stage setting but the act as well.   The acquirement of organic vigor, neuromuscular skills, and desirable social behavior is vital and important.   But also vital to satisfactory learning and to the future of physical education is the pupil, as he progresses through school, increasingly recognizes the values of physical education in terms of mankind, constructs his own values of physical education, develops new and favorable attitudes toward physical education, and better understands its scope, nature, and purposes.   Of the proposed outcomes mentioned in this paragraph, only a very few may be quantitatively measured.

The desire to *evaluate* physical education frees one's ideas for a consideration of major objectives, their scope and nature.   The idea of evaluating physical education rather than measuring it indicates new areas of emphasis, new possibilities, new basic purposes, a few of which have been indicated.

Evaluation and conduct.   Among other things, evaluation starts the teacher observing the behavior, the conduct, the actions, and reactions of the pupil as he participates in a physical education activity.   That is, through evaluation the teacher becomes interested in: what happens to the *whole* pupil when he participates; what, besides skill performance, he does with what he learns; what he does in the varied and many situations in and out of class; whether and in what ways he is maturing in his decisions, system of values, understandings, and self-responsibility; whether symptoms of integration or frustration can be observed, attempting to maintain the former and prevent or remedy the latter; the ways in which the pupil is growing and developing in his social relationships; and the ways he is acquiring such qualities as reliability, ingenuity, and emotional stability.   Do these acquirements exist?   Can they now be measured?   Is it worth while that we find out as accurately as possible these aspects of the growth and development of the pupil that may help us better to understand the pupil, to guide him, and to check on the results of our teaching?

Methods of evaluation.   Fortunately, most teachers are curious to know the ways that evaluation can be conducted.   The known methods do not yield equated units of scientific data.   They are merely common-sense ways of trying to secure information.   In fact, these methods of evaluation are not new.   Some teachers have used them for years.

One of these methods of evaluation is *observation*.   In this case, the name of the method is quite respectable in "scientific" circles, but the interpretation of what is observed is open to question.

Observation as a method of evaluation must be carefully applied. Some suggestions are enumerated here:

1. Observation includes more than merely looking out, gazing, and watching; it also includes the use of all the senses, not just the eyes.

2. Experience in physical education is no guarantee that the teacher will observe the significant symptoms, but the person inexperienced in physical education seldom observes traits of conduct that relate directly to physical education.

3. Even temporary conclusions should be drawn with great caution. One observation of an expressed behavior trait may mean nothing. Several observations of the same symptom under similar circumstances *may* be indicative. On the other hand, observation of some nontypical behavior *may* yield a lead to further understandings, to solutions of other problems.

4. We interpret our observations in terms of personal experiences, which may be incomplete, inadequate, or of an inappropriate type.

5. We are apt to think we understand behavior merely because we observe expressions of it.

6. The observer should know what he is looking for without seeing into the situation that for which he is looking.

7. Observation always gives way to more valid, accurate methods of collecting information.

Other methods of evaluation include *interest-inventories, checklists, questionnaires, score cards, rating scales, personality inventories, interviews, estimates, appraisals, photographs, moving pictures, judgments; tests of such phenomena as attitudes, social maturity, emotional stability, and the like; diaries, anecdotal records, case studies, autobiographies, committees, inspection, group discussions, self-ratings and self-appraisals.* Such methods are used in securing from and about pupils essential and vital information not available through more objective methods such as the health examination and tests of traits that are purported to exist in some amount. The information resulting from these and similar methods of evaluation serves as a check on what is being acquired by the pupil as he develops. It also helps us help him understand and analyze his needs, reset his goals and values, identify and take steps to solve his problems, recognize his attitudes with possible resultant changes, and make ever increasingly reliable self-estimates.

In closing this section, let us remind the reader that in the preceding section we assumed a critical attitude toward tests and measurements for certain stated purposes. In this present section we have distinguished between evaluation and measurement for the purpose of emphasizing the possibilities of and opportunities for gaining information often frowned upon by test enthusiasts in physical education.

Before proceeding to a brief discussion of measurement, you should understand that evaluation is an area of investigation that gives way to measurement when tools are invented to measure scientifically the phenomena now covered by evaluation.   The authors readily recognize that either measurement or evaluation may be considered as inclusive of the entire gamut of scientific measurement and unscientific appraisals.   By creating differences between the meanings of the two words we have sought to emphasize the importance of and value in the evaluation type of information, as a counter-offensive against the exaggerated claims made in the name of tests and measurements in physical education.

MEASUREMENT

In spite of what has been said and more that might be said in a criticism of measurement, it deserves the active support and active cooperation of every teacher of physical education.   Why?   Because existing tests and devices, as instruments of measurement, symbolize the best we have in an attempt to secure facts instead of guesses, and to approach the truth regarding measurable phenomena instead of being satisfied with mere assumptions.   The data resulting from responsible measurements in physical education are the most concrete, verifiable, provable phenomena in the field.   As such, measurement is valuable to the teacher in several ways.

Purposes of measurement.   What are some of the ways that tests and other devices of measurement and their results may be valuable to teachers?

1. Bases of estimates of achievement or improvement of one pupil, class, or school.
2. Bases of justifiable comparisons of ability, achievement, or potentiality between pupils, classes, or schools.
3. Diagnoses of difficulties, weaknesses, and gaps in the learning and experiences of a pupil, class, or school.
4. Bases of grading, promoting, or classifying pupils.
5. Bases of teaching emphases and methods.
6. Bases of pupil guidance.
7. Bases of motivating learning, review, drill, practice.
8. Bases of teacher self-appraisal.
9. Bases of checking on the acquirement of measurable outcomes.
10. Sources of quantitative information about the pupil.
11. Bases of new knowledge for the profession through research.

Tests also have other uses, including those valuable to the supervisor, the school administrator, and the research worker.

Kinds of measurement.   In physical education, the kinds of measurement receiving most attention have followed the emphases in physical education during particular periods.   Roughly, kinds of measurement in physical education may be classified as follows: *anthropometrical, strength, cardio-vascular condition, athletic achievement, physical growth, neuromuscular control, physical efficiency and ability, sport technique, general motor capacity and ability, endurance, special abilities, motor learning, posture, character, personality and adjustment,* and *attitudes.*[3]   Obviously, kinds of measurement need not follow emphases in physical education.   Increasing attention to measurement for research purposes should yield results that may very well give rise to new emphases in physical education.

Selecting the tool of measurement.   As indicated previously, if one decides to use a standardized test or a test devised by another, considerable caution should be exercised in its selection.   We might borrow a leaf from the physician's book in this instance.   After he decides what it is he wishes to know, he selects the best available and appropriate measures and methods for securing his information. Testing for the sake of testing, or because it is modern is expensive in terms of the taxpayer's money and of the teacher's and pupils' time and energy.

In selecting a test the teacher should consider, among other criteria: (1) the purpose for which a test is needed; (2) the purposes and value of the content of the test; (3) validity; (4) objectivity; (5) reliability; (6) economy in money and time, other factors being equal; (7) ease of scoring and administration; (8) appropriateness to the locality and group; (9) existence of alternate or equivalent forms of the test; (10) bases for and aids in interpretation; (11) durability; and (12) convenience of test equipment for handling.

The value of local tests.   Some of the limitations of the standardized test have been mentioned previously in this chapter.   Recall that the test may be and often is utterly unrelated to the local situation in such test essentials as (1) content, (2) length, (3) organ-

---

[3] Charles Harold McCloy and Norma Dorothy Young, *Tests and Measurements in Health and Physical Education* (New York: Appleton-Century-Crofts, Inc., 1959).

ization, (4) norms, and (5) difficulty; and in such essentials related to the pupils as (6) their background in the phenomena to be tested, (7) their attitudes toward some or all of the factors of the test, (8) their rate of performance, and (9) their quality of performance. Certainly in a standardized test no claim is made by its makers for validity in terms of the local course of study and points of emphasis. And certainly the teacher earnestly desires a test that comes as close as possible to measuring that which it purports to measure.

Almost invariably the teacher desires to know the degree to which the pupil has learned what the teacher has presented and emphasized; how much a given pupil has improved from time to time in his traits and abilities; how a pupil in a given class compares with classmates in that which is taught and emphasized locally; and what particular difficulties a given pupil is having in what is being taught and emphasized locally. Satisfactorily prepared local tests, particularly those used for showing the pupils' achievement in the local program of physical education, are on the increase. And while local tests will not replace standardized tests, chiefly because of their dissimilar purposes, the local test is becoming an invaluable tool for instructional purposes. The standardized test, with its general content as a basis for school-to-school, city-to-city, and local-to-national comparisons is useful for administrative and research purposes. The local test, with its specific, appropriate content and application, is useful as a basis for grading, for diagnosis of individual difficulties, for individual motivation, and for measuring class achievement, in addition to the values already mentioned.

Guides in local test construction. The teacher who is devising a local test and does not take all possible and appropriate steps used in constructing a standardized test is wasting his time. Tests can be localized and at the same time devised in such a way as to conform appropriately to the criteria of acceptable test construction. The following are some of the guides to be used by the teacher in the construction of local tests:

1. Achievement test items should range in difficulty so that those with least ability can successfully perform some of the test items and those with greatest ability cannot successfully perform all of the test items. In a diagnostic test the purpose is usually to find out the inadequacies in pupil learnings. That is, the test is devised to find out where remedial teaching is necessary.

2. The test items of an achievement test should be arranged in order of increasing difficulty.

3. The number of test items should be large enough to provide a representative sampling of the important factors or phases of that which is being tested, and at the same time give a fair and accurate picture of the pupils' ability. The number of test items, of course, should be limited by the length of time pupils require to take the test, the percentage of total class time to be devoted to testing, and the length of the class period.

4. The scoring of the test items should be as objective as possible.

5. Any local test should be supplemented by a carefully planned set of directions, with illustrations or demonstrations if the pupils lack experience in the type of test given. If a specific time limit is set for taking the test, the directions should include this information. The pupil should also be informed of the general plan of scoring so that he may know where to direct his attention and energy.

6. The teacher should make up his mind as to the trait or ability he purports and attempts to measure by means of the test. He should also decide the type of test—e.g., diagnostic or achievement—because the test items selected are related to the type of test. The validity of the test is dependent upon such factors.

7. The test should be as valid as possible. Earlier in the chapter some difficulties in this phase of test construction were discussed. The teacher must not conclude that a test *made* up of the most valid test *items* will make the most valid *test*. Many of the items may measure the same basic aspect; items showing less item validity may spread the scope of the test and make the total test more valid.

8. The test should be as reliable as possible—that is, it must accurately measure whatever it does measure.

9. The test should attempt as directly as possible to measure the trait or ability that is supposed to be measured.

Factors governing the installation of a testing program. Here are some of the factors related to the plans for a testing program. They should be carefully considered by the teacher, and most of them should be discussed with the school administrator before introducing a test or installing a testing program.

1. The purposes of this plan of testing program.

2. The attitude of the community toward testing.

3. The attitude of the school administrator toward testing.

4. Appropriateness and desirability of the test in terms of the pupils. For example, the teacher would avoid a test which involves potential bodily strain without first knowing definitely the health status of the pupils through a good health examination.

5. Adequacy and availability of facilities and equipment for conducting the testing program.

6. The type of physical education program used previously and at present.

7. The teacher's preparation for the *entire* task planned.

8. The teacher's knowledge of the pupils to be tested.

9. Justification for using the teacher's and pupils' time in such a project.

10. The amount of time available for the program.

11. Possible availability of assistance of test experts.

12. The possibility that better tests are available to accomplish the main purposes of the testing program.

13. The disposition of the results in terms of teaching and learning.

14. Cost of the testing program.

15. Possible attitude of pupils toward the testing program.

16. Claimed purposes of the tests to be used.

17. Recency of norms of the tests to be used.

Guides in selecting a standardized test. The teacher about to select a standardized test should first ascertain certain information about the test. Money spent on the purchase of a test, much less equipment, is wasted unless it is as satisfactory as can be expected. Publishing companies or the test devisers themselves can furnish important information about a given standardized test. They can explain the costs, equipment, and background information needed to administer the standard test; they can explain the test's purpose, applicability, validity, and reliability; and they can furnish scoring instructions. Often they will make available comparative information on other similar tests.

Classification. Individual human beings defy exact classification. *Precise,* homogeneous groupings of individuals into physical education classes or into groups or squads within classes is impossible in most all situations. Attempts at classification of individuals in physical education are usually on the basis of easily measured factors such as height, weight, age, and strength, or upon more difficult factors such as physical capacity, motor ability, and achievement in specific activities.

Let us examine the easily measured factor of height and the validity of this factor in classification or grouping. Obviously, we may rather accurately measure a pupil's height and find that he is almost identical to some others in the group. The pupil may be equal in height, but will most certainly be unequal in weight, unequal in length and size of various body parts, unequal in coordinations, unequal in ability to learn, unequal in speed of contraction, unequal in range of movement, endurance, strength, and many personality factors. Obviously, the use of the height measurement has serious limitations in grouping individuals. Many other easily measured factors have serious limitations as well. For example, individuals who are equal in chronological age can almost certainly be expected to be dissimilar in many other aspects of ability and maturation. Because of the reasons described above, any system of classification admittedly lacks precision and in some individual cases may be grossly inaccurate.

Classification, even though it very roughly groups people for instruction and competition, may be better than no classification at all. A number of leaders in physical education question the principle of dividing pupils according to ability groups because such grouping of pupils does not represent life situations. Some people would not have any classifications in physical education. They feel that pupils must learn to live with others of differing proportions and abilities; they feel that depriving pupils of this opportunity to understand and deal with others who are quite different is an unwise educational limitation. This viewpoint seems to be strongly held by some women teachers of physical education. Possibly it is less important to classify and group girls than boys. This is because of the greater intensity with which boys compete and because of the nature of the activities often included in the physical education program for boys.

The ingenious teacher of physical education, however, classifies pupils within a given class so as to facilitate instruction. In swimming we have beginners, intermediate, and advanced groups; wrestlers are preferably divided according to weight; some other athletes according to ability and maturity. In athletics, the attempt to safeguard the individual from injury is an important consideration.

The flexible squad system within a class lends itself admirably to classification for purposes of safety, equality of competition, and for purposes of instruction. At the present time we are not prepared to request of the school administration that pupils within a given grade be sectioned into separate physical education classes according to any plan except possibly on the basis of the health examination. We are, however, prepared to request that pupils at a given grade be sectioned into a given class period. The practice in some small high schools of sending high school girls or boys from all grades to the same physical education class should not be condoned. Precisely how a teacher of physical education is to teach a program that leads on to richer and better experiences, in such a situation, has never been answered by school administrators.

Situations such as these and others almost as lamentable bring home the fact that often the teacher's chief task aside from doing his best, is to educate the educator, his administrator. In the meantime, we suggest that the teacher make the best of a bad situation. For example, ingenious teachers who have groups of pupils from several grades may use to advantage squad systems and plans which apportion floor or field space and which divide pupils according to their needs and abilities. In some activities, which are conducted primarily for social purposes, a group may participate as a whole. In other activities the teacher may actually have several programs of activities going on at the same time. Individualized teaching may not be a characteristic of such work, but ingenuity and intelligent efforts are the chief factor in gaining the principal's sympathy, respect, and, finally, action toward rectifying the situation.

The experienced teacher realizes that no system of classification can completely equalize pupils for competition. Too many unmeasurable factors are involved. Many teachers of physical education will, however, continue to have creditable types of the classifications for several purposes within the classes, so that learning is facilitated and enriched and pupil growth and development are promoted.

GRADING

Most school systems require that marks or grades be assigned in physical education just as they are in other subjects. Pupils and parents are interested in these grades. They become a prestige symbol for pupils and parents alike. Assigning grades is usually a perplexing difficulty for beginning teachers because many aspects of pupil development must be reduced to a single letter or number. It is difficult to know what this letter or number represents and what it should represent. Marks should be based upon the objectives sought, and the goals for a given mark should be in terms of the abilities, needs, and interests of the group at hand. But these are over-simplifications of a task that has proved to be a problem for experienced as well as beginning teachers.

Many prospective teachers are critical of courses in evaluation and measurement. After completing such classes, they say, "I've learned a lot about educational statistics, I can find means, medians, and compute standard deviations, but I still don't know how to grade my classes." This common criticism requires an answer. Professors and books cannot and should not tell students specifically how to grade classes. No effort is made in this chapter to describe how to grade any individual or class. It cannot be done. Programs differ, emphases differ, pupils differ, and under these situations the system used to determine grades also should differ. The best answer to the criticism above, therefore, is that your evaluation course gave you the tools that you need to adapt your grades to your particular grading situation.

This section of this chapter is intended to be a *critical* approach to several ideas about grading in physical education. In this section we will examine the bases used by many teachers to arrive at grades and make an effort to determine whether the various factors are fair and justifiable means of assigning these marks.

Basic questions. Any broad-gauged discussion of grading or marking physical education is charged with controversy. Why do we give grades? How important and valuable are these reasons? Is it possible to accomplish these purposes without using letter or number grades? Do grades shift the pupil's attention from the value of learning to the acquirement of grades? Is the basic idea of orthodox grading a product of or related to agrarian individualism or industrialism with its emphasis upon efficiency and cooperation? Should grades be based only upon objective measures, or is it justifiable to include information gained from evaluation? Should grades consider a pupil's level of ability as compared to others in the class?

Should grades be chiefly an expression of the acquirement of specific measurable bits such as isolated skills or chiefly the functioning of the skills such as the playing of a game made up of these skills? Should grades be based upon ability, improvement, potentiality, or actual achievement? Should such acquirements as knowledges and attitudes be considered in grading? To what extent should attendance enter into arriving at a grade? Is it possible to give grades but so emphasize the fundamental, valuable learnings that pupils will not seek grades as ends?

Should grading in physical education correspond to grading in other school subjects?   Regardless of one's answers to the questions in the above paragraph, the teacher usually must cooperate with the school administration in using the grading plan in operation in the school system. This, however, is no reason for not knowing some of the characteristics of a few of the grading plans being used, and examining some of the basic ideas of those who advocate that grading procedures be eliminated or modified.

Usually educators maintaing that the pupil should be graded in physical education as he is in other areas of the educational program. That is, grades of the same type (A, B, C, D, F, for example) should be given, and these grades should be awarded in the same proportions as they are in other subjects. This means that rather arbitrary standards of performance and achievement must be established so that discriminations can be made in the proper proportions.

Many beginning physical educators feel that grading according to arbitrary standards helps the pupil understand his own limitations and abilities. The novice teacher may assume that since the pupil is usually graded on how well he performs in mathematics, science, or other subject matter fields, he is logically graded on the basis of his *level of performance* in physical education. These young teachers seem to fail to realize that the pupil probably has a fairly accurate idea of his limitations in physical education without being graded. In many aspects of physical education he has rather accurate notions of his limitations even without organized efforts at self-evaluation.

In most schools, physical education teachers do not award grades in the same proportions as they are assigned in other subjects. Some teachers of physical education are reluctant to admit that they depart from the curve usually employed in other subjects (they assign a greater per cent of higher grades and fewer low grades). The grade of *B* is more common in many physical education programs than the grade of *C*. Often there are more *A*'s than *D*'s and usually very few failing grades. Physical educators are sometimes criticized for such proportions in assigning grades. Let us examine one point of view concerning the appropriateness of such a practice.

Some leaders in the field maintain that departure from the curve used by some other subjects in the school is proper. These persons say that physical education serves a general education function, that it does not play the role of being a specific prerequisite for professional or vocational programs. These persons insist that the concern of physical education is with the personal and life adjustment of the individual. They say that not only is it difficult but it is *usually unnecessary* to contrast one person with another in this respect. *It is important to help the pupil and his parents to understand the progress that is made by the pupil by seeing the progress that he, as a unique individual, might reasonably be expected to make.*

This point of view hold that grades should not indicate where the pupil is in comparison *with other students'* traits and skills and qualities, but that grades should indicate the *progress* and *development* and *learning* of *the pupil,* during the given period of time. In other words, grades should indicate improvement in contrast with the individual's *own potential.*

Persons who hold this point of view say that grading should accomplish different purposes at different times and in the different subject matter fields. They contend that physical education grading does not have to be based on the same elements as grading in other areas of the educational program. They admit that one purpose for the grading in some fields is to determine which pupil is equipped to advance to more complex subject matter and to what degree he is equipped. In some subject fields, they say, discriminating by the use of grades is extremely important. For example, if the pupil is not equipped to accomplish the elements of mathematics surely he is not equipped to study chemistry. And without this background he may not study organic chemistry in college. And without this he may not enter a pre-medical course and study advanced physiology. And without this he may not gain admission to medical school and become a Doctor of Medicine.

Mathematics or chemistry, under such circumstances, becomes a vital step in the sequence of experiences that lead into certain professional areas.   Under these conditions the pupil is quite properly graded, failed, or redirected if such a course of study is not successfully completed.   A course such as this may properly be used to select or eliminate pupils.   Such a course has great social and personal consequence.

Other courses are of great social and personal consequence as well, but may not need to be graded in the same way.   Physical education may be one of these.   Figure 15-1 shows graphically this

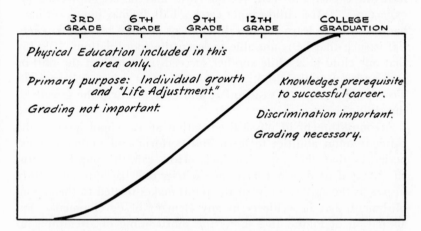

Fig. 15-1. *Illustration of the viewpoint that pupils should not be contrasted with each other or with group standards for grading in physical education. Physical education as an area of study remains in the upper left portion of the course offerings from elementary school through college.*

point of view.   The *upper left* portion of the rectangle depicts those subject areas in which no contrast or comparison need be made between pupils.   The *lower right* portion indicates those subject areas in which pupils should be properly graded, detained, failed or reguided if the courses are not successfully completed.   Note that as the child progresses through school from the elementary to college level and becomes more mature, grading for purposes of selection becomes more important in more areas of the school program.   For example, the physical education major student should be graded so that professional standards might be maintained and elevated.   If he were not graded and carefully appraised, those *not* prepared to assume the important responsibilities of teaching might be allowed to enter the profession. An example from elementary school physical education may serve to further clarify this point.

An elementary teacher said, "To contrast one elementary school child with another is unethical. Comparing small children with each other on the basis of their ability to perform is unfair because the contrast is being made in terms of aspects or factors *over which the child has little or no control.* If he lacks the readiness to read, he should not fail in reading. He is not in a position to achieve as yet; perhaps he has limited ability to do so. He does not yet have the capacity to read, yet the child may be accomplishing *his* expectancy." If a child cannot catch a ball, he may not as yet have had the time to learn the coordination or perhaps his motor potential is such that he is not able to learn the coordinations. To say that one child fails while another succeeds is to look at the skill or goal and not at the child. Persons do not fit arbitrary standards. To expect them to do so is unfair and does not help the growth of the child.

Accomplishment in physical education at all school levels is dependent upon abilities to learn and perform and upon *prior* experiences that the pupil has had. How can the pupil perform effectively if he does not have the capacity and background? *Only in part* is the application that the pupil makes related to the accomplishment that he achieves in any element of development. Examination of Figure 15-2 shows the shortcoming of attempting to apply arbitrary standards to individuals. Achievement is dependent upon both potentiality or capacity and upon application. Some pupils work up to capacity while others do not, yet, their grade based upon arbitrary standards may be the same.

Improvement as a basis for grading. Some teachers realizing the weaknesses of grading on arbitrary standards attempt to base their grades upon improvement in various elements of development. Some teachers interested in equalizing the opportunity for students of various capacities to earn superior grades feel that grading on the basis of improvement makes their grade more justifiable and fair. But there is a weakness to this approach as well. What does improvement mean? Many persons who advocate this approach fail to realize that students with the greatest capacity, who may score higher on initial tests, actually improve more than pupils who score lower on initial tests. The beginning teacher may assume that since

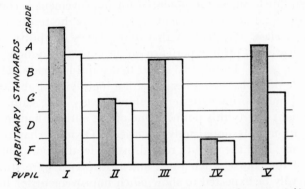

Fig. 15-2. *Possible potentialities (black bars) and achievement (white bars) of pupils in contrast to arbitrary standards. The potentiality of pupil I exceeds the standards and his achievement; pupil III works to capacity and achieves nearly the same point on the arbitrary standard, but is short of an A grade.*

some pupils start lower on the scale they have more room for improvement. This is true.

But actually those pupils with the most capacity show more gain in the acquisition of skills—even though they may start higher they also show greater gain. Figure 15-3 shows that improvement does

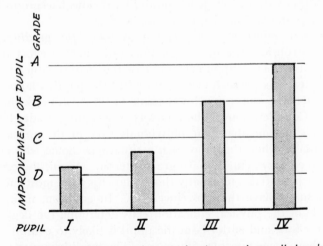

I. High level of ability to perform; much prior experience. II. Low level of ability to perform and learn; much prior experience. III. Low level of ability to perform and learn; no prior experience. IV. High level of ability to perform and learn; no prior experience. **Fig. 15-3.** *The effects of equal application and effort on improvement in neuromuscular skills is a function of the ability to learn and perform and the amount of prior experience or learning of the skill.*

not mean much unless the *potential* for improvement is considered. Obviously, final accomplishment is not always the result of *what* is learned in class. Students with varying levels of ability and with varying degrees of prior experience can be expected to show different amounts of gain. Figure 15-3 shows that pupil IV made the greatest gain while pupil I (having begun with a high level of ability to perform and much prior experience) showed very little gain. An example might clarify this point. One of the authors had in a physical education professional activities class an Olympic champion who, at that time, held the world's record in the decathalon. During the period of the course when track and field events were studied, he could hardly be expected to show much improvement for he was so near performing at his capacity. His level of performance was, of course, superior to all other members in the class. Some members of the group, having had little experience in track and field activities, showed great improvement in all events during the course. With relatively equal application of effort by all students in the class, how is it possible to assign a grade on a basis of improvement? Some pupils have capacity to improve, some already have prior experience and may not be able to improve appreciably. These characteristics might be expected in most physical education classes in which there are various levels of ability, various backgrounds of experience, and various degrees of application.

Interest, effort and enthusiasm as bases for grading. Some teachers consider the interest, enthusiasm, and the effort put forth by pupils as factors upon which to base the physical education grade. These teachers use such factors to reward the pupils who possess the characteristics and assign lower grade to those who lack these qualities. Consideration of these factors in assigning grades has shortcomings. Remember that individuals vary in the *appearance* of enthusiasm when they approach a situation. Some who are quite restrained may actually have great interest. Again, those with the highest potentials are usually those who enjoy the most success and will usually have the most incentive. In addition, many stimuli outside of the physical education class determine the degree of interest, effort, and enthusiasm the pupil is likely to exhibit. Figure 15-4 shows some possible influences. The pupil brings to class himself and his many attitudes and points of view, which are developed outside of class by various environmental forces. To base a large portion of the grade on such factors seems inappropriate.

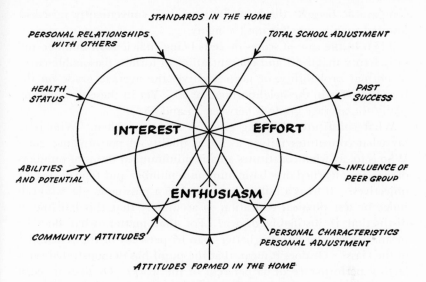

Fig. 15-4. With so many outside influences affecting the student's attitudes, his grades cannot be appropriately based on his interest, effort, and enthusiasm.

The per cent system of grading. The per cent system is still a common grading plan in spite of the fact that it has repeatedly been shown to be one of the poorest ways of marking. In this system, the pupil is marked on the basis of 100. What does 100 represent? Does it represent perfect performance in skills in the activities offered? Best performance in the class? Satisfactory performance? Mastery of skill and knowledge and demonstration of desirable attitudes? Greatest improvement? Highest attainment?

The letter system of grading. The letter system is probably the most common type of grading now in use. It is related to and developed from the per cent system. In the letter system, usually, *A* represents 95 to 100, *B* represents 85 to 95, *C* represents 75 to 85, and so on. This system avoids the difficulty of a teacher's virtually claiming the ability to distinguish between performances of 82 and 83. However, it fails to avoid this same difficulty at the joints—i.e., 94–95, 84–85, 74–75, and, further, it overemphasizes differences in scores near these joints.

Neither the per cent nor letter systems permit valid comparisons between marks given by different teachers or between schools. For that matter, one teacher's marks at different intervals are not validly comparable because the level for passing is conveniently raised or lowered to fail some but not too many.

Then in the case of scores on tests being sufficient in number and satisfactory in spread and concentration to form a reasonable curve of normal probability, or normal curve, the average grade on the basis of 100 is in the neighborhood of 50.   Yet in these two grading plans, the average grade is between 75 and 85.

What constitutes a failing grade is also a problem.   Who is to say what constitutes failure as far as quality of performance goes? Who is to say what constitutes a basic minimum in terms of numbers of activities learned or a basic minimum number and type of specific objectives?   If 64 is a failing grade and 65 a passing grade, who can judge or test physical education so accurately that this hairline of distinction is justifiably drawn?   For that matter, what does 65 mean?   That the pupil is better than 65 per cent of the remainder of the class?   Or does it mean that the pupil has demonstrated satisfactory performance in 65 per cent of the work?   Or does it mean that he is 35 per cent less than perfect?

These questions and the other indicated weaknesses are some of the reasons for the recommendation to discard the per cent and letter plans of grading.   The teacher of physical education who finds himself in a school system using either of these systems refrains from any verbal criticism or critical attitude.   Rather, he grades as best he can, attempting to avoid or repair the weaknesses.   New teachers can easily bring the displeasure of both their colleagues and the administration by expressing or showing a critical attitude toward the way things are done.

Pass or fail systems of grading.   Some physical education teachers maintain that grades should be simply divided into two classifications: pass or fail; or satisfactory and unsatisfactory; or some such two point scale.   This system obviously presents some of the same difficulties as the per cent or letter systems.   What is failing?   What level of attainment must be reached to be considered satisfactory? What kind of attainment is to be measured?   How is it to be measured?   This system has the advantage of eliminating three of the joints described above in the letter system.

Standard scores used in grading.   Suppose a pupil kicks a soccer ball 88 feet, makes 14 baskets in one minute, scores 63 on a knowledge test, and scores 41 on a test of throwing for accuracy.   Is he, therefore, best in soccer kicking and poorest in basketball shooting? Is it possible that he is equally effective on all tests?   Examination of the raw scores alone does not enable us to answer these questions. However, it is possible to compare achievement if a standard-score scale (z score scale) is employed.

This system of marking may be used where there are a large number of pupils, or where the teacher has available the scores of several smaller groups so that a normal curve is approximated.   These standard scores are based upon the standard deviation (sigma).   One of the chief advantages of this plan is that the scores on different tests or tests with different means and standard deviations are comparable.

Assuming that the number and distribution of the scores justify statistical computations such as standard deviation, the finding of a pupil's standard-score is a simple process.   Let us suppose that the mean score in the soccer kick for distance for a group of twelve-year-old boys was 75 feet, and that the standard deviation was 12.   What is the standard-score of a boy who kicks 99 feet?   We simply subtract the mean from the score received by the boy, which is 24, and then divide by the standard deviation.   The answer is plus 2σ, or 2 standard deviations above the mean—and the standard-core is plus 2.

The sigma score of a boy who kicks 50 feet is: $\dfrac{50-75}{12} = -2.08\sigma$

or 2.08 sigmas *below* the mean.

To make the standard-score more easily understood by pupils, frequently the standard-score of 0, or where the mean lies, is moved down 5 standard deviations below the mean since this distance below and above the mean is apt to include the poorest and best achievements.   Five standard deviations below the mean gives us a kick of 15 feet.   A kick of 75 feet, or the mean, then has a standard-score of 5σ; the kick of 99 feet, 7σ; and the kick of 50 feet, 2.75σ.   These are then multiplied by ten, since the pupil can easily think in terms of 100, or parts thereof.   The average kick is then scored a 50; the 99-foot kick, 70; and the 50-foot kick, 27.5.

Scores derived in this manner are comparable from year to year, from test to test, and from pupil to pupil.   If the teacher desires that part of the semester grade to be based upon achievement in tests, the derived standard-scores would be averaged—that is, totaled and divided by the number of tests.   The standard-scores for the more important achievement tests might be weighted before averaging, so that the more significant measures have greater influence on the semester grade.   Standard-scores for various tests may be used in a pupil's profile graph.   Several excellent textbooks on the use of statistics in education and psychology give more detailed explanation of the use and limitations of standard-scores.

Point systems as a basis for assigning grades.   To grade objectively and fairly, some beginning teachers prefer to gather data such as: seventy-five per cent on X test of neuromuscular potential, throw or distance at 110 feet, 60th percentile in basketball shooting, 5 feet 7 inches tall, fair human relations, showers daily, two absences, tardy once, good self-control, usually cooperative, properly dressed at each meeting of class, weighs 140 pounds, 51st percentile in enthusiasm and interest, 77 points on knowledge test.   The teacher then prefers to punch these data on an IBM card, wait patiently for a few seconds until a card comes out stamped with the appropriate grade. Such a system is of course somewhat absurd.   Grading can never be that simple.   The problem is too complicated.   It is truly difficult for the teacher to know a few students in a small class well enough to grade effectively.   Large classes become increasingly difficult.   In schools in which quarterly or mid-semester grades are needed, teachers often have difficulty knowing their students well enough to grade fairly by the end of the first grading period.

Some teachers anxious to devise systems of grading that are readily understood by students, that are manageable, and in an effort that make grading fair, have developed elaborate *point systems*.   Some of these involve an approach in which the pupil begins the semester or unit of work with a given number of points, say 100, and as the unit of work progresses he may lose a certain number of points for failure to accomplish stated goals or for inappropriate or substandard behavior.   In this system the teacher must be vigilant in finding faults, in fact, his attention as he evaluates for the purpose of grading is to find what is wrong.   A *second* point system employs the same general idea but involves awarding pupils points for superior accomplishment.   In this way superior behavior or performance gains for the pupil more points.   A *third* system is a combination of the above two and involves both bonus and penalty points.   Lack of purposefulness or misbehavior detracts from the total point score while superior effort and conduct add bonus points.

Using the methods described above, some novice teachers feel that numbers makes grading objective.   What these teachers may fail to realize is that the particular weighting that they assign to each of the factors is a *subjective* step in the process.   How much the grade is to be based on each factor is a matter of *judgment*.   And merely translating factors into numbers does not rule out the *subjectivity* of initially weighting the factors or determining their importance.

Factors that teachers base grades upon.   The following are some of the considerations used by various teachers as bases for assigning grades.   These considerations overlap in many respects and their classification in the following outline is merely for convenience. This list is not intended as a guide in deciding which factors should be the basis for a grade—rather, this is a listing of factors commonly used.

1. Potential or capacity—individual aptitude to achieve the stated objectives.
2. Level of attainment in:
   a. Movement skills
   b. Social skills—personal-social adjustment
   c. Knowledge and understandings and information
   d. Group or team success
3. Social considerations, such as:
   a. Citizenship and democratic values
   b. System of values
   c. Social relationships and social skills
4. Interest and effort as reflected in:
   a. Attitudes
   b. Extent and intensity of participation
   c. Regularity of attendance
   d. Punctuality-tardiness, and the like
   e. Regularity in dressing
5. Improvement in elements such as:
   a. Skills
   b. Fitnesses
   c. Knowledges of the activity
   d. The use of knowledge, how it is applied
   e. Making decisions
6. Understanding of techniques, rules, and strategy as appraised through:
   a. Performance tests
   b. Written tests
   c. Oral work

7. Personal qualities as evidenced by:
    a. Efficient work habits
    b. Responsibility
    c. Self-direction
    d. Self-control
    e. Cooperativeness
    f. Sportsmanship
    g. Team work
    h. Leadership
8. Rating of the pupil by others in the group on various factors.
9. Self-rating or self-evaluation by the pupil.
10. Subjective estimate of the teacher.

Grades used to motivate and control.   Some teachers grade on bases unrelated to the objectives of the course or subject.   They state objectives that determine course emphases, but they give weight to other factors in grading.   They say, for example, that 30 per cent of the grade will be based on improvement in skills, 20 per cent on level of performance, 20 per cent on behavior qualities, and 15 per cent on enthusiasm and effort, and 15 per cent on knowledge tests. But how are these various factors actually weighted?   Which skills are selected?   How are they measured and weighted?   What behavior qualities?   And, how is improvement measured?   Many teachers use grades as a lever to control student behavior.   In fact, some teachers grade more on behavior qualities than on anything that resembles the objectives of the subject.   They pretend that the mark indicates achievement, but actually they use the grade as a whip to guarantee class control. Professor Rudolph Pintner's (Teachers College, Columbia University) unpublished findings show that of the fifty-one fears held by school children the greatest is the fear of failing.   In fact Pintner specifically states: "The excessive worry of these children about school items would seem to indicate that our school system lays too much emphasis upon failing a test, having a poor report card. . . ."   Other teachers use the grade in physical education as the chief basis of motivation, with the result that the children may be grade-conscious throughout the physical education class period.

The teacher realizes that grading helps to motivate and control. This can be a useful factor in the control of student behavior especially in very large physical education classes.   We hope that students participate for reasons other than the grade they receive, but the fact remains that grading does help to motivate and to guarantee control. However, grades should be used as little as possible as levers of this nature.

Grading remains a personal responsibility of the teacher. No test or group of tests yet devised (nor in all probability will such a battery of tests be devised) can replace the effective teacher's estimate of the potential of the *whole pupil in action.* The responsibility of grading and evaluating, then, rests squarely on the teacher. This responsibility can never be shifted to a system, a group of tests, or any electronic device. The teacher is the expert in understanding pupils, their learning, and their potential. Human estimates are vital to evaluating pupil progress and cannot be avoided. Fair grading must be based on the teacher's judgment of each situation surrounding each pupil. Motivating and promoting interest in physical education through sensible, understandable grading is as important as developing the prestige of physical education through a rigid system of tough grading. Making physical education a hard subject in which to earn a high grade may result in motivating a few pupils, but it would be disheartening and discouraging to most.

In contrast to more conventional marking systems, descriptive sentences can also be used. In descriptive sentence marking, the teacher merely indicates on the report card pertinent points worthy of emphasis. For example: "A is average in her group in hockey. She has learned the elementary skills very quickly and easily. She seems very interested in physical activities, and she is always willing to take advantage of opportunities for self-improvement. A is a very enthusiastic member of the group, but there are times when she could exert more self-control for the good of the group as a whole." [1] The use of such statements does not mean that the teacher fails to measure and evaluate. As a matter of fact, such a statement needs to be based upon something besides an end-of-semester's musings. Such a statement might very well be an interpretation of test scores, appraisals, estimates, observations, anecdotal records, and the like.

Marking must be based partly on objective measures of knowledges and performance. But it also should represent the actual

[1] Rosalind Cassidy, *New Directions in Physical Education* (New York: A. S. Barnes and Company, Inc., 1938), 139.

progress the student has made toward his potential accomplishment of all of the objectives. Obviously, then, *subjective judgment is of value* in this process. The student's ability to take responsibility, and his attitude, as expressed in his behavior and his leadership ability, are two factors for which there are no objective tests. The teacher's responsibility is to attempt to evaluate the growth and needs of students in all pertinent areas of behavior. And, obviously, the basis of marks might differ in various phases of the program.

In physical education every game is a test—every performance a kind of measurement. Controlling the measurements that should be made is sometimes impossible, but the continual observation by an effective teacher is valuable in determining the grade the pupil should have. Students and parents should understand upon what basis grades are to be assigned. They would be helped to understand what grades mean. They should understand that grades are an appraisal of the *whole* student's performance and achievement in contrast to his own best ability and potential.

As long as grades are given, they should represent the estimated degree of achievement the pupil has made of the outcomes of physical education, toward which teaching and learning have been directed. Obviously, this includes testing the kinds and amounts of knowledges acquired, estimating social behavior, attitudes, personality development, as well as testing skill, endurance, speed, and strength. Goals for each grade could be set up by the experienced, well-trained teacher, with guided pupil participation. The report to the parent and school administration then would be in terms of goals accomplished and not accomplished. No uniform set of goals for a given grade is advocated for the country at large. Rather, the goals for a given grade would be in terms of the abilities, needs, and interests of the group at hand.

SAMPLE TEST ITEMS

True-False

1. Physical educators have been pioneers in some educational movements.
2. Physical educators lead other educators in the testing field.

3. All persons who have devised tests are test experts.

4. All test devisers possess a scientific attitude toward testing.

5. A standardized test is objective in every respect.

6. A test may lack complete validity and yet be of some value.

7. Man has many isolable, measurable traits.

8. Whatever is measurable is worth measuring.

9. All tests are fallible in some respect.

10. Scientific measurement is not open to criticism.

11. Experts in the field of educational measurements appear to be more critical of their field than experts in physical education measurements.

12. Evaluation and measurement may be used to mean the same thing.

13. Evaluation is unscientific and, therefore, has no place in modern physical education.

14. Observation as a method of evaluation is free from weaknesses.

15. The purpose of testing is measurement.

16. In selecting a test, the teacher should know its purpose.

17. Locally constructed tests are unscientific and should not be used by teachers.

18. Pupils are tested; hence they should have nothing to do with test construction.

19. Since there are no guides to test construction, only experts should devise tests.

20. If a pupil is average in physical education, he should receive a grade of 50, which puts him below passing.

21. Classification of pupils in physical education is related to their safety.

22. Agreement as to the precise meaning of many traits which we attempt to measure is difficult.

23. A standardized test will be appropriate to any local situation.

24. Securing agreement on what things are of sufficient worth to justify the establishment of national norms is relatively easy.

25. Measurement fails to include the not-yet-measurable yet valuable phases of physical education.

26. The statistical aspects, such as the mean, tend to direct attention away from the individual pupil.

27. The teacher who devises a local test and does not take all of the appropriate steps used in constructing a standardized test is wasting his time.

28. Individuals defy exact classification into homogeneous groupings.

29. Measurements of improvement provide a sound basis for contrasting pupils and assigning grades.

30. Translating factors used as a basis for grading into numbers fails to rule out the subjectivity of initially selecting and weighting the factors.

BIBLIOGRAPHY

Adams, Georgia Sachs, and Theodore L. Torgerson, *Measurement and Evaluation for the Secondary School Teacher*. New York: The Dryden Press, 1956.

American Association for Health, Physical Education, and Recreation, *Measurement and Evaluation Materials in Health, Physical Education and Recreation*. Washington, D. C.: The Association, 1950.

American Association for Health, Physical Education, and Recreation, Research Section, *Research Methods Applied to Health, Physical Education, and Recreation*, Rev. Ed. Washington, D. C.: The Association, 1952.

Barrow, Harold N., *Motor Ability Testing for College Men*. Minneapolis: Burgess Press, 1957.

Bovard, John Freeman, Frederick W. Cozens, and E. Patricia Hagman, *Tests and Measurements in Physical Education*. Philadelphia: W. B. Saunders, 1950.

Bradfield, James M., and H. Stewart Moredocks, *Measurement and Evaluation in Education*. New York: The Macmillan Company, 1957.

Broer, Marion R., "Are Our Physical Education Grades Fair?" *Journal of Health, Physical Education, and Recreation*, 39:27, 84 (March, 1959).

Cumbee, Frances Z., "Factorial Analysis of Motor Coordination," *Research Quarterly*, December, 1954, 412.

Greene, Harry A., Albert N. Jorgensen, and J. Raymond Gerberich, *Measurement and Evaluation in the Secondary School*. New York: Longmans, Green and Co., 1954.

Hunsicker, Paul Alfred, and Henry J. Montoye, *Applied Tests and Measurements in Physical Education*. Englewood Cliffs, N. J.: Prentice-Hall, Inc., 1953.

Jordan, A. M., *Measurement in Education*. New York: The McGraw-Hill Book Company, Inc., 1953.

Knapp, Clyde G., and E. Patricia Hagman, *Teaching Methods for Physical Education, A Textbook for Secondary School Teachers*. New York: The McGraw-Hill Book Company, Inc., 1953.

Kozman, Hilda Clute, Rosalind Cassidy, and Chester O. Jackson. *Methods in Physical Education*. Philadelphia: W. B. Saunders Company, 1958.

Larson, Leonard August, Morey R. Fields, and Milton A. Gabrielsen, *Problems in Health, Physical and Recreation Education*. Englewood Cliffs, N. J.: Prentice-Hall, Inc., 1953.

Larson, Leonard, and Rachel D. Yocum, *Measurement and Evaluation in Physical Health and Recreation Education*. St. Louis: The C. V. Mosby Company, 1950.

Mathews, D. K., *Measurements in Physical Education*. Philadelphia: W. B. Saunders Company, 1958.

McCloy, Charles Harold, and Norma Dorothy Young, *Tests and Measurements in Health and Physical Education*. New York: Appleton-Century-Crofts, Inc., 1958.

Michaels, William J., and M. Ray Karnes, *Measuring Educational Achievement*. New York: The McGraw-Hill Book Company, Inc., 1950.

Oberteuffer, Delbert, *Physical Education, A Textbook of Principles for Professional Students*. New York: Harper & Brothers, 1956.

Scott, M. Gladys, and Esther French, *Measurement and Evaluation in Physical Education*. Dubuque, Iowa: William C. Brown Company Publishers, 1959.

Stroup, Francis, *Measurements in Physical Education: An Introduction to Its Use*. New York: Ronald Press Co., 1957.

Weiss, Raymond Allen, and Marjorie Phillips, *Administration of Tests in Physical Education*. St. Louis: C. V. Mosby Co., 1954.

Wrightstone, J. W., J. Justman, and I. Robbins, *Evaluation in Modern Education*. New York: American Book Company, 1956.

16

Adjustment and guidance
in physical education

*In a democracy, the individual and
his personality are of primary
concern.—*

THE AVERAGE PERSON HAS BECOME AWARE OF THE HIGH
incidence of maladjusted persons in the nation's population. This national problem has been brought to the consciousness
of teachers, many of whom in the past avoided any responsibility for
helping to develop the human personality.

While physical education teachers are not mental health experts,
any *good* teacher has common sense and human understanding that
form some of the basis of sound mental health. A good teacher is
alert. He becomes aware of the earlier stages of maladjustment before professional attention is demanded. On the other hand, this
alertness to *possible* problems results in too many teachers mistaking
normal problems and minor maladjustments of youth for symptoms
of serious mental or emotional disorders. Some misbehavior is to
be expected in any normal youngster. Some changes in mood and
temperament will be observed. Unless conditions such as this *persist,* the teacher should be cautious in drawing the conclusions that
the observed behavior is personality maladjustment. All young

402

people have some problems of adjustment.   Growing up is difficult.
For many of them these problems are not serious; for some, they are.
The teacher must avoid any temptation to indulge in amateur psy-
chiatry.

The physical education teacher has a place in the guidance program of the school.   He must realize, however, that he has limitations as a counselor.   The goodness of his intentions has nothing to
do with his fitness for counseling.   He must understand the need
to refer the suspected maladjusted pupil to the counseling service
of the school.   This is his part in the counseling sequence.

For too long we have been concerned with bits of knowledge, small
skills and part skills, and the establishment of a myriad of other
minutiae *as habits.*   For too long we have not been concerned
enough with whether the student could make sense out of this patch-
work, with whether he could put the parts of the jig-saw puzzle together, with whether all necessary pieces are at hand, or with whether
it really matters.   Formerly, the profession was overly concerned
with "let's-do-something quick" and, too frequently, disregarded the
consequences upon the pupil.

Sharp distinctions mark the concern of the educator of today
compared with that of his professional brother of yesterday.   And,
little wonder.   Certain facts and factors point directly and drama-
tically to the need for using the tools and forces of education in
integrating, not disintegrating, the pupil's personality, and in furthering his integration in society.   Let us consider a few of these
facts and factors.

In spite of a higher standard of living, inventions for the pleasure
and comfort of man, new ways of enjoying one's self, more and
better social services, all that education has to offer, and a form of
government that is most concerned with the welfare of the individual, Americans are said to be disintegrating in nervous instability.
Mentioning the large but inadequate number of clinics and hos-
pitals for the mentally ill and emotionally disturbed is sufficient
example.

These facts with supporting data are common knowledge.   A
human being's biological organism has not changed perceptibly
since its earthly origin.   This human organism, which developed
to meet and adjust to the simple life and environment of that day,
quite suddenly found itself face to face with conditions and circum-

stances for which it was not adapted.   The Industrial Revolution and the space age are closely related to a revolution within man's personality and within his social life.

Compared with the long stretch of time that measures man's development, it was but a moment ago that the man's biological organism found itself "restlessly speeding in motor cars from nowhere to nowhere"; fighting or dodging traffic, flying vast distances at many times the speed of sound, receiving through an audition system (built for the environment of 2,000 decades ago) the wild, irritating confusions of urban sounds, and the crash and clatter of the steel on steel of the factory and mill.   Urbanization has brought with it the chatter, laughter, and very presence of a great many persons imposing and projecting themselves upon others.   The devitalizing effects of daily meeting many persons, the hypertensions that accompany the necessary day-to-day adjustments to others, the great difficulty the individual has in closing out the world for very long are examples of the experiences of millions of Americans.   Thousands of stimuli today incessantly peck away at our senses.   Millions tend to react by living at a tempo that the human organism was not made to stand for long.

This discussion is no pessimistic mirroring of contemporary life. The point is that modern civilization seems to keep us continually between an emotional shiver and a nervous sweat with little opportunity for that splendid serenity that marks the stable, integrated personality.   Certainly the conduct of some of our physical education programs demonstrates that we have ignored the common-sense demand to counteract some of the results of the rustle, rush, and run of this modern age.

In spite of technological advances and the resultant increase in human productivity, the decrease in working hours, the existence of plenty in goods and services, the increase of leisure; in spite of rapid transportation and the means for rapid distribution of goods; in spite of highly educated economists, sociologists, engineers, and scientists of various kinds with the benefit of implements and processes with which to apply their advanced knowledge; in spite of the extension of the number of years of required schooling, the expansion of school services, and the liberalization of the school curriculum; in spite of all this and more, we do not feel secure.   Many American youths and their parents do not face today and tomorrow with the steadying hand of hope, calm countenance of faith, or the zestful eye of enthusiasm.

What is education, what is physical education doing to ease the ordinarily difficult task of growing up now that it has become so much more difficult?   What is education, what is physical education doing to help satisfy the personality needs, the integration needs, the emotional needs, the social needs of the offspring of the atomic and space age?

Youth wishes for the respect of others, for success, for exercise of his capabilities, for security, for affection, for belonging, for self-direction, for an optimum balance between rest and activity, for faith in ultimate survival of the right, for being like others of the group in basic ways and yet an individual personality—in short, for *self-realization*.   These physiological, social, and psychological needs of youth show the necessity for integration.   Physical education *must* help in this process of integration; it *must* help youth solve some of his pressing problems.   The following are examples of the common difficulties to which *some* young people need to adjust. The physical education teacher and the physical education experience can help, at least in part.

1. Difficulties concerning participation in school social life—difficulties in adjusting to school requirements—difficulties in relationships with teachers.

2. Difficulties in the home concerning relationships with parents, siblings, and aging relatives.

3. Difficulties in relationships with peers of both sexes—making and keeping friends—developing social skills, and desirable personality traits.

4. Difficulties concerning personal appearance—problems of adjusting to and accepting characteristics that cannot be changed.

5. Difficulties in making worth-while use of out-of-school free time.

6. Difficulties concerning personal behavior—moral and ethical areas that seem confused.

7. Difficulties in establishing goals—personal, vocational, or educational plans beyond high school.

8. Difficulties and concerns over matters of health.

Guidance through and in physical education.   Guidance is achieved *through* physical education when the pupil is helped to maintain, gain, or regain balance and soundness in personality by means of participating *under the teacher's guidance* in physical education experiences. Here the experienced teacher uses physical education, or experiences related to physical education, that are selected, managed, and conducted so that the *participation* itself and the outcomes lend stability and balance to the pupil.

Guidance is achieved *in* physical education when the pupil is enabled to be ready for, to be receptive to, and willing to try out suggestions and viewpoints that will help him have the most desirable and need-satisfying experiences in physical education.   In this sense the teacher guides the pupil in preparing for the new, difficult, and unfamiliar experiences he will encounter.   The teacher also prepares him to meet complex experiences.   The teacher plans and helps the pupil meet and cope with success or failure; praise or criticism; problems that require reasoning, judgment, reflection; a wide variety of skills, strengths, and endurances of various kinds and degrees.   The teacher helps him learn to become more self-responsible, more self-directing, and at the same time helps him avoid frustrating thwarting experiences that come too often, last too long, or are too much for him.

Adjustment and guidance begin with the teacher.   The effective guidance of young people is dependent upon the mental and emotional health of the teacher.   Maladjusted teachers cannot properly use the techniques of guidance.   Menninger has neatly said, "Neuroticisms are more catching than measles!"   The teacher must practice good mental health.   He sets the example.   He controls the atmosphere of the environment.   He guides the selection of goals as well as the experiences through which to reach them.   The teacher's personal adjustment is shown in part by the degree to which he likes people and is able to cooperate with and believe in them; by the extent to which he is optimistic and enthusiastic; by his qualities of sympathy, understanding, and patience; by the degree to which he achieves a balance between work and play; and by the extent to which he is sensible about self-set goals and their achievement.   How can a maladjusted person spread anything but maladjustment as he engages in well-intentioned guidance of young people?

What the teacher can do.   The paragraph above describes roughly what the teacher should *be,* if he is effectively to guide pupils. Let us now consider what, in general, the physical education teacher can *do* to help the adjustment of adolescents. The following are some suggestions:

1. Teach activities in such ways that pupils have respect for you, so that they admire you.

2. Perform activities in such ways that pupils gain further respect and admiration.

3. Participate in such ways that pupils *know* you experience sheer enjoyment in participation, in playing, in sports competition, in being a good sportsman, *et cetera*.

4. Give each pupil every desirable and possible opportunity to participate, to be helped *personally*, to be successful at something in which he desires to be successful, to be recognized favorably by the group, to become and remain a part of some group.

5. Select experiences that are appropriate to *this* child and to *these* children in *this* class. Set up reasonable goals toward which the pupil may strive, thus satisfying personal and group motives.

6. Establish with each pupil the proposition that you are there to help, to protect, to cooperate, to guide, to enable him to have fun, to learn, to let himself go within *reasonable* limits.

Phases of personality needing emphasis. An almost universal weakness in human personality is the tendency for one to feel inferior. In order to assuage inferiority feelings, the individual must be helped to attain a reasonable amount of successful accomplishment and social approval. The student must be guided into activity in which his abilities make possible successful accomplishment. The competition must be commensurate with his abilities. He must learn self-confidence.

Acceptance in social groups and success in social situations is, to a large degree, dependent on the *skills* of the individual. To swim, to play tennis or golf, to dance, to bowl, or to participate in the team games implies adequate skill. One psychologist found that participation in games and sports was usually accompanied by personality development. To get along well with the other sex implies skill in co-recreational activities. Skill in music, skill in sedentary games, in dramatics, or in leading a discussion may secure social acceptance for the adult. Youth prizes the more active type of social, recreational, and co-recreational skills. With the modern emphasis on pleasurable physical activity for tension releases, these active types of social recreation are increasingly becoming a part of the adult social milieu.

Intelligence, unless given artificial erudition emphasis, means the ability to deal with the perplexities and problems of one's daily life. These problems may be social, physiological, emotional, academic, or economic. In the first three aspects, the teacher of physical education can be of great help. He can foster co-recreational activities, healthy and vigorous physiological development, and stabilizing emotional experiences. He can help the child attain the socio-motor skills. In other words, the teacher can help the child improve in confidence, skill, and emotional balance and, hence, increase his ability to meet daily problems.

Energy is a highly desirable attribute of personality. An energetic personality is colorful. Mental and physical health habits foster the generation of this dynamic element. The industry and perseverance necessary to succeed and the will to achieve are manifestations of this energy properly directed. The sparkle of wit is a phase. The buoyancy of spirits that is supposed to characterize youth is a joyous expression of excess energy. The elusive aura of personal magnetism possessed by striking personalities is this energy suffusing their social behavior. Evidence shows that energy is related closely to personality development.

Emotional stability is one of the objectives of personality development. Emotional stability means the ability to act intelligently under duress, to work in spite of discomforts, to maintain outward calm and intelligent action in the midst of crises. Pupils will differ widely in their sensitivity to emotional stimuli. All must strive for intelligent control of emotions. Those of the more sensitive nature are not necessarily the most unstable. They may even acquire adequate behavior more quickly. Ability to feel deeply is very desirable. Life would be colorless without emotion. The overt expression of emotion is what needs to be dominated by intelligence and reason.

Techniques and activities should be arranged so as to foster sociality in the student. Ability to get along with others agreeably and harmoniously must be developed. Wide experience in associating with others is the major way to acquire this ability. One must learn: (1) to see the other fellow's point of view, and (2) to see one's own behavior objectively. Optimism, cooperativeness, a sense of humor, freedom from intolerance, and a sincere interest in others are elements of sociality.

Health habits, knowledge and attitudes, available energy, organic vigor, skills for body control, safety, recreation, and social conduct and attitudes are general objectives and, of course, should be included in drawing up the program for the school year.   Specifically desired personality traits and specific situations in which each trait is to obtain developmental experience must be listed; for example, one might list honesty as a trait and, as specific developmental experiences of honesty, list care of equipment, behavior during examinations, giving credit to the other fellow when he deserves it in the give and take of play activities, care of public property, honest score-keeping, exact accounting for team, class, or club monies when handled, and the like.

In order to make such teaching effective, the teacher and students should discuss the *specific* objective, and approve and adopt it as a part of the development plan.   An instance of the use of this procedure is frequently observed in the teaching of sportsmanship.   The customary way is for the teacher to hold a group discussion of the attitudes toward opponents, officials, and guests during the week preceding some form of interschool contest.   The group discusses the situation as it exists, desirable changes, and methods of instituting them.   The group then draws up plans for achieving these changes.   Some guidance and encouragement are given during a preliminary tryout of the plans in an intramural activity period. Needed revisions of plans may become apparent.   The revised plans for achievement of this phase of sportsmanship are then tried out at the inter-school contest.   After the experience of the real contest, summary notes are recorded by student committees.   On the following day, the class discussion is led by the student committee chairman.   The results are discussed, suggestions are drawn up for future progress, and needed committees are elected.   The motivation for this type of lesson needs to be as great as possible, but it must be indirect.   The teacher must do his teaching by suggestion and example.   The project must be voluntarily and enthusiastically undertaken by the students if the lesson is to be effective.

If the class can be motivated to undertake the development of a certain personality trait, they will then seek suggestions from the teacher.   The teacher, with his greater breadth of experience, can suggest and arrange for varieties of pertinent activities. A personality trait needs to be expressed several times in a variety of situations before it begins to take on the nature of generalized habit. The situations must be real and lifelike, not artificial and funereal.

Personality factors such as abundance of energy, emotional stability, sociality, self-confidence, optimism, tolerance, and sense of humor should be definite student-approved objectives; they should be given due weight in selection of appropriate activities; they should be reworded by the student in terms of the desired outcome for the specific activity; and, following the activity, they should be evaluated by the student as to outcome. Evidence of lack of such personality factors is easily detected. Even the students can recognize lassitude and indolence, fits of anger, stage fright, seclusiveness, bullying, cliques and snobbishness, race and religious antagonisms, and inability to see a joke on oneself. The teacher's responsibility is to guide the student into *conscious* practice of behavior which will replace lethargy with energy and urge for activity, which will substitute emotional control for fits of anger, and which will change social maladjustment into tolerance, kindliness, sociality, self-confidence, and objective self-insight.

The value of teacher example for personality development cannot be stressed too highly. The child learns by his association with others, by reading, by observation of adults, but chiefly by active practice and self-direction in an attempt to emulate those he admires. The teacher may be his model.

Principles of personal integration. The following principles concerning personal integration outline the concern of the teacher in the broad aspect of developmental guidance in and through physical education. The principles are worded so that they serve as guides to action.

▶ **The teacher should realize that the individual attempts to attain selfhood, to gain purposes, to reach self-set goals, in spite of the obstacles set by his environment and his biological heritage. The extent to which a youth will go to satisfy a desire, such as to be recognized and respected by members or a member of his group, is sometimes remarkable, amusing, tragic, or shocking.**
▶ **The teacher should help the pupil understand himself and find himself in his social group and life.**

▶ The teacher should be aware of and ready to help the pupil who is attempting to make adjustments to problems and obstacles too great for him to solve and surmount. At the same time, the teacher should refrain from assigning projects, tasks, and performances beyond the ability of a pupil. The school and the teacher do not educate. They do all they can to make education possible, but the pupil is the one who educates himself. The challenge and enjoyment of meeting and solving problems are eliminated when the teacher assigns too difficult a task. The child feels thwarted and frustrated. To maintain a feeling of integration within himself, the child adopts some behavior (often misbehavior) which helps him keep a balance between tensions and releases, instabilities and stabilities.

▶ The teacher should assist each child and provide opportunities for him to develop and mature in his emotional actions and reactions.

▶ The pupil should be guided to examine discriminately his system of values and should be led to raise them to higher levels—in fact, to find out what these higher levels are. The pupil should grow in ability to reexamine his system of values as he gains experience.

▶ The teacher should understand that the average child tries to do all that is necessary to be able to think well of himself, to feel that he is worthy of his classmates, to believe that they think well of him and that they expect something of him, to try to measure up to what he thinks these expectations are.

▶ When a pupil fails in his attempt at successful performance in an activity, the teacher should help him assume a mature attitude toward the failure. If the child seeks to be successful in some other project as an escape from and a substitute for the failed performance, as he attempts to maintain integration, the teacher should aid him in being successful in the substitute performance. The teacher should also appropriately guide him back to the original task if he gives promise of being successful after conscientious and intelligent effort.

▶ The pupil should be given opportunities to develop and follow ideals, loyalties, and other appropriate aspects of the aesthetics of life.

▶ The pupil should be aided in appreciating his strengths and weaknesses as well as the limitations and advantages of his environment. The pupil transferring from another school often becomes maladjusted because the new environment sets limitations and demands which he does not recognize or sense. A pupil must be helped to learn to survey and appraise a situation and a group to know what is required to adjust to them.

▶ The teacher should be alert to and guard against expression of his own personal tensions, instabilities, or maladjustments so that they will not be projected to the members of his classes. This restraint is not easy because some symptoms of maladjustment in one's conduct may persist undiscovered and unexamined. Furthermore, even if such instabilities are discovered, the teacher is apt to excuse them as being justified. The teacher who fails to receive a promised raise in salary becomes disgruntled. The innocent but indiscreet teacher, who is talked about, rebels, suffers a persecution complex, or enjoys an orgy of feeling sorry for himself. These states are unfortunate enough in themselves but become serious, socially and educationally objectionable faults if imposed, either consciously or inadvertently, upon the pupils.

▶ The teacher should help the pupil in knowing when and how to adjust to others and to his environment, and when and how to take the initiative in pursuing his purposes. One of the major lessons in adjustment is to learn when to give and when to take.

▶ The teacher should understand that when a pupil is facing a serious adjustment problem as, for example, pumping up a deflated ego, he is apt to be oblivious to the accomplishment of other tasks. The athlete or student who is intensely worried over finances or personal relationships usually fails to measure up in his respective specialty. Such adjustment problems may cause the pupil to engage in anti-social conduct, apparently ignore the pressing needs of school situations, break the rules of the school, and the like. That is, when the pupil is unable to fulfill a cherished desire common to persons of his age, he may rebel or try to balance the tension by compensative behavior of some kind.

▶ The teacher should make certain that, as the program progresses through the year and from year to year, the pupil is prepared to cope with the new. This not only facilitates the learning process but helps avoid unnecessary experiences and feelings of failure with resultant disintegration. Obviously some failures are expected as a part of development.   When they occur, the teacher's task may be to help the pupil find or develop new ways to overcome or get around failure and to achieve some successes.

▶ The pupil should be led to appreciate his dependence upon the other members of an athletic team, other members of his class, the school staff, his home relationships, the members of the community and their respective enterprises as contributors to the welfare of the individual.   This appreciation not only helps him better understand his world but helps him arrive at that point of maturity when the center of the universe is visualized at some other place than within himself.   Such appreciations help the pupil understand the vast scope and significance of society.   Such appreciation makes him more willing to adjust to the social order, more intelligent in adjusting to and being a part of his social group.

▶ Some teachers work in communities that provide an environment that encourages maladjusted children.   If such conditions prevail, the teacher should understand the causes of disintegration, do what he can to maintain integration, cooperate with the school administration in controlling conduct, and do what he can to improve conditions.

▶ The teacher, in promoting the integrated personality, should make as certain as is possible, by means of a health examination, the health status of the individual.   A related step is to adopt measures that will prevent conditions and circumstances that may be injurious to the pupil's health.   A third basic step is to help remedy or correct conditions, found during the health examination, that are deleterious to the child's health.

▶ The pupil should be helped to feel confidence in himself and his ability and system of regulating his inner life.   He may need some help in establishing and working out a system so he is justified in being self-confident.

▶ The teacher should be alert to and adopt measures to find pupils' talents.   He should provide outlets for creative abilities.   Pupils should receive the satisfaction of creating new rules for games, new games with familiar equipment.   If we had listened to pupils, we would have introduced long ago such innovations as smaller-sized basketballs and footballs for the later grades in elementary school and earlier grades in junior high school, and lower goals for basketball in the junior high school.

▶ Efforts should be made as early as nursery-school age to develop cooperation with others and to develop other social traits as opportunities arise.   By the time the pupil is a senior graduating from high school, he should be a young adult in social maturity and stability.   We teachers of physical education as a group have not contributed toward such a goal in proportion to the opportunities provided in physical education.   Regardless of essential skills, fundamental skills, and basic activities, an important obligation of physical education is to join other educators in the development of personality and character.   An integrated personality is dependent upon the ability to deal intelligently with problems involving social *adjustments.*

▶ Teachers should not establish too many codes of conduct.   Integration is worth while if opportunities are provided for the individual and the group to pursue modes of action which are best for them in the long run, regardless of the teacher's need for expediency.

▶ Backward, clumsy children should be given more opportunities than other children to realize success and to achieve in physical education activities.

▶ Pupils who are highly skilled and well coordinated should be presented with activity situations and skills that are extremely challenging, or given other challenging tasks, such as trying to be successful activity leaders or squad leaders.

▶ Physical education for high school seniors (and perhaps some juniors) should be planned chiefly by them in terms of their life needs now and next year, as well as in terms of their interests. Physical education takes on meaning and value to these young persons if it is seen in relationship to adult life, as a means of belonging to a local community or as necessary for college.   Physical education should satisfy the *actual* social and personality needs as well as the biological needs of any pupil if we are to contribute to the individual's integration.

▶ The teacher of physical education should cooperate with other teachers in aiding the pupil to view his life as a set of unified experiences and, if they are not unified, to help him find ways of accomplishing an optimum degree of integration.

▶ The teacher, who wants to help a pupil continue to be an integrated personality, should not try to eliminate all obstacles and problems in the pupil's pathway. The teacher should not try to eliminate failure from the child's life and experience. Rather, the teacher should try to prevent failures and thwartings from occurring too often, continuing for too long a period, being too large or difficult to surmount or solve. We learn through failures, dilemmas, and disturbances as well as through their opposites. We attain integration momentarily by adjusting. We learn to adjust by adjusting. We prepare ourselves for future adjustments by seeing the necessity for adjustment, by having varied experiences in adjusting, by developing originality and initiative in solving our adjustment problems, and by taking the responsibility for the consequences of our attempts at adjustment. The teacher, therefore, aids the pupil in solving adjustment problems; he helps him to develop self-reliance in meeting, overcoming, or getting around obstacles; and he helps him in meeting the uncertain future, its problems and difficulties, with confidence.

▶ Teachers should find the type of pupil whose ambitions overshoot his abilities. Such a disjointed condition means maladjustment whenever, wherever, and as long as it exists. The substitution or sublimation process usually should be gradual and imperceptible so that further disintegration is avoided.

▶ The pupil should be led to appreciate the place of his wishes and interests in relation to those of his group and those of larger units of society. He should understand that most of his wishes are fulfilled and his interests satisfied chiefly through cooperation with others.

▶ The teacher should use available means of determining the present status of the child's maturity as well as his rate of maturing. Differences in degree and rate of maturation form the seat of some disintegrations, particularly if the teacher fails to adjust appropriately the program and his teaching.

▶ The teacher should find out the types of needs and cherished wishes among his pupils and try to satisfy them. The reticent, backward girl needs to participate in social situations. The weak, underdeveloped boy needs to participate in strength-building activities. The clumsy child should be helped to become as skillful as possible in appropriate activities.

▶ The pupil should be given opportunities for discovering, for adventuring, for meeting situations that demand courage and ingenuity. Teachers who were denied a normal childhood or who have forgotten it, tend to lay the pallid hands of restraint, caution, safety-first, and conservatism upon the activities of adventuresome boys and girls.

▶ Children should be given opportunities to gain distinction while continuing to be like others in basic respects. One way for them to gain these desired differences is by making decisions and selections, being as self-directive as their maturity and the circumstances indicate. This is fundamental to an integrated personality and demands a teacher who can judge the maturity of a pupil regardless of age.

▶ The teacher should make certain that the pupil knows what the school and teacher expect of him. A sense of security is partially attained through such understanding. He should know the type of work, quality, amount, the speed at which he is expected to work, and ways of attacking the work. This principle does not preclude the pupil participation in planning work; rather the teacher guides the pupil's estimates, standards, and judgments as he participates in planning.

▶ A pupil sometimes becomes extremely interested in a given activity. His interest may become so deep and enveloping that he is thoroughly absorbed in what he is doing. At such times he attains an integrated personality—he is at one with the world and himself. Such centers of integration tend to change from one activity to another. The teacher should guide the pupil in not becoming too deeply engrossed and fixed in one center for too long a period, if this participation does not lead to further and higher activities. This principle is based on the assumption that a balanced, well-rounded personality is a worth-while goal. Furthermore, if a child is limited to one center of integration, he is due for a severe and disintegrating shock if this center of his interest and attention is suddenly removed. The old adage, "Don't put all of your eggs in one basket," takes on meaning in any discussion of integrating the individual.

▶ The teacher should do what he can to secure the pupils' cooperation in making class and the school authority assimilable and agreeable to the individual. When this condition does not prevail, the individual becomes disintegrated. His resulting behavior upsets the equilibrium of the environment, which is at best delicately poised between balance and unbalance.

▶ The teacher should set an example to pupils by the ways he adjusts to life's tensions, instabilities, and obstacles. (Read that again!)

▶ The teacher, alone, should not tackle the task of preventing or remedying maladjustment. Rather, the aid of other teachers, the other school personnel, the community, and the home should be secured. If these other sources of influence are lacking, the lone teacher should not give up. He can accomplish something. In fact, if the pupil has but one person whom he trusts, whom he believes understands and likes him, and in whom he can confide, he may be prevented from becoming maladjusted—if he does not become too dependent on one person.

▶ The teacher should understand that the justification for rules, regulations, and other limitations of pupils' conduct is that pupils benefit from being protected from injury, are enabled to enjoy their participation in activities, and are enabled to realize other values of physical education impossible without such restrictions. The youth, therefore, should *understand the purposes and values of limitations* to his behavior in school. This understanding helps prevent his feeling that the school and the teacher are trying to thwart the accomplishment of his purposes, the realization of his desires. It is most advantageous to secure the understanding and cooperative effort of pupils in discovering the need for *necessary* rules and regulations. This is the case not only because it increases conformance to rules by pupils but also because such cooperative and creative participation is one way to aid the integration of the pupils' personalities into a social group.

Selective teacher recruitment. One important function of secondary education is vocational guidance. Though teachers of physical education usually are not primarily concerned with vocational guidance, they are in a unique position to help young people explore the opportunities and advantages of selecting physical education as a career. In fact, the influence of physical education teachers on young people who consider entering this field is usually more important than the influence of vocational counselors.[1]

[1] Marillyn Jane Nass, "A Survey of the Factors Which Influence Girls in the Choice of Physical Education as a Major Curriculum" (Unpublished Master's Thesis, The Pennsylvania State University, 1955), and Walter C. Crowe, "Identification and Evaluation of Some Practices of Selective Recruitment of Male Physical Education Teachers" (Unpublished Doctor's Dissertation, The University of Southern California, Los Angeles, 1957).

For many years, the continuing shortage of qualified teachers has been of great concern. During recent years, this problem has become increasingly acute. Secondary school population has increased. This increase in school populations has not had a corresponding increase in high school graduates entering the teaching profession. As shortages of teachers in some high school subjects became acute and as enrollments increased steadily, many other subject areas were affected. The field of physical education for men has not had serious shortages in the past. During some periods, the supply of men has exceeded the demand. There have, however, been periods of a serious shortage of qualified women teachers. Even without possible teacher shortages in physical education, the problem of assuring improved *quality* of persons entering the field would remain an important concern of teachers of physical education.

The manpower pool of *highly qualified* young people is short for most fields. And competition for available manpower is becoming keener every year. Many young people who initially intend to become teachers never do enter the profession because they are diverted to other attractive occupations. Therefore, teachers in the field of physical education must take an active interest in procuring the most highly qualified people available. Such selective recruitment is one of the best steps yet proposed to improve the supply of teachers. Influence being exerted and pertinent information being given to high school youth by physical education teachers are not only beneficial in the guidance of young people but also important to the profession.

The National Commission on Teacher Education and Professional Standards has consistently maintained that the high standards approach is the only long-range solution of the continuing problem of teacher shortages:

A basic obligation of any profession is to exert every effort to assure a continuing and adequate flow of qualified practitioners into the profession. This obligation rests with especial emphasis upon the teaching profession, and the emphasis should be on selective recruitment.[2]

[2] National Commission on Professional Education and Standards, *An Action Program For Selective Recruitment* (Washington, D. C.: National Education Association, 1953).

To effectively recruit teachers and provide adequate vocational guidance, factors that are associated with pupils' interests in physical education as a career must be identified.   Just how it is best to appeal to youth is not clearly known as yet.   Teacher recruitment efforts have been generally pointed at the appeal that teaching may have at all levels and in all subject areas.   Evidence indicates that interest in specific subject areas is a very important aspect in the selection of high school teaching as a career by young people.[3]   Probably, a *general appeal* to youth on the part of all areas of education is *not* as effective and as attractive to youth as *specific appeals* in individual subject fields.   Physical education is one of these.

One of the authors studied the factors and influences which seem to be associated with interest in or the selection of public school teaching and, more particularly, physical education teaching as a career by scholastically qualified young people.[4]   The study showed that the status and prestige attached to the occupation of physical education teaching by young people who were interested in considering this field was higher than the status attached to other teaching fields.   Consequently, specific emphasis on this area of teaching should have more appeal than associating this field with areas of teaching which have less status in the opinions of young people. We also found that the field of physical education appeals to high school pupils in ways quite different than those in other subject areas and levels of teaching.

Let us examine the type of young people who are most likely to be interested in entering the physical education profession and some possible steps to cause them to seriously consider this area of teaching as a career.

1. A great many young people qualified to enter college have not completely rejected the possibility of physical education as a career. There is, therefore, a large group of possible candidates as potential

---

3 Melbern S. Clark, "Analysis of the Motives for Entering the Physical Education Profession" (Unpublished Master's Thesis, Utah State University, 1954).

4 Earl L. Wallis, "Factors Related to the Recruitment of Young Men For Physical Education Teaching" (Unpublished Doctor's Dissertation, University of Southern California, 1957) and Earl L. Wallis, "Factors Associated With the Recruitment of Women Physical Education Teachers" (Unpublished research report presented at California Association for Health, Physical Education, and Recreation, Annual Conference, San Mateo, 1958).

teachers in this area.This means that many young people who are qualified to enter college *may* be interested in considering this area as a vocational choice.   The most highly qualified should be encouraged and supplied with information and guidance which will help them to make wise career choices.   Specific recruitment procedures aimed at the intellectually gifted should be a measure in improving standards in physical education.

2. A high percentage of young people whose parents are teachers indicate that they are interested in teaching.   Some recruitment appeals might be made to young people through their teacher parents.

3. Appeals were effective to those young people who have had sustained successful experience in high school athletics.   The young people who win the most awards and recognition in athletics are particularly receptive to recruitment appeals.   In many cases they appear to be interested in a career in physical education teaching or coaching.

4. Efficient appeals should be directed toward the groups of young people who have the distinction of having been elected captains of teams or who have been selected to serve in other leadership positions.   These experiences also are associated with interest in considering physical education as a career.

5. Physical education teaching and coaching enjoy higher status than other fields of teaching, in the opinions of groups of young people who are interested in this career area.   For this reason, general recruitment appeals (directed toward young men and women for *all teaching fields*) would be less effective than specific appeals directed specifically toward young men and women for physical education teaching or coaching.

6. Further interpretation of the purposes and values of physical education and of the needs and opportunities in the field should be given to potentially interested young people.   Many young people do not understand the need or the opportunities.

7. Earlier recruitment efforts at the junior high school level could assist young people in defining their career objectives.   Additional appeals seem to be indicated in the later high school years when interests are more clearly defined.

8. Young people very frequently state that poor pay is an important disadvantage of teaching careers.   However, these young people generally indicate *little understanding of the actual earnings*

of beginning or experienced teachers.   Recruitment appeals should clearly explain the potential earnings of teachers and coaches and contrast these earnings with other vocations.

9. Recruitment procedures might include appeals directed to parents and teachers due to the extent of influence these persons apparently have on the vocational decisions of young people.

10. Generally improved public relations would increase the possibility of highly qualified young people selecting physical education as a career.   For example, better public relations will influence favorably the opinions of persons who are influential when assisting these young people in making vocational choices.   Efforts can be directed at the opinions of friends, teachers, and parents of young people with qualifications for physical education.

11. Greater emphasis should be placed on providing qualified youth with occupational information so that they have a more realistic understanding of employment opportunities in the field of physical education.

12. Consideration should be given to special appeals that physical education seems to have.   Existing recruitment procedures should be examined to determine if the elements are included which have the greatest influence on pupils and which would cause them to consider physical education as a vocation.   Many concepts, which cannot be applied to public school teaching in general, are thought to be advantages of physical education teaching by many young people.[5]   Some of these ideas are: working out-of-doors, the opportunity to maintain physical condition, interest in sports, and athletic coaching opportunities.

A *guidance approach* to recruitment is indicated.   Pupils should not be exposed to biased or extreme appeals.   Rather, they should have the opportunity to explore their interests.   Physical education teachers should supply them with information to help them wisely choose their careers.   The professional obligation of teachers is to encourage those who appear to be highly qualified to teach and to redirect those who are not qualified.

5 Blodwen Corlee Munson, "Factors Affecting the Recruitment of Girls' Physical Education Teachers" (Unpublished Master's Thesis, University of Washington, 1956).

SAMPLE TEST ITEMS

True-False

1. Some misbehavior is to be expected in any normal youngster.

2. The physical education teacher should avoid functioning as a guidance worker.

3. Guidance *in* physical education is achieved when the teacher prepares pupils to be ready for and receptive to complex and difficult situations in the plan of experiences.

4. Guidance *through* physical education is achieved when the pupil is helped to maintain or gain soundness of personality by means of participating in physical education.

5. The mental health of the teacher has relatively little effect on the effectiveness with which he may employ guidance techniques.

6. The tendency to feel inferior is an almost universal weakness in human personality.

7. Most young people do not face serious emotional problems in growing up.

8. Aspects of emotional stability are the abilities to work in spite of discomforts and to act intelligently under duress.

9. The manpower pool of highly qualified young people is short for most fields.

10. Teachers of physical education and other subject fields seem to select teaching as a career for much the same reasons.

11. A professional obligation of teachers is to assure a continuing flow of qualified young persons into the teaching profession.

12. Pupils desire to be appreciated and wanted by others.

13. Feelings of happiness, satisfaction, and joy are essential to the integrated personality.

14. Man's nervous system is biologically adjusted to modern civilization.

15. Integration is more preached than practiced in physical education classes.

16. Teachers should establish many codes of conduct.

17. The teacher should set an example to pupils by the ways he adjusts to life's tensions, instabilities, and obstacles.

18. Before participating in a new activity, pupils should be encouraged to ask many questions.

19. Before introducing a new activity to be learned, the teacher should find out in great detail the ability of each pupil in the new activity.

20. The teacher, who is interested in helping a pupil continue to be an integrated personality, tries to eliminate all obstacles and problems in the pupil's pathway.

21. The teacher, alone, should not tackle the task of preventing or remedying maladjustment.

BIBLIOGRAPHY

Association for Supervision and Curriculum Development, *Fostering Mental Health in Our Schools*. Washington, D. C.: National Education Association of the United States, 1950.

Association for Supervision and Curriculum Development, *Guidance in the Curriculum, 1955 Yearbook*. Washington, D. C.: National Education Association, 1955.

Bennett, Margaret E., *Guidance in Groups*. New York: The McGraw-Hill Book Company, Inc., 1955.

Bernard, H. W., *Toward Better Personal Adjustment*. New York: The McGraw-Hill Book Company, Inc., 1957.

Carroll, Herbert A., *Mental Hygiene, The Dynamics of Adjustment*, 3rd ed. Englewood Cliffs, N. J.: Prentice-Hall, Inc., 1956.

Cassidy, Rosalind, *New Directions in Physical Education for the Adolescent Girl*. New York: A. S. Barnes and Company, 1938.

Gordon, Ira J., *The Teacher as a Guidance Worker*. New York: Harper & Brothers, 1956.

Harsh, G. M., and H. G. Schrickel, *Personality: Development and Assessment*. New York: Ronald Press, 1950.

Jennings, Helen H., *Sociometry in Group Relations*. Washington, D. C.: American Council on Education, 1948.

Kluckhohn, Clyde, and Henry A. Murry, eds., *Personality in Nature, Society, and Culture*. New York: Alfred A. Knopf, 1956.

Knapp, Maud Lombard, and Frances Todd, *Democratic Leadership in Physical Education*. Palo Alto: National Press, 1952.

Kozman, Hilda Clute, ed., *Group Process in Physical Education*. New York: Harper & Brothers, 1951.

LaSalle, Dorothy, *Guidance of Children Through Physical Education*, 2nd ed. New York: Ronald Press Company, 1957.

Layman, Emma McCloy, *Mental Health Through Physical Education and Recreation*. Minneapolis: Burgess Publishing Company, 1955.

Lehner, George F. J., and Ella Kube, *The Dynamics of Personal Adjustment*. Englewood Cliffs, N. J.: Prentice-Hall, Inc., 1956.

Little, Wilson, and A. L. Chapman, *Development Guidance in Secondary School*. New York: The McGraw-Hill Book Company, Inc., 1953.

McDaniel, Henry B., and G. A. Shaftel, *Guidance in the Modern School*. New York: Dryden Press, 1956.

Murphy, Gardner, *Human Potentialities*. New York: Basic Books, Inc., 1958.

Ohlsen, Merle M., *Guidance, An Introduction*. New York: Harcourt, Brace and Company, 1955.

Rothney, John W. M., *Guidance Practices and Results*. New York: Harper & Brothers, 1958.

Traxler, Arthur E., *Techniques of Guidance*. New York: Harper & Brothers, 1957.

Wattenberg, W. W., and Fritz Redl, *Mental Hygiene in Teaching*. New York: Harcourt, Brace and Company, Inc., 1951.

Part Six

YOUR RELATIONSHIPS,
YOUR JOB, YOUR FUTURE

17

Public relations for the physical education teacher

"When your work speaks for itself, don't interrupt."
—Henry J. Kaiser.

EDUCATION WAS THE LAST OF THE PROFESSIONS TO COMPETE for the time and support of man as a worth-while major activity and social institution. But, rapid strides to catch up are being taken in most phases and levels of education. Even those in the most cloistered teaching situations are beginning to appreciate that public relations is not some objectionable process borrowed from the tainted market place. They are coming to see it as a social process that is as good as its purposes, means, and outcomes—like any other social process.

Education joins the other pursuits of man that have worthy goals and ethical means of reaching those goals. It also competes against an ever-growing body of forces whose means and ends are destructive of man's efforts to improve. People continually need to be made aware that they must make choices as to how they spend their time, money, energy, and thought. For through these choices their destinies—the very destiny of man—are determined. For people to be made aware, they have to be *reached*. This is the task of public relations. If education or physical education wants to give people correct, adequate information about what it is trying to do and why, if it is to rectify misunderstandings and mistaken ideas, and if it is to gain the active cooperation and support of individuals and organizations, people have to be *reached*.   And, in the meantime an increasing number of other forces and fields also are trying to reach these same individuals and groups.   Public relations has become a *necessity* in today's world.

Administrators in all fields long ago realized that while the *responsibility* for public relations is put upon their shoulders, most of the program of public relations in education is performed by *all* personnel who meet the students, parents, and members of the other publics.   It has been estimated that the nonadministrative staff has *five hundred times* greater opportunity to practice public relations. Not only are there more nonadministrative staff members, but they also have many more face-to-face meetings.   Too, these meetings are apt to be in such an atmosphere that *reaching* a given public's representative is easier.   An office girl who answers the telephone can destroy in one minute the public relations that her employer took one year to build.

PERSONAL RELATIONS, THE FOUNDATION

Every teacher in physical education inescapably is a public relations agent.   Those who serve more actively and more consciously in a department's public relations program soon become aware that some persons may prove to be inept in such a program.   For, a person must have the desire and ability to have good relations with other human beings.   Not all persons seem to possess the necessary aptitude and know-how.   Most of us have to be reminded of what we, as human beings, are like underneath the social protective veneer that we build.

A foundation in personal relations needed.   The following suggestions make no claim at comprehensiveness.   They are listed here partly because they might be overlooked by the average teacher, overlooked because a good many teachers deal considerably with but two publics, their colleagues and students.   Neither of these two publics is typical or representative enough of the many other publics to give teachers an adequate acquaintance with the abilities needed in the wider concept of personal relations.

First and most fundamental, you must really like people, believe in them, be outgoing toward them, overlook their shortcomings. Success in personal relations rests in part on your ability to make friends. This means that you must be worthy of the friendship of others. It means that you have the capacity to give friendship (some persons lack this ability, according to Menninger). Aids to acquaintanceship include such familiar practices as finding out beforehand about a person's interests and hobbies, his name (and remembering it together with some key things about him). What has he done that he considers important? For what is he striving? Best yet, permit him to do a favor and especially to return one.

To be effective in public relations, occasionally you must gain and retain the attention of the other fellow. In addition to the more common steps, try using the technique of arousing a person's curiosity in something in which he already has interest, then giving him the new point, asking the searching question, or making an attention-getting comment. Usually, you must speak the other person's language. Here is one area in which teachers are apt to lose the other person quite early. But because of the general interest in sports, this is an area where most coaches and physical educators excel in holding attention. Related is the use of statements that touch on the vivid experience of the other person. Sometimes his attention may be won by making your point *connect* with one of his values, one of his goals, one of his hobbies. Certainly all of us have resistance to others until we feel no further need to be wary. One of the surest ways to remove the veil of resistance is to talk of the other man's cherished interests. These, to change the metaphor, are the chinks in his armor. We must allow him to talk about these favorite hobbies. We must ask questions about them, permit him to tell of his achievements in them.

One basic reason the teacher establishes good working relations with members of various publics is not just to expand the number of his friends and acquaintances but also to gain their cooperation in being active supporters of physical education. The taxpayer, the parent, the union leader, politician, or civic leader who reacts to the physical education story with the yawning jaw and drowsy eye can hardly be said to have been reached. Some of the personal relations items that help you gain the other person's cooperation are: empathy; understanding; and respect of others. The ability to put yourself in the other fellow's place is difficult because we tend to be cocooned in our own concerns, and *empathy* requires the outpouring of your interest into the other fellow's reservoir.   We must *understand* the other fellow and his doings, aspirations, and concerns, or we fail to have *respect* for his peculiarities, wishes, actions.   Failing this respect, we cannot show respect for others unless we become hypocritical.   Lacking this understanding of the other person, we also cannot genuinely show what we believe is important and valuable.   When we truly understand, we can sincerely show that the other counts, that he is indeed a unique personality, that we respect him for what he is.   Above all, respect of another demands that we trust him, that we have confidence in him.   Parenthetically, throughout all personal relations, the assumption must be that the other fellow is Mr. Everyman or his wife, daughter, or mother.   The chances are that you will seldom if ever encounter a scoundrel as you pursue your public relations tasks or the personal relations that support them.

When teachers find themselves in a leadership role, it becomes more important than ever that practice in personal relations show a feeling toward and for the other person.   What are a few of the ways you may demonstrate this kind of understanding?   A long established but often violated rule is to permit the other person always to keep his self-esteem, to save his pride.   This means he is never belittled.   And, on the other side is the truism that he should be given a bit more credit than he deserves; honors are shared with him, publicity and whatever limelight there may be should encompass him.   Another guide is to let the other person know that his work and abilities are important in as many ways as honestly possible.   Thus he is helped to take pride in his work, particularly if you are quick to point out some phase which means a good deal to him and equally quick to show appreciation for any special ability, thought, or effort.   You must also be a good listener, easily approached, easy to see, even easy to make complaints to.   Letting him get it off his chest is therapeutic, and it provides the chance for you to be on hand to do something about the matter.   This keeps the other person's confidence where it should be.   Whatever his troubles and problems may be, you should show sympathy and understanding.   Offer to help him work out some possible solution if any exists after he sees that his welfare is of personal concern to you.   He should be complimented about the kinds of things he wants to have recognized (if you can do it truthfully) but not overcomplimented. In times of stress, display confidence and poise and conceal worries, doubts, and fears.

Finally, in spite of all these efforts to treat the other person with fairness, occasionally someone may turn violently against you. A few suggestions fit all cases of this type. Usually it is best if you take temporary defeats and work for eventual understanding. Be sure you understand the other person's case. Seldom if ever should you become engaged in an argument of any kind in these cases. Avoid any but fair, calmly worded, reasonable statements. In fact, the best policy is to say only the fine things about the other person.

PUBLIC RELATIONS

Before looking at the meanings of and details about public relations, let us examine the ten things that you as a physical education teacher can do about public relations:

1. Make certain that your own personal behavior, speech, and appearance are assets to the department, the school, the profession, the students, and yourself.

2. Have or develop traits that inspire confidence by others in what you say, do, and are.

3. Initiate and maintain the best possible program.

4. Teach the best you know, in the best way that you know, for the best reasons you know.

5. Help with school and community causes concerned with the welfare of others.

6. Communicate with others (using their language) so that they have affirmative attitudes toward physical education.

7. Secure the support of others who are in key positions by first getting them involved in some way in the program.

8. Be readily available to help boys and girls, school personnel, and community groups engaged in worthy projects.

9. Present an occasional exhibition or demonstration that uses many children and that is of interest to their parents.

10. Cooperate with the school's public relations program.

What is the meaning of P.R.? Public Relations, or P.R. as it is called, is actually a misnomer. There are *publics*, not *a* public. Here are eleven typical definitions of P.R.:

1. Simply and broadly, P.R. consists of all that one does, as a

representative of some organization, that influences persons favorably or unfavorably toward that organization.

NOTE: "All that one does" refers to *words,* written or spoken, *attitudes* taken, *acts, feelings* shown, *gestures,* and the like.

2. Using all the communications media for interpreting the physical education program to the pupils, parents, and publics.

3. All of the forces and factors which influence the attitudes, beliefs, reactions, and activities of any persons outside of the profession.

4. Any contacts of any professional person with any person outside of the profession.

5. The process of keeping informed persons who have an interest in education.

6. Procedures used to interpret the program to the lay public.

7. The sum total of all activities furthering the knowledge of the public about physical education.

8. Making people understand the values in physical education, and causing them to believe in the importance of it, and supporting it when help is needed.

9. Translating with good taste and good sense, the activities and aims of the program in terms found understandable to other groups.

10. The utilization of all means whereby the public is able to acquire an understanding of the nature and purpose of physical education and its particular values.

11. The aggregate of attitudes toward, opinions concerning, and beliefs about physical education derived from direct and indirect information, observations, and experiences related to the specific program as influenced by previous and current observations and experiences in related areas.

What are P.R.'s functions?   The authors prefer the first definition but the others represent other justifiable views.   Another way of looking at the meaning of P.R. is to examine its *functions.*   Ten of these functions are:

1. Finding, clarifying, and changing the attitudes of pertinent publics toward one's field.

2. Interpreting the reasons for, the goals, programs, and methods of one's field.

3. Disseminating information about physical education.

4. Making available facilities, personnel, and services to publics.

5. Helping publics in the understanding of changing patterns.

6. Recognizing pressures from certain quarters and reacting intelligently.

7. Showing the various publics how physical education serves.

8. Making use of related personnel and organizations, as well as outside agencies who may be of help.

9. Correcting mistakes made by one's department or field.

10. Rectifying misunderstandings.

What are the purposes of P.R.?   There are three *major* purposes of public relations. These are:

1. *Informative*—To inform and help pertinent groups of professional (and departmental) personnel understand policies, programs, events, services, planned revisions and additions, status, reasons for, values, and the like. To anticipate change and the new and get the publics ready.

2. *Ameliorative*—To rectify mistakes, explain misunderstandings, eradicate negative attitudes, remove deterrents to and create good will, guide and promote favorable and supportive public opinion and action.

3. *Cooperative*—To enlist and give assistance and cooperation to pertinent groups and individuals, to make available professional (and departmental) resources to suitable groups, to participate.

Purposes of P.R.   If these three major purposes are broken down into more detailed ideas for the sake of gaining some concreteness, we can say that twelve of the *purposes* of P.R. are:

1. To create good will with all pertinent publics (pupils, parents, school personnel).

2. To help pertinent publics understand the reasons for and values of physical education.

3. To inform pertinent publics of present programs and planned changes in programs, policies, etc.

4. To inform pertinent publics of services rendered by the department, and its willingness to serve.

5. To inform pertinent publics of events that have occurred and will occur.

6. To encourage participation in suitable activities related to the program and in the use of available facilities.

7. To inform the publics of the expenditure of funds (probably through the superintendent's annual report).

8. To enlist assistance in suitable projects and other help.

9. To encourage and publicize activities that are as self-supporting as possible.

10. To show reasons for greater financial support if needed (and if approved by the school administration).

11. To rectify mistaken ideas, remove misunderstandings, erase negative attitudes.

12. To guide and promote public opinion in favor of worthy programs of physical education.

The need of P.R. in physical education. As a special project, several graduate classes comprised of experienced teachers in physical education over a period of four years asked a total of 3,000 persons in three different states, "What's wrong with physical education?" These 3,000 men and women represented sixty-three different vocations, all of which are common to our every day lives, such as barbers, fishermen, truck drivers, beauticians, clerks, and so on. While this was a leading question and seventeen persons said that they did not think anything was wrong with the field, almost all of them replied promptly with answers. Their replies fell into the following six categories:

1. Teachers are lazy, indifferent, weak, poor disciplinarians.

2. Public does not know what the program does, is for, can do.

3. Poor organization and administration, e.g., scheduling, assignments, budgets.

4. Facilities and equipment inadequate and in poor repair except for athletes.

5. Program inadequate, one-sided, narrow, unproductive.

6. Accomplishments of program and values to student only a guess for lack of proper evaluation and measurement.

Although not all of these errors of omission and commission can be rectified by a good program of P.R., most of them can. The three states in which the project was conducted have long histories of acceptable programs of physical education.

What is the scope of P.R.? A good many people think of P.R. as mostly publicity and selling. Actually, P.R. also includes advertising, distributing information, interpreting information, and propagandizing (although this latter is not included in P.R. connected with education and its branches).

Seen in a different way, P.R. includes: consumer relations (the pupil), public opinion (the parents), government relations (state and county and local town or city), community relations (the taxpayer and parents), and business relations.   This list omits propaganda.

Furthermore, the prospective teacher should remember especially that P.R. has for its foundation human relations, personal relations, and ethical conduct.   Thus, regardless of how fine a P.R. program may look on the surface, it cannot be sound unless human and personal relations are worthy.

Kinds of publics served by P.R.   The point was made earlier that P.R. deals with various publics, not with the public.   What are some of these publics?   The two most important ones, of course, are the pupils and their parents.   Also of top importance are school administrators, school faculties, and taxpayers.   Then, there are religious groups, taxpayer groups other than parents, service and civic groups, fraternal orders, chambers of commerce, manufacturers, businessmen, professional men, labor unions, and so on.   The reason for mentioning several of these publics, which obviously overlap, is to point out that a given man or woman may have to wear different hats on different occasions in the same community.   Each of the publics has to be reached in different ways, with different appeals. And, all the time the physical educator knows that a given man or woman has to be appealed to in several ways if she or he does belong to several publics.

Who are P.R. agents?   Formerly, public relations was considered to be something that the head office did, for, to, and with publics. Today, it is an acknowledged obligation that all physical educators serve as public relations agents.   The office girl, the custodian, and the equipment clerk are also agents, as are the students.

True, the superintendent of schools, the principals, and department heads are held *responsible* for P.R.   But how successful they are depends on the extent to which they receive active cooperation of students, teachers, custodians, food handlers, bus drivers, and *all others* connected with the schools.   As mentioned earlier, nonadministrative staff members can more than *cancel* the good public relations work of the head office.   They can create bad public relations through the way they communicate over the telephone, handle visitors, and deal with students and faculty members who come to the office.

Students are in a strategic position.   Not only do they form the first line of the publics, but they constitute one of the most powerful agents. They should be accurately informed about the program and its purposes. They should be served by this program through activities and in a manner that gains their respect. They should understand the services meant for others in the community besides themselves. Any area of the school program that neglects to develop students into effective P.R. agents can expect trouble, eventual extinction, or both.

SOME DISCUSSION QUESTIONS

1. Why is the old story about "he who builds a better mouse trap" not practical today?

2. Is it difficult to influence people? Why?

3. What is lost in an undemocratic country where the support of the public is ignored?

4. Why do you think P.R. will become a sure-fire process in the foreseeable future?

5. Of the general ways that P.R. functions, which one works best with you as a member of one public? Why?

6. Is there any enterprise's P.R. program in this country that you take with a grain of salt? If your answer is yes, Why?

7. Which is preferable, a P.R. program with good purposes and poor outcomes, or one with poor purposes and good outcomes?

8. Of the general purposes of P.R., which is most necessary? Easiest to accomplish? Most difficult to accomplish? Most worth while to schools?

9. To what publics do your parents belong? Do you plan to belong to the same publics when you are their ages? Why? To what publics do you now belong? What are the disadvantages of belonging to one public? Several publics?

10. In physical education, which publics are most essential to reach? Which publics are apt to be most difficult to reach?

11. Which enterprise, organization, or group, that you know about, has the most effective P.R. program? Can you explain this success?

12. What experiences have you had with persons in subordinate positions who were P.R. liabilities for the enterprises that employed them?

13. Are public school teachers good P.R. agents of the schools? Give an outstanding example to support your opinion.

14. Should time be taken to train stenographers and custodians in P.R.?

15. Would you take steps to dismiss a stenographer or a custodian who was a P.R. liability and openly refused to change?

16. How would you go about having students become good P.R. agents?

17. What would you do about a few students who became annoyed with you and were potential P.R. liabilities as a result?

Methods, Techniques, and Devices. For the sake of definiteness and clarity, let us define *methods* as general ways of doing things; *techniques* as refinements or specialized applications of these methods, and *devices* as objects or tools upon which the methods or techniques are used.

P.R. being what it is (using acts, attitudes, and words to influence people), *different means of communications* constitute three methods of using P.R. media. These, with some of their subsidiary techniques and devices, are:

1. *Verbal-audio-visual communications:* The press, radio, TV; movies, slides, film strips; public addresses and sermons; printed and mimeograph materials, such as booklets, handbooks, pamphlets and leaflets; letters, newsletters, postal cards, reply cards; telephone calls; exhibits; testimonials; canvasses, polls, questionnaires, opinionnaires, interviews; maps, charts, diagrams, tables, photographs, sketches, cartoons, transit advertising cards; directories, schedules, yearbooks, calendars, scrapbooks; home and school visits; annual reports, researches, surveys, studies; signs, poster, notices, placards, displays, advertisements, sign and bulletin boards.

2. *Group action communications:* Study and discussion groups, councils, conferences, assemblies, forums, mass meetings, town meetings; committees; and special committees in a community's various organizations, agencies, clubs, lodges, and the like.

3. *Dramatic communications:* Celebrations, parades, bands, demonstrations, contests, campaigns; plays, skits, songs, entertainments, parties, special events; tours and field trips.

The effectiveness of these media depends on how techniques and devices are selected to best fit each given public and on *how* they are used. For example, a public address may be very well fitted to a given public but lose its effectiveness by *how* it is given.

The conclusion should not be drawn that a P.R. program must use all of the many techniques and devices listed above. This list provides a variety of tools or avenues by which a public or all the publics may be reached and influenced. And, variety is one of the guideposts in this effort.

Someone has said, "There is nothing sillier than a plumber running around with a kit of tools he doesn't know how to use." To this could be added, "Or, using the wrong tools on things that need to be fixed." Certainly the names of some of these techniques and devices falsely promise success because of their appeal, their popularity. And, confidence may be wrongly placed in some of these media because someone else used them successfully in another situation. The tools must not only fit the public but the agent using them. All of us have to learn to use such tools. Developing know-how benefits the profession as well as one's self in working with people.

DISCUSSION QUESTIONS

1. Which techniques and devices could you now use rather well?

2. Which of the tools work best on you as a member of what public?

3. Which of the media have been used on you in such a way that you reacted negatively or indifferently?   Reacted positively?

Relations with the press.   One of the oldest and most helpful public relations media is the press. Here are a few hints gleaned firsthand from frank talks with newspaper men.

1. Never dodge. Be straightforward.

2. Never ask for or expect favoritism.

3. Find out about the paper, its deadlines, its policies, its workings.

4. Anticipate the press's concern for knowing about important events beforehand. Give all local papers the story about two weeks beforehand.

5. Know the code of ethics of the journalist.

6. If you have to, or if it is desirable, take the newsman into your confidence. Tell him you are doing this. He will keep it.

7. Go see the editor or suitable substitute. Tell him your story. Seek his advice.

8. Never try to use the newspaper. They want news (period).

9. Don't show biases.

10. Check and doublecheck and triplecheck your story for accuracy.

11. Most misinterpretation laid at the foot of the press is the fault of the person who gave the story.

12. Names make news but big names make bigger news. Learn what else makes news. Learn to sense news stories in commonplace happenings.

13. Keep improving. Ask for appraisals of the quality of your work.

14. It's a good rule but not followed by all newspapers: The Big Six Rule: Who, Where, When, Why, What, and How.

15. Don't use the ancient approach (fancy adjectives). Instead, use *action* verbs.

16. Human interest stories usually are sure-fire.

17. Give the press some stories that are not dated and can be used as filler.

18. Every story should have at least one public in mind—perhaps parents, perhaps taxpayers, but beam it.

19. Keep a store of photographs on hand.

20. Don't expect the press to remember. Write it down for them.

Informal, friendly relations with the press is an example of the kind of experiences needed by those of us who teach. One's hour-by-hour, day-by-day contact with children and with parents who want to talk about their children—and with other adults who also teach—*tend to stereotype one's personality and outlook.* Courage and initiative to avoid this stereotype is needed in schools and communities where the pattern is set for teachers to teach (period)! On the other hand, if the school administration prefers that teachers not have direct relations with the press, that policy should be followed as long as one works in that situation. Finally, those writing for newspapers should avoid playing up themselves and their accomplishments. That kind of publicity backfires.

The bulletin board. One of the most frequently used public relations devices in the school is the bulletin board. It also is one of the most ineffective! The chief reason for its usual ineffectiveness is lack of organization of materials on the board and lack of imagination in preparing the materials. The acid test of an announcement, a poster, a placard, or other displayed material is *whether it is read and understood!* This means that it has to have stopping ability. Too often students *walk past* the bulletin board. Experience has taught them that it seldom displays materials of interest to *them.* Often students have to *search* for some announcement in which they are interested and have heard is posted on the bulletin board.

The basis for an *organized* bulletin board (or boards) is the principle made throughout this chapter, namely, *beam public relations to each of the publics.* Not all students are interested in all phases of the school program—nor should this be expected.

Those elected or assigned to maintain the bulletin boards should plan and prepare *carefully* each change of bulletin board materials, and there should be frequent changes. Constant checks or surveys should be made to ascertain how effective the materials are.

Each item on the bulletin board should carry a caption, label, or heading. Most of the items should use the newspaper technique of enabling the reader to get the essentials quickly. The use of attractive colors should be a guidepost. Each item and the entire display should have balance. Cooperation of the English and art departments in following these suggestions is apparent.

Reading material should be as brief as clarity permits and should be in letters large enough *to be read easily from a distance of two or three feet.* Sketches, cartoons, art work, photographs often may be used to tell or illustrate part of the story. The bulletin board should have adequate lighting and be placed where it will be seen by the most students during the day.

Those responsible should post suitable results, outcomes, accomplishments of activities, often including the names of the participants. The bulletin board also should carry announcements of things to come, activities currently in progress, and matters of a relatively permanent nature.

No bulletin board is complete without presenting in various ways such matters as the underlying purposes of the program from time to time. Other heavy items such as the potential benefits of participation in various kinds of activities and the services rendered by the program also should find an occasional spot. Assuming that the bulletin board is changed on the average of once a week, there usually should be *one* heavy or serious item. Admittedly, serious items are the trickiest to present. Here, indeed, is the test of imagination and ingenuity! A photograph, a water color, a sketch, a placard carrying a tersely worded but catchy statement or question, a cartoon—these and other media seem to be best received by students. A student committee can be very helpful in this kind of project.

A word of caution. In presenting a purpose, a benefit, a service, and the like, make certain that the claim is accurate. At least all participating in a given activity should recognize that the attempt is being made to *actualize* the claim.

Twenty years ago some physical educators were aghast at the idea of selling physical education or some phase of it. There was concern about bringing the taint of the marketplace into the sacred halls of education.   For all concerned, fortunately this attitude has changed.

STEPS IN SALESMANSHIP

Every man, woman and child is a salesman of himself and all that he represents every waking moment of his life.   What, then, are the steps in selling?

The *first* step is to be sold personally on the product.   The teacher is bound to believe in the product because it represents his best thinking and his best efforts.

The *second* step is to study the customer.   What are his special interests, hobbies, and peculiarities?   Interests are the weakest point in one's armor of sales resistance.

The *third* step is to decide on the most advantageous way of presenting the product.   What points should be mentioned first? Should one keep an ace in the hole?   What points will appear because of the customer's standards or his system of values?   Is the customer the type that wants the cards laid on the table at once or is he the more sociable type?   What objections will possibly be raised and how shall they be answered?

The *fourth* step is to select a time and place advantageous to selling the customer.   He should be free from distractions and irritating disturbances.   Is he in a better state of mind in the morning or the afternoon?

The *fifth* step is the approach, wherein the information gained in step two is put into operation.   (This step is presented in detail later in this chapter.)

The *sixth* step is the presentation, in which the plans made in step three are carried out with modifications.   (This step is presented in detail later in this chapter.)

The *seventh* step is the sale, in which the customer is led to make a favorable decision.

Seeking the best.   After the attention of a public is obtained, answers to such questions as the following should be anticipated. Of what benefit or value is the idea?   What or whom will the idea improve, help, satisfy, protect?   What will it cost in time, money, energy?   Any public that must be sold on an idea, a program, a purpose is apt to have resistance.   The public needs confidence in the department.   They also want the facts.   Statistics and drab details should be avoided.   Facts that appeal to feelings as well as to reason should be presented.   Most facts can be restated in new ways, in ways that are interesting to *this* public.   The key value or benefit (for this public) must be stressed again and again—*each time in a different way.*   This public must be certain of exactly what is being sold and why.   Use specific, concrete, definite examples.

The point cannot be overstressed that the selected public must be known so well that its major wants, wishes, problems, needs, and lacks are appreciated.

In all forms of public relations communication, negative approaches should be avoided.   The assumption should be felt and expressed that this public wants the best, wants to support, wants to start helping, wants to cooperate.

Education is in competition with other forces for the energy, time, and minds of young America.   Education's competitor is anti-educational forces.   The school increasingly includes activities that are attractive, interesting, satisfying.   By its very nature and through its fine personnel, physical educators should have few difficulties selling their purposes and program.

Difficulties in selling.   Some ideas are easier to sell than others. Physical education may be difficult to sell for some: *first,* because of prejudices against physical education and because of willy-nilly programs; *second,* because physical education is still a relatively new addition to the curriculum and may receive the raised eyebrow of skepticism; *third,* because physical education deals with the physical, which still conflicts with the mental in the thinking of some; *fourth* because convincing results have been difficult to show because of a lack of tests or the failure to use them; and *fifth,* because physical education fails to draw the favor that athletic sports enjoy with many publics because of its lack of entertainment appeal and social prestige.

Gaining confidence.   Even though someone is skeptical of physical education *per se,* or if he hesitates to approve an enriched program, he is apt to tolerate it at least, providing he has confidence in the teacher.   The need for confidence by others makes the task of the new teacher difficult because he has not yet had an opportunity to establish himself.   The young teacher's lack of judgment because of insufficient knowledge of pupils, school, and community often results in lessened confidence in him.

One way to gain and maintain confidence is to demonstrate good judgment. This judgment results from basing a decision upon all pertinent information and viewing the many possible consequences of the decision. When a teacher exercises good judgment, it is apparent in his appearance, conversation, and personal relationships, as well as in his program of physical education. At first it *pays* to seek the help of older, wiser colleagues.

A *second* way to inspire confidence is to prove to be reliable. The teacher must show even in minor tasks that he can be counted on, that he can carry responsibility through to the desired end, that he is worthy of trust, and that his word is accurate and free from emotionalisms. Such attributes should be started long before taking one's first job.

A *third* trait that begets confidence is to demonstrate an understanding attitude, which is basic to intelligent cooperation. This characteristic shows a willingness to put yourself in another's place and to compromise for the welfare of those concerned. Teachers who show this quality also demonstrate their recognition of the importance of establishing cordial relationships with others.

A *fourth* way the teacher may stimulate the confidence of others is through careful preparation. The person who plunges into a task unprepared can expect to encounter trouble. Preparation means being forearmed, anticipating difficulties, being foresighted.

The closed door. If one planned to pass through a door, you would expect him to notice whether it was open or closed before he tried to go through! Yet, P.R. too often ignores this simple precaution. If even a modest program is to operate, the door to the selected public must be open. One of the most frequently overlooked reasons for failure of P.R. is that the selected public has the closed door attitude. That is, P.R. sometimes fails because it never had a chance, never got started because the door was closed.

Some of the reasons for such a situation and attitude are: (1) The selected public, unknown to the staff, harbors suspicion or wariness based on some long forgotten episode. (2) Unknown to school authorities, undesirable rumors may be circulating. (3) Reliance may be placed on the judgment of a few selected persons who purport to be, *but are not,* leaders of that public. (4) The actual nature and reactions of a public may have changed recently, unknown to the staff. (Even famous national agencies make errors in estimating a public; these mistakes invariably have resulted from a public or two having changed its views unknowingly.) (5) Cooperative relationships among the publics served may have broken down. These publics may be thought of as a team. We know what happens when bad relationships arise among team members. In the case of publics, one of them is apt to withdraw support merely because the public(s) it dislikes is *for* physical education!

Some further reasons for the closed door are: the staff's smugness about its work (too common); neglect (probably imagined) of a given public; failure to be in direct touch with an adequate number of a given public's members; or making public relations too obvious or too sweet.

Techniques of opening the door.   When the door is closed, the first step is to find out what the trouble is and its causes. This task requires the selection of someone who is sympathetic toward the offended public. He must want to understand the whole problem. He must know *how to listen* and how to ask questions intelligently and tactfully. He must know and have a feel for the public in question.

This contact person will understand that this public wants its place in the sun, that it wants recognition of its importance, contribution, and rights. He knows that if he can reach this public, the energies now directed in negative attitudes and acts can be changed to support. He must believe sincerely that these people are good, worthy people.

The contact person also must be a good appraiser of what is said and of what is not said. He must find how to get the ear of this public's representative(s). If he fails in this, he is only talking to himself when he tries to talk to them. We humans have a way of filtering what we hear. We think we hear and understand what is said. Inevitably, we *interpret* what is said. And, if our minds are closed, if emotions enter in, we hear *mistakenly,* we blur what we see. We, perhaps unintentionally, misinterpret.

Sometimes the persons who hold the offices are not the ones who really lead a public. In such cases, some behind-the-scene person(s) must be reached. If properly approached, he may react favorably to having been recognized and selected. He may be pleased to be asked for advice.   Such affirmative reactions may not be apparent, may be concealed at first by reticence, wariness, with a what do you have up your sleeve attitude.

Nevertheless, if his respect and confidence are gained, the ground-work is laid.   A way now must be found to reach his public, to find a way for it to change its position honorably, retaining its pride and self-respect.   If there are untrue rumors and false ideas about physical education, ways must be found to correct them.   Further, ways must be developed for this public to work and serve and lead in the program.   In all of these steps the selected representative(s) will be extremely helpful.   Above all, at no time in any way can there be even a hint or gesture of pressure, anxiety, or of a deal.

SOME DISCUSSION QUESTIONS

1. It is said that many public school teachers are afraid of the press.   How do you account for this?

2. If several persons are members of a staff, would you favor one of them writing all newspaper copy instead of each one having this experience?

3. Assuming that most taxpayers read the newspaper, what appeal would you make to sell them the idea that physical education pays?

4. If you were placed in charge of bulletin boards, what would you do to make them really effective?

5. What stops you, and makes you start to read material on a bulletin board?

6. Do you think the bulletin board should be a place where anybody could post anything, or should it be supervised?

7. Do you know someone who really is a very fine person but who does not know how to put across his fine qualities?   How could he be helped?

8. Do you like the idea of inescapably being a salesman of everything you represent—family, hometown, state, country, profession, et cetera?   Why?

9. Of the seven steps in selling, which one is most essential?

10. How does one gain the confidence of a public so that its members are more receptive?

11. In a school's program, with what is physical education in competition for the students' time, interest, support, and goodwill?

12. In your home community, with what forces is physical education in com-petition for the energy, time, and support of its adult citizens?   Its teenagers?

13. What besides vocabulary is involved in speaking a man's language?

14. Why are we so slow in showing recognition of the other fellow?

15. Can we understand the other fellow if we fail to put ourselves in his place?

16. From a practical viewpoint, what is accomplished by trying to see ourselves as others see us?

17. What would your reply be to an acquaintance who said, "Personal relations are okay, but are actually impossible to accomplish?"

18. Would you ask a staff member to perform a task, e.g., to be in charge of a radio program, if he were not interested in it?   Why?

19. What would you do with a staff member who had no talent for any part of a P.R. program?

20. How would you go about effecting a change in a stenographer whose voice and manner over the telephone were unquestionably irritating to the other parties?

21. What proportion of a department's problems would you guess had public relations implications?

22. If you were a member of an offended public, what would determine whether you were willing to reverse your stand?

23. For what kind of public would you be a good contact person?   Why?

24. How would you go about talking to a person whom you knew would not at first listen to you?

25. What is the *essence* of avoiding being a misfit in a group?

26. Why is a person who immediately agrees with a remark you've just made apt to misunderstand you?

Ten steps in initiating a P.R. program.   In order to help the novice anticipate and prepare to help out in a departmental P.R. program, the following steps are suggested as *one* outline of work to be done.

1. Whatever else, start slowly and quietly. Avoid temptations to show off immediately.

2. Begin close to home with a favorable public. Move to a related one and so on outward—like the expanding wavelets from a stone dropped in a pond.

3. Start with identifying the publics; then identify the problems or issues that eventually need to be solved or resolved with each public.

4. Select one public and one related problem—usually a pressing problem or issue that *can* be met successfully or that must be tackled now.

5. Outline several tentative plans of solution, with their probable difficulties, and probable results. Then select the best plan, or best combination.

6. Carve out the first year's work—exactly what is to be done.

7. Figure out cause(s), characteristics, probable solutions, and probable results of *each* phase of this first year's work on the selected public.

8. Have a master file for each problem for each public and all that goes with it. File the information from step seven, and any pictures, press releases, reactions, or reports.

9. Have this file available to all departmental personnel. (Keep confidential matters out of the file.)

10. Get under way:

Call a meeting of all persons who could be involved in departmental P.R. Educate them in the purposes of P.R. Go over some problems with them, step by step, giving the *why's*. Get them to express views on the problem that should be tackled first. Ask for suggestions about solutions. Integrate your and their ideas, and ask for further ideas. Leave the door open for additional ideas.

Select the problem to be attacked. Work out with them each step in any proposed solution. Get volunteers for each step. Assign work to others or at least give them a chance to help.

Keep a careful log of work done: who, what, when, results. Keep all informed, if they should be informed, of plans. Don't be afraid to change your attack, and help staff adopt the same attitude. In the last analysis, one person must be responsible, and the staff should know that. Do not expect teachers to give too much time, but remember that P.R. is hopeless without them.

Report the year's work—evaluate. What was actually accomplished with the publics? Plan the next steps. Adopt 3-5-7-year tentative program.

Evaluation steps. The following questions are helpful in a *general* evaluation of a P.R. program: Was each pertinent public studied adequately? Were all possible agents used effectively, cooperatively? Did school and community members help plan the P.R. program? Was the P.R. program successful in meeting major interests and wants of each pertinent public? Approximately what per cent of each pertinent public knows and supports the program? What potential services are still unrealized? Have all closed doors been opened? Is there a core of enthusiastic, dependable supporters in each pertinent public? Approximately what per cent of the community's other agencies and organizations have committees or projects devoted to your field, at least indirectly? What P.R. attempts have failed? Why? Is a continuous evaluation program in operation? What techniques and devices were unquestionably successful with what publics?

Some musts. Here are twenty tasks that must be performed if a department wishes to maintain an effective P.R. program:

1. Sense the significance of small events.
2. Be alert to trends and dangers.
3. Develop: a philosophy, purposes, policies, plans, and a program of P.R.
4. Learn attitudes and degree of understanding of each public.
5. Get parents to help.
6. Know what and how a public thinks.
7. Find out and reach the opinion-makers in a public.
8. Get or develop more qualified agents.
9. Have and show confidence in a public.
10. Get the information to the public the way they like to get it.
11. Ferret out and correct misunderstandings.
12. Collect and use evidence that elicits respect.
13. Find out what a public believes in.
14. Help gain cooperation from community.
15. Whatever the P.R. phase, have someone responsible.
16. Gear P.R. to each public.
17. Learn opinions of publics.
18. Select and adapt devices and media to each public.
19. Keep personal relations on a high level.
20. Develop and use features and continually search for new features.

*Some principles of public relations.** The following principles of public relations are worded impersonally in order to leave the assignment of responsibility open. These principles are given here as indicative of the concern an alert department must have for its public relations. The authors acknowledge the work of Eugene Stemm in formulating these principles. Public relations should:

▶ **Keep the publics informed concerning the purposes, accomplishments, and needs of physical education.**
▶ **Gain for physical education the confidence of the publics.**
▶ **Develop a public awareness of the importance of physical education.**

* Principles formulated by Eugene Stemm.

▶ **Correct misunderstandings of the aims and objectives of physical education.**

▶ **Result in an improvement in the quality of physical education.**

▶ **Involve the publics in the work of the school and in helping to solve physical education problems.**

▶ **Be honest in intent and skillful in execution.** Public relations should be identified with honesty and integrity; the public relations worker should have knowledge of the various tools and skill in their use; a specific P.R. program should be the result of cooperative planning by those concerned in the program.

▶ **Be a continuous process.** Public relations should be promoted at all times and in all situations, and its intensity should be suited to the situation.

▶ **Be planned to improve physical education.** Public relations should provide opportunities for the publics to understand the values of physical education and aid in making desirable changes in physical education policies and practices.

▶ **Be sensitive to the publics.** Public relations should be responsive to the needs and desires of the publics, be adaptable to the particular public situation, and should provide a two-way process between physical education and the publics.

▶ **Be comprehensive.** Public relations should be concerned with all phases of physical education; it may sometimes neglect to conform to a public and even neglect to seek its support for a period of time.

▶ **Communicate and interpret.** The ideas and the methods of communicating ideas should be easily understood by the publics. Public relations should establish channels of communication and interpretation and use varied media of communication, but the media of communication should be suitable to the particular public and situation.

▶ **Be an intrinsic part of planning and maintenance of the physical education program.** P.R. should truthfully represent what is attempted and/or accomplished in physical education; it should be a part of the total education process, subject to constant evaluation and the responsibility of each physical educator.

Ethical relationships. Self-imposed ethical standards are the mark of any profession. Ethical behavior is an obligation of a responsible member of a profession. Ethical relationships between the professional person and various publics is a necessity in effective public relations. The public attitude toward the teaching profession is shaped by the standards of conduct of individual teachers.

Even though the reader, throughout this book, has been made aware of the importance of high standards, ideals, and ethics, special attention is now called to certain aspects of these ethics. Concern for professional ethics is vital if the teaching profession is to continue to improve. The teacher, in his various roles both as educator and as a member of the community, has obligations to carry out his relationships with others in an ethical manner. The beginning teacher must understand the importance of these agreed upon standards by which he should live.

Acceptable standards of approved behavior for the professional practitioner are determined by professional action, tradition, and common sense. Professional ethics involve a code of conduct for professional persons. These are the distinguishing customs and attitudes to which professional persons are obligated to adhere. An older but still most adequate statement of the importance of ethical standards in professional practice is implied in the following description of a profession by Tawney: [1]

A profession is not simply a collection of individuals who get a living for themselves by the same kind of work. Nor is it merely a group which is organized exclusively for the economic protection of its members, though that is normally among its purposes. . . . Its essence is that it assumes certain responsibilities for the competence of its members or the quality of its wares, and that it deliberately prohibits certain kinds of conduct on the ground that though they may be profitable to the individual, they are calculated to bring into disrepute the organization to which he belongs.

The values of a guiding code of ethics are, first, the code protects the profession by helping to guarantee the effectiveness of its members; and, second, it establishes high-minded standards which are intended to improve the services it provides. A third value of self-imposed professional standards is that they prevent state and local government agencies from attempting to regulate the profession.

To these ends, codes of ethics have been developed by various teacher groups. But as yet there is no one code to which all teachers

[1] R. H. Tawney, *The Acquisitive Society* (New York: Harcourt, Brace & Company, Inc., 1920), p. 91.

might be expected to adhere since all teachers do not belong to a single organization.

In contrast to the profession of medicine, which has the 2,500 year-old Oath of Hippocrates and a modern code of ethics which dates from 1848, the teaching professions have only recently developed codes of ethics. Although various state education associations developed standards around the turn of the century, not until 1929 did The National Education Association adopt a code of ethics, which was revised in 1952.[2] Since the N.E.A. represents the largest teacher group in the nation, its code most nearly approaches a code for all teachers. At present all state education associations have either adopted the statement of the N.E.A. or have developed statements of their own. The field of physical education has also developed a code of ethics.[3]

A professional code of ethics for teachers is important because the average citizen cannot judge the quality of professional services rendered. The public should be able to rely upon the integrity of the practitioner. The persons who are in the best position to make a fair and effective appraisal of the quality of services rendered are other expert practitioners.

Such strong professions as medicine, law, dentistry, and engineering control the standards and practices of their respective members. Correspondingly strong control has never been evidenced by the teaching profession. Though there are several state and national committees on ethics, they have little power for enforcement or discipline of teachers who violate the code. The field of teaching values academic freedom too highly and has not been willing to be responsible for the professional behavior of its members. And this is among the reasons why teachers have not been able to win the wholehearted respect and support of the public. So far the teaching profession has not produced a statement of professional ethics with sufficient impact to cause teachers to rise to the challenge of truly professional conduct. The real test of any ethical statement for teachers must have as its basis the responsibility the profession assumes for being of service to young people.

[2] National Education Association, *NEA Handbook for State and Local Association* (Washington, D. C.: The Association, 1953–54), 346–48.

[3] Committee on Professional Ethics, "Suggested Code of Ethics for Teachers of Physical Education," *Journal of Health, Physical Education, and Recreation,* June, 1950, 323–324, 366.

Merely because some people lack standards or because some people do not know the standards does not imply that standards are unimportant. Professional people must not lose their ideals. Even if, in some instances, the ethic is violated or distorted, the ethic remains unchanged. No teacher has a right to be a poor teacher, to short-change youth, or to lower professional standards. The profession has the obligation to prevent persons from entering or remaining in the profession who are or might be poor teachers, and who do or may lower professional standards.

Statements concerning a few areas of ethical conduct appear below. These are not intended as a comprehensive code of ethics; the reader may find those elsewhere. These statements are intended to focus the attention of the student on some of the ethical obligations of the beginning teacher of which he may be unaware.

1. It is the obligation of the teacher to respect the dignity and individuality and basic worth of his students, avoiding disparaging, insulting, lowering techniques in his relationships with young people.

2. It is the obligation of the teacher to provide every child with a reasonable share of his time and attention avoiding disproportionate attention to the highly skilled.

3. It is the obligation of the teacher to deal with students in an unbiased and unprejudiced manner regardless of their mental or physical abilities, or their racial, social, or religious backgrounds.

4. It is the obligation of the teacher to refrain from using his position of prestige and influence in the school to promote any political or religious view or any personal view which would result in his personal gain.

5. It is the obligation of the teacher to avoid any actions or inferences which would lower the student's estimation and confidence in his own home or parents.

6. It is the obligation of the teacher to hold personal information about students in confidence unless it is for the best interest of the student or the school not to do so.

7. It is the obligation of the teacher to avoid involvement and interference in relationships between other teachers and students.

8. It is the obligation of the teacher to render assistance to other teachers, to share and make public effective techniques, methods, and information which will contribute to the welfare of youth.

9. It is the obligation of the teacher to avoid making or repeating criticism or speaking disparagingly about another member of the profession. Exceptions to this point occur when the criticism is made directly to the one being criticized or to his superior with the expectation that the person being criticized will have the opportunity to explain his position.

10. It is the obligation of the teacher not to engage in unjustified criticism of members of the profession or of the profession itself.

11. It is the obligation of the teacher not to endorse products or receive any payment or other compensation from vendors of school supplies or teaching materials.

12. It is the obligation of the teacher to support the policies of the school and to continue to do so as long as they remain in effect. But it is a further obligation to inform responsible school officers about conditions which may be detrimental to the welfare of students and the effectiveness of the school system, or that may be damaging to the profession.

13. It is the obligation of the teacher to conduct business of the school through the proper channels, not to go over the head of the person immediately responsible.

14. It is the obligation of the teacher to refrain from using his position in the school for personal advantage, that is, he should not tutor his pupils for pay nor should he bring any pressure to bear upon them which would result in a personal advantage to him.

15. It is the obligation of the teacher to be a responsible, socially conscious member of the community, a contributing, participating citizen.

16. It is the obligation of the teacher to inform local, state, or national committees or commissions on ethics of all instances of unethical practices.

SAMPLE REVIEW QUESTIONS

1. What is P.R.?   Why is it a misleading term?
2. Why is P.R. far from being a sure-fire process?
3. What are the major functions of P.R.?
4. Upon what bases are these functions to be judged?
5. What are the purposes or objectives of P.R.?
6. What publics does physical education serve?

7. What are the advantages and disadvantages of people belonging to several publics?

8. Should the department head be the number one P.R. agent?   Give five examples of agents.

9. Why are students in a strategic position?

10. Why should P.R. training begin at the bottom?

11. What are the three major methods used in P.R.?   Give five examples of each method.

12. How can a technique or device be judged as good or bad?

13. Is another person's success in the use of a technique a sure sign it is good for you to use?   Why?

14. Why is a P.R. program always in the process of development?

15. What are five do's and five don'ts one should observe in relations with the press?

16. Why should public school teachers have the *kind* of experience one has in relations with the press?

17. Why is the bulletin board usually an ineffective device?

18. List ten techniques that may help make the bulletin board more effective in P.R.

19. Why is a discussion of selling important?

20. What are the seven steps in salesmanship?

21. What kind of questions may a public ask which relate to selling?

22. Explain why knowing your customer is so important in selling.

23. What kinds of competition make it essential to know how to sell effectively?

24. What kinds of difficulties regarding P.R. are common?

25. What are ten essentials in the operation of a P.R. program?

26. Why cannot a department run its own show in P.R.?

27. Why should human relations undergird P.R.?

28. What complaints do some people make about physical education?

29. What causes a public to have the closed door attitude?

30. What steps can be taken to open the closed door?

31. List ten principles of P.R.

32. What steps would you take in building a P.R. program?

33. What steps would you take if a colleague of yours were unethical?

34. Why is it important for a profession to enforce its code of ethics?

BIBLIOGRAPHY

American Association of School Administrators, *Public Relations for America's Schools, Twenty-Eighth Yearbook.* Washington, D. C.: National Education Association, 1950.

Brownell, C. L., L. Ganz, and T. Z. Maroon, *Public Relations in Education.* New York: The McGraw-Hill Book Company, Inc., 1955.

Harlow, R. F., and M. M. Black, *Practical Public Relations.*   New York: Harper & Brothers, 1952.

Lane, Howard, and Mary Beauchamp, *Human Relations in Teaching.* Englewood Cliffs, N. J.: Prentice-Hall, Inc., 1955.

18

Securing a position

*Inescapably, we are salesmen of ourselves and all that
we represent—our backgrounds, our educations, our
alma maters, our professions, our abilities, and our
potentials.*

Adapted from Charles Schwab.

THE PARAPHRASE FROM MR. SCHWAB REMINDS US THAT WE
must be able to sell in addition to having something to
sell, if we are to be successful in obtaining a position.

There is quite a difference between getting *a* job and getting *the*
job. Getting the position you *deserve* is a still different idea. And,
securing the position for which you are *qualified* is an idea that differs from the others.

Competition for the better, more promising positions occurs with
each vacancy. And, usually, one particular job is most preferred.
Few indeed are the physical educators who are ambitionless enough
to be satisfied with just *any* job. Even when vacancies are few, one
would like to have the best possible among the positions available.

Be realistic. Although a few persons in physical education are
without ambition, some are so ambitious that they are unrealistic
about themselves. They overlook two unavoidable conditions that
must be considered. First, what are the qualifications of the candidate? Second, what are the demands of the job? The unrealistic

ones also expect their major professors to forget or gloss over weaknesses, lacks, and the like.   They expect strong recommendations regardless of *the record,* regardless of possible personality gaps or traits which are not promising.   Still more unrealistically, they expect the local school officials to overlook the disparity between their qualifications and the demands of the position.

At this time, reconsider your self-appraisal (see Chapter 3) and review the formal and informal ratings from time to time.   Review of the general qualifications demanded of any position also are a basic part of realistic preparation for a job hunt.

Occasionally, a senior says, "But you should have told me about all of this earlier."   When reminded of occasion after occasion when suggestions were given, some of them come back with, "Oh!   But I was so young then.   I didn't get the point."   And "Why didn't you *force* me to do the smart thing?"

On the other hand, almost all major students by the time they are in their last college year are realistic enough to say something like this: "I'd surely like to get that job at Blank Hi.   Do I have what they want?"   That says it in a nutshell!   Do I have to sell what they want to buy?   Then, can you *sell* yourself better than the other fellow whose abilities are similar to yours in quality and amount?

Be prepared.   Securing a position is a process.   It is an operation.   It also serves as a bridge between professional education and professional practice.   We have had a good deal of discussion in this volume about what to teach, whom to teach, how to teach, and when to teach.   All this is useless without an answer to: *where* am I going to teach?   The question points up its own crucialness.   No one faces the question without preparation for this process, this operation.   For, preparation for job-getting diminishes the element of chance.   It also helps *build* the bridge between college and professional practice.

Preparing for this final step before one launches full-fledged into his profession is unlike any other kind of preparation.   It involves a number of steps.   Here are the main ones: *

1. Answers are needed to such questions as:
   a. Do I really want this job?   Why?
   b. What are its demands?

* For special emphasis: consult your instructors as to how early in the year you should start seeking a position.

    c. Do I have the qualifications?

    d. If not, what are my qualifications?

    e. How do I go about getting this or another job?

    f. Do I really want to do all this work?

    g. When am I ready to start going after a job?

2. Map out a detailed attack:

    a. Obtain criticisms of your plan of attack from your instructors.

    b. Obtain help in writing and *perfecting* a preliminary resumé letter.

    c. Obtain help in anticipating questions that may be asked in an interview.

    d. Obtain help in anticipating other experiences before, during, and after the interview.

    e. Obtain help in answers and reactions about which you wonder or have doubts.

    f. Obtain all essential information about the job, the community, the school officers, and the probable interviewer.

    g. Lay out a time schedule (tentative) for each step in your plan.

    h. Obtain help in identifying your skills, traits, abilities, and the like.

3. Assuming an interview-appointment, *practice:*

    a. Practice answering anticipated questions (realistic role-playing).

    b. Practice asking questions you will ask.

    c. Practice walking in and out of an office.

    d. Practice being seated in a chair.

    e. In short, practice, again and again, *each* step and phase in an interview.

    f. Obtain help from different persons who will objectively appraise your interview skills.

4. Work for finesse:

    a. Work for effectiveness, evenness, balance.

    b. Work for unaffectedness.

    c. Work for results

5. Review.*

6. Have the interview. You have prepared well. Now take the view, "Whatever else, I'll give it my best."

7. Send a thank-you note, if appropriate, after the interview.

8. Keep at least one instructor informed of how things are going.

So helpful are some of the practice steps listed above that some major departments make arrangements for persons on and off campus to receive and criticize practice letters of students, to grant them practice interviews with a subsequent rating on a scale worked out by the class, and so on.

* Note: Two reasons for this emphasis on practicing each phase of the interview are: (1) confidence will come with improvement in performing these skills; and (2) confidence will help bring naturalness and overcome fear, the destroyer of a candidate's poise, control, and alertness during an interview.

The student should understand that in all practice of this kind, he should not pretend to be someone he is not. Nevertheless, he certainly should be helped to permit persons to see him at his best, and he can learn to improve himself in most ways.

Have empathy.   One reason a candidate for a position some-times makes a poor showing is that he lacks empathy. He does not put himself in the other fellow's place. The candidate gains new insight into job-getting by saying to himself, "If I were the principal (or superintendent), what would I like to see in someone I'd want on my faculty?" Would you like someone who spoke distinctly and in good English? Would you like him to be enthusiastic? Pleas-ant and agreeable? Reasonably confident? Possess vigor and drive? Have determination without being inflexible? Show good judg-ment? Be punctual and reliable? And, even though he were just out of college, would you wish him to have taken every possible ad-vantage in and out of school to gain teaching and leadership ex-periences?

Furthermore, would you select a person for a position in physical education who obviously practiced the self-disciplines and controls that underlie a good figure, good posture, and carriage? Closely related, you certainly would select a person whose appearance and all-round grooming left little to be desired. You also would expect a man or woman in this field to have good tone, texture, flexibility, and modulation of voice.

Another way of saying these things is to say, "look in the mirror" in the role of employer and permit your reflection to be you. Then say, "What are the qualifications of this person?" "What has he done with the 'knock down parts,' the building blocks, the pieces of the jigsaw puzzle which he began to fit together four or five years ago?" "What has he constructed?" "Did he start with little and develop and improve a great deal—or vice versa?"

This looking-glass technique, this practicing empathy goes far toward *helping* one to see himself more clearly, as the administrator will see him. This trait of empathy helps you become more objec-tive about yourself to see to what degree you are actually fitted for a given position. What does the cold eye of objectivity see in your background, educational achievement, experience? In the cold light of facts, what are your aptitudes, temperament, and character traits?

Are your interests confined chiefly to the athletic-physical education area? And, what of your specialties—are you a one-sport man or woman? What about *effectively* teaching anything else? Or, are you the jack-of-all-trades-and-master-of-none kind of physical educator?

What we are saying is that we must be honest with ourselves, that we take a good look at what we want to sell, as we prepare to seek a position. We should do this in order to visualize ourselves as the employer sees us. But, we should not be discouraged with what we see! In most cases it isn't too bad, even though it is not as roseate as it would have been without empathy.

Letter of application. If, after finding out all essential information about a given vacancy an interest remains in the position, a brief letter of application is in order. That is, such a letter should be sent if one's major advisor or instructor suggests it. In some situations it may be ill-advised, but in most situations, the employing official(s) prefers that a letter of application first come from the candidate. In most instances these letters should be brief, concise, simple, and well organized. This letter, brief though it is, can be attention-getting. It can use the employing official's language. It can indicate enough to arouse the interest of the recipient so that he wants to interview the candidate. The tone of the letter may be coldly factual or full of human interest and thus more informal. It should avoid being too novel in style.

In many communities, the employing agent of the school does not expect more than three, four, or five brief paragraphs in a letter of application. In other communities, a brief letter is expected, accompanied by a resumé presenting in detail the personal, educational, and professional data about the applicant.

In any case, any letter of application should indicate (at least in general) the candidate's special abilities. Previous experience should be indicated, even if the inexperienced man or woman must mention experiences in and out of college which have provided only chances to teach informally and serve in small leadership roles.

The foregoing paragraphs about a letter of application (or letter of inquiry), as well as those suggestions on preparation for a position, may be inappropriate in some localities. The major student's instructors can guide him properly. Here again we take advantage of the opportunity to encourage the student to *talk things over with your instructors.*   Too many major students in too many colleges and universities are prone to seek the advice of their peers on professional matters about which the peers know little more than those who ask the questions.   *Decreasing the chances of making mistakes* whenever possible is a symptom of a mature person.   Another symptom is to seek advice from the person best prepared to give it.

Face-to-face contacts.   As has been indicated previously, procedures to follow in securing a position vary considerably from one area to another.   For example, in some areas twenty to thirty school superintendents select an employing agent.   Sometimes this may be one of their own number.   This man travels about the country for weeks during the spring, visiting colleges and universities, interviewing prospective teachers.   Sometimes previous correspondence with either the department or the placement bureau of the institution sets the stage for a series of interviews with graduating students who most closely fit the demands of the vacancies.

Institutions usually provide fine placement bureaus.   The major student who plans to teach, or who wants to be considered for better positions as he gains experience, should make sure to carry out all instructions which this bureau sends out each year.   Many beginning teachers obtain their first positions through such a bureau. Here they meet the interviewing agent (often the superintendent), and the interview is held in one of the rooms provided.   One of the obvious advantages of this plan is that members of the major department may be readily contacted if the employing agent wishes to ask questions about the candidate and his work.

Some school administrators write to the placement bureau, requesting the credentials of candidates with specified preparation specialties and temperament.   In such a case, the individual whose record seems most promising is contacted indirectly through the placement bureau and requested to write a letter of application.   If this letter is satisfactory, usually he is invited to visit the school for an interview.   School administrators now are placing a good deal of importance upon the letter of application, short though it may be.   It is one added bit of evidence to form the picture of the candidate.

When a candidate is asked to visit the school, he may expect to have more than one interview, even though all of them may not be formal.   In addition to the superintendent and principal of the high school (where the candidate will work if he gets the position), interviews will probably be held with at least some staff members of the department of physical education. Not infrequently, the candidate is invited to stay long enough to meet members of the department; often he has lunch or dinner with them. In some schools, an administrative officer, usually the assistant superintendent in charge of employing personnel, conducts a formal interview. This is followed by meeting the departmental staff, sometimes in the administrative officer's office but more frequently in one of the departmental staff offices. One reason the latter practice is preferred is because the candidate can see the facilities, ask professional and technical questions, and satisfy himself that he would like to work in that place with those people under those conditions.

In some areas the candidate will find that a committee does the interviewing. Such a committee might include such persons, besides the principal and physical education representatives, as the dean of girls or dean of boys and someone from the guidance department.

In some areas the interviewing agent is the board of education. In such cases the candidates whose application letters are most promising are invited to visit the board at a given time and place. Here, one at a time, the candidates are interviewed, and the successful one is notified by mail later.

In some of the larger cities, the practice is for those who wish to become candidates for the vacancies or who wish to get on the list for future consideration to gather at a designated place to take a written examination and a practical examination. Usually, the examining team also conducts interviews, and candidates fill out all forms during the same day. Assignments to the various schools are made by the personnel office, in order to bring objectivity to the assignment (under the assumption that some schools are preferred by most candidates, and, some candidates are preferred by most principals).

This by no means exhausts all situations that are provided for helping schools find out all they can about a candidate before hiring him. Note that all plans call for at least the interview. Letters of application can be made to misrepresent the writer. Few indeed are the letters of recommendation which do not attempt to give the best possible picture of the candidate. In the first place, the candidate is not likely to ask persons for letters of recommendation if he thinks they will not or cannot write somewhat complimentary things about him. Even tests can be misleading. Perhaps the candidate is exceedingly expert in the specialty for which the department is seeking a teacher but rather inexpert in other activities. Perhaps the kind of questions asked on the written test were not emphasized at the candidate's major department. Such things occur often enough to force most schools to place great emphasis on the interview and the face-to-face opportunity which this occasions.

This is understandable. Personality not only is the one most promising predictor of teaching success, it also is the one most promising factor in indicating whether the candidate will fit into the department.

Sometimes, in some places where teacher shortages exist, some prospective teachers can obtain a position without much difficulty. Nevertheless, if they have weak or poorly executed interviews, not only do they cast unfortunate reflections upon their major department, but they also inescapably cast unfortunate reflections upon themselves. A socially mature person, who learns a few technicalities about the interview, usually performs admirably in an interview.   On the other hand, those who go to college without learning office decorum, who have not learned to express themselves under pressure, still may make fine teachers.   Thus, a major department should do what it can to help prepare its students for the all-important interview.

THE INTERVIEW

To discuss the interview, we found it necessary to adopt one of the varying plans briefly discussed above. The one selected (because it is usually the most difficult) is the situation in which the candidate has an appointment for an interview with the school superintendent or the principal at his office. Although all the details do not fit every interviewing situation, the suggestions and the ideas behind them provide material for modification by the class instructor.   It is he who is able to inform the upper division major student of the particular plans for job-getting most common in the local area.

Usually, an appointment for an interview follows the candidate's letter of application. Sometimes this appointment is given as a result of some other kind of preparatory action by the candidate or by the employing agent. (In most communities a candidate is ill-advised to telephone a school employing official about matters related to vacancies or positions.)

Preliminaries

Details.   The candidate will carefully note the *hour, day, date, location, and building* (and possible *room number*) at which the interview will take place. Being on time is an *obligation* on the part of the person seeking the job. Nor can he break an appointment except under the most extenuating circumstances. Most experienced candidates have found that arriving several minutes beforehand pays. In fact, should it be necessary to drive fifty to a hundred miles, allowing time for such an emergency as changing a tire and tidying up afterward is the kind of precaution that experienced job seekers take.

Appearance.   It hardly need be mentioned (and yet school administrators continue to report the necessity for it) that the candidate make sure of all phases of grooming.

Placement record.   Normally, the candidate who has an appointment for an interview knows that the interviewer has seen his credentials. This is sometimes requested, however, *after* an interview because the school officer originally was not interested in the candidate.

When the student fills in these various forms, he should remind himself that, next to the interview, many school administrators place most weight on the record in helping them select the candidate. This is one reason the *typical* passport photograph is unsuitable for one's placement record.

Letters of recommendation.   The applicant usually can count on having letters of recommendation arrive at the school before the interview (a part of the credentials sent by his school placement bureau).   The references selected for letters of recommendation should represent *at least* three general types: namely, a character reference; one or two major department references (possibly one who will write about quality of scholarship and general preparation, and one who will write about specialties); and (if possible) one reference with prestige in the applicant's community, such as a president of a business, a bank, and the like.   Preferable *types* of references may vary from locality to locality.   One's instructors also are helpful here.

Interviewer unprepared.   Another preliminary point should be considered by the candidate.   Even though the one being inter-viewed must be on time, the interviewer may not be.   Further, even though the interviewer is in his office, the interview may start later than planned.   Then, sometimes the interviewer may not have had time to study the candidate's credentials, including the letters of recommendation.   In such instances, the candidate can expect ques-tions that are answered in his records.   Sometimes the interviewer will ask such a question only as a springboard to encourage the candidate to discuss certain matters.

As a rule not only is the school official ready, but he also is an astute interviewer.

Interviewer and role playing.   The candidate should be aware that some school officials sometimes play roles in their interviewing in order to gain reactions from the interviewer.   This is one way of finding out a little more about him.   On the other hand, some school administrators' genuine behavior is quite unusual and unex-pected.   For example, some administrators are the "I am a very, very busy man" type.   Some of them are gruff and abrupt.   Others throw the weight of carrying the entire interview upon the applicant. Still others fire one question after another at the candidate, without giving him a chance to ask questions until toward the end of the conference.   We hasten to say that for a candidate to assume that any interviewer is playing a role is disastrous.

Technicalities

Office etiquette.   Most of us are embarrassed for an acquaintance or friend if he is unintentionally discourteous.   Some of us may recall with chagrin an occasion when we inadvertently broke some rule of social behavior; and some of us have experienced that feel-ing of uncertainty that accompanies a lack of information as to what to do next in social situations.

Those who have not worked in offices or are unfamiliar with office procedure may overlook the importance of knowing the ac-cepted practices in office decorum.   Yet, the office secretary and the administrator are likely to form an opinion of the teacher's social background from the way he conducts himself in the office.   A lack of knowledge regarding proper office decorum is an excuse, but it is a somewhat embarrassing one for a teacher to have to admit even to himself.   What are some of the practices that should be observed?

Upon entering the office, the teacher makes his business known to the secretary or office attendant.   Usually, he will be asked to be seated.   At any rate, he refrains from wandering about the room. If he must wait a few moments, this time can be used to review his approach, or simply to relax.

He refrains from taking the secretary's time by needless talking, although he is cordial in responding if she wishes to talk a little. Sometimes a secretary's reactions to candidates are valuable to her employer.   In such cases, the secretary may say things in order to gain better insight into the candidate's politeness, responsiveness, and the like.   Never, under any circumstances, should a candidate, by look, act, gesture, or word be anything but courteous toward the secretary.   Shy, easily embarrassed candidates must guard against seeming to be superior, smart-alecky.   Being unsure of themselves, they try to cover up their lack of "sophistication" and overdo the casual act.

The candidate can properly ask the secretary for the *correct* pronunciation of the person whom he will be interviewing in a moment.   If there is the slightest doubt, this is a must.   It is also appropriate to ask the secretary's name, after the candidate has given his, if she fails to give this information.

Assuming that the administrator's office is separate from the reception room or outer office, as the secretary shows the candidate into the inner office, it is proper to thank her.   Repeating her name at this time is smart manners.

In the office.   When shown into the administrator's office, the candidate remains standing until asked to be seated.   If a man, he remains standing until the administrator is seated if the latter is standing, or he is asked to be seated.   A woman may be seated unless she wishes to show her respect by waiting for the administrator to be seated.   In the case of a man, after he is seated, he may place his hat on the floor near his chair if no hatrack is provided in the outer office and if the administrator does not offer to take care of it.   In any case, hats, coats, umbrellas, and other personal belongings are *not* placed on tables, desks, chairs, or other office furniture unless such a request is made by the administrator.

The applicant avoids lolling or sprawling in his chair.   On the other hand, he avoids a stiff, West Point posture.   He avoids placing his feet, hands, or elbows on the office furniture.   If and when he is standing, he should not lean against the chair, desk, or other office equipment.

During the course of the conference, the candidate guards against absent-mindedly glancing at papers and correspondence that may be in view on tables or desks.   He avoids nervous mannerisms that tend to detract from what he is saying, or, worse yet, those that disturb the administrator.   If a telephone call interrupts the conference, the time should be used in looking away, planning the next step in the discussion.   At any rate, one gives no sign that he has heard the telephone conversation.

Throughout the discussion the candidate keeps his voice modulated, even if situations tend to make him emotionally upset.   Lack of poise is a sign of lack of confidence, a feeling of defeat, or at least a sign of being on the defensive.   The candidate avoids *talking* out the window, a sure way of making points lose their forcefulness.   It is tactful and courteous to avoid *listening* out the window.   As a rule, one looks at the person who is speaking.

The candidate may have a card on which he has a list of important items.   Usually, these words remind him to find out certain information about the position and perhaps about the community. Some candidates have found it helpful also to include a word of encouragement to themselves such as: Smile!   Be yourself!   Relax!

The person being interviewed should be alert for any intended or unintended gestures by the interviewer that the interview is about to close.   Most interviews for positions in schools last *about* twenty minutes.   The candidate should begin to be particularly alert after fifteen minutes (approximately).   Then, as he makes a gesture to leave, if the administrator cares to extend the interview, the candidate might well feel a bit encouraged.   At least the administrator wants to know more about him.   But remember, the interviewer, not the candidate, is the one who officially terminates the interview.

Throughout the conference, the candidate must remember to: (1) give and gain attention; (2) give and gain interest; (3) maintain a pleasing manner; (4) show enthusiasm when it is appropriate; (5) avoid any semblance of argument; (6) avoid shading the truth; (7) avoid being evasive; (8) feel free to ask for a restatement of any question if it is not understood or if it is complicated or if time is needed to quickly think of a judicious answer.   Again, empathy helps.   If the candidate can remember that the interviewer is simply trying to know him better, he can help the administrator see what a fine, capable, pleasant person he really is!

At the conclusion of the conference, the candidate thanks the administrator for his time, for making the interview possible, and for interest in selecting him to help in the education of the youth of that community.

Leaving the office. Leave-taking should be *definite, brief, businesslike,* and at the same time *cordial.* As the candidate leaves the outer office (if that is the procedure in that office), he again thanks the secretary for her help.

Filling in the local application form often is done before the candidate leaves the outer office. These forms as a rule have been revised many times *for the sake of clarity.* School administrators report that *many* college seniors ask needless questions about filling in these forms. They also report failure to fill in some of the blanks. They often eliminate candidates who omit filling in *any* blank or requested information.

In most situations the secretary can be asked about possible *appropriate* next steps in following up the seeking of the position.

After an interview is over, sometimes the candidate in thinking it over (and this may be on his way home or it may be a year later), says to himself, "I didn't realize such-and-such would be regarded as important." Or, "If I'd only been prepared for that one!" Here, then, are a few examples of questions that a candidate might be asked (others that more closely fit local situations are available from instructors):

1. "Would you like to live here?" ("Yes, sir.") "Why?"
2. "Do you like our school system?" ("Yes, sir.") "Why?"
3. "Do you know of our sick leave plan?" ("Yes, sir.") "Do you consider these days permitted for sick leave as days teachers should take advantage of, even though they are not ill?" *(Look out!)*
4. "What books besides those connected with school work have you read in the past six months?" (Your answer.)
   "What do you think of the way the author handles _____ in this book?"
5. "Do you feel teaching is a profession?" ("Yes, sir.") "What

is the chief difference between a profession and a trade?   Between a profession and business?"

6. "In what are you most interested?"
7. "What TV programs do you enjoy watching regularly?"
8. "With what racial, religious, or other groups would you expect to have most trouble?"   (Your answer.)
   "*Why* do you think it would be *that* group?"
9. "What is the most valuable thing in life to you?"
10. "What is your philosophy of physical education?"
11. "We have two positions open in our school.   Are you interested enough in our school and community to accept the less attractive of the two assignments?"

Do's and don'ts relating to employment interviews.   Here are some things to do in job-seeking, which were suggested by a school administrator who considers about 6,000 applicants a year.

1. Do make available a complete and legible application which can be reviewed by the administrator and assist him in the interview with you.
2. Do be sure that confidential letters of recommendation are supplied the school district prior to your interview appointment.
3. Do appear for the interview dressed neatly and conservatively. Most school administrators will want to see you *a shade better* than you might expect to appear for school.
4. Do go into the interview with a congenial attitude of friendliness and security.
5. Do seat yourself comfortably and retain the composure befitting the position for which you are applying.
6. Do be prepared to answer questions related to teaching experience, special interests, hobbies, *et cetera*.
7. Do be prepared to meet and talk with several persons in the school district who would be involved with your employment *besides* the interviewer.

The following are some don'ts:

1. Do not fail to fill in all blanks on an application for employment.
2. Do not present letters of the "To Whom It May Concern" type.

3. Do not supplement your application with data sheets of your experiences, qualifications, courses of study you have developed, and the like.

4. Do not oversell yourself. Permit your preparation, experience, and personal qualities to speak for you. Do not push!

5. Do not expect an offer of employment at the close of your interview.

6. Do not telephone to inquire about the status of your application unless someone in authority instructs you to do so.

Unethical procedures in securing a position.   Certain procedures are considered proper when the teacher secures or changes positions. The following statements of what should *not* be done may guide the beginning teacher toward acceptable professional conduct.

1. It is considered unethical for the teacher to give the names of his superiors as references (or any other references) without first asking for their permission to do so.

2. The use of any kind of pressure on school officials through groups or individuals to secure a position is considered unethical.

3. It is considered unethical for the teacher, when he is a candidate for a position, to underbid knowingly another candidate or to agree to accept a salary which is less than that which is to be provided according to the recognized salary schedule of the district.

4. It is considered unethical for a teacher to apply for a specific teaching or coaching position when that position is presently held by another person.

5. It is unethical if the teacher, when he has accepted a position with a school district, fails to contact all other districts to which he has applied to inform them that he is no longer available as a candidate for a position in their district.

6. Once the teacher has a position, it is considered unethical for him to apply for another position that he does not intend to accept for the purpose of bringing pressure to bear upon his employing school district to increase his salary.

7. It is considered unethical for a teacher, when he has accepted a contract, to fail to adhere to all of the obligations of the contract until it is dissolved with the consent of the employing district.

8. It is considered unethical for a teacher, when he is under contract, to seek other positions without notifying the school officials of

his present district of his intentions to explore opportunities in other districts.

9. It is considered unethical if a teacher, when under contract, fails to give his employing district the earliest notification possible when he intends to resign from his position.

DISCUSSION QUESTIONS

1. Why should girls applying for a physical education teaching position follow such suggestions as those given about the interview when there are so few of them available for the many vacancies? They can get positions without bothering to be courteous and businesslike!

2. Is it fair for one's major professors to stick to the record so carefully instead of being good sports enough to forget some of the mistakes of young people?

3. What suggestions in the chapter do not fit the local situation when one applies for a position?

4. Why doesn't the employing officer also have to practice empathy?

5. Would a mimeograph brochure about one's self, sent to all the schools where one would like to work, be a good idea?

6. Isn't the thank you business with reference to an office secretary at the time of the interview a bit overdone?

7. Would you prefer to work in a given community and school and take a less desirable position, or, to work at certain assignments (e.g., head of dance, head coach of a given sport) in a less desirable type of community and school?

8. Would you favor a position with higher pay in a less desirable community and school over a position that paid $1,000 less per year in a community and school that you would like?

9. Since most persons are average, why not be satisfied with being competent?

10. Of the twenty-five indices of a truly professional person, which one do you think is most difficult to do?

11. In what order would you rank these factors related to a position: salary, departmental colleagues, climate, facilities and equipment, and school administrator?

19

And now what?

"Not I, nor anyone else can travel that road for you.
You must travel it yourself.
You are asking me questions and I hear you.
I answer that I cannot answer you, you must
Find out for yourself."

—Walt Whitman, A Song of Myself.

AT THE CONCLUSION OF THE LAST PRACTICE SESSION PRIOR
to the first game of the season, a head coach at a major
university addressed his team: "During the past weeks we of the
coaching staff have done everything humanly possible to prepare
you. We have planned carefully, conditioned you to use the best
techniques known, arranged practice sessions so that best performances become habits. The trainer has used all of his skill to keep
you fit. We have provided the best medical care possible. Nutrition and health and fitness have been considered in every way.
Now what?"

Stopping his remarks here made an impact on his team. He
made the point with each athlete, "Now it's up to me." What
would the boys do for themselves? What were they *willing* to do
for themselves? The responsibility was inescapably theirs.

A teacher education program resembles these preparatory activities of the skilled coach. The major professors do all that they can
in the training period, but what the young teacher does subsequent

472

to his graduation and certification is largely dependent upon what he chooses to do with his professional life—what he is willing to do and what he is willing to *sacrifice* for it.

No book or group of books, no person or group of persons can tell the teacher all he needs to know about teaching in physical education. Some things he must find out for himself. He must have experience and learn from it. He must deal with real people on the job. He must deal with actual not hypothetical problems. He cannot pretend to chart the course that he would take. He must indeed be practical. Precisely what should be done and how it should be done in these actual situations is not easily determined only through examination of literature. The value of this literature is that it affords guidance to the beginning teacher, not that it is an exact formula of how to function precisely. To find the best solution to many questions takes more than a brush with reality.

Once the teacher has secured his first position, he is confronted with both opportunities and obligations. While he is carrying out his responsibilities, he is faced with the personal question of "Will I be asked to return for a second, third year?" In addition he may wonder, "How long is it smart to stay on this job?" Matters of *professional advancement* and *promotion* also cause concern.

Little help can be given a teacher in finding an answer to how long he should stay on a job. Further, it little concerns the major student. Only this, except in bad times, no teacher should accept a position knowing that he will remain there, regardless, only for a year. Nor should he find himself building a *pattern* of flitting from one short-time job to another. On the other hand, the case of an extremely fine teacher who is successively offered increasingly better positions is understandable. Even then some professional persons believe he should pause for at least a few years (say, three) at each location. Thousands of teachers who lost years serving in the military and naval services usually disagree with such a view.

The competent teacher, not enough. Regulations of state departments of education and requirements and opportunities of one's major department are beamed at turning out graduating seniors who are competent. The dictionary gives such definitions as these for the word competent: adequate, capable, rightfully belonging, able, and legally qualified.

Even superficial reading of this volume cannot help but give the impression that competency is the *bottom* rung of the professional ladder! In fact, the word competent, as used to refer to teachers, has resulted in many teachers being satisfied with being legally qualified! At what point above *mediocrity* is the teacher directed by such words as capable, adequate?

Nor is that all. Many an excellent teacher *began* by being only an *adequate* teacher. But somewhere along the line, someone grasped his shoulder and gave him the idea of *going beyond the call of duty.* He caught the ideal of—not merely rightfully belonging—but *doing his best to make the effort to improve!* And then some time later, at another of those golden moments, he caught another ideal, *aspiring* toward the *best!* And, his idea of what was best continually moved up, because of his aspirations.

A simplified answer. The two paragraphs above say, in effect, you will be asked to return for a second year if you prove to be professionally competent. That is all there is to it! Just do an *adequate* job. Just do a *capable* job. In fact, a young person prepared in a four-year major curriculum in an accredited institution has to be a bull in the China shop, socially; a dullard, academically; a ne'er-do-well, professionally, in order not to be invited to return. Of course, in most communities any *one* of these negative conditions would be enough to result in his losing his job long before the first year is over!

A not simplified answer. Fortunately for physical education and for the youth of this country, not many major students in this field want to be a mediocre *anything!* One of the noblest, indirect learnings of this profession is the striving for excellency. That is the warp and woof of professional fabric; it is that for which we stand.

Thus, we can give the following kind of answer to the question of *promotion* and *advancement:*

1. Strive to become the best teacher you can be.

2. Make the most of it if administration claims most of your time. Remember that the acid test of administration is the degree to which those under your leadership *grow and develop to the heights of their potentials.*

3. Find ways of evaluating yourself and all that you do.

4. Keep abreast or ahead of the times, particularly in the field of research in and related to the field.

5. Work out *in writing* a detailed statement of your philosophy of physical education (continually revise it).

6. Select a half dozen fields of human knowledge and read copiously from their pages.

7. Serve your own professional organizations as occasion may provide, but avoid being an office-seeking politician.

8. Be willing to help establish real lines of communication and service with related fields.

9. Remain or become creative, speculative.

10. Work for an ever-improving program.

11. Become acquainted with real leaders, without pushing.

12. Work toward improving professional preparation. (Sometimes this opportunity comes during one's first year as a teacher, for one's alma mater may seek help from its alumni.)

13. Write, when you have something that *must* be written.

14. Improve your ability in public address, including radio and TV.

15. Remain or become experimentally minded; conduct your own research (get expert help in planning it).

16. Try out new devices, ideas, gadgets with an open mind.

17. Develop an ability to speak their language when interpreting physical education to outside persons.

18. Develop the reputation that you produce quality work, no matter how small or large the assignment that you have accepted.

19. Become known as a positivist—not starry-eyed—but avoid self-pity, being misunderstood, not giving due credit, hurt feelings, and the like.

20. Act as you think the finest professional person should act. *Think* that way. *Be* that way!

21. Retain perspective. Some things are more important than physical education. Some things are more important than education, than becoming known, than politics, than being elected president of a professional organization. One of those things is self-respect, another is integrity, another is being ethical.

22. Help recruit persons for the profession who will serve it well, advance it, and be happy in so doing.

23. Continue to be unafraid of having ideas that are different. (Let the plant gain stature and roots before discarding it.)

24. Apply the wisdom gained from using a key in a locked door. Jamming, rush, force *postpones* its opening.

25. Strive to meet the acid test of a profession: *quality* of service.

Improvement means change. Previous chapters of this book were designed to aid the teacher in developing his understandings, skills, and attitudes toward better teaching of youth in physical education. These chapters are not presumed to have all of the answers or the final answers. Such a presumption would be impossible. All of the facts are not in—all of the truth not discovered. In fact, the student should realize that this book is but one point of view however objectively the authors may have dealt with the ideas discussed.

Some beginning teachers are distressed by such a statement. They would prefer that their field be a precise, exact body of knowledge that they need only memorize and use. Some beginning teachers become worried and uncertain when they find that even the experts do not take an absolute, definite stand on all of the issues and do not have a ready supply of pat answers. This is not at all abnormal or a cause for concern. The important step is to determine what kind of person you wish to be; then you may determine your own goals, define your responsibilities and obligate yourself to the kind of service that you believe is significant.

The young teacher must define his measure for success in the teaching field. The definition will, of necessity, vary with persons. This definition is a problem that each teacher must solve for himself. However success is defined, it is seldom served on a silver platter. It involves effort, challenges, and responsibilities.

Whatever his definition of success, the young teacher must learn for himself the value of the urge to progress—to be better. This is a characteristic that is not unique to, but that is certainly abundant in, physical education majors. Usually they have had a background of satisfying competitive experiences that enables them to transfer this approach into other life situations. With this natural desire for improvement and perfection, it is difficult to understand why some young teachers become *status quo* teachers. What happens that causes ambitious, energetic, competitive people to become complacent? Why should they become easily satisfied with conditions, standards, and practices as they exist at present? Would anyone deny that teaching can always be improved? *Further change is needed.* The facts, near-facts, principles, and points of view that have been outlined in this book need fresh examination, new criticism, close scrutiny by the new teacher. Through such evaluation, in time new facts will replace the old, and some suggested principles will become dated—and practices will change.

The responsible professional person *cannot* fold his hands and wait for improved practices to be discovered by someone else. He must assume a share of this responsibility. These things he must find out for himself.

The above discussion implies that more good new ideas, more creativity, less dependence upon traditional activity and practice, and more innovation are needed. We do not want to imply that the young teacher should be insistent upon change merely for the sake of change. But, he should be a tactful proponent of change when alterations in ideas and practices may result in improvement of the educational service to young people. The young teacher might ask, "How might I know what changes would be best? We already know what works, why change?" This is a timid view. New questions should be raised, new answers should be sought. How else can a profession be improved?

The potential and opportunity for new discovery in all fields of man's endeavor staggers the imagination. The field of physical education is not an exception. The new knowledge of how things might be done better is the result of learning, research, and thought. The stimulus for such new knowledge results from the desire to progress. This desire is only possessed by those who are unwilling to be bound by the *status quo.*

Acceptance of the broad view and utility of research becomes a responsibility of the professional person. The importance and significance of research is not always clearly understood by persons who use the term. Research applies to an approach or way of thinking as much as it does to any precise process. It applies to elementary things as well as those that are very complicated. The noted C. S. Kettering provided an enlightened definition of research:

"Research" is a high-hat word that scares many people. It needn't. It is rather simple. Essentially it is nothing but a state of mind. . . . A friendly, welcoming attitude toward change, going out to look for a change instead of waiting for it to come. Research for practical men is an effort to do things better and not be caught asleep at the switch. The research state of mind can apply to anything; personal affairs or any kind of business, big or little. It is the problem solving mind as contrasted with the let well enough alone mind. It is the composer mind instead of the fiddler mind. It is the tomorrow mind instead of the yesterday mind.[1]

In this quotation can be found one path to professional progress. Experimentation, innovation, planning with vision become a way of life for the responsible professional person. Such activities become a necessary element in carrying out day-to-day obligations. It becomes a matter of doing today's task and at the same time creatively thinking ahead.

The purposeful professional person is aware that he is engaged in a project of lifelong learning. He realizes that completion of his college course work is by no means the end of his education. If he realizes this continuing nature of learning, he knows that he is daily maturing on the job. He would have little respect for the physician who, upon completion of his formal medical training, determined that he would engage in no further study. He would not consider entrusting his health and welfare to the hands of such a person. He would undoubtedly agree that the physician has a responsibility—*an obligation* to keep abreast with the new developments in his field. The obligation to keep up is one that is shared by all professional persons. Who can ever say that he knows enough, that he is satisfactorily informed, that he has a right to be complacent?

Without question the young teacher is expected by others to be growing and advancing on the job. More important, he should *expect himself* to grow and advance on the job! In addition to the opportunities to grow through experiences in teaching classes and dealing with students, he should expect to gain much from the staff meetings he attends, the professional conferences to which he will be welcomed, visitations he has the occasion to make, in-service education of which he may avail himself, graduate study that he may undertake, and the professional literature which he may read to keep abreast with the advances in his field.

The teacher as he matures learns that he must formulate his own goals. For only if he does, can he be elevated by the power of his purpose. The professional person realizes that he must go beyond

---

[1] Charles S. Kettering, as told to Neil M. Clark. "More Music Please, Composer!" *The Saturday Evening Post*, September 10, 1938, Vol. 211, No. 11, p. 33.

what others might expect him to do. He must not do his work *merely* to please and satisfy his department chairman, his principal, or his supervisor; he must please and satisfy himself. As he matures, he learns that his conduct and activities are shaped as much from his attitudes of mind as from his *knowledge* of the principles which underline his field.

As he matures, it becomes increasingly obvious that his system of well developed, well tested beliefs and purposes become as important in determining his direction as *any other factor*. The young teacher may hasten this professional maturation as he critically and continually examines his values in an effort to build a stronger personal and professional philosophy. Only in this way is he building a professional career and not just doing a job. It is his *obligation* to gain this larger view.

And finally, two measures of the value of the knowledge, gained in a teacher preparation program, in the larger areas of a college education, and in the still broader experiences of life, come from the *use* that is made of the knowledge and the *direction* it is given. *This use and direction must be determined by the teacher himself.* The young teacher is again reminded that his professional obligations are best met if he is able to "keep the composer mind instead of the fiddler mind—the tomorrow mind instead of the yesterday mind."

Through such considerations the beginning teacher is helped to build a vehicle for the voyage ahead. To see this vehicle as a spaceship is a fitting analogy. For, if he is to escape the beckoning of mediocrity, the teacher's use and direction of accumulated knowledge and experience must press beyond the limits of the ordinary.

All that has gone into the preparation years, and all that is gained therefrom, serve to bring the prospective teacher to the threshold of himself. If he is to continue to build toward better teaching, he must become aware of healthy discontent, doubt, and curiosity about today's *way*.

These evidences of thinking, leading toward more mature values, together with a deepening belief in the high potential in man's reach and vision, indeed send the individual back again to the threshold of himself. And, here he will find, as he matures, that easily lost secret of every profession. Man—and all that this implies—is a foundation to, transcends, and permeates the *professional* self. As he strives to improve his special discipline and technique, he will find the talisman only when he brings the humanness and humaneness of man to the greatest and the most trivial of his every task. This talisman unlocks the wisdom needed to select ever-finer goals, and, the integrity to choose means that reflect man at his best.

BIBLIOGRAPHY

Huggett, Albert J., and T. M. Stinnett, *Professional Problems of Teachers*. New York: The Macmillan Company, 1956.

Knapp, Clyde, and Ann E. Jewett, *Physical Education: Student and Beginning Teaching*. New York: The McGraw-Hill Book Company, Inc., 1957.

Murray, Ruth L., and Delia P. Hussey, *From Student to Teacher in Physical Education*. Englewood Cliffs, N. J.: Prentice-Hall, Inc., 1959.

Wilson, Charles H., *A Teacher Is a Person*. New York: Henry Holt and Company, 1956.

INDEX

INDEX